W9-BBA-724

THE VARGAS REGIME

Institute of Latin American Studies
Columbia University

THE
VARGAS
REGIME

THE CRITICAL YEARS, 1934-1938

by Robert M. Levine

COLUMBIA UNIVERSITY PRESS 1970

New York and London

ROBERT M. LEVINE is Assistant Professor of History at the State University of New York at Stony Brook.

Copyright © 1970 Columbia University Press
Standard Book Number: 231-03370-2
Library of Congress Catalog Card Number: 78-115222
Printed in the United States of America

THE INSTITUTE OF LATIN AMERICAN STUDIES of Columbia University was established in 1961 in response to a national, public, and educational need for a better understanding of the nations of Latin America and a more knowledgeable basis for inter-American relations. The major objectives of the Institute are to prepare a limited number of North Americans for scholarly and professorial careers in the field of Latin American studies, to advance our knowledge of Latin America through an active program of research by faculty, by graduate students, and by visiting scholars, and to improve public knowledge through publication of a series of books on Latin America. Some of these studies are the result of research by the faculty, by graduate students, and by visiting scholars. It was also decided to include in this series translations from Portuguese and Spanish of important contemporary books in the social sciences and humanities.

Robert Levine began his direct acquaintance with Brazil in the summer of 1964 as a young Princeton graduate student in history; he went to Brazil as a participant in the Metropolitan Graduate Summer Field Training Program administered by Columbia University. He defined his interest in recent Brazilian history, especially the Vargas era, and has pursued that interest to the extent of uncovering new and essential sources on subjects whose origins have been only imperfectly understood.

During that summer of 1964, Dr. Levine proposed, organized, and contributed to a volume of field research essays written by Brazilianist graduate students, which was published by this Institute as BRAZIL: FIELD RESEARCH GUIDE IN THE SOCIAL SCIENCES. Dr. Levine has maintained close contacts with Brazil and has most recently returned to Brazil in 1969-70.

The publication program of the Institute of Latin American Studies is made possible by the financial assistance of the Ford Foundation.

To My Parents

ACKNOWLEDGMENTS

Field research for this study was carried out chiefly in the Brazilian cities of Rio de Janeiro, Recife, and Natal. A grant from the Henry L. and Grace Doherty Foundation for the 1964-65 academic year and supplementary aid from the Ford Regional Studies Fellowship Program of Princeton University and the Research Foundation of the State of New York maintained the author during the tenure of the project.

The documentary material cited in the text includes data located in the archives of the Civil Police in Rio de Janeiro, Recife, and Natal, the Superior Military Tribunal (now located in Brasília), the National Library, the Brazilian Academy of Letters, the National Historical Museum, and the Brazilian National Archives. The author wishes to express particular gratitude to the families of Getúlio Vargas and Oswaldo Aranha for permission to use their archives, as well as to Caio Prado, Jr., Roberto Sissón, José Soares de Maciel Filho, and Padre Ponciano Stenzel dos Santos for their personal papers.

I would also like to acknowledge the generous help and advice received from the following Brazilians: the National Library's capable Dona Zilda Galhardo de Araújo; Anísio Teixeira; the late Leoncio Basbaum; the late Agildo Barata; João Café Filho; the late Astrojildo Pereira; Enélio Petrovich of the Historical Institute of Rio Grande do Norte; Hélio Silva; and Hercolino Sobral Pinto, defender of civil liberties in Brazil since 1920. Also Eurico Bellens Pôrto, Hercolino Cascardo, Danilo Nunes, Pedro Vilela Cid, José Américo de Almeida, Aron Neumann, José Augusto Bezerra de Medeiros, José Honório Rodrigues, Sérgio Buarque de Holanda, Vamireh Chacon, Nelson Werneck Sodré, Oswaldo Torres Galvão, Malvino Reis Neto, Wandenkolk Wanderley, and João Baptista Galvão.

For counsel received in the United States the author acknowledges the contributions of Thomas E. Skidmore, Francis D. McCann, Jr., Joseph Love,

John D. Wirth, Paulo Singer, Octavio Ianni, Gabriel Bolaffi, Brady Tyson, Robert Conrad, Timothy Harding, Judith Collins, and my Stony Brook colleagues Kenneth P. Erickson, Thomas Mermall, David Burner, and Herman Lebovics. Professor Stanley J. Stein, of Princeton University, offered wise and generous professional guidance for which I am highly grateful. None of these persons, of course, bear any responsibility for errors or misinterpretations that may appear in the text.

My wife, Gracia R. Levine, typed most of the drafts of the manuscript and provided consistent support and affection, for which no acknowledgment can suffice.

ROBERT M. LEVINE

Stony Brook, New York
August, 1969

NOTE

Brazilian public figures are usually referred to by abbreviated versions of their full names. Thus Antônio Carlos de Andrada becomes Antônio Carlos; Pedro Aurélio de Góes Monteiro is referred to as Góes Monteiro or Góes; João Alberto Lins de Barros becomes João Alberto. Variations of names and places are frequent, reflecting in part the orthographic reform of Brazilian Portuguese which took place in the late 1930s. Names in the text will be spelled as they generally appeared during their time (e.g., Juracy Magalhães, Afrânio de Mello Franco) but geographic place names will be modernized (Niterói, not Nictheroy). Titles will be spelled as they appeared at the time of publication.

CONTENTS

THE VARGAS REGIME

ABBREVIATIONS
USED IN TEXT AND NOTES

AIB	Ação Integralista Brasileira (Brazilian Integralist Action)
ANL	Alliança Nacional Libertadora (National Liberation Alliance)
APRA	Allianza Popular Revolucionária Americana (Popular Revolutionary American Alliance [Peru])
AS	Alliança Social (Social Alliance [Rio Grande do Norte])
BC	Batalhão de Caçadores (Artillery Battalion)
CP	Caio Prado, Jr. archive
DASP	Departamento Administrativo do Serviço Público (Administrative Department of Public Service)
DIP	Departamento de Imprensa e Propaganda (Press Information Service)
DNP	Departamento Nacional de Propaganda (National Department of Propaganda)
GB	Gustavo Barroso archive
GV	Getúlio Vargas archive
HAHR	*Hispanic American Historical Review*
IBGE	Instituto Brasileiro de Geografia e Estatística (Brazilian Institute of Geography and Statistics)
IPC	*International Press Correspondence*
OA	Oswaldo Aranha archive
PCB	Partido Comunista Brasileiro (Brazilian Communist Party)
POL	Partido Operário Leninista (Leninist Workers' Party)
PP	Partido Popular (Popular Party [Rio Grande do Norte])
PRF	Partido Republicano Federal (Federal Republican Party [Rio Grande do Norte])
RA	Archive, Delegacia de Ordem Social e Investigações, Natal
RC	Archive, Secretaria de Segurança Pública, Recife
RI	Regimento da Infantaria (Infantry Regiment)
RP	Archive, Departamento Federal de Segurança Pública de Polícia Política e Social, Rio de Janeiro
RS	Roberto Sissón archive
STM	Supremo Tribunal Militar (Supreme Military Tribunal)
TSN	Tribunal de Segurança Nacional (National Security Tribunal)
UFB	União Feminina Brasileira (Brazilian Federation of Women)

INTRODUCTION

On November 3, 1930, one month after the formal outbreak of hostilities against the federal regime, a military junta installed the defeated candidate for the presidency, Getúlio Dornelles Vargas, as provisional chief of state of Brazil. This act terminated the Old Republic, bringing to a close a forty-one-year-old era controlled by the rural landholding oligarchies of the leading states and their political machines. The new provisional regime, a diverse coalition of forces united chiefly by their opposition to the ousted government, unfolded a new, aggressive chapter in Brazilian life: dynamic, professedly revolutionary, and reflecting the aspirations of newly emerging social forces. Yet at the same time, Brazil from 1930 to 1945 remained inherently conservative, paternalistic, and dominated by the personal rule of one man, Getúlio Vargas. In any case, as an observer has remarked, 1930 represented a "turning point in the Brazilian mind."[1]

The economically strongest states of the center-south—São Paulo, Minas Gerais, and, to a lesser degree, Rio Grande do Sul—had dominated the First, or Old, Republic (1889-1930). The broadly federal 1891 constitution had apportioned extensive fiscal, juridical, and administrative powers to the states, in part as a result of the reaction of the members of the 1890–91 Constituent Assembly to the highly centralized system under the Empire. *Panelinhas*, or groups of persons linked by mutual self-interest and influence drawn from the socioeconomic elite, controlled the hierarchies of the powerful state political parties, which in turn chose candidates representative of their personal interests for public office.[2] Only when the elite divided over political issues did open presidential campaigns ensue: in 1910, between Marshal Hermes da Fonseca (supported by Minas Gerais, Rio Grande do Sul, and the military) and Rui Barbosa (backed by São Paulo and his own state, Bahia); in 1919, when Rio Grande do Sul supported Paraíba's Epitácio Pessôa, the only northerner to hold office during the Old Republic;

in 1922, when Artur Bernardes (Minas Gerais and São Paulo) opposed ex-President Nilo Peçanha (Rio Grande do Sul, Rio de Janeiro, Pernambuco, and Bahia); and in 1930, when Vargas, the candidate of Rio Grande do Sul, Minas Gerais, and Paraíba, faced Júlio Prestes, the protégé of incumbent *paulista* Washington Luís, who considered Prestes the most likely to maintain his administration's fiscal program.[3]

The governments of four other Latin American republics fell to military coups in 1930. In neighboring Argentina the army toppled Hipólito Irigoyen's middle-class Radical Party after fourteen years in power. Many other countries in the hemisphere felt the strain of the worsening world agricultural market and the emergence of domestic nationalism, particularly among the armed forces. In Brazil, military strength had been traditionally divided among the states, whose well-armed militias often stood in contrast to the officer-heavy, poorly equipped federal army. Dissent within the military first appeared publicly in 1922, when a revolt at Rio de Janeiro's Copacabana Fort over an alleged affront to the armed forces by President-elect Artur Bernardes was suppressed at the cost of the lives of sixteen young officers who refused to surrender. Their resistance gave birth to the *tenente* (literally, lieutenants) movement among young officers opposed to the planter-dominated federal system. After a second revolt in July, 1924, the tenente leaders were driven into the interior by pursuing troops in a chase which precipitated a heroic guerrilla march through 24,000 kilometers of Brazilian territory; rarely stopping more than two days in a single place, the tenente expedition marched from Rio Grande do Sul to the northeastern *sertão* (backlands) and back into the tropical interior. The band of between 800 and 1000 men was commanded by its "general," cavalry major Miguel Costa of the São Paulo state militia, and was supported by four tenentes who held the rank of colonel in the column— Siqueira Campos, João Alberto Lins de Barros, Djalma Dutra, and Oswaldo Cordeiro de Farias—each of whom commanded his own detachment of troops. Captain Luís Carlos Prestes, the executive officer and a leading personality in the movement, gave his name to the expedition although he remained subordinate to Costa even after being made a "general" on January 20, 1926. The Prestes Column harassed landowners and federal authorities until three of the four detachments entered Bolivia with Costa and Prestes on February 3, 1927, and the fourth, led by Siqueira Campos, was driven into Paraguay seven weeks later.[4] A popular mystique immediately developed around the adventure and its leaders acquired the stature of national heroes. Many of the tenente officers of the march returned from exile as the 1930 presidential election approached, placing themselves at the disposal of Vargas' advisers and offering to lead a military revolt against the incumbent regime.

The tenentes generally came from the lesser or declining states of the Old Republic: Ceará (Juarez Távora and Juracy Magalhães), Pernambuco (João Alberto), and Mato Grosso (Felinto Müller, later Vargas' confidant and chief of police). Others (Prestes, Cordeiro de Farias, and Baptista Luzardo) were from Rio Grande do Sul, a state on the fringe of the São Paulo–Minas Gerais Republican axis, and one which more than any other had been ridden by conflict and which had chafed at its peripheral political role for more than a century.

By 1930, most tenentes still showed their youth and political inexperience. Many had suffered bitter exile in Uruguay and Argentina, which was possibly the cause of their authoritarian "mentality" and their idealistic willingness for patriotic self-sacrifice.[5] The tenentes represented a status-incongruent elite in terms of their middle-class origins and the secondary place the states of their birth held in the political hierarchy of the Republic.

Alienated from the civilian administrations in power from 1922 through 1930, the tenentes had been contemplating armed insurrection since at least September, 1929, when Prestes had conferred with Vargas and Oswaldo Aranha but had refused to accept the command of the military forces of Vargas' Liberal Alliance, which had been equipped with arms purchased from Czechoslovakia by Aranha in his position as secretary of the interior of the state of Rio Grande do Sul. When Colonel Euclides Figueiredo and a third candidate also declined the offer, Aranha, in the aftermath of the disputed presidential election which gave the victory to the official candidate, reached an agreement with Lieutenant Colonel Pedro Aurélio de Góes Monteiro, a professional soldier from Alagôas who had fought for the federal government against the Prestes Column but who now set out to organize the revolt. Aranha, Vargas, Góes (who had attended military school in Rio Grande do Sul and who considered himself a *gaúcho*), João Neves da Fontoura, Baptista Luzardo, Lindolfo Collor, and Maurício Cardoso all helped give the Liberal Alliance a distinctly gaúcho flavor.

Fewer than two million adult males voted in the presidential elections of March, 1930—out of a total population of more than forty million. The paulista candidate, Júlio Prestes, had campaigned in orthodox fashion in spite of the devastating effect on agricultural prices caused by the depression. Although Vargas had promised direct federal relief to planters (and appealed to urban groups with promises of electoral reform and social welfare legislation), the incumbent administration exploited its control of the electoral machinery, allowing Vargas' Liberal Alliance victory only in the three states which had backed his candidacy. In Vargas' home state of Rio Grande do Sul, he collected 287,000 votes to a recorded 789 for his opponent—a testimony to the power of his state's own political machine. In all, Júlio Prestes carried the popular vote by a ten-to-seven margin, and was proclaimed President-elect.[6]

The Liberal Alliance subdivided into two factions following its defeat: the tenentes and their civilian allies, and a wing comprised of anti-Washington Luís politicians (led by gaúcho chieftain Borges de Medeiros and *mineiro* Antônio Carlos de Andrada) which advocated accommodation. In the ensuing period of indecision, many of the tenentes abandoned their plans and drifted back into exile. After Luís Carlos Prestes publicly condemned the Liberal Alliance and issued his own revolutionary manifesto (from Buenos Aires), Aranha resigned from his state post. This gave relief to officials of the Washington Luís administration, who, aware of the revolutionary threat, nonetheless continued to attack Liberal Alliance congressional strength.[7] The probably unrelated assassination in July of Vargas' running mate, Governor João Pessôa of Paraíba, suddenly reversed the situation: it united the Liberal Alliance and revived the plans of the conspirators. On October 3, rebels in the south led by Aranha, João Alberto, and General Antônio Flôres da Cunha of the Rio Grande do Sul state armed force raised the banner of revolt and seized Pôrto Alegre. With Vargas as titular head, Góes Monteiro, Aranha, and tenente Juarez Távora, who led the campaign in the northeast, executed strategy. Faced by the desertion of his general staff in the federal capital in late October, President Washington Luís resigned, turning over the national government to a three-man military junta. Tenente João Alberto took control of the government of São Paulo and Vargas triumphantly entered Rio de Janeiro on October 31, 1930, accompanied by three thousand gaúcho state troops.

The composition of Vargas' initial cabinet illustrated his reliance on diverse sources of support: Aranha as minister of justice; author and engineer José Américo de Almeida from the state of Paraíba as the successor to Juarez Távora, who relinquished the public works post after three weeks; the young mineiro lawyer Francisco Campos as minister of education; Lindolfo Collor, the author of the Liberal Alliance program and a protégé of Borges de Medeiros, as first minister of labor. The cabinet also included two senior career military officers, neither of them tenentes, as ministers of war and the navy; respected jurist Afrânio de Mello Franco as minister of foreign affairs; and José Maria Whitaker, a São Paulo coffee banker and director of various foreign business enterprises, as minister of finance. Had Vargas been elected and taken office legally, these cabinet choices probably would not have raised the least comment, save possibly the mere single post conceded to São Paulo and the three granted to Rio Grande do Sul, although one of these, the Ministry of Agriculture, went to Joaquim Assis Brasil, the former chieftain of the Federalists, the state's opposition party. Paulista Whitaker was forced out of the Finance Ministry after a year by tenente opposition to his efforts to balance the federal budget, his insistence that the foreign debt should rigorously be honored, and his resistance to large-scale spending on public works. Vargas replaced him with Oswaldo Aranha, his chief troubleshooter between 1930 and 1934.

As president, Vargas concentrated his initial efforts on consolidating his coalition and creating a popular base, but he made no attempt to formulate a consistent program or political ideology. On November 11, 1930, he issued a decree law which granted virtually dictatorial powers to the provisional government. It also dissolved the National Congress and state and municipal legislative bodies, and granted the president absolute powers to name and dismiss all public officials. Vargas' public statements appealed to the hostility of the middle class against the rural oligarchy and reiterated promises made during his electoral campaign for social legislation to aid the working classes. With great fanfare he inaugurated two new ministries: Labor, Industry, and Commerce, and Education. To rescue the states from financial insolvency the national government assumed all prior state debts. The government named federal interventors to replace the governor of every state except Minas Gerais. For the most part the appointees were tenentes, the youngest being twenty-six-year-old Juracy Magalhães in Bahia. Although the interventors attempted to remain aloof from local political issues, most became embroiled in state politics. As a result, many failed to govern effectively despite their power to rule by decree; the rate of turnover among the federal interventors was high.

Vargas, who remained an enigmatic political quantity throughout the early days of his administration, faced a major test posed by the continued division of his own bloc, the Liberal Alliance. On one side stood the tenentes, committed in principle to national reorganization and hostile to any return to pre-1930 orthodox liberalism. The tenentes controlled the state interventorships and, through tenente-convert (and newly promoted) General Góes Monteiro, exerted growing influence in the army. The state political leaders of Rio Grande do Sul and Minas Gerais (and the non-tenente members of the cabinet) made up the competing constitutionalist wing of the Vargas coalition, agreeable to political reform but anxious to end the dictatorship and return to constitutionalism, with, of course, their own state parties sharing power with the federal government.[8] The first major confrontation between the two groups occurred over plans elaborated in December, 1930, by the tenentes and their civilian supporters, who included Aranha, to prolong the provisional regime and create revolutionary organizations, or legions, to mobilize support for the regime. The legions, semi-fascist in form, would establish local tenente power bases in place of the old state parties. All, however, failed, victims of the tenente leaders' inability to organize and their unwillingness to delegate authority to civilian aides. The new organizations included Francisco Campos and Gustavo Capanema's khaki-shirted Minas Legion (Legião Liberal de Minas), Oswaldo Aranha's October Legion (Legião de Outubro), established in São Paulo and the Federal District of Rio de Janeiro, and Miguel Costa and João Alberto's Revolutionary Legion (Legião Revolucionária) in São Paulo, whose manifesto was written by a young intellectual, Plínio Salgado.[9] Tenentes also formed the Third of October Club, created in Rio de Janeiro as an attempt to consolidate the bloc's national political influence, already exerted through Vargas' so-called black cabinet of informal advisers, which included Aranha, Távora, Góes Monteiro, José Américo, João Alberto, and the Federal District's interventor, Dr. Pedro Ernesto Baptista.

Internal dissent over ideology, however, split the Third of October Club and shattered its façade of unity. Radical tenentes led by Miguel Costa and Hercolino Cascardo eulogized the revolutionary spirit of the Prestes Column and saw socialistic reform as the precondition for the destruction of oligarchic control. Conservative (or hard-line) tenentes, led by club president Góes Monteiro, favored the continuation of government by decree and advocated corporatist-influenced programs of national development. Both groups paid lip service to rural land reform, but the issue dropped from sight soon after the Liberal Alliance came to power. The club exercised veto powers over Vargas' naming of federal interventors, and loudly attacked economic schemes judged detrimental to the national interest, one such being the controversial Itabira Iron project which had first been proposed in the 1920s by American engineer Percival Farquar.[10] Impressed by the club's seeming influence, officials of the United States Embassy in 1932 privately called Vargas the club's figurehead.[11] This did not prove to be the case. By mid-1931, internal battles within the club prompted Góes to resign its presidency. Increasingly, Vargas ignored the club, weakening its influence and depriving the tenentes of a potential source of institutional power.

Getúlio Vargas' tenure as chief of state from 1930 to 1945 can be examined in the context of his administration's efforts to experiment with new forms of national organization in the face of post-1930 domestic and external pressures, and in the context of his own efforts to consolidate his personal political power. The mood of Brazil during the 1930s reflected the frustrations and conflicts of the times. To a certain degree, the differences between the Washington Luís and Getúlio Vargas administrations are paralleled by those between Herbert Hoover and Franklin D. Roosevelt in the United States. Washington Luís undermined the coffee sector and its support of his administration when he refused, out of economic principle, to commit the federal government to massive remedial action, while Vargas pledged aid to the planters and viewed problems in national terms, not being hesitant to increase federal power to seek solutions when such a procedure seemed necessary.

The impact of the depression and the lesson of Brazil's vulnerability as an exporter of raw agricultural produce generated demands for economic independence and diversification fostered by government initiative, issues which underlay the principal conflict of the early Vargas years: state power versus centralized authority. The voices of influence around Vargas included cotton growers and the increasingly important manufacturing sector.[12] Those reflecting the nationalistic tenente ideology—military officers, intellectuals, industrialists, and politicians from the less powerful states—surrounded the President and urged direct action at the expense of the broadly federal structure of the Old Republic and its commitment to orthodox economic liberalism. In opposition stood the anti-tenente liberal constitutionalist bloc, headed by former mutual adversaries Borges de Medeiros and Raul Pilla of Rio Grande do Sul, the São Paulo Democratic Party, and mineiro political spokesmen Antônio Carlos and ex-President Artur Bernardes.

Tensions between liberal constitutionalists and tenentes rose through 1931 and early 1932. After an attack in February, 1932, on the offices of the pro-constitutionalist newspaper *Diario Carioca* by Third of October Club partisans, several high officials of the administration resigned, including cabinet ministers Collor, Cardoso, and Assis Brasil, Rio de Janeiro police chief Baptista Luzardo, and João Neves da Fontoura, an adviser to the Bank of Brazil. In the wake of this attack a deeper crisis exploded in São Paulo. Since 1931 residents of the state had been angered by the creation of its Revolutionary Legion, whose ranks had been filled by Miguel Costa with unemployed workers, by the unpopular and authoritarian interventorship of tenente João Alberto, and by Vargas' appointment of an elderly civilian successor, Pedro de Toledo, who was not permitted to nominate officials loyal to the state's United Front (Frente Única) coalition to his secretariat.[13] Underlying the matter was São Paulo's demand that constitutionality be restored and the provisional government be terminated.

Vargas narrowly prevented full-scale civil war when open conflict erupted in July, 1932, by successfully convincing Rio Grande do Sul, its armed forces controlled by federal interventor Flôres da Cunha, to remain neutral, despite public appeals by Borges de Medeiros, Raul Pilla, and Baptista Luzardo to come to the aid of the constitutionalist revolt. The rebels, led by Euclides Figueiredo (the colonel who had refused command of the Liberal Alliance forces in 1930), anti-tenente General Bertoldo Klinger, and General Isidoro Dias Lopes, the veteran of the uprisings of 1893 and 1924, held out for nearly three months before they capitulated on September 29.[14] With the seizure and exile of Borges de Medeiros, the former influence of his state Republican Party disintegrated. Control of the state passed to Flôres da Cunha, whose maintenance of order had prevented an alliance with São Paulo and who therefore had saved the union.[15]

With the cessation of hostilities, Vargas resisted tenente pressure to punish the rebellious paulistas; instead, he dealt lightly with the insurrectionists. Appealing for national unity, he reconfirmed that elections for the national Constituent Assembly would be held in May, 1933, and directed the Bank of Brazil to absorb the war bonds which had been floated by the defeated paulistas. Vargas' act demonstrated compassion and hard political acumen.

The long-awaited Constituent Assembly gathered in Rio de Janeiro's Palácio Tiradentes, in November, 1933, having been selected by an electorate of nearly one and a half million Brazilians, including women and persons over eighteen. Its preliminary eight-man constitutional commission, which was presided over by Afrânio de Mello Franco, rejected Vargas' class representation scheme whereby forty at-large deputies would be chosen by occupational constituencies. But Vargas—who knew that these deputies would remain loyal and thereby would offset the voting strength of the larger states—overruled the decision. Voters elected 214 deputies to the state delegations, and forty more, under the close supervision of the Ministry of Justice, were "elected" to represent employer groups (18), employees (17), the liberal professions (3), and civil servants (2).

Vargas' long address to the Assembly's opening session recalled the Liberal Alliance victory of 1930 and set forth his blueprint for constitutional reform: the adoption of codes of social welfare and electoral justice; reorganization of the police and the armed forces; permanent class representation; broad federal powers to control public works, transportation, and drought relief; and aid to agriculture, education, and public health. In addition, he advocated fiscal reform, immigration quotas, and relief to depressed agricultural producers, chiefly coffee planters.[16] He did not, however, speak on the major issue which would face the Assembly during the seven months of its deliberations: the balance of power between the executive and the legislature, and between the states and the national government. The lines of debate became clearly drawn as soon as the hearings unfolded. The government program was supported by a coalition of class deputies, tenentes, minority deputies from the larger states, including two self-proclaimed socialists, and delegations from the smaller states. Most of the representatives from São Paulo and Minas Gerais, as well as states' rights advocates from such states as Bahia, Pernambuco, Rio de Janeiro, and Rio Grande do Sul—the liberal constitutionalists—allied themselves in opposition.

In the long months of Assembly hearings, deputies submitted more than five thousand amendments to the Assembly's constitutional body, the Committee of Twenty-six. This committee hammered out the new constitution behind closed doors under the direction of its president, Carlos Maximiliano, a leading constitutional authority from Rio Grande do Sul, and its two subofficers, Levi Carneiro and Raul Fernandes, both skilled in public law and both representing the state of Rio de Janeiro. By the middle of the deliberations, states' rights forces realized that they could not gain a majority, a situation which was reflected in the departure from the Assembly of Rio Grande do Sul's minority United Front deputy, Joaquim Assis

Brasil, perhaps the most famous non-paulista spokesman for the liberal constitutionalist position. Led by the so-called United Slate (Chapa Única) bloc in the São Paulo delegation, the states' rights deputies unsuccessfully attempted to monopolize debate and reverse the direction of the Assembly. When the final draft was ratified on July 16, 1934, it satisfied no group entirely, although it represented a clear victory for Vargas on every issue but executive power. Of greatest concern to the states was the fact that the federal union won the right to restrict state duties on exports to a maximum of 10 per cent *ad valorem*. For their part, the states' righters preserved—for the time being—the federal-based legislative system.

Two days before the final vote on the constitution Vargas issued more than fifty executive decrees under Article 18 of the draft constitution—the so-called Indemnity Act—a cleverly designed measure which approved retroactively all actions of the provisional government since 1930 and removed them from judicial review. The act infuriated Vargas' opponents, but they remained divided. On July 17 he was elected by the Assembly as constitutional president to a four-year term, by a margin of 175 votes to 59 for gaúcho Borges de Medeiros and 4 for General Góes Monteiro.

Advocates of constitutional reform welcomed the new sections which incorporated most of the provisional government's social and welfare codes decreed since 1930, as well as constitutional revisions which had been initiated nearly a decade before, in 1926. The document sanctioned the free establishment of political parties under new organizational statutes, limited the authority of the federal Senate (except where that body was given the right to review foreign loans by states and municipalities), and established technical advisory councils to work with the various ministries and the legislature. Tenentes and their allies welcomed the concept of corporatist labor organization incorporated into the document that granted government protection to unions but also placed them under paternalistic control. Urban deputies applauded provisions protecting working-class employees, prohibiting child labor, and guaranteeing an eight-hour workday, paid vacations, pensions, and minimum wages.

The wordy constitution also preserved the class system of representation by which fifty at-large deputies representing professional, employer, and working-class groups would be elected in addition to the three hundred fifty deputies sent to the federal capital from the twenty states. The new constitution also approved the right of religious instruction in the public schools (a practice tacitly permitted by Minister of Education Francisco

Campos since 1930), thereby modifying the doctrine of separation of Church and State which had been in force since 1890 and granting the Church and its lobby, the Catholic Electoral League, a victory. It also embodied such nationalistic themes as immigration restriction, exclusion of non-native-born Brazilians from elected office, and the "two-thirds" rule for employment, measures supported by spokesmen for the tenente position.

The constitutional mandate that permanent federal legislators and state constituent assemblies be elected during 1934 and 1935 precipitated a flurry of new political activity across the nation. The general amnesty proclaimed by the 1934 constitution allowed the political exiles to return: their arrival in July and August, 1934, heightened the feeling of excitement. In Minas Gerais, a gathering reportedly eighty thousand strong heard returning ex-President Artur Bernardes pledge to carry forward the banners of the opposition Republican Party of Minas (Partido Republicano Mineiro, or PRM) into the Congress. In Bahia, all commercial enterprises closed to allow employees to honor the arrival of venerable constitutionalist Otávio Mangabeira, who emotionally promised to wage a massive legislative struggle for states' rights.[17]

Tenente partisans complained bitterly that Vargas was opening the door for the oligarchy to regain power in the states and thereby erase all revolutionary gains. The election to the presidency of the Chamber of Deputies of Antônio Carlos, the aristocratic mineiro whose rejection by Washington Luís for the presidential succession in 1930 had helped precipitate the Liberal Alliance revolution, cheered opponents of the federal administration and spurred efforts on the part of local politicians identified with the pre-1930 status quo to reactivate their political machinery and to work for the reconquest of power in the coming elections.

Vargas forcefully exercised his executive authority, particularly in the economic sphere. Most reforms quietly extended the reach of the federal government. In 1931 he established federal regulation of monetary exchange; in 1933 he forbade private speculation in gold, although his decree was withdrawn after a year but was revived in 1937 after repeated claims of abuse. Efforts at fiscal regulation resulted in the delegation of strong authority to the Bank of Brazil and gave impetus to the creation of numerous federal agencies, particularly after 1937 under the *Estado Nôvo*. Vargas initiated strong measures to save coffee planters, who were faced by an approximately 280 per cent drop in prices between September, 1929, and September, 1931. Between 1931 and mid-1941, Vargas' National Coffee Institute destroyed 78,000,000 sacks of coffee, while coffee exports numbered only 12,000,000 sacks annually through 1934 and less than 15,000,000 for the remainder of the period, a result of the new uneasy equilibrium between the growing world demand for coffee and the growing competition from other Latin American and East Asian coffee-producing nations.[18]

One of the chief effects of the decline of Brazilian foreign trade and the depression of the agricultural sector was the expansion of industrialization and the rapid growth of the domestic market, in part as a result of what economist Celso Furtado calls the "pump-priming unconsciously adopted . . . as a by-product of the protection of the coffee interests," and in part as a result of conscious administration policy.[19] Imports, on the other hand, fell to half of pre-1929 levels. By 1932, exports had declined by two thirds, even though Brazil signed most-favored-nation treaties with several dozen foreign countries in an effort to stimulate sales of cotton, frozen meat, and cocoa as well as coffee. Vargas' General Tariff Act of 1934 revised tariff rates upward and decreased rates on essential raw materials and semi-manufactured goods unavailable domestically. Oswaldo Aranha's Trade Agreement Act, which took effect at the onset of 1936, reduced duties on sixty-seven tariff classifications and encouraged the importation of machinery not prohibited by the 1931 decree against imports by industries judged overproductive.[20] But within two years the Aranha Plan was abandoned; Vargas suspended payment on the foreign debt in early 1938. He justified his action in terms of the national economic interest.

The decline of the tenente Third of October Club by 1934 signaled the departure of individual figures prominent in the early phases of the provisional government. Oswaldo Aranha, who had studied in Paris and who was fluent in French, although he knew no English, left for Washington as ambassador in mid-1934 after having served in the cabinet since late 1930 in the justice and finance posts. Labor Minister Lindolfo Collor had resigned in early 1932 over the São Paulo crisis, as had Maurício Cardoso, minister of justice from December, 1931, through September, 1932, and Baptista Luzardo. Unsuccessful tenente interventors such as João Alberto (São Paulo) and Hercolino Cascardo (Rio Grande do Norte) fell from influence. The small faction of radical tenentes turned to the still-exiled Luís Carlos Prestes, who in 1931 had publicly embraced communism, had

left Argentina for residence and training in the Soviet Union, and had been
seated as the Brazilian representative to the Executive Committee of the
Communist International—the Comintern—in Moscow.

The pattern of a new Vargas coalition emerged as individual political
fortunes ebbed. Increasingly, Vargas acquired public identification with
business and industrial spokesmen favorable to enlarged federal initiative.
The middle class welcomed the expansion of the federal bureaucracy and
sided with Vargas' interventions in the states against attempts of local
oligarchic interests to regain power. The northern and northeastern states,
traditionally neglected under the Old Republic, responded to Vargas' ability
to distribute patronage and firmly backed the President, who, in turn,
offered generous encouragement to the Ministry of Public Works and
Transportation under José Américo de Almeida and its comprehensive
program of drought relief for afflicted areas. Coffee planters watched with
hope as the government wrestled with their problems; as the decade
progressed, planters welcomed the new federal institutes for sugar, alcohol,
cocoa, coffee, food oils, alkalis, and salt which amounted to production
cartels, and the government's efforts to promote crop diversification, stimulate domestic consumption, and increase agricultural output.

The urban working classes gradually responded to Vargas' attention,
although he lacked personal magnetism and did not willingly seek public
acclaim. The government instituted social security and pension benefits
through federal institutes, provided for paid vacations and sick leave, and
protected workers—particularly government employees—from dismissal, in
part as a sop to their low salaries. In later years, Vargas' progressive public
employee codes, which coexisted with surviving traditional attitudes
equating public offices with remunerative sinecures, contributed to the growing morass of Brazilian bureaucracy. This occurred in spite of the fact that
entrance to the civil service initially was governed by merit examination,
installed for the first time in 1936 and subsequently administered by Vargas'
newly created Administrative Department of Public Service, the Departamento Administrativo do Serviço Público, or DASP.

On the other hand, Vargas rarely reached the mass of rural sharecroppers
(*moradores*) and peasants; nor did he seem to be publicly aware of the
growing numbers of unemployed squatters who fled to urban slums from
the impoverished interior. Politically, the growing arm of the federal government influenced traditional mores in rural areas: politics came to depend
less on crude power and more on a complex network of patronage-based

relationships on local and state levels.[21] Federal troops stationed in the *sertão* helped to reduce banditry and to enforce scrutiny of border territories.

The national armed forces lent their support to Vargas throughout the 1930s in exchange for the President's efforts to build military power and his willingness to accept military counsel. Góes Monteiro remained the most influential military officer. Although several different men occupied the War Ministry post under Vargas' tenure, Góes, as chief of staff, dominated the armed forces' hierarchy and commanded its unquestioning loyalty.

The insistence of the stronger states on maintaining individual militia and police forces in defiance of federal authority increasingly irked military leaders and administration officials as the decade progressed. The state of Rio Grande do Sul, after 1932 dominated firmly by its interventor, Flôres da Cunha, drifted steadily away from the federal administration and forged alliances with anti-Vargas factions across Brazil. Flôres enraged military leaders when he purchased extensive weaponry, including tanks and field guns, from European suppliers and attempted to smuggle them into his state. Between 1933 and 1937 Flôres waged a silent war against the federal government, ostensibly to counter its growing power but probably to further his personal political ambitions as well. At the same time Vargas availed himself on the federal level of the services of other gaúchos: nine different men from his own state received cabinet posts between 1930 and 1937, as compared with seven from Minas Gerais, seven from São Paulo, four from the Federal District, three from northeastern Ceará, two each from Alagôas, the state of Rio de Janeiro, and Mato Grosso, and one each from Bahia and Paraíba.[22]

Major issues raised by the 1930 coup still remained unresolved by 1934: state versus national power, Vargas' ideological direction, the role of the armed forces, and the question of the aspirations of the groups which emerged out of the ruins of the Old Republic. After 1934, Vargas gingerly manipulated his administration under an atmosphere of rising strife and conflict between newly emerging nationalistic groups on the far right and far left and state and local factions loyal to the government and opposed to them. Following armed rebellion from the left in November, 1935, Vargas consolidated his power, silenced potential sources of opposition, and sacrificed civil liberties in order to achieve stability and national unity. Ironically, the very acts of the government in 1934 and 1935 to restore democratic procedures through free elections threatened to return state control to the rural oligarchies, which, through alliances with local bosses, or *coronéis,* generally controlled local voting.[23] The fear that the groups identified with the pre-1930 order might return to power so upset the urban middle class that it willingly relinquished the luxury of democratic niceties in exchange for strong state power in an authoritarian framework.[24]

The turbulent course of events between 1930 and 1935 determined, to a large degree, the coloration of the Estado Nôvo, the highly centralized regime imposed in 1937 which condemned liberal democracy and adopted centralized planning in the name of development and national unity. The years between 1934 and 1937 witnessed the last struggle for state independence and the victory of a new administrative ideology underlying Vargas' one-man executive rule. By November, 1937, the states were relegated to little more than administrative divisions subordinated to federal interventors and a hierarchy of bureaucratic agencies.[25]

1

THE SOCIAL
AND IDEOLOGICAL SETTING

Approximately 41,500,000 inhabitants populated Brazil in 1935, 93 per cent being clustered along the 3,517-mile-long coastal belt stretching into the Atlantic from Amapá to Rio Grande do Sul.[1] Three million—mostly of Indian and *caboclo* stock—occupied the remaining two million square miles of territory. In 1920, 65 per cent of all adult Brazilians could not read or write.[2] Two decades later, two thirds of Brazil was still classified as rural; only two cities, São Paulo and Rio de Janeiro, boasted more than one million residents.[3] The rural interior, dominated by the social framework of a declining monoculture, languished barely aware of urban Brazil, much less the outside world.

Malaria, schistosomiasis, Chagas' disease, beriberi, plague, smallpox, typhus, and intestinal parasites ravaged the countryside and appeared even in urban centers. The monotonous lower-class diet of manioc flour, black beans, and jerked beef (*charque*) rarely exceeded two thousand calories daily.[4] Of the twenty states in the federal union, three (São Paulo, Minas Gerais, Rio Grande do Sul) produced more than a half of Brazil's gross agricultural and industrial output.[5] Thousands of migrants from afflicted agricultural areas flocked to the major cities, particularly after the severe drought of 1931-32, peopling the *mocambos* in Recife, the *favelas* of Rio de Janeiro, and the *malocas* in the south. Few government services were tendered to the urban poor; the Catholic Church, led by the dignified but cautious Cardinal Leme, sought no major progressive social role.

Despite scattered efforts at reform after 1927, public education remained as archaic as it was inadequate to Brazil's growing needs. Teacher preparation consisted of four years of "normal school," usually completed at the age of eighteen, but of the 74,000 primary-school teachers in 1937, 65 per cent lacked even this training.[6] While the Ministry of War took one fourth of the federal budget during the 1930s, the Ministry of Education, Public Health, and Culture barely received 5 per cent. Table 1 summarizes the result in terms of school enrollment according to age group.

TABLE 1

SCHOOL ENROLLMENT, 1889-1940
(in per cent)

Year	7-11 Age Group Enrolled in Primary School	11-17 Age Group Enrolled in Secondary School	18-21 Age Group Enrolled in Higher Education
1889	12.4	n.a.	n.a.
1910	18.4	n.a.	.044
1920	26.4	n.a.	n.a.
1930	39.0	1.7	.063
1940	46.0	3.5	.058

Source: Robert J. Havighurst and J. Roberto Moreira, *Society and Education in Brazil* (Pittsburg, 1965), pp. 85, 187; adapted by Nathaniel H. Leff.
n.a. = Not available.

Primary education was roughly divided between Church-run private institutions and poorly equipped state schools, 90 per cent of which in rural areas were one-room structures without sanitary facilities. Secondary education, with rare exceptions, remained privately administered, thereby effectively excluding the lower classes, who could afford neither books and uniforms nor tuition charges. *Colégios* prepared their pupils exclusively for the rigid entrance examinations to the tuition-free, university-level faculties (or *faculdades*). Even the military academies demanded rigorous proficiency in languages, geography, history, the physical sciences, and mathematics; but civil and military schools alike stressed memorization and suppressed creativity. Brazil followed the traditional outlook that considered learning a grace acquired by the elite, not a key to social mobility but an exercise to broaden and cultivate the mind.[7]

Even in the larger cities, the old social traditions dissolved slowly. Respectable families kept three or four servants; the wealthy imported European governesses and engaged French- or English-speaking tutors for their children. Social distinctions remained sharpest in the north, where the influence of the *coronel* continued strong. In the south, newly rich industrialists, many of them immigrants, entered the elite through marriage or through achieving commensurate status by the acquisition of great wealth. In São Paulo more than two thirds of a sample group of industrial firms in 1935 were found to be owned by immigrants or their immediate heirs. While the affluent escaped taxation, wage levels remained pathetically low even in industrial areas.[8]

The Brazilian upper class, described by Thales de Azevedo as the socially "white" descendants of the traditional planter aristocracy (and which included, by the 1930s, the most successful businessmen, industrialists, bankers, and professional men, government personalities, and the top echelons of military and ecclesiastical life), resided for the most part in the fashionable residential neighborhoods of the cities.[9] High society in the federal capital, Rio de Janeiro, played host to an international set; it lionized the Braganças, the Brazilian royal pretenders, as well as the remnants of the Imperial nobility. The 1935 opera season featured twenty-three productions imported from Europe—considerably more than thirty years later although a sharp decline from the grand days of Brazilian opera, the immediate post-World War I years, when as many as seventy-three performances were held at Rio de Janeiro's Municipal Theater.[10] Social life revolved around the nightclubs and restaurants, the three beach-front casinos, the clubs, and embassy row. During the summer months the wealthy deserted the stifling city for their villas in Petrópolis and *sítios* in the mountains across Guanabara Bay.

Cultural institutions carried on their activities in the pattern of the nineteenth century. They included the French-styled Academy of Letters, which by 1935 was installing its second generation of literary "immortals," the Portuguese Literary Lyceum, the National Museum of Fine Arts, and the Institute of History and Geography, established by Emperor Pedro II. But the private clubs, erupting annually in lavish extravagance during the pre-Lenten Carnival, dominated society and brought together the most prominent names in government, finance, and public life. The most exclusive were the Gávea Golf Club, the Jockey Club, and the Country Club of Leblon; others included the Paissandú (with its British clientele), the Fluminense, the Military and Naval Clubs, and the Club Ginástico Português.

Rio de Janeiro's striking new architecture and high-rise beach-front apartment buildings added to the visual impact of urbanization. Automobile registrations jumped from 8,900 in 1925 to 25,700 in 1935, all vehicles being imported from the United States and Europe. The Federal District boasted 13 radio stations, 45 telephones per 1000 population—the highest rate in

EQUATOR

Manaus

Amazon River

PARÁ

Belém

São Luís

AMAZONAS

MARANHÃO

Teresina

CEARÁ

Fortaleza

RIO GRANDE
DO NORTE · Natal

TERRITORY
OF ACRE

Rio Branco

PIAUÍ

PARAÍBA · João Pessoa

PERNAMBUCO · Recife

ALAGOAS

Maceió

SERGIPE

Aracajú

GOIÁS

BAHIA

MATO GROSSO

Cuiabá

São Francisco River

Salvador

Goiânia

MINAS GERAIS

ESPIRITO SANTO

Belo Horizonte

Vitória

SÃO PAULO

RIO DE JANEIRO

São Paulo

Niterói

TROPIC OF CAPRICORN

PARANÁ

Rio de Janeiro

Curitiba

SANTA
CATARINA

BRAZIL, 1938

◉ Federal capital
◉ State capital

Florianópolis

ATLANTIC

RIO GRANDE
DO SUL · Pôrto Alegre

OCEAN

Brazil—and 19 newspapers. The mass media helped transform the urban style of life. Cinemas in 1935 offered a solid fare of foreign movies, including such films as Jean Harlow's *Reckless* and Douglas Fairbanks' *The Private Life of Don Juan*. Women's magazines titillated housewives with stories of movie stars and glamorous love affairs. Advertising agencies, new to Brazil, ballyhooed a host of modern products, many manufactured locally by foreign manufacturers, including Quaker Oats, Flit, Gillette (soon to enter the Portuguese language as a noun) and Colgate Dental Cream. Café Condor, in a vivid green bag, heralded its presence with an unmistakable NRA eagle.[11]

While the 1934 constitution guaranteed liberal democracy in its traditional Brazilian form, a relatively small percentage of Brazilians exercised political influence. Women did not vote until after 1932; in the 1930 elections in the Federal District only 140,000 adult males registered to vote, 10 per cent of its adult male population. However, only 60,000 actually voted. The 1932 Electoral Code inaugurated electoral reforms but most subsequent elections were indirect, and no national political parties were formed. While the expanded electorate freely chose the national Constituent Assembly in 1933, fewer actually went to the polls than three years before. In rural areas, *coronéis* and other local dominant interests continued to control voting and political activity.

A subtle hierarchy of racial values based on economic conditions and subsurface prejudice permeated social relationships. Middle-class culture displayed embarrassment at primitive survivals in its midst, such as spiritistic *umbanda* and *macumba*. Contestants chosen for international beauty contests were invariably Caucasian, reflecting the elite's desire to avoid the stereotype of the mulatto abroad.[12] To be sure, no legal barriers restrained nonwhites from social or economic advancement: to the contrary, intellectuals expressed pride in the theme of successful Brazilian racial amalgamation as expounded by sociologist Gilberto Freyre and suggested a generation earlier by Affonso Celso. Yet invariably businessmen, university professors, diplomats, and high government, Church, and military officers were white, usually descended from the Portuguese colonists; the servile classes, on the other hand, consisted of blacks, poor whites, and the full range of mixtures in between.[13]

Uneasiness about Brazil's racially heterogeneous heritage persisted in private circles and cast a pall over conversations on the future of the nation. "We need," Ambassador Oswaldo Aranha wrote from Washington in 1935 to a friend, "a Brazil of white men . . . nothing of other races."[14] A letter removed clandestinely from a diplomatic mail pouch provoked rage when the press was informed of a Chilean air aide's remark that the Brazilian armed forces were filled with "Indians and Negroes."[15] Aranha repeatedly praised the United States as a "Nordic society," often lamenting with Vargas over the weaknesses in the Brazilian character, urging that diplomatic personnel be selected with an eye to the impression they might make.[16]

An undercurrent of xenophobia and anti-Semitism rose to the surface in the early 1930s, particularly among those members of the intellectual elite increasingly disconcerted by the specter of Marxist-influenced internationalism. Brazil's Jewish population, estimated at 7,000 in 1917, grew sevenfold between 1928 and 1934, although restrictions on further immigration in the 1934 constitution severely reduced quotas on Jews fleeing Nazi Germany.[17] While the Vargas era by no means fostered anti-Semitism, it tolerated the rise of such activity, particularly by the fascist Integralists, whose virulent anti-Semitic campaign borrowed directly from Nazi propaganda materials. Some government officials echoed the atmosphere of the times by remaining silent on the issue publicly, but attacking Jewish activities in their private correspondence.[18]

In *Preparação ao nacionalismo* (1934), Affonso Arinos de Mello Franco catalogued centuries of agitation by Jewish enemies of the status quo: Marx; Weimar Jewish internationalists; such "Jewish" French revolutionaries as Marat ("Mosessohn"), Danton ("David"), Robespierre ("Rubin"), and Rousseau. The author, a generally respectable social critic, relied on such scurrilous anti-Semitic tracts as the Portuguese Mario Saa's *A Invasão dos judeus* (1926), a work popularized by the Nazis. "This weak [Jewish] race," Mello Franco declared, "incapable of producing economic wealth but prodigiously able to enrich itself through transactions . . . [and] with [this] capital, [it] realizes its ambitious dream to dominate other peoples."[19]

Xenophobia dominated the debates over immigration restriction in the 1933-34 Constituent Assembly, where deputies led by physician Miguel Couto, armed with extensive pseudo-scientific data, condemned non-European immigration, particularly Japanese. Speakers attacked the alleged clannishness of Japanese agricultural settlers, their failure to adopt Brazilian ways, and their loyalty to Imperial Japan. Others warned of the "yellow peril." An earlier survey of predominantly rural attitudes toward race and immigration showed that, while 97 per cent of those queried favored continued immigration of Europeans to Brazil, preferably Italians, Germans, and Portuguese, only 45 per cent would permit Asiatics to enter. Although virtually all respondents paid homage to the value of the Negro's services rendered as slave and free laborer, only 18 per cent declared their willingness to permit black immigration.[20]

A self-conscious cry of distress over the national identity emerged after 1930 among certain intellectuals. Influenced by the earlier writings of Euclides da Cunha, Graça Aranha, Alberto Torres, and others, they were labeled Brazil's *jeunesse dorée* by sociologist Guerreiro Ramos. Included were Alceu Amoroso Lima and his theme of neo-orthodox Catholicism (moral, not structural, reform); Affonso Arinos de Mello Franco and his goal of modernization by an elitist aristocracy; and Octávio de Faria and his pessimistic view of unredeemable national corruption.[21] These writers rejected the naïve glorification of Brazil typified by Affonso Celso's *Porque me ufano do meu paiz* (1901), and the idealization of the Indian as the "noble hero of the jungle" in the poems of Gonçalves Dias in the 1840s and José de Alencar's novels *O Guarani* (1857) and *Iracema* (1865).[22] The Indian, Mello Franco wrote angrily in 1936, contributed only "improvidence and dissipation" to the Brazilian character; the Negro gave it its "preoccupation with sexuality," its occultism, and its obsession with "cabalistic numerology." Brazil was doomed, he concluded, "to a state based openly or secretly on brute force."[23]

Anxiety plagued the new sociology. Many Brazilian intellectuals avidly read the works of such European racists as Gustave Le Bon and Ludwig Gumplowicz. Euclides da Cunha's eloquent *Os sertões* branded the Brazilian mulatto as inferior, a concept shared by Francisco José Oliveira Vianna, a brilliant and conservative critic of the Brazilian political structure and a self-proclaimed disciple of Alberto Torres.[24] In 1928 Paulo Prado's widely successful *Retrato do Brasil* identified sensuality and greed as the twin pillars of the historical past. The "Blue Series" (Coleção Azul), edited by Augusto Frederico Schmidt, produced five books of criticism (two others originally chosen for publication appeared independently), all of them efforts to evaluate the dilemma of the times, as had been fashionable during the previous decade in Europe.

The first book in the series, Martins de Almeida's *Brasil errado*, published in October, 1932, lamented Brazil's lack of ideology and its disorganized currents of public opinion. The Brazilian government, Almeida declared, had been an "organizational disaster," based upon tribal relations among parental clans. At fault were the Brazilian's passive resistance to the nation's vast potential, Brazil's subtropical environment, and its topographical obstacles to the penetration of the interior.[25] Affonso Arinos de Mello Franco's *Introdução à realidade brasileira* urged that the intellectual assert himself in political affairs and combat regionalism and internationalism.[26] Virgínio Santa Rosa attacked the middle classes as pauperized and divided among themselves: as a result, he wrote in *O sentido de tenentismo*, the tenentes must consummate, not abandon, the revolutionary task initiated by the seizure of power in 1930.[27] Echoing the spirit of the series, Azevedo Amaral, writing in 1935, placed the roots of distorted social evolution in the recent past, asserting that since the beginning of the nineteenth century Brazil had suffered progressive denationalization and, as a result, lacked national consciousness. What was needed, he advised, was an economic state "oriented and directed exclusively by those representing the productive forces of the nation."[28]

But the post-1930 critics made few attempts to remedy the national condition through specific measures for reform, prescribing instead sweeping theoretical panaceas. Those who did take an active political stance in the mid-1930s generally joined one of the two movements of the times which advocated radical change—the Integralists or the popular front National Liberation Alliance (Alliança Nacional Libertadora, or ANL). Other intellectuals avoided political involvement but expressed their search for national self-examination in such analytical works produced during the 1930s as sociologist and folklorist Gilberto Freyre's *Casa Grande e senzala* (1934) and *Sobrados e mocambos* (1936), and Sérgio Buarque de Holanda's *Raízes do Brasil* (1936), published as the initial work in the new Documentos Brasileiros series, which joined the Coleção Brasiliana founded in 1931 and which eventually reached one hundred volumes on all phases of Brazilian studies.

To be sure, the period between 1930 and 1935 exuded a feeling of change, rooted in the new political innovations in the areas of social, welfare, and nationalistic legislation. The wage earner, who, according to Octávio Ianni, prior to 1930 had been to government authorities a "question of law enforcement," now became a "question of politics."[29] Gilberto Freyre, Artur Ramos, Edison Carneiro, and Antônio Silva Mello probed aspects of social history unrecognized in earlier decades. Fiction by Jorge Amado, Érico Veríssimo, José Américo de Almeida, Graciliano Ramos, Carlos Drummond, José Lins do Rêgo, and Raquel de Queiróz created new interest in local and regional themes. Social awareness leaped from the canvases of Emiliano di Cavalcanti and Cândido Portinari; interest in Brazilian folk culture was stimulated by the musical compositions of Heitor Villa-Lobos. The establishment of modern university structure dates from 1934-35 when unified faculties of Philosophy, Arts, and Letters were created in São Paulo and Rio de Janeiro. In São Paulo, authorities invited teams of professors from France, Italy, Germany, and the United States to counsel university officials and to lecture: the new university became a symbol for paulistas of their efforts to maintain their personal initiative. Academic visitors to São Paulo included T. Lynn Smith of Louisiana and French scholars Emile Coornaert, Jean Gage, who inaugurated a graduate degree program in history, and Paul Bastide, who spent four years in the state as a consultant on yellow fever eradication. In the Federal District, educator Anísio Teixeira, fresh from a Master's degree from Teachers College, Columbia University, under John Dewey, planned dramatic advances in the areas of public education and pedagogical reform. But unlike the paulistas, Teixeira was forced to work on the federal level, where, for reasons to be discussed later, his reforms were distrusted and opposed.

The urban middle class generally shared the same values and aspirations as the upper-class elite. This group, comprising members of the government bureaucracy, commercial proprietors, the clergy, the middle-level military officialdom, and the white-collar sector, stubbornly resisted or remained oblivious to the need for social change. Fearing lest Vargas stir the working classes, the middle class passively accepted the squeeze of low wages and high consumer taxes to which it was subjected.[30] Negroes, mestizos, and caboclos, as well as some whites on the lowest economic levels, filled the ranks of the lower class, itself divided into urban and rural sectors. The urban working class, despite the slow growth of industrialization through the 1930s, remained relatively small: from an estimated 275,000 at the time of the 1920 census, it rose to approximately 700,000 by 1938.[31]

Although Vargas had established a ministry of labor at the outset of his administration and decreed extensive syndical privileges, organized labor remained largely impotent. Only one union per trade was recognized by the Labor Ministry, a reflection of the corporative nature of Vargas' early social legislation, and all other unions passed into renegade status.[32] Only members of recognized unions could bring cases to the newly established labor courts. In early 1934 the administration decreed mandatory annual paid vacations, but only for members of government-sponsored bodies. The 1934 constitution permitted plural unionism and expanded the coverage of the Labor Code, but under the Estado Nôvo in 1937 unions were again restricted to one per category. Although that oppressive regime allowed no syndical freedom, the Labor Ministry's share of the federal budget tripled, to a total of 3.85 per cent, between 1936 and 1940.[33] Industrial wages were generally highest in São Paulo, where they averaged 10$000 per day according to official statistics, whereas in Rio de Janeiro state factory workers received 6$100, and in Pará, 5$800—one milréis (1$000) being equivalent to approximately 7 cents (U.S.). Factories offered no compensation for work layoffs; employees suspected of extralegal union sympathies were summarily dismissed. The industrial wage index jumped from 230 to 315 (1920 = 100) between 1930 and 1938, but the cost of living index also rose, from 290 to 490.[34] In 1937 a kilo of medium-quality rice cost 1$600 in Rio de Janeiro; a kilo of sugar could be bought for 1$100; a pair of shoes for 16$000. Communists dominated some nongovernment syndicates, chiefly in the transport and utilities industries in Rio de Janeiro and São Paulo. Labor unrest in rural areas—especially in the north, where such activity was considered rebellion against local authority and was generally suppressed militarily—received no publicity, being reported only in the press of the radical left and occasionally by foreign correspondents, most notably by those representing *The Times* of London. Federal legislation regulating wages and labor did not extend to rural agricultural workers, some of whom, according to an observer in 1935, earned 1$400 daily in the rubber fields or collecting cashew nuts.[35]

Some illegal strikes occurred in urban areas during the 1930s, but the news media ignored them, as if by silent agreement among editors. Few newspapers were sufficiently strong financially to stand alone: most had to accept subsidies and bribes from private interests, politicians, and foreign consulates. Of the several dozen Rio de Janeiro newspapers, only five— *A Noite, O Globo, Jornal do Brasil, Correio da Manhã,* and *Jornal do Commercio*—enjoyed financial independence.[36] Virtually all leading newspapers throughout Brazil heavily stressed international and local coverage, usually limiting their treatment of national affairs to news of ministerial functions, pronouncements, and new fiscal policies. The single national wire service, Havas (which was in part controlled by German capital), competed with the overseas wires of the Associated Press and United Press. Two firms, Havas and the completely German-owned Transocean, shared the telegraph service. Many local newspapers across Brazil were linked into one of the several national chains, such as Assis Chateaubriand's *Diários Associados.*

While the bulk of public opinion occupied the middle range of the ideological spectrum, a variety of positions competed for public attention in the relatively free atmosphere in the aftermath of the 1934 constitution. But by November, 1937—or by May, 1938, with the effective destruction of the Integralist movement—the furthest of these extremes had collapsed, although Vargas quietly adopted some of the nationalistic measures advocated by radical right and left.

On the far right in 1935 lay the small but potentially powerful domestic Nazi and fascist groups, Italian, Polish, and German, poised throughout southern Brazil among its unassimilated immigrant populations. These organizations, not directly linked with the generally indigenous Brazilian Integralist movement, received financial support from the foreign governments involved and from within the local communities. Nazi propagandists claim the presence of between 800,000 and 1,000,000 *Volksdeutsche* Brazilians, although only approximately 100,000 still retained their German citizenship, 220,000 having been born in Germany.[37] The majority of German immigrants came to Brazil between 1855 and 1934, mostly as agricultural settlers in the southern states. Italian immigration during the same period represented the largest single bloc of arrivals, followed by the Portuguese, Spaniards, Poles, Japanese, and Arabs. Many of the newcomers took up residence in the state of São Paulo.

The Italians, Portuguese, and Spanish, in general more effectively assimilated than the other immigrant groups, avoided fascist militancy, although Italo-Brazilian cultural groups cheered Mussolini and received his envoys. Facing rising organized hostility toward themselves, Japanese community leaders concentrated upon the administration of their agricultural settlements in the south and in the Amazon, most of which, after a study tour under the auspices of the Japanese ambassador to Brazil in 1927, planted and cultivated cotton. A Japanese trade mission visited Brazil in 1934 and signed minor agreements for cotton exports. Upset at the rise in Japanese settlers—one half of all immigrants to Brazil during the three-year period 1931-34 came from Japan—the Constituent Assembly fixed a quota for Japanese immigrants at 2,711 persons annually, a reduction of 82 per cent from the 1924-34 level.[38] The Poles, the Germans, and, to a much lesser degree, the Italians operated primary and secondary schools in their own languages, a factor which restricted cultural assimilation until such foreign-language schools were curtailed by Vargas at the end of the decade. In 1927, 1,177 German-language private schools functioned in the south: 937 in Rio Grande do Sul, 180 in Santa Catarina, and 60 in Paraná. By 1937 there were at least 2,500 German-language schools, most of them affiliated with the Rio Embassy through city- and statewide *Deutsche Schulvereine*. The German-language press comprised ten daily newspapers and a total of forty cultural, agricultural, and fraternal publications, most of which were soon suspended by government decree after the imposition of the Estado Nôvo.

The Germans staffed twenty-nine diplomatic legations in Brazil during the 1930s, second only to the Italians' fifty-three. The German Embassy, Rio de Janeiro's largest, administered a broad range of cultural and propaganda programs; it ran the offices of Lufthansa and Luftschiffbau Zeppelin, the German airlines, as well as the German Railways Tourist Bureau, and supervised the commercial activity of the *Reichsdeutsche* community through its Foreign Trade Office. By mid-decade the German Embassy controlled most of the 2,000 *Volksdeutsche* organizations in Brazil, the largest being the Brazilian *Verband Deutscher Vereine* in São Paulo, which numbered more than 15,000 members.[39] Youth movements trained Teuto-Brazilians in the handling of small arms and in military encampment, and sent the most promising to Germany for additional instruction. The federal police, which employed 5,000 agents in Rio alone, closely surveyed Nazi activities, although its chief, ex-tenente Felinto Müller, sympathized with Hitler's government and maintained frequent contact with Reich officials.[40] By early 1938, Vargas decided to suppress the *Volksdeutsche* movement as a threat to national security; arrests of Nazi leaders in February were followed by a decree on April 18 outlawing all foreign-based political organizations. Brazilian-German relations reached their nadir following the attack on the President in May in which German nationals were implicated; relations gradually improved between 1939 and 1941, only to collapse in early 1942 with the formulation of the Roosevelt-Vargas alliance.

Polish fascists were active in Brazil primarily during the period of the Pilsudski government, operating in collaboration with Polish consulates in São Paulo and Curitiba. Occasionally they received financial aid from Nazi sources as well.[41] Agents collaborated with the Polish clergy in Paraná, working out of the Central Union of Poles in Brazil, located in Curitiba.

The Polish paramilitary youth (*Junak*) society operated eighty-four separate groups in the southern states in 1933-34. Polish fascist activities declined, however, after the death of Pilsudski in May, 1935.

The domestic Integralist movement (Plínio Salgado's Brazilian Integralist Action [Ação Integralista Brasileira, or AIB]) dominated the far right of the political spectrum. It originated in 1932 among conservative intellectuals in São Paulo, an heir to the cultural rebellion first articulated during São Paulo's Modern Art Week in early 1922. The Integralists rekindled interest in the past, championing indigenous Brazilian culture, and launching a dogma dedicated to the establishment in Brazil of an "organic" authoritarian and political order disciplined by ritual and absolute allegiance to the supreme national chief. The middle classes, academicians, Brazilians of German and Italian origin, and the armed forces (most notably the tradition-centered navy) provided the movement with its most ardent supporters; it also attracted financial backing from industrialists and businessmen. It boasted such prominent adherents as author San Tiago Dantas; poet Augusto Frederico Schmidt; historians Hélio Vianna, Américo Lacombe, and Gustavo Barroso; the brilliant young jurist, Miguel Reale; and Father Dom Helder Câmara, in later years a progressive archbishop and spokesman for the Catholic left.

But the main body of Brazilian conservatism lay outside of formal political movements. Unmeasurable and only occasionally expressive publicly, it reposed in the traditional sectors of society: the Church, the military, and the rural landowners. The Brazilian Church defended the traditional system although, despite the professed Catholicism of an overwhelming percentage of the population, its power was restricted by organizational weaknesses, small numbers of priests, and the countering influence of spiritism, in both its African and its European forms.[42] Generally, the Church blamed the abuses of liberal democracy for the ills of modern life. Cardinal Sebastião Leme of Rio de Janeiro spoke for the Church in official circles; he was close to Vargas and often dined alone with him. Leme sponsored a militant lay organization, the Catholic Electoral League (Liga Eleitoral Católica), which lobbied in the Constituent Assembly and was instrumental in winning constitutional approval for religious instruction in the public schools, but in 1934 the Cardinal allowed its political influence to diminish by incorporating it into the less militant Catholic Action (Ação Católica).[43]

In the army, the victorious tenentes purged many of the older, inactive officers following the Liberal Alliance coup, forging a *modus vivendi* with the other officers who adopted their philosophical outlook. The exposure of the military to the rigid methods of the French military mission which had been invited to Brazil prior to World War I (and under which Góes Monteiro as a cadet had been trained) contributed to the army's readiness to accept the tenente outlook. Vargas' response to tenente demands to build up the strength of the federal armed forces further unified the military command, although some officers, including Góes Monteiro himself, felt at times the process was excessively slow. A wide gap separated enlisted men and their officers; military officials knew that poor conditions in the barracks and low pay undermined morale, but efforts at reform were sporadic. The navy, the most traditionalist of the armed services, remained the least sympathetic to Vargas and the call for change. Some naval officers backed the reactionary Brazilian Monarchist Party, which called for the restoration of the Empire and the reunification of Church and State, separated in 1890 by the founders of the Republic.[44]

The uncertain atmosphere between 1930 and 1936 and the wide divergences within the coalition hindered any elaboration of political consistency behind the banners of the Liberal Alliance. The constant pressure upon the President accentuated his ideological eclecticism and forced him to manipulate among interest groups, earning him a reputation for opportunism and deviousness. But this unpredictability disarmed his opponents and provided him with the weapon of surprise, a factor which contributed positively to his political longevity as the years progressed. In the absence of national parties—a phenomenon which lasted until 1945—local political factions often formed around old, dominant families or personalities instead of substantive ideological issues. Most of the state parties paid lip service to the principles of classical liberalism while reflecting the interests of the local elite, differentiated less by ideology than by the ins and outs of power. In this context Vargas thrived, served by his ability to moderate divergent internal elements and to discern the forces of political ascendancy and incorporate them into his personal political orbit.

Increased industrial growth and the federal government's efforts to expand commerce and promote fiscal growth shaped the formation of an influential group of businessmen around the President. In 1930 Vargas had been initially hostile to the industrial sector, which distrusted, among other things, his attempt to make himself the *patrão* of the working class, his December, 1930, "two-thirds" law which regulated the employment of non-Brazilian nationals by industrial firms, and the federal government's tax on transmission of profits abroad and its efforts to reduce tariff protection for "artificial" industries (those utilizing protected imported raw materials for domestic manufacture). But by 1934, relations had improved markedly. Employees warmed to the effects of government-controlled unionism and the officially sanctioned industrial associations, which institutionalized the earlier strike-breaking, price-fixing activities of such formerly private organizations as the São Paulo Textile Industrial Center. And with the effective transfer of initiative in fiscal and industrial matters from legislative to executive auspices under Vargas, cooperation between businessmen and the government now became a political necessity.[45]

By 1935 the President's inner circle had acquired many spokesmen for foreign and domestic industrial and commercial interests. Included were the Guinle family—Carlos, Octávio, and Guilherme—with holdings in metals, textiles, hotels, and banks; paulista José Maria Whitaker, his provisional government's first finance minister and personal agent for various British and French firms; João Daudt de Oliveira of the Rio de Janeiro Commercial Association; lawyer and industrialist José Carlos de Macedo Soares, later a cabinet minister and a would-be successor to Vargas in 1937; industrialist, planner, and publicist Roberto Simonsen of São Paulo; Eugenio Gudim, representing Lazard Brothers of London; Valentim F. Bouças, Vargas' golf crony, son of a Spanish immigrant and representative of the Hollerith and IBM corporations; Euvaldo Lodi of the Brazilian Federation of Industry; and newspaper baron Francisco de Assis Chateaubriand, a lawyer for numerous foreign business interests including Itabira Iron, later to become Vargas' implacable opponent.

The Brazilian government traditionally balanced its budget by contracting foreign loans, which resulted in extensive foreign influence domestically and placed Brazil in dependence upon foreign sources of capital. Efforts of Oswaldo Aranha in 1933 to negotiate loan repayment without new borrowing made him unpopular among foreign capitalists and may have contributed to his removal from the treasury post in 1933.[46] British firms dominated foreign investment in Brazil until approximately 1930, when the United States became the single largest investor.[47] British groups exercised control of several major railroads in Brazil, including the Great Western Railway in the northeast and the Leopoldina, São Paulo, and Vitória lines in the center-south.[48] Other British firms operated port facilities in Manaus, Recife, and Rio de Janeiro, power and light utilities in various cities, meat processing plants, the Western Telegraph Company, and banking facilities. Investment activities of United States–based corporations included Amazon rubber production; port operations in Pará and Salvador; gas and power in Maranhão, Bahia, and São Paulo; meat packing in the south; and coffee distribution and export. United States companies in Rio de Janeiro by 1941 included the Companhia Nacional de Cimento Portland (entirely owned by the Lone Star Cement Company), General Motors, Ford, Westinghouse, Singer, General Electric, and Sinclair Oil. French firms were involved in sugar, coffee, and salt production and controlled the port of Angra dos Reis in the state of São Paulo. Japanese and Italian investment was less developed. German firms expanded their activities after 1930, especially in banking, pharmaceuticals, beverages, and air transport. Krupp, Siemens, Stinnes, and Bayer were represented with local factories by 1935. Of Brazil's nine major airlines in 1936, eight—Air France, LATI, Pan American, Varig, Vasp, Luftschiffbau Zeppelin, Deutsche Lufthansa, and Condor—were foreign-owned or -controlled, the last four by German interests. Of 362 new corporations authorized by the administration in 1936, it is alleged that only 121 were clearly national in ownership, although many named Brazilian businessmen to directorships.[49]

While the government consistently welcomed foreign investments, weighing carefully, for example, a comprehensive offer from a German trade mission in late 1934 for bilateral trade based on nonconvertible currency, increasing numbers of spokesmen within the administration demanded a more nationalistic economic policy as the decade progressed. As early as 1931 the War Ministry established a commission to investigate possibilities for the creation of a national steel industry; in 1932 José Américo de Almeida called for a state steel complex; and Góes Monteiro, the chief advocate of economic nationalism in the armed forces, repeated the request in 1934. The industrial and manufacturing associations favored cooperation with the government in economic planning and favored centralization of political administration.[50]

Formal opposition to Vargas' leadership primarily reposed in the Congress after constitutional government was restored in 1934. The so-called parliamentary opposition bloc included diverse political personalities united chiefly by their dislike of the government and their desire to restrict federal power. Led by ex-President of the Republic Artur Bernardes of Minas Gerais, Borges de Medeiros and João Neves da Fontoura of Rio Grande do Sul, and Otávio Mangabeira of Bahia, the bloc adopted the classical liberalism of Washington Luís and sympathized with the São Paulo revolt of 1932.

Although the opposition included a small radical group headed by deputies João Café Filho of Rio Grande do Norte, Abguar Bastos of Goiás, and Senator Abel Chermont of Pará, few genuine ideological differences separated the legislative opposition and the administration. Socially, members of the opposition retained their membership in the pleasant social set frequented by high government, business, and military officials. The opposition bloc regarded its criticism as constructive. Its members, led on the floor by João Neves da Fontoura, a deputy from Vargas' Rio Grande do Sul and an eloquent orator, protested individual political acts of the administration, mostly in the sphere of civil liberties, but offered no basic policy alternatives of their own.[51] In equal measure, the public media reflected the aspirations of the government and the political elite, although no consensus existed until Vargas temporarily forged it by authoritarian methods after 1937. Between 1930 and 1937, the President's name rarely appeared in the daily press except in connection with state functions and official ceremonies. Even Vargas' opponents generally shared his advocacy of controlled reform and his goal of political and economic stability.

No significant moderate left flourished save for such individual voices as Café Filho (who, as he gained political experience, methodically gravitated to the center) and a few liberal newspapers such as Rio de Janeiro's *A Pátria*. The federal intervenor in the capital, Dr. Pedro Ernesto Baptista, orchestrated numerous public works programs and assumed a progressive posture, but his lack of political sophistication made him vulnerable, and Vargas easily deposed him in 1935.

A vocal but small and largely ineffectual radical left occupied the furthest pole of the political spectrum. Its press, centered in Rio de Janeiro, buoyed up the movement by tireless attacks upon government authorities and the prevailing social and economic system, particularly emphasizing foreign influence and documenting working-class suffering. This press encompassed several dozen newspapers, the most important of which were the Brazilian Communist Party's *A Manhã* in the capital, *A Platéia* in São Paulo, and the underground *Classe Operária*. As a movement, however, the radical left suffered from uncontrolled internal division. Lacking a trade union base, it appealed chiefly to middle-class intellectuals and urban immigrants from Central and Eastern Europe. The Brazilian Communist Party (PCB), organized in the aftermath of the Russian Revolution, constructed its base out of remnants of the small anarchosyndicalist movement active in Brazil since the turn of the century, but it did not digest these elements easily. Angry conflict between Stalinist and Trotskyite factions hindered the party; the Washington Luís administration outlawed the PCB in 1927, although the Leninist PCB, led by Octávio Brandão and the sensitive and brilliant young theorist, Astrojildo Pereira, remained dominant by establishing the Brazilian General Workers' Federation (CGTB) and a brief-lived electoral front, the Worker's and Peasant's Bloc, the party's first attempt at mass political participation.[52]

But police repression and continued ideological schisms weakened the radical left under Vargas. Purges from 1931 to 1934 expelled many of the older party leaders and alienated many potential adherents. Strikes, often violently suppressed by the police, occurred more frequently than most Brazilians recognized, since the daily press generally excluded such coverage. In late 1934, authorities arrested Worker's and Peasant's Bloc-supported candidates and imprisoned them in spite of habeas corpus writs submitted to the judiciary by their attorneys.[53]

A feeling of uncertainty slowly expanded in the wake of the animosities and sporadic acts of violence which accompanied the statewide election campaigns in late 1934 and early 1935, particularly after a number of pro-Vargas state electoral slates, some headed by federally appointed interventors, were defeated by hostile opposition parties identified with the pre-1930 status quo. Foremost among those expressing cynicism with regard to the political climate was Oswaldo Aranha, who, now Brazilian ambassador in the United States and frustrated by the isolation of his post, voiced despair at the course of events in Brazil. Aranha, Vargas' close lieutenant in Rio Grande do Sul, the leading civilian tactician of the 1930 Revolution, and finance and interior minister under the provisional government, had, some said, been exiled from Brazil because he posed a threat to Vargas' popularity; he often could not gain the Foreign Ministry's ear, a frustration which encouraged his extensive correspondence from Washington with Vargas and other confidants. "Our politicians are masochists and sadists," he wrote to deputy João Mangabeira in June, 1935; "Brazil is too large for its future to be left to them."[54] "The civil, military, and economic weaknesses of our country," Aranha complained to War Minister Góes Monteiro, "are the fruits of ignorance, sickness, and lack of personal capacity." If Brazil did not rid itself of internal disorganization, he warned, it would follow in the footsteps of Italy, Germany, and Russia.[55] General Góes Monteiro, too, spoke darkly, attributing the tendency to authoritarianism to the basic lack of credence in the capacity of the Brazilian people to govern themselves. Only a government which "attends to current realities and resists national decomposition," he added, could overcome Brazil's "fatalistic nature."[56]

More ominous clouds gathered as 1934 progressed. The left made preparations to organize under a mass political front, to counter domestic fascist influence, and to attack what it considered the domination of the Brazilian economy by foreign capitalist interests. Integralist ranks swelled, feeding on reports of growing communist strength. Armed clashes between Integralists and communists threatened public order and justified strengthened internal security measures by government officials, leading to the closing of the left's popular front, the ANL, in mid-1935. An abortive insurrection in the name of this movement in late November left the nation under a partially suspended constitution and a decreed state of siege. The signs that Brazil might abandon liberal constitutionalism entirely were becoming apparent by early 1936. In March of that year, Viriato Vargas wrote to his brother from Pôrto Alegre, citing Nietzsche, and calling "democratism" a form of "decadence" and the "decomposition of organized force."[57]

2

THE VARGAS
ADMINISTRATION

Getúlio Vargas dominated Brazil during most of the period between 1930 and 1954, when he abruptly took his own life in the bedroom of the presidential palace. His ability to hide behind a shield of inscrutability has magnified the enigma of his personality. Vargas' calculating ability to judge events and to retain power puzzled observers who dismissed him as a pawn of vested interests, a small man obsessed with power. Relentless yet good-natured, crafty yet bland, Vargas viewed the presidency as a vehicle for authoritative rule but not personal aggrandizement.

Vargas was born on April 19, 1883, in the bellicose frontier town of São Borja, Rio Grande do Sul. He was the third of five sons born to rancher and local political boss Manuel do Nascimento Vargas and Dona Cândida Dornelles Vargas. His father, named an honorary general by Marshal Floriano Peixoto for service during the Paraguayan War and for his continued loyalty in the 1890s, faithfully followed positivist state chieftain Júlio de Castilhos. As a youth, Getúlio enlisted in the local Sixth Infantry Battalion to facilitate his admission to the military academy at Rio Pardo. He studied briefly at the Ouro Prêto Preparatory School in Minas Gerais but departed with his older brothers Viriato and Protásio when they became involved in a conflict which led to the death of a classmate. Two years later he joined the Twenty-fifth Infantry Battalion in Pôrto Alegre, the state capital. At the same time he enrolled in the local Law Faculty and became a member of Castilhos' Republican Party.

Vargas did not expect to be mobilized, but a sudden crisis between Bolivia and Brazil over the territory of Acre resulted in his transfer to the Mato Grosso border as a sergeant with his unit. Quickly disillusioned, he abandoned his military career and returned to law school, where he was elected class orator. He received his degree in 1909, a year after party leaders—prodded by Vargas' father—named him state attorney general. The young attorney quickly became known as a protégé of party chieftain Borges de Medeiros. He rose quickly, earning a reputation for brightness and loyalty. Vargas progressed to the state assembly, to its presidency, to the federal Chamber of Deputies in 1922, and, in 1926, to finance minister in the Washington Luís government. In the tradition of gaúcho state politics he inherited the command of São Borja's Seventh Corps of pro-visional troops (*provisórios*), and set out—as his faithful daughter Alzira has noted—to defend the ideas of his party.[1] If Vargas objected to his state's tradition of bossism and one-party domination, he did not show it publicly.

He returned to Pôrto Alegre in 1928 to become state governor, using his good relations with the federal administration to secure favors for gaúcho interests. He obtained aid for failing producers of dried meat (*charque*), who were unable to halt the flow of contraband goods shipped across the border from Uruguay and Argentina. He also established the Bank of Rio Grande do Sul to provide agricultural credit. A popular governor, although under Borges' shadow, Vargas received the nomination of the Liberal Alliance as its compromise candidate in late 1930. Notwithstanding a lack-luster campaign, the Liberal Alliance coup catapulted him into the presi-dency despite his narrow but decisive defeat at the polls.

By mid-1934, with the armed forces standing silently behind him, Vargas retained firm control of the national administration. His revised coalition now included formerly hostile manufacturers and growing numbers of federal-level bureaucrats, the latter the by-products of the administration's courting of the urban middle classes and its use of federal services to counter traditional state and regional loyalties. Although future political trends remained cloudy, the growing influence of the military and the use of censorship and police repression foreshadowed later developments, in particular the consolidation of government power at the national level.

A pedestrian figure unmarked by personal eloquence, Vargas worked late over administrative matters and avoided public exposure. His five-foot-four-inch rotund figure clothed in baggy white linen suits and his fondness for small jokes and black cigars invited newsmen to parody his personal appearance.[2] He rode horses on his family ranch in São Borja, but he confessed to friends that riding made his backside sore. Taking up golf in the mid-1930s, he laughed at his haplessness—but he used the fair-ways for private negotiations. He frequently sounded out his aides on political issues during midnight poker sessions. He attended only one opera in his life, a Wagnerian performance at the Municipal Theater which he left after the first curtain. He rarely relaxed at his desk, constantly sifting a large volume of reports on all aspects of political and economic matters. He maintained an extensive correspondence with friends and members of his family. Military and police officials provided confidential reports which included data gleaned from letters and telegrams intercepted indiscriminately from persons loyal to the federal government and those opposed to it.

Vargas was a curious blend of positivist and *caudilho* attributes, so audacious that in the largest Catholic country in the world he named one son Luther and another Calvin.[3] Oswaldo Aranha likened Vargas at his presidential desk to "a Christ among thieves."[4] Few men enjoyed close relationships with him, even high government officials. Aranha, the leading civilian ally of the tenentes and assumed by many to be the President's heir, was sent brooding to Washington in 1934 in an ambassadorship which amounted to political exile. By 1935 thirty-four different men had occupied the nine cabinet posts and ninety-four had governed the twenty states and the Federal District as interventors, a high rate of turnover for any regime.[5] Each administrative change precipitated flurries of intrigue as each state jockeyed for patronage. States unofficially staked out individual ministeries: Pernambuco generally sought labor; the northeast, public works; São Paulo, justice and foreign affairs; and Minas Gerais, agriculture and education. Newspapers publicized rumored realignments with intense interest, an activity indicative of the survival into the 1930s of the forms of the Old Republic's state-oriented politics—and one which afforded Vargas a clear field in which to exercise his political acuity.

As president, Vargas closely supervised his administration, aided by Luís Vergara, chief of his personal staff from 1935 to 1945, and his administrative alter ego. Vargas ruled over his cabinet by dealing with each minister separately in a personal and paternalistic manner. Often he exasperated officials by announcing new policies for their departments without first notifying them. The presidential coterie of cronies and aides sheltered him from unwelcome intruders and isolated him from the day-to-day world. His daughter Alzira and his three brothers—Benjamin (Beijo), Protásio, and Viriato—all served him through his tenure as chief of state.

Although he regularly scanned the press, he rarely reacted visibly to journalistic criticism.[6] He never put on airs as president; frequently he met visitors to his Petrópolis summer residence in his pajamas, an old rural

Brazilian custom. Vargas earned a reputation for treating his associates well, but there is no evidence that he accumulated personal wealth as a consequence of his position. He was probably as honest as any civilian president of the country.

Vargas' keen ability to maintain his political balance and to anticipate developments failed him only in 1945 when he lost the support of the armed forces. As president, he proved himself neither liberal nor inflexibly conservative. He supervised innovation, but he did not become known as an innovator; rather, he exploited existing trends, and rarely created new ones.[7] No sentimentalist, he sacrificed his own friends and the very tradition of state autonomy which launched his own career when this seemed politically expedient.

His handling of the civil war in 1932 boosted his political reputation and won him the respect of many of his former critics, who now spoke of his backbone of "cold steel."[8] Opposition politicians demanded that the federal government reveal its ideological goals; in response, the administration simply retreated even further from public view. By 1934, Vargas governed from behind closed doors, occasionally meeting with businessmen and other visitors at the Jockey Club or similar private places. To the public Vargas maintained silence.

At the outset of 1935 Vargas wrote pessimistically about coming events, remarking to Oswaldo Aranha that the year was beginning "in an atmosphere of doubt and fear."[9] The state electoral campaigns revived the out-of-power local oligarchies and confronted several federal interventors with probable defeat, now that the law required assemblies to elect governors. Held fast by his public commitment to constitutionalism though he reportedly considered the new constitution inefficacious and unworthy of enforcement, Vargas chose to watch and wait.

The congressional opposition bloc justified its refusal to support administration policy as being necessary to prevent new incursions of federal power against the states and individual civil rights. To be sure, opposition spokesmen documented abuses committed by the government. But their stakes were larger: whether openly or in unspoken terms, most congressional opponents desired the protection of local prerogative and, in many cases, the return to preeminence of political groups identified with the pre-1930 order. This was clear in the platform of the São Paulo *bancada* to the 1933-34 Constituent Assembly, the majority of whose members later remained in the Congress as paulista representatives. Planks of this platform included the preservation of the traditional system of state and municipal autonomy; direct presidential elections; religious instruction in the public schools; the right of states to maintain militia; opposition to the proposed constitution's Indemnity Act (upholding retrospectively all acts of the provisional government); and amnesty for political exiles and enemies of the regime.[10] Only in the area of immigration restriction did São Paulo side with the tenente bloc, its *bancada* being particularly militant (with the exception of one deputy) against the Japanese.

The larger states consistently argued for state and municipal autonomy and for control of the sources of tax revenue, while the smaller states advocated such measures as agrarian credit for small landholders, aid for the development of port facilities, drought relief, and federal aid to education. The failure of the Congress to achieve unity, the absence of national political parties, and the persistence of deputies in putting forward the demands of their own states left Vargas disgusted while the legislators continued to orate. As the Congress produced little reform legislation through 1935 and 1936, critics began to consider means of circumventing it.

What the administration regarded as the fulfillment of the Liberal Alliance's revolutionary program emerged through a series of executive decrees, dating from November, 1930, to the establishment of the *Estado Nôvo* and beyond. The radical left attacked the measures as hollow betrayals, pointing to their evasive wording and their special ends. The new labor ministry, it charged, used its regulatory codes as a vehicle to circumscribe syndical freedom and to require police registration of labor union activists. As late as 1941, moreover, a survey uncovered extensive violations of work and hours legislation in São Paulo, the most advanced industrial state.[11] Nonetheless, Vargas' decrees between 1930 and 1936 represented a broad range of innovation:[12]

November 12, 1930
First labor minister named
November 14, 1930
First minister of education and public health named
December 12, 1930
Immigration of alien workers restricted
December 17, 1930
Retirement pension institutes created for state, municipal, public utility, transport, and communication workers

March 28, 1931
Regulations for workers' vacations standardized
August 29, 1931
Administrative norms for states and municipalities established
August 31, 1931
Charitable organizations, technical and general educational establishments regulated

February 24, 1932
Electoral reform code promulgated
March 21, 1932
Professional licensing established
April 27, 1932
Pension and retirement institutes empowered to write mortgages and provide loans for housing
May 4, 1932
Working hours for adult males regulated
May 17, 1932
Conditions for employment of adult women specified
September 26, 1932
Pension and retirement institutes empowered to provide emergency health and hospitalization coverage

October 29, 1932
Commercial establishments regulated
November 3, 1932
Conditions specified for employment of minors
July 10, 1934
Industrial disability insurance established
November 12, 1935
Night work for minors regulated; benefits to women before and after childbirth specified
January 14, 1936
Commissions to set minimum wages created
October 23, 1936
Civil service reform enacted (Readjustment Law)

In the economic sphere, fiscal problems continued to plague the government in 1934 and 1935. Bank of Brazil exchange director Marcos de Souza Dantas reported at the outset of 1935 that the federal government would not be able to meet its debt obligations specified by the schedule adopted in February of the previous year. The announcement provoked numerous outcries at home and abroad; as a result, Vargas resumed payments on the debt and Souza Dantas resigned. Vargas immediately dispatched a mission abroad to renegotiate the debt and arrange new loans. It was headed by his finance minister, Artur de Souza Costa, formerly the general manager of the leading Rio Grande do Sul bank. The mission signed a trade agreement with Washington by which Brazil received most-favored-nation status in exchange for mutual reduction of tariffs and guarantees that the nation's debt obligations would be met. The Vargas administration honored this agreement until November, 1937, when it again suspended payments. Souza Costa continued on to Europe, where he negotiated for credit with the Rothschilds and other private banking firms.[13] At home, the financial community looked with favor upon Vargas' efforts to achieve recovery through economic negotiations, while it counseled prudence: "The remedy against extremist desperation," José Bento de Monteiro Lobato, the modernist author and spokesman for natural resource development, wrote to Vargas in February, 1935, "must be . . . good economic sense and the restoration of prosperity."[14]

Whereas the collapse of world agricultural prices and the subsequent fall of the Old Republic stripped the rural landowning class, particularly the coffee planters and their allies, of its former political preeminence, industrialists, buoyed up by the inability of the economy to support prohibitively expensive imports, acquired increasing political influence through the new decade. Domestic iron and steel consumption, which dropped to 36 per cent of the 1929 level by 1931, fully recovered by 1935. The textile sector, spoken for by manufacturing associations in Rio de Janeiro and São Paulo, demanded continuous protection from the government to relieve pervasive industry-wide sluggishness, which manufacturers attributed to "overproduction" in spite of seemingly propitious conditions for growth. None of the textile producers publicly recognized the deeper reasons for their lethargy: the characteristic unwillingness of Brazilian industrialists to adopt technological processes and their conscious neglect of the need to expand the domestic market, in spite of the accession to textile manufacturers' demands for high tariff duties, restricted importation of industrial machinery (achieved after 1931), and, later, government support to facilitate exports.[15] Manufacturers failed to view their own workers as potential consumers; the survival of traditional paternalism in employer-employee relations precluded the award of higher salaries, training programs to expand the tiny skilled labor force, or the reduction of dependence upon unskilled manpower, as well as upon women and minors.[16]

But low agricultural prices and the inability of the planter sector to recover tied Vargas' hands. Until 1941 the government maintained the policy of destroying coffee surpluses. Meanwhile, the cruzeiro dropped yearly in value (see Appendix D). Other factors, including an often bitter arms race with Argentina, contributed to the air of uneasiness. To this must be added growing restlessness in the armed forces, sporadic strikes in the rural north as well as in São Paulo and in the Federal District, the continued growth of the Integralist movement, and, in early 1935, the emergence of the left as an active national political force.

The armed forces held the balance of power during the Vargas period, although restlessness stirred continually within military ranks. Trouble became public in 1934 when more than 600 cadets at the federal military academy struck in protest against José Pessôa, its commander (and the brother of Vargas' assassinated vice-presidential running mate). Pessôa was named to the command of the Military Academy (Escola Militar) at the end of that year. Having served with the French army from 1914 to 1918, the new director, appalled at the school's disorder, immediately announced a program of reform. He recruited top-flight officers for the faculty, initiated a campaign for cleanliness, and, introducing French training methods, imposed a stern program of physical exercise and discipline. But while standards rose sharply, his vanity and his martinetish passion for obedience aroused hatred in the cadets and provoked unrest.[17]

Early in 1935 a crisis broke out at the top of the military hierachy when the legislature refused to pass a bill increasing military salaries and granting related privileges. At about the same time, an investigation revealed an abortive antigovernment conspiracy among a group of discontented officers, involving among others the commander of the First Infantry Brigade.[18] On May 8, amid extensive public debate, War Minister Pedro Aurélio de Góes Monteiro resigned and was replaced immediately by General João Gomes, an officer considered unshakably loyal to Vargas. Góes explained his departure to Aranha and others on the grounds that he could no longer tolerate abuse reputedly leveled at his office; that left-wing officers had inflamed the atmosphere in the Military Club (Clube Militar); and that the army was becoming demoralized, presumably over the rejection of the military pay increase bill.[19] But the real reason arose from Góes Monteiro's abortive attempt to humiliate the legislature and increase the power of the military.

A month prior to his resignation, Góes had outlined a confidential plan to all active generals by which his departure would be used to force the government to override the legislature's defeat of the military privileges bill. All generals would refuse nomination to the ministry, thereby creating a crisis which would give Vargas no choice but to restore order.[20] Lack of unanimous support among the generals had destroyed the scheme. Even José Pessôa had demurred, saying in a letter to Góes Monteiro that "all possible measures for a just and humane settlement have not been exhausted." Góes replied pleadingly that the army should maintain solidarity for the "cohesion of the military class."[21] Defeated, and having threatened resignation publicly, Góes stepped down in early May.

A frustrated conspiracy within the military uncovered in March had shaken morale and prepared the atmosphere for Góes Monteiro's scheme. Vargas, kept informed by his agents, easily suppressed it.[22] Whatever the war minister's role had been, it did not ingratiate him with Vargas, who told Aranha that Góes, at odds personally with one of the other conspirators, had exaggerated the gravity of the conspiracy.[23] But the President held his temper following Góes' resignation. "I am a friend of [his], as you are," he told Aranha. "We know his defects and his qualities. He left in peace and will be given another position."[24] Others, citing Góes Monteiro's attempt to meddle in the government, were less kind. "Either [he] is abnormally unconscious," Luís Simões Lopes told Aranha, "or he is perverse, devoured by unlimited ambition."[25]

Military unrest continued through the remainder of 1935. Isolated barracks disturbances caused frequent changes in local command and worried federal officials. Newspapers reported renewed insubordination among military academy cadets.[26] On November 16, War Minister Gomes refused to elevate the controversial, pro-Integralist Colonel Newton Cavalcanti to general over forty-eight other officers on the promotion list despite heavy pressure from ultraconservatives. But in the aftermath of the insurrectionary revolts at the end of the month, Calvalcanti was promoted quietly and without opposition.

Crises in the states harassed Vargas through 1934 and 1935 and occupied most of his attention as president. The absence of national political parties worsened the situation, which produced a variety of strange alliances rooted in the desire of traditional state machines to regain control of patronage. Ambitious local politicians lent support to antigovernment groups. In some cases, the President postponed state elections to prevent open warfare between hostile factions.

The conflict in Rio Grande do Norte which followed the 1934 legislative mandate for state elections typified the federal government's difficulties. This northeastern state had languished in obscurity since the gradual decline of sugar agriculture after the seventeenth century, a decline compounded by the loss of slave labor through abolition and by the recurrent droughts cruelly afflicting the region into the twentieth century.[27] Cotton, the leading crop, yielded minimal profits in the 1930s, in the face of depressed prices, inadequate transportation (700 kilometers of semipaved roads and a skeletal railroad network which failed to link the western part of the state with Natal, the capital), primitive farming methods, a severe drought in 1931-32, and growing competition from São Paulo and Paraná as well as from neighboring Ceará and Paraíba. Natal, the principal port, stricken by a malarial epidemic in 1929, subsisted on small commerce and a bloated bureaucratic payroll. Steady emigration from the region and a rate of 42 deaths per 1000 population (1931)—50 per cent of those who died were children less than one year of age—restrained population growth despite a high birth rate. Abject poverty flourished in the state, only 19 per cent of whose land earned the classification "fertile."[28]

A rough synthesis of the frequently conflicting available data on education reveals that less than 2 per cent of the state's 22,000 enrolled primary school students in 1934 could hope to reach Rio Grande do Norte's twenty-one secondary schools. The 1920 census classified 81 per cent of the state's people as illiterate. The most notable schools in the state were Natal's Rio Grande do Norte Academy, with about six hundred male and female students, chiefly from the families of the local elite, and the Domestic School, founded in 1914, an impressive two-story institute which prepared half of its women students for teaching, the other half in sewing, music, and handicrafts. In 1926 the state, following no Latin American precedent, gave women the vote, although the event was tempered by the fact that a single political party, the Federal Republican Party (Partido Republicano Federal, or PRF), the instrument of the state's oligarchy of planters, ranchers, salt producers, merchants, and professionals, dominated political life down to 1930. There was no university: sons of the elite traditionally pursued higher studies elsewhere, mostly in Recife, but occasionally in Salvador or Rio de Janeiro.[29]

The Vargas coup upset the political oligarchy for the first time in a century, the PRF having continued as the successor to the Empire's Liberal Party (Partido Liberal). José Augusto Bezerra de Medeiros dominated the PRF. His maternal grandfather had directed the Liberal Party during the monarchy before serving as federal senator during the first sixteen years of the Republic—encouraging young José Augusto to adopt his mother's name, Medeiros, rather than his father's, Araújo. The PRF chieftain governed according to an orthodox liberal program which stressed public works, administrative reform, and economic improvement. The party attempted to aid cotton production through state aid to growers and, in the 1920s, to establish the state as a commercial aviation center. The state government constructed an airport and an aero-club with rest facilities for pilots and passengers, but the airport was rendered obsolete when larger airplanes bypassed Natal, although Air France, Lufthansa, and Pan American used its facilities until 1940 and it remained a major base until the end of the war. The PRF ignored the lower classes, lagged in education, public health, and transportation, and generally governed for its own sake.

Generations of social isolation in a poor, underpopulated state produced a closely knit social and economic elite. The political control of the oligarchy, however, was broken after 1930, and the federal interventors named by

Juarez Távora were outsiders—Irineu Joffily, a civilian from neighboring Paraíba; Aloísio Moura, later commander of the local Twenty-first Artillery Battalion (Batalhão de Caçadores, or BC); and Hercolino Cascardo, national chairman of the popular front National Liberation Alliance in 1935. Vargas broke the pattern when, in 1933, faced by continual hostility from PRF partisans, he named a *potyguar* (state resident) to the interventorship— Mário Raposa da Câmara, grandson of a leader of the old Liberal Party and the son of Augusto Leopoldo Raposa Câmara, José Augusto's vice-governor during his administration. Mário Câmara belonged to the state elite, but, as a federal treasury official in Rio de Janeiro at the time of his appointment, he was not identified with the PRF. Once in office, Câmara initiated a campaign against the remnants of PRF influence, disclosing such evidences of nepotism as the case of Juvenal Lamartine's six relatives— two sons, a brother, a nephew, and two sons-in-law—who had been named by him to government positions. Some of these relations, it should be noted, were highly qualified (two were agrarian economists specializing in cotton cultivation and a third, a physician and epidemiologist, served on a dollar-a-year basis as director of public health), but Câmara dismissed them all.[30]

The personal career of José Augusto illustrates the rise of political leadership during the Old Republic from within the state oligarchy. The boy, born in 1884, was the grandson of a Liberal Party stalwart and the son of a baccalaureate degree-holder (*bacharel*) from the interior town of Caicó. He entered the Rio Grande do Norte Academy in Natal when his father moved there as state deputy and later customs collector. In 1905 the youth took a law degree in Recife and returned to his state to teach history and geography at his old secondary school; at the age of twenty-seven in 1911 he became a municipal judge. In the following year he was named interim state police chief. He became a state deputy and assembly leader in 1913, a federal senator from 1915 to 1923, governor from 1924 to 1928, and senator again in 1928 when he exchanged positions with his colleague (and relative by marriage) Juvenal Lamartine. Other members of the PRF oligarchy associated with José Augusto were Aldo and Rafael Fernandes, young men from a powerful family of cotton brokers and exporters; Alberto Roselli, a lawyer and journalist for the PRF's *A República*, son of Colonel Angelo Roselli, and a student in Zurich before matriculating at the Recife Law School; Colonel Francisco Cascudo, editor during the Old Republic of an independent newspaper, *A Imprensa*; and the Rosado family, headed by a powerful merchant from the state's northern second city, Mossoró, who named all the males of his twenty-one children Jerônimo and all of the females Isaura, each followed by the number, in French, of the order of his or her birth. Jerônimo Dix-sept later became governor of the state; Vingt a federal deputy.

In 1932 PRF interests not only applauded the constitutionalist rebellion in São Paulo but dispatched local cowboys (*sertanejos*) to fight against the federal forces. In February, 1933, José Augusto founded the Popular Party (Partido Popular, or PP) as the formal successor to the old PRF. With the return of parliamentary government in the following year, José Augusto won election to the federal Congress, where he became subleader of the opposition. At home, the anti-Vargas Popular Party advocated municipal autonomy, the secret ballot, agrarian credit and efficient utilization of the land, free public education, free association of persons, protection of private property, and guaranteed civil rights.[31] It pledged itself to the repression of rural banditry, still a problem in part of the interior of the state. But as soon as it gained power, the PP ignored its program and made no visible effort to change the status quo beyond attempting to reestablish its old hegemony.

Vargas was awakened to the threat to the prestige of his government when three of the four Popular Party candidates were elected to the national Constituent Assembly in May, 1933. He named Mário Câmara as interventor in July and visited the northeast in September; but the sudden death of the governor of Minas Gerais in late 1933 turned the President's attention from the region, and he left Câmara to his own devices. Although Câmara proved an effective administrator, he drew growing attacks from the PP and from a new minority party in the state which was led by federal deputy João Café Filho. An articulate reformer, Café Filho was the son of a state treasury official and had been instructed as a boy by José Augusto at the Rio Grande do Norte Academy. He never progressed beyond the secondary level of education, although he served as president of the Republic after Vargas' suicide in 1954 (and was awarded several honorary degrees). In the late 1920s he originated so-called Natal Workers' Leagues among stevedores and laborers, an activity which won him the label of radical agitator. A conservative, although socially conscious and dedicated to civil liberties, Café Filho represented the only truly populist element in his state's political spectrum.[32]

The announcement of state elections scheduled for October, 1935, set intense political activity in motion. In early 1934 Câmara and José Augusto discussed a possible truce through the creation of a single, neutral state party, but negotiations failed. Vargas attempted to encourage a settlement through the good offices of Juarez Távora, who was a friend of the Fernandes family of the PP, but Távora informed the President in June, 1934, that his efforts had not succeeded.[33]

To forestall certain electoral defeat, Câmara turned to his erstwhile adversary, Café Filho, and informed Vargas in August of the formation of a new party, the Social Alliance (Alliança Social, or AS), a "tactical convergence of two forces with similar objectives."[34] The aim of the two forces was to keep the oligarchy out of power. In outlook, however, few differences distinguished the AS from the PP. Each bloc comprised similar elements—businessmen, officials, and literate white-collar workers. Ranchers and rural landowners generally favored the PP while the small middle class more frequently backed Câmara. But old family ties and animosities blurred party loyalties, and the mass of the state population, more than 90 per cent disfranchised, paid scant attention to either party.[35]

The Popular Party nominated physician Rafael Fernandes for the governorship and the Social Alliance named Interventor Câmara. Both candidates sponsored caravans of speakers which traveled through the small towns of the interior in their behalf. As the elections neared, increased reports of violence accompanied the campaign. Popular Party spokesmen claimed that one of their municipal chieftains had been murdered, and dozens of beatings and acts of intimidation were charged against both sides.[36]

As interventor, Câmara fully utilized the power of his office, dismissing public employees suspected of disloyalty and hiring rural undesirables (jagunços) to fill the ranks of Natal's Civil Guard, which at any rate was normally composed of drifters impressed into the regiment.[37] Sensing the strength of the opposition, Câmara maintained steady correspondence with federal officials through mid-1935. At Vargas' request Governor Carlos de Lima Cavalcanti of Pernambuco visited Natal in September and advised the President to remove certain officers from the local military post, the Twenty-first BC, who allegedly favored the anti-Vargas forces.[38] As a result the War Ministry transferred the suspected men, including the battalion's commander.

State officials remained outwardly cheerful but privately doubtful as the election neared. Câmara's brother wrote to Vargas in early October, suggesting that the elections be suspended, that a compromise candidate be named interventor, and that Mário be rewarded with a judgeship on the federal Financial Tribunal (Tribunal de Contas). In return, the Popular Party would be given one of the two federal Senate seats.[39] But Vargas ignored the request. On election day, October 14, civil war nearly erupted in the state as each side claimed victory in terms of a majority of electors to the state assembly. Finally, after a brief but heated dispute, the federal Electoral Tribunal ruled in favor of the candidate of the oligarchy, Rafael Fernandes. The winning margin was fourteen to eleven.[40]

On October 20 Câmara and his advisers discussed the possibility of armed resistance to Fernandes' inauguration as governor, but they were discouraged by reports that the Twenty-first BC would remain loyal.[41] The War Ministry sent General Manoel Rabello, commander of the Seventh Military District in Recife, to observe the situation and preserve order. Câmara left Natal for Rio de Janeiro, but not before his party was fired upon at dockside. Federal troops from Paraíba guarded the inaugural ceremonies, having accompanied Popular Party officials who had fled to the south after election day, fearing violence.[42]

President Vargas did not intervene in the state although the victory of the opposition represented a clear defeat for his administration and demonstrated that the federal government, in spite of its new powers, still lacked authority in the states. If Flôres da Cunha had meddled in Rio Grande do Norte, Vargas would have acted, since the military was eager to confront Flôres' obstructionism with federal power. But the military command apparently saw little difference between Câmara and Rafael Fernandes, even if the government had suffered a bitter blow to its prestige.

Another internal disturbance erupted in Pará, the vast state at the mouth of the Amazon and the gateway to the jungle interior of Brazil. Vargas' interventor, Major Joaquim Magalhães Barata, a protégé of Juarez Távora, faced certain defeat at the hands of an anti-Vargas coalition comprised of members of the state Liberal Party and others identified with the pre-1930 regime. Liberal Party deputy Abel Chermont, the coalition's candidate for federal senator, led the opposition.

While Abel Chermont later earned a reputation as a liberal spokesman for civil rights, there is no evidence that his party consciously sought liberal reform, in spite of its name. Opposition to Barata, an aggressive politician, arose from personal grounds, and it was rumored, but not proved, that British commercial interests in the region supported the opposition Liberal Party bloc.

As the election in the legislature approached, Barata took matters into his own hands: he surrounded the assembly building with militia and barred entrance to the Chermont delegation. Fearing personal injury, the opposition deputies took refuge in the nearby army barracks, where they telegraphed Rio de Janeiro for assistance. The legislature, sitting in rump session, elected Barata governor by a 14-0 vote, ignoring the sixteen deputies absent from the session. Barata cynically wired Vargas that "all those present" had elected him governor unanimously.[43]

War Minister Góes Monteiro told the press in Rio de Janeiro that order would be restored if Belém, the state capital, had to be blown sky-high; but he did not indicate his position toward Governor Barata. Vargas remained silent.[44] Late in the following afternoon, the opposition delegation left the barracks under a writ of habeas corpus from a federal judge, and approached the assembly building. The militia opened fire, gravely wounding three deputies and killing several bystanders.[45] The local army commander placed the capital under martial law. Weakly, Barata accused the opposition of having hired assassins to provoke conflict.[46] Vargas replaced Barata with a new interventor who supervised the election and inauguration of a compromise gubernatorial candidate after a month. Abel Chermont's reward for his cooperation was a senate seat in Rio de Janeiro.

Conflicts between loyal and opposition factions erupted in almost every other Brazilian state as well. The small northeastern state of Alagôas underwent a comic-opera insurrection in March, 1935, during which a band of rebels, reportedly including Sylvestre Góes Monteiro, the brother of the war minister, unsuccessfully besieged the governor's residence in Maceió, then retreated to the city's leading hotel, where loyal troops encircled them.[47] In neighboring Sergipe, the pro-Vargas party faced defeat in the state assembly; friends of the interventor implored Vargas to intercede lest the state revert to reactionary control.[48]

In Bahia, Interventor Juracy Magalhães remarked to Vargas in January that the political atmosphere in his state was so quiet that he felt apprehensive; his election as constitutional governor in April united his adversaries, who boycotted the legislative assembly in protest.[49] São Paulo's Armando de Salles Oliveira, allied with his state's industrial and business interests, was elected governor in early April with little difficulty. A military plot allegedly allied with interests hostile to the state administration was uncovered in Pernambuco in March, part of the larger conspiracy which shook the federal military command.[50] In February, the Bahian interventor wired

Vargas that federal intervention in Ceará might be necessary.[51] Enmity between the federal government and the Pedro Ernesto administration in Rio de Janeiro grew unchecked.[52] Political disturbances occurred as well in the backwater states of Espírito Santo, Maranhão, and Mato Grosso.

The federal interventor in Santa Catarina was defeated in May by Nereu de Oliveira Ramos, a moderate who quickly moved to challenge Nazi and Integralist influence in his southern state. Two factions contested political power in Minas Gerais: the so-called Progressives, headed by Gustavo Capanema, later federal minister of education; and the opposition Republicans, led by Virgílio de Mello Franco and ex-President Artur Bernardes, and allied with opposition groups in São Paulo and Rio Grande do Sul. In mid-1935 the Progressives held a 34-to-14 edge in the assembly, but opposition attacks provoked continued irritation.[53]

Only Amazonas, Paraná, and, to a lesser degree, Pernambuco did not face internal disorder. Crises in the remaining two important states, however, threatened to undermine the continued stability of the Vargas government. The state of Rio de Janeiro, the small, agrarian state wedged between Minas Gerais, São Paulo, and the Federal District of Rio de Janeiro, became the chief pawn in the struggle between Vargas and Flôres da Cunha, the flamboyant interventor and later governor of Rio Grande do Sul. That southernmost Brazilian state, since the fall of the Empire, had produced an impressive number of national political figures, including Júlio de Castilhos, Pinheiro Machado, Borges de Medeiros, Oswaldo Aranha, Lindolfo Collor, and Vargas himself. Colorful and wily Flôres da Cunha now pitted his personal strength, backed by well-armed gaúcho troops, against the President. The struggle, perhaps the last major state offensive against federal hegemony in modern Brazil, came to light following the restoration of institutional government and was resolved only by the assertion of national control with the Estado Nôvo coup of November 10, 1937.

The heated recent history of Rio Grande do Sul has not been told fully.[54] The state, bitterly divided into warring factions during the Farrapo rebellion between 1835 and 1845, remained split between two camps through the Old Republic: the Federalists, or *libertadores* (also known as *maragatos*, their red shirts allegedly providing inspiration to Garibaldi during his stay in southern Brazil), and the Republicans, or *chimangos*. Family rivalries contributed to the feud, as did the tradition of bellicosity allegedly inherited from the region's history of frontier violence and independence.[55]

A new generation of political leadership emerged in the aftermath of the

Empire's collapse, recruited largely from the cattle-ranching and landowning elite. Júlio de Castilhos, who, like many of his gaúcho contemporaries (Assis Brasil, Pinheiro Machado, Borges de Medeiros), returned to Rio Grande do Sul after law studies in São Paulo, led the chimangos against the maragatos in a bloody war which lasted from 1893 to 1895. Castilhos, a strong military commander allied with the federal government, prevailed, although both sides together suffered as many as 12,000 casualties, about 12 per cent of the total state population. The chimango leader ruled the state single-handedly as governor and Republican Party chieftain until 1903, when he died undergoing surgery; he was succeeded by the efficient but less colorful Borges de Medeiros, a member of the Comtian wing of the party. From 1893 through the 1920s, the Rio Grande do Sul Republicans defended fiscal orthodoxy and expansion of domestic markets (for the by-products of the cattle-based economy), and jockeyed for political power within the Old Republic, abandoning after 1910 their earlier policy of isolation from the affairs of the federal government by shifting the state's political weight within the Minas Gerais–São Paulo elite whenever appropriate. The Republican Party campaigned against increased federal authority (the key to its refusal to support Artur Bernardes in 1922) and fought to keep the new Liberator (*Libertador*) coalition of Federalists and antipositivist Republicans, after 1897 headed by Assis Brasil, a brother-in-law of Castilhos, out of power.[56]

Renewed clashes after a contested gubernatorial election in 1922 brought a new group of Republican Party leaders to the fore, including Oswaldo Aranha, Flôres da Cunha, Getúlio Vargas, and Baptista Luzardo (of the Liberators). Other names emerged at the first Republican Party convention: João Neves da Fontoura, Maurício Cardoso, Lindolfo Collor. Together, they became known as the "Generation of 1924." Flôres, a fiery militia officer in the mold of Pinheiro Machado, fought against the tenente uprising in 1924, joined with the Liberal Alliance in 1930, and, a trusted friend of Oswaldo Aranha, was named gaúcho interventor in that year. Flôres, a violently independent, emotive man, soon broke with the dissident constitutionalists in his state, remaining loyal to Vargas in 1932 during the São Paulo revolt. A new gaúcho political lineup emerged: Flôres, backed by a portion of the landowning elite, was opposed by a united front of the states' rights Republicans, including Borges, who lost personal control of the machine after having supported the rebellious paulistas, and Raul Pilla, the head of the opposition.

Although Vargas aided his native state's failing economy through the extension of credit for agricultural development, Flôres, deeply resentful after his unrewarded loyalty in 1932, began to attack Vargas for alleged neglect of Rio Grande do Sul and for his efforts to reduce state independence. At the 1933-34 Constituent Assembly, the thirteen Republicans elected to the state's sixteen-deputy delegation allied themselves with São Paulo and Minas Gerais, opposing the transfer of former state sources of tax revenue to the federal government and, while defending the President's social welfare program, demanding constitutional guarantees of states' rights.

Flôres' professed control of 26,000 Rio Grande troops provoked the federal armed forces and further strained relations between Pôrto Alegre and the federal capital.[57] In 1934 Flôres publicly backed Vargas during the Minas Gerais succession crisis, but he subsequently broke with the pro-Vargas faction and allied himself with the disappointed opposition bloc, headed by Virgílio de Mello Franco. Renewed friendship with São Paulo, pastoral Rio Grande do Sul's natural trade partner, gave Flôres sufficient leeway to pursue an independent position and to seek potential allies in the nationwide electoral campaigns prescribed by the 1934 constitution. In his personal correspondence with Vargas he retained normal cordiality; but Getúlio began to grow wary, exacerbated by Góes Monteiro's open hostility to Flôres.[58]

Only the fact that the states' rights legislative opposition was headed by anti-Flôres gaúchos Borges de Medeiros and João Neves da Fontoura precluded the formation in later 1934 of a congressional alliance potentially disastrous to the Vargas administration. Because Vargas well understood this he avoided a formal rupture with Flôres, despite pressure on him from the military. In July, 1935, when Flôres visited the President to confer on means of dealing with legislative obstructionism, his newspaper chain, based in Rio Grande do Sul and linked with dailies in Rio de Janeiro and São Paulo, loudly publicized the governor's demands for new federal credit and state autonomy.

Flôres da Cunha's interference in the unstable politics of the state of Rio de Janeiro foreshadowed his coming rupture with Vargas. In the very first year of the Liberal Alliance provisional government, five different *fluminense* interventors came and went; peace arrived only in December, 1931, when naval commander Ary Parreiras took office, instituting an honest and efficient state administration. But Parreiras, angered at the opposition's bitter attacks, refused to run for election in 1935 when required to do so by the constitution. At one point, in early 1935, he tendered his resignation, desiring to leave office altogether, but Vargas declined to accept it.[59] During the electoral campaign Parreiras refused to participate in the selection of his successor; in so doing, he divided the pro-Vargas camp, and control of the state assembly passed to the opposition in April by a two-vote margin. As in Pará, the political climate turned ugly and the victorious deputies sought refuge in military headquarters to escape violence. Adding fuel to the fire, agents from Rio Grande do Sul openly conferred with opposition leaders, reportedly offering financial support for their antiadministration campaign.

In September, Vargas reacted publicly, indicating his personal candidate for the governorship, Admiral Protógenes Guimarães, the former navy minister. But the opposition retaliated, disrupting efforts in the assembly to reach a vote. Finally, backed by federal officials of the Ministry of Justice, Guimarães won a narrow victory and prepared to assume office in October. Legal disputes and public outcry stirred by the anti-Vargas, pro-Flôres press delayed his inauguration until early November.

Allegations that the federal government had imposed its candidate's election provided a moral victory to Flôres, who, assuming the posture of a wounded innocent, offered reconciliation to prevent further injustice. In October he wrote to Vargas in his own hand: "You can be assured with reference to my [supposed] intrigues . . . [that they] cannot separate us, nor prejudice the support I have always given to you . . . . You know that Rio Grande asks little."[60] But Vargas was annoyed: "I am arriving at the limits of my patience," he confided to his brother Protásio on the same day.[61]

A month later Flôres instructed his congressional bloc to vote with the opposition against the federal administration.[62] Newspapers loudly displayed the news, while government leaders, gravely upset at the potential loss of the administration's legislative majority, conferred anxiously among themselves. The neutral O Radical of Rio de Janeiro called the new political atmosphere "the darkest imaginable"; O Imparcial warned that the crisis threatened "armed conflict."[63] Deputy Prado Kelly of the state of Rio de Janeiro opposition party flew to São Paulo to meet with a Flôres emissary. Talk of civil war filled the air.

The crisis persisted. Flôres reportedly approached Armando de Salles Oliveira of São Paulo, offering economic concessions such as the lease of the São Paulo–Rio Grande do Sul Railway to Salles' state in return for his support.[64] A portion of the congressional opposition declared its solidarity with Flôres, creating the threatened anti-Vargas majority. On November 16, in retaliation, Vargas dismissed General Pantaleão Pessôa, who was close to Flôres as well as a reputed ally of the right-wing Integralists, from his post of army chief of staff. Several of Vargas' friends rushed to his side to forestall disaster. It seemed that 1932 would repeat itself before the year's end.[65]

The turbulence produced by the state elections tempered alliances and brought some political figures closer to Vargas. Among these were Benedito Valladares, the rather colorless governor of Minas Gerais; Felinto Müller, the chief of the federal police; and Francisco Campos, the keenly intelligent lawyer who ultimately would play a major role in the establishment of the Estado Nôvo. By mid-November, 1935, Brazilian politics was sunk in confusion and uncertainty.

Yet, save for Flôres da Cunha's brief flirtation with Armando Salles in November, São Paulo remained conspicuously removed from what proved to be the final struggle between advocates of a strong central government and their adversaries in the states. The reasons for this included the fact that the state seemed to be preoccupied with its massive economic and industrial growth. São Paulo supported the highest standard of living in the country in the 1930s, although its population had by no means become "industrialized" in the European sense. Most factory owners, reluctant either to adopt new technological processes or to train their own workers, preferred to import foreign technicians, terming their own underpaid employees indolent and unproductive, although some relied on the graduates of the São Paulo Polytechnic School, which had been founded by positivists at the end of the last century, and whose Technological Research Institute served the entire paulista industrial sector and contributed to its development.[66]

São Paulo prospered after the 1890s, with the advent of free labor, the availability of raw materials, and economic autonomy under a federal system largely dominated by the state after the fall of the Empire. The coffee sector buoyed up São Paulo more than it did any other Brazilian state. Between 1872 and 1935, the state population jumped from 800,000 to an estimated 7,800,000; the municipality of São Paulo, with 372,000 inhabitants in 1920, leaped to more than a million fourteen years later.[67] The first impetus for industrial development in the state came from the coffee planters, who, with the emergence of an urban market, participated in railroad construction and subsidized immigration and others plans to develop public utilities, food-processing plants, credit facilities, and, in order to clothe the population inexpensively, textile mills. By World War I, São Paulo achieved virtual economic independence, having come to dominate a national market tied to it by transportation lines extending beyond state boundaries to northern Paraná, the Minas triangle, and into Mato Grosso. Between 1889 and 1945 the state produced half of the total value of Brazil's industrial output and half of its exports.

Intermarriage and a gradual confluence of interests of coffee entrepreneurs and the newer, largely immigrant industrial elite, which included such names as Matarazzo, Klabin, Jafet, Lundgren, and Pignatari, produced a powerful industrial group, thrust into prominence with the collapse of the power of the rural planters after 1929 and closely organized in industrial, commercial, and manufacturers' associations.[68] Its interests defeated in 1930, the state chafed for two years under the stewardship of the provisional government. But following the 1932 paulista rebellion, Vargas offered peace by the selection of popular industrialist Armando de Salles Oliveira as interventor, appointing other paulista figures to important fiscal posts, and offering guarantees to the international economic community of Brazil's intention to maintain monetary respectability. In exchange, São Paulo tacitly accepted the situation whereby it was asked to supply significantly less than its proportional share of national political leadership in terms of its economic power.

The role of the groups which rose to challenge the prevailing system between 1934 and 1938 is the final factor to be considered in this description of the political climate after the adoption of the 1934 constitution. The absence of truly structural change alienated the more volatile elements of the political spectrum; to its critics the Liberal Alliance had abdicated its revolutionary responsibility. This opinion was expressed by Carlos Lacerda, a radical student leader in the early years of his stormy political career, who, with the advantage of hindsight, attempted to recall his disenchantment as a youth in the 1930s: "The Brazilian reality was wretched and despondent; liberal opposition a fiction; politics no more than . . . careerism; the dominion of foreign interests in Brazil permanent; the lack of a cause for the young . . . [created] one single option: communism or fascism."[69]

But Vargas avoided doctrinal confrontation with the far right or left, relying rather upon force whenever his government's interests seemed to be threatened. The administration publicly considered social protest subversive; and the elite did not oppose this policy. Of the visible threats to the existing order, the specter of international communism was feared most by Brazilian authorities. To be sure, many sensitive Brazilians naturally opposed Comintern policy fostering socialist revolution. Yet Vargas' anticommunist campaign touched more than the small number of communists in Brazil: it offered a facile peg upon which conservatives could hang their assault on left-oriented advocates of change. The threat of communism assumed inflated proportions in Brazil in the years between 1936 and 1945.

The activities of the federal police, under the widely feared and seemingly omniscient Felinto Müller, characterized the administration's growing reliance on repression after 1935. Emerging from relative obscurity after the São Paulo insurrection in 1932, Müller soon answered only to the President. He commanded the Political and Social Police and its undercover branch referred to only as S-2; both were technically under the auspices of the Ministry of Justice, but Müller was completely independent. Surveillance extended to all members of the government, even including cabinet members and officials of the diplomatic service.

Complaints of police harassment increased as the Integralists and the National Liberation Alliance grew in influence through 1935. Repression was sporadic, calculated to frighten potential adherents. Most complaints occurred on the left of the radical spectrum; police authorities worked out a *modus vivendi* with Integralists in many local areas and few difficulties with the right were reported. Police agents often raided the presses of antiadministration newspapers, seized and destroyed objectionable issues, and arrested editorial staff members without formal charges (releasing them after several days of pointless interrogation and confinement). Occasionally police or thugs would invade a printing plant or a trade union headquarters and smash furniture and equipment.[70] So-called preventive arrest was increasingly employed by the police as 1937 approached.

The federal government also applied censorship to all means of communication. Brazil's press, boasting more than a dozen dailies in Rio de Janeiro and several hundred smaller newspapers nationally, encompassed a remarkable range of opinion, from the fascist foreign-language press to clandestine communist sheets produced in factories and military barracks. Foreign correspondents complained of censored dispatches and the unwillingness of government sources to issue important economic data.

Yet Vargas officials allowed newspapers as volatile as Recife's *Fôlha do Povo* and Rio de Janeiro's *A Manhã* to publish, applying mild post-factum punishment for extreme articles. Rio de Janeiro's *A Nação,* loyal to Flôres da Cunha and caustically opposed to Vargas, operated with relative freedom in spite of its editorial policy.

The antiextremist campaign which government officials gradually elaborated through 1935 unsettled the mood of stability. While Vargas and his aides remained silent in the face of growing unrest, pessimism about the fate of Brazilian democracy increased publicly and privately. In this atmosphere, the Integralists and the National Liberation Alliance raised their voices. The left attempted to meet the challenge of fascism with a mass popular front, but it failed to win a national following, and succeeded only in strengthening Vargas' position.

3

THE LEFT AND THE
NATIONAL LIBERATION ALLIANCE

Crimson are our Brazilian souls,
Erect, brave, and handsome youth,
Of clear minds and strong physique,
We fight for bread, land, and liberty.

ANL march, to the tune of the
Brazilian national anthem

Historians of the Brazilian left cite the unsuccessful Rio de Janeiro–São Paulo Workers' Congress of 1892 and the 1895 Santos Socialist Center, founded by Spanish longshoremen, as the earliest precursors of Marxist organizations in Brazil. In 1902 European immigrants organized a Socialist Party in São Paulo and published a newspaper in Italian, *Avanti!*, until the party disbanded a year later. In 1906 socialists established the Brazilian Workers' Confederation, patterned after the anarchosyndicalist French General Workers' Confederation. It sponsored a newspaper, *La Parola dei Socialisti*, published in São Paulo, and, in 1912, *A Voz do Trabalho*, the first socialist journal written in Portuguese. The Brazilian Workers' Confederation claimed fifty syndical groups from Pernambuco to Rio Grande do Sul as members. It charged that police constantly harassed them and that employers fired members as a means of retaliation.

After the turn of the century labor protests included such events as several violent railroad strikes, one of the largest being that against the Paulista line in 1901; a march in 1904 against compulsory vaccination and to secure the rights of non-Brazilian nationals; and antiwar marches in early 1915, which were accompanied by small public rallies throughout the country. But the labor movement remained weak, its high point coming in 1917 with a major strike to win recognition for unions in São Paulo. Although some businesses were closed for as long as thirty days and amnesty guarantees were promised to the strikers, leaders were seized by police as soon as order was restored and most of them were deported as aliens.

Small, unaligned communist groups met to discuss the events of the Russian Revolution as early as 1918; perhaps characteristically, most of them considered the revolution a victory for anarchosyndicalism. The Communist League of Livramento, founded in that same year in Rio Grande do Sul, probably constituted the first formal communist party in Brazil. The movement grew slowly. In November, 1921, the communist organization in Rio de Janeiro subscribed to the principles of the Third International, and, in turn, sponsored a national party congress in Rio de Janeiro and Niterói in late March, 1922. Nine representatives of the party's tiny membership, joined by a Comintern observer and a comrade from the Uruguayan Communist Party, formally ratified Lenin's twenty-one points in order. The Brazilian Communist Party subsequently was admitted to the Comintern as a full member.[1]

In January, 1922, the PCB established a monthly publication, *Movimento Communista*, which shifted to a biweekly basis after eleven months. Party fortunes dimmed in the wake of the national state of siege declared after the unsuccessful Copacabana Fort uprising in July, and the party failed to win legal status; but during the presidencies of Artur Bernardes and Washington Luís it was not persecuted widely. The Communist Manifesto was published by the party in serial form in a weekly newssheet, *Voz Cosmopólita,* which was issued by PCB hotel, restaurant, and café workers. After the party's Second National Congress in 1925, organized by its secretary-general, Astrojildo Pereira, it initiated a sophisticated weekly newspaper, *A Classe Operária,* although the PCB claimed only 350 to 500 members at this time. Through the remainder of the decade it followed Comintern policy faithfully, purged suspected deviationists, and warred against the remnants of "pseudo socialism"—anarchosyndicalism—within its ranks.

Party theorists rarely devoted their energies to the application of party doctrine within the context of the Brazilian environment, although cadre leaders wove a skeletal network of cells, regional commissions, and secretariats across Brazil in the anticipation of mass activity. Heated semantic disputes rent party unity while leaders ignored the realities of recruitment, communications, and finances. As a result, the PCB was ill-equipped to undertake organizational work when the decision to do so was made in the late 1920s and early 1930s.

The Comintern, for its part, paid scant attention to its Latin American units prior to 1933 or 1934. Moscow's Latin American contact point was the Iuyamtorg Corporation (Prima S/A), the Soviet agency established in Buenos Aires in 1926 as an arm of the Amtorg Trading Company of New York. After its banishment by the Uriburu government in 1931, the agency moved to Montevideo, which subsequently became a center for communist activities in the area.[2] To direct its operations, the Comintern sent to Uruguay a forty-year-old Bolshevik named Guralsky, who spent most of his time traveling through South America under the pseudonym "Rústico." The Brazilian police asserted that the PCB received instructions and financial aid from Iuyamtorg, but the extent of this support is unknown and was probably slight.[3]

After its Third National Congress held during December, 1928, and January, 1929, the PCB formed its General Labor Confederation, which soon claimed 60,000 members nationally. It also founded a political arm, the Worker's and Peasant's Bloc, a reconstituted front group which was first created in early 1927. The bloc produced propaganda directed at the electorate and backed local and state candidates acceptable to the party; occasionally it nominated its own candidates. But the bloc met with little success: the public ignored it, and some communists attacked the bloc's attempts to organize rural workers, whom they considered reactionary. Dissidents in São Paulo deserted the PCB and formed a Trotskyite movement among old anarchosyndicalists and young Marxist intellectuals.

The PCB slowly warmed to the need for mass appeal as other tactics failed. In 1927 it dispatched Astrojildo Pereira to Bolivia to visit Luís Carlos Prestes, although party leaders expressed doubts about the probable success of the mission. In 1929 the PCB offered Prestes its nomination for the Brazilian presidency, but the tenente hero refused, offering instead a program, issued publicly, for social justice and civil liberties which the Leninist PCB rejected. In May, 1930, Prestes issued a second document, this time condemning Anglo-American imperialism in Brazil, but the PCB attacked him in *A Classe Operária* as a "bourgeois *caudilho* opportunist."[4]

Between 1930 and 1932, Worker's and Peasant's Bloc spokesmen accused Vargas of betraying the promise of his revolutionary cause. The bloc demanded agrarian reform, the confiscation of foreign-controlled businesses, and the socialization of heavy industry and domestic transport. Functioning as a political party, it represented the Brazilian Communist Party's first (and virtually last) effort to treat rural as well as urban problems, but few Brazilians understood the stilted rhetoric in which the bloc couched its programs. It disappeared unmourned in 1934 when Vargas outlawed it.

In July and August, 1935, the Comintern's Seventh International Congress in Moscow adopted the policy of the popular, or people's, front, having experimented previously with the concept of the "proletarian united front" whereby communists allied themselves with socially conscious reformist and antifascist groups in a common effort against the established order. Bulgarian theorist Georgi Dimitrov announced the new goal: the formation of people's fronts of all groups and individuals willing to unite against fascism, regardless of their ideological posture. Members would expose fascist influence where it existed and prepare the masses for popular front governments poised to defend the Soviet Union and all democratic peoples against fascist aggression. To establish such a regime, Dimitrov listed three essential conditions:

1. To "sufficiently disorganize and paralyze" the existing state apparatus by popular front agitation.
2. To lead the masses to a state of "vehement revolt against fascism and reaction, although not ready [to] fight under Communist Party leadership for the achievement of Soviet power."
3. To demand "ruthless measures against fascists and other reactionaries."[5]

The Brazilian effort, as we shall see, fell clearly short of these prerequisites. What prompted the PCB to act largely unprepared is a matter for speculation and puzzlement.

To execute its new popular front policy in Brazil, the Executive Committee of the Comintern turned to Luís Carlos Prestes, the Brazilian "Cavalier of Hope" who had served his Soviet apprenticeship and who, in 1934, as the most influential Latin American convert to communism, had been named the titular head of the Brazilian communist movement. Forced to reverse its former hostility to Prestes, the PCB dutifully welcomed him. A host of purges and voluntary departures from the party accompanied Prestes' appointment.

A number of foreign Comintern officials—including Harry Berger, a former German Communist Party Reichstag deputy whose real name was Arthur Ewert, the Argentine Rodolfo Ghioldi (like Prestes a member of the Comintern Executive Committee), and Leon Valée, a Belgian assigned to handle fiscal details through contacts with agents passing through Brazilian ports—arrived in Brazil in early 1935. Simultaneously, the PCB initiated massive campaigns for membership among workers, among members of the armed forces, and in rural areas. The party publicly outlined its new approach at its Fourth National Congress in July, 1934, and pledged to send four delegates to attend the forthcoming Comintern meetings and to confer with Prestes, still unable to return to Brazil without facing immediate arrest as a deserter from the armed forces. The PCB warned of the need for unity in the face of the coming "deep revolutionary crisis" in Brazil.[6] Nine months later the PCB embraced the new National Liberation Alliance, an antifascist popular front organization dedicated to national unification of all liberal Brazilians under the banner of "bread, land, and liberty."

But only three months after the inception of the ANL, Prestes and his advisers suddenly demanded a popular front revolutionary government, an act which provoked immediate reaction from waiting civil officials and thereby effectively undermined the ANL as a potentially independent mass movement. The turn to militancy, probably the result of heady optimism among PCB leaders, signed the popular front's death warrant and prejudiced the security of all those actually or potentially attracted to its socially conscious, nationalistic program, at least until Vargas' ouster in 1945.

In retrospect, the Communist Party's organization proved inadequate for the task which would be entrusted to it under the new popular front strategy. The party's membership was clustered in the Rio de Janeiro–São Paulo region, with a skeletal network in other areas. Labor activities, save for sporadic attempts to establish permanent workers' federations, languished under government repression. Party officials lamented the state of its middle- and lower-level leadership. "We have too few comrades . . . who have read more than five Marxist-Leninist books," one wrote in late 1934; "many of us cannot read at all."[7]

The line adopted at the outset of 1935 stressed the presence of foreign imperialists and the failure of the Vargas administration to reach the people. It categorized Brazil as semicolonial, more advanced than most other "dependent" countries, but controlled by a feudal bourgeoisie, subservient to its own greedy upper class, and victimized by international cartels and economic monopolies. It identified preconditions for revolution within Brazil's recent past: the tenente movement, and the Prestes Column's heroic resistance against authority. It advocated solidarity with the working man and the rural sharecropper. In addition, the party pointed to the need for tactical diversity. "We cannot offer a recipe that can be applied in all cases," a spokesman wrote. "In each concrete case we should put forward concrete demands."[8]

"Our mission," another wrote, "is the destruction of the latifundia and the division of the land among the peasants." He continued:

It is to annul the [foreign] dividends and confiscate the enterprises of the imperialists who channel out rivers of gold with the sweat and effort of the working classes; it is to develop the natural riches of the country; it is to liberate the oppressed nationalities (indians) [sic]; it is to establish a democratic and popular government. Its transformation to the socialist stage is a dialectic process dependent upon the realization of the democratic-bourgeois tasks of the revolution, the strengthening of the proletariat, and international conditions.[9]

Unfortunately for the PCB, its first fifteen years of experience in Brazil did not prepare it adequately for its new, activist orientation. Officials, failing to understand the apathetic and unpoliticized nature of the lower classes, made little effort to alter their own language, tactics, or organization in order to reach the general population. Yet one aspect of the PCB had changed by 1934 or 1935: a new leadership cadre was emerging to replace the older group which had dominated in the 1920s.

The new leaders in the early 1930s looked less to ideology for inspiration than to social distress and the tangible example of the Prestes Column a few years before. Many came from the more backward urban areas in the states of Minas Gerais, Rio de Janeiro, Espírito Santo, and Bahia, but few claimed rural origins. Most seemed to be of lower middle or middle-class stock, of Portuguese or light-skinned mulatto background, and reasonably well educated by the standards of the day. Rarely were PCB regional or district officials more than thirty or thirty-five years of age in 1935.

Honório de Freitas Guimarães, a rising party leader in the mid-1930s, represented a new type of PCB member: the disenchanted bourgeois coming to the communist movement out of failure to cope with the environment or disgust with the prevailing system. The following brief history, summarized from his autobiography written during his long imprisonment at the end of the decade, illustrates such a career.[10]

Guimarães was born in 1902 into a middle-class family. His grandfather was a "sick old man who liked music"; his great-grandfather had been an army officer who emigrated from Portugal to Brazil for undetermined reasons. The boy's father, the only one in his family to complete a secondary education, had struggled through law school, and, upon graduation, had been given a minor sinecure in the municipality of Friburgo, a quiet mountainside town in the state of Rio de Janeiro originally settled by Swiss and German colonists. He married, but when he supported the losing presidential candidate during the electoral campaign of 1910 (Rui Barbosa), he lost his job. The mother's family supported the couple henceforth, and she used this pressure to force Honório's father, a freethinker, to observe Catholic ritual with the rest of the family.

The mother, who came abruptly into a considerable inheritance when the boy was about nine years old, took her two children to Paris for three years. When World War I broke out, she moved to England and enrolled Honório and his younger brother at Eton. The boy was ridiculed for being Brazilian. He was timid in nature, and his years at the school were unhappy ones, although at graduation in 1919 he won several academic prizes and finished near the top of his class. He returned alone to Brazil to study engineering, only to find that his mathematical preparation at Eton had been inadequate. He barely passed the entrance examination to the Technical Academy (Escola Técnica), and soon abandoned his course of studies. To rid himself of economic dependence on his parents and what he termed the atmosphere of "semifeudal externals" in Brazilian life, he sat for officer candidacy and was commissioned an army lieutenant.

Three months later the Copacabana Fort revolt shook the armed forces, but Guimarães did not recall that he noted its nationalistic content. He remained loyal to the army during the disturbances in 1924, but was personally offended by what he considered the immoral behavior of his fellow officers, many of whom sacked opposition strongholds and carried off personal property. The young lieutenant was still highly idealistic, and he began to take interest in the case of his future brother-in-law, who had been arrested and jailed for alleged conspiratorial activities in conjunction with the tenente movement. The experience of the Prestes Column awed Guimarães. By 1930, he wrote, he had become frankly sympathetic with Prestes and communism, and, with his brother-in-law, he refused to join the general mobilization to defend the Washington Luís administration, resigning his commission.

Returning to civilian life and still attempting to avoid the necessity of accepting money from his family, Guimarães joined a mining expedition to

Minas Gerais, where he lived off the land for two years but finally returned when he found that his partners would not pay him his share of the profits. Now thirty years old in 1932, he used his mother's connections to find a job as overseer on a fruit plantation owned by the Guinles in the state of Rio de Janeiro. He borrowed money to export oranges grown on his own plot of land, but a bad crop ruined him. The experience taught him, he said, that he was "simply not capable of earning money under the existing capitalistic system." He vowed that he would not try to do so again.

Guimarães then became a full-time member of the party. He settled down briefly with his wife on a small farm inherited from relatives, but he chafed at his inactivity. With his brother-in-law, he traveled to Buenos Aires and stayed three weeks among the exiled community of Brazilian communists. On his return, he and his wife moved to the Federal District, where they joined the regional party committee. He served as mimeograph technician and general worker. Once he was arrested for helping to defend a PCB meeting against armed attack. Eager to suppress his bourgeois background, he identified with the cause of the downtrodden although admittedly he never had contact with them. By early 1934 he had risen in the party and was exiled by Federal District police to Bahia, where he avoided arrest and helped organize a regional conference.

He returned clandestinely to Rio de Janeiro, and, when factional dissent rent the top leadership, he was placed in charge of the important railroad workers' cell, which boasted over a hundred adherents. In July, 1934, he was elected to the PCB's central committee and was given his own code name to use in party correspondence: "M." In addition, he served as secretary of the regional secretariat and was its financial commissar. He had become a full-time revolutionary worker. He remained loyal to the party through 1935 and helped plan the uprisings which took place in November. Party officials murdered sixteen-year-old Elza Fernandes, the companion of party secretary Adalberto Andrade Fernandes, in Guimarães' quarters.[11] If, after his arrest in 1936 following the proclamation of a national state of siege, he had become disillusioned in any way with the party apparatus or its way of life, he never admitted it to himself during his years of imprisonment.

In keeping with the new Comintern line, the PCB initiated several local antifascist and anti-imperialist groups in 1934 in response to the growing influence of the Brazilian Integralists and the ideological climate in Europe.

Foreign events received major attention in the communist press, particularly the Spanish Republican cause. Domestic fronts organized by the PCB included the Committee Against Imperialistic Wars and Fascist Reaction, a National Antiwar Congress, the Society of Friends of Russia, the paulista-based Common Antifascist Front, a Fifth of July Civic Legion, and the largest of the organizations, the Popular Front Against Fascism and War.[12] These groups welcomed all Brazilians; they addressed their public appeals to the unpoliticized urban working class. Intellectuals, however, came to dominate them. Party officials performed administrative services, but generally left the organizations to their own devices and to fend for themselves against virtually incessant police harassment, a factor which crippled efforts to recruit extensively.

In March, 1935, the PCB encouraged the formation of the National Liberation Alliance, Brazil's first nationwide popular front, organized according to the principles of the Comintern's new international policy. Brazilian subservience to the international capitalistic system; character- The ANL's nationalistic program reflected the domestic left's view of istically, it did not demand that oppressive Brazilian-owned businesses be confiscated or nationalized. In addition, ANL statutes championed civil liberties in general and the interests of the working classes in particular, calling for higher salaries, lower consumer taxes, land reform, and nationalization of subsoil wealth. The ANL press, comprising several dozen newspapers formerly operated by the PCB or sympathetic to its cause, singled out the enemies of the Brazilian people: the foreign companies (Brazilian Traction Light and Power, the Great Western of Brazil Railway, Standard Oil) and their agents; the latifundists; the Integralists and their allies.[13]

Most of the ANL's founding officials came from outside the Communist Party, which considered the ANL not primarily an ideological vehicle but a device for agitation, a means of constructing a receptive atmosphere for later, party-led revolutionary activity.

Of the six principal organizers of the ANL, three were military officers identified with the radical wing of the tenente movement. The ANL's president, navy captain Hercolino Cascardo, had led the 1924 revolt of the dreadnaught São Paulo against the Bernardes government, served as federal interventor in the northeast under Juarez Távora, and helped organize the Third of October Club, from which he later resigned. Cascardo's Italian-born father was a merchant and a socialist; in Uruguayan exile between 1924 and 1930, Cascardo became a successful businessman himself.

Although a victim of the post-November, 1935, campaign of repression, Cascardo ultimately returned to acceptability. Before he died in 1967, still a socialist, he achieved the rank of Fleet Admiral in the naval reserve.

Roberto Henrique Sissón, also a naval officer (and, as the secretary-general of the ANL, its most active director as well as its organizational link with the PCB), came from a wealthy Spanish-French-Portuguese background, although his father, who achieved high rank in the Brazilian navy and became wealthy as secretary of a naval shipbuilding mission to Europe, died impoverished after having failed in business as a civilian. The organization's vice-president, army captain Amorety Osório, a spiritist and successful merchant in later life, similarly was identified with the Prestes–Miguel Costa tenente wing.

All three civilian founders—Benjamin Soares Cabello, a journalist from Livramento, Rio Grande do Sul; Manoel Venâncio Campos da Paz, a physician from a distinguished Republican family of physicians (and real estate dealers); and Francisco Mangabeira, a lawyer for the Public Savings Institute (Caixa Econômica) and son of the wealthy and respected Otávio Mangabeira, several times deputy from Bahia and foreign minister under the Old Republic—reflected privileged origins within Brazilian society and the air of respectability which clothed the ANL, despite its subsequent dogmatic rhetoric and radical political base. The ANL's Mangabeira served as president of the government-owned petroleum monopoly, Petrobás, under President Quadros, although he was shorn of his political rights after the 1964 coup; Campos da Paz, at the time of his death, was vice-president of the Federal District's (Rio de Janeiro) Municipal Legislature; Soares Cabello held high-level federal administrative positions after World War II.

The national directorate of the National Liberation Alliance met for the first time on March 12, 1935, in Rio de Janeiro. Those present, in addition to the six principal founders, included Ivan Pedro Martins, a law student and fiery orator; deputy Abguar Bastos, of Goiás; Rubem Braga, a young journalist from a good family; and several army officers who had participated a decade earlier in the Prestes Column.

To provide a financial start, the organizers drew up three lists of names, according to which donors would be asked to contribute either 50$000 (U.S. $3.50), 20$000, or 10$000 monthly. The assembled group discussed a manifesto through which it would disclose its public program, and was informed that permanent office space had been secured in the suite formerly occupied by the Third of October Club.[14]

The ANL held its first public rally on March 30 at the João Caetano auditorium, near Praça Tiradentes. Federal district Prefect Pedro Ernesto authorized the use of the municipally-owned theater, although he requested that none of the orators attack the administration. An invited representative of the federal government attended the rally. Two or three thousand people, overflowing into the street, watched the proceedings, during which a young law student and colleague of Ivan Pedro Martins, Carlos Lacerda, nominated Luís Carlos Prestes as honorary president to acclamation by the assembly.[15] Near the end of the scheduled speeches, fighting broke out in the crowded theater entrance. Police, who stood in the crowd, made several arrests; ANL officials charged that the disturbances had been staged.

If there had been any doubt regarding the probable attitude of Vargas administration officials toward the new movement, the symbolic nomination of Prestes sealed its fate. The man who had defied federal authority for three years after 1924 and who had embraced communism in Russian exile had become a living legend among much of the Brazilian population. Five days after the inaugural ANL rally, the government issued its National Security Law, termed the "Monstrous Act" (*Lei Monstro*) by ANL partisans. The law was subsequently used to harass communist labor organizations (for example, the United Trade Union Confederation); later, in 1936, it was cited when ANL members were charged with subversion.

To officials and the public, Prestes' name linked the ANL with the Communist Party, in spite of denials by ANL officials. Prestes himself, allegedly in Europe, entered Brazil secretly with his German-born wife on a forged passport in April, 1935. His physical presence defeated any possibility that the ANL would be able to function independently of the party. On May 3 the radical press published Prestes' statement accepting the honorary presidency of the movement, a stirring charge which was read to ANL rallies across Brazil on the anniversary of the abolition of slavery in the penultimate year of the Empire:

I join the ANL in order that in its ranks, shoulder to shoulder with all who have not sold themselves to imperialism, I may fight for the national liberation of Brazil, for the abolition of feudal conditions, for the defense of the democratic rights of the Brazilian people menaced by fascist barbarism. . . . Every honest Brazilian has the profound feeling that national liberation is impossible without the annulment of foreign debts, without the confiscation and nationalization of the imperialist factories, [and] without the expulsion of the emissaries of imperialist capital from Brazil. . . . Join the ANL![16]

The nationalistic ANL grew rapidly in April and May; after three months of existence it claimed several hundred thousand members (although it is unlikely that the figure represented any more than exaggerated guesswork). Roberto Sissón directed most of the activity of the national secretariat. Cascardo, the titular president, played a considerably lesser role in planning and organization. The ANL adopted a cellular format within a hierachy of municipal, regional, and national secretariats. Each cell of ten or more members, organized either residentially or by occupation, elected its own officers and delegates for "propaganda and general organizational work."[17]

ANL cells generally reflected the environment within which they operated. Professionals and white-collar workers dominated the fashionable urban residential cells, while groups in industrial areas or in the interior attracted low-income, often illiterate, membership. The ANL remained basically urban during its short existence; middle- and lower middle-class elements predominated in spite of attempts to build a working-class base. The cell in Gávea, then a partially industrial (now wholly residential) neighborhood in Rio de Janeiro, boasted a barber, a watchmaker, a mechanic, and three other workers on its executive secretariat; but its real mentors were Captain Henrique Oest of the national directorate and Alexander Varela, a municipal functionary. In Rezende in the state of Rio de Janeiro, Lieutenant Aristóteles Roriz, listed as a "small farmer" but at the same time an officer on active duty, headed the local cell.[18] In many regions PCB activists assumed positions of leadership when adequately qualified persons could not be recruited from the local area. From the inauguration of the popular front movement, party members were instructed to join and support local ANL cells.

For the Federal District, ANL membership lists indicate the following approximate breakdown of membership during 1935:[19]

Businessmen, professionals, and commissioned officers	37%
Workers and soldiers	52%
Unclassified (including 1.5% "agricultural")	11%

Yet ANL statistics are difficult to interpret. They combine all wage earners as "workers," making no distinctions among factory, unskilled, or white-collar employees. Some observers, doubting ANL claims of working-class participation, estimate that as much as 70 per cent of ANL membership was middle class.[20]

The movement did attract less affluent segments of the population in nonurban regions. In Itajaí, Santa Catarina, a clerk and a stevedore presided over the ANL municipal cell, while three truck drivers and a shoemaker constituted the executive secretariat.[21] A regional committee in Bahia listed sixteen municipal cells with a total of eighty-nine members, 95 per cent of whom, it claimed, were such representatives of the working class as longshoremen, telegraph operators, bakers, and carpenters.[22] São Paulo's ANL membership, as a result of deliberate efforts by state ANL leaders, heavily reflected the industrial nature of the region, although intellectuals held official positions. Of 412 persons imprisoned in São Paulo during 1936 for having belonged to the ANL, 65 per cent claimed working-class status. Of these, approximately 90 per cent were skilled workers, chiefly in the graphic, electrical, and building trades.[23]

The ANL's favorite organizational device was the outdoor public rally, held with considerable advance publicity and capable of attracting passers-by as well as regular members. Batteries of speakers, representing various labor, military, and civilian groups, harangued the audiences, usually shouting, and always invoking the name of Prestes, the honorary president. Speeches usually adapted themes of local interest to the general ANL program. Officials of the regional directorate checked all speeches before delivery and exercised veto powers as specified by formal organizational instructions.[24]

The ANL national directorate dispatched personal representatives to the interior in order to inaugurate local cells and advertise the movement. Its officials followed whirlwind schedules, installing more than two dozen local secretariats in the space of a week in two or three adjacent states. The traveling representatives paid their own transportation expenses or were reimbursed from the pocket of Roberto Sissón, who served as the ANL's private emergency financier. Sissón, whose relatives and first wife were relatively wealthy, at one point turned over his Petrópolis house with swimming pool to PCB officials, while he shared quarters with other ANL officials in Rio de Janeiro. The national directorate and local contributors financed the caravan of speakers sent to the northeast in June, 1935.

The mid-May installation of the Baurú municipal cell in the state of São Paulo was typical of ANL procedures. A makeshift band from a local labor syndicate opened the session by playing the national anthem. Sissón welcomed the new chapter into the movement in the name of the national directorate; in turn, local representatives welcomed the visitors. Sissón and São Paulo state ANL president Caio Prado followed with short speeches, and officials read congratulatory telegrams from Cascardo, neighboring ANL cells, and Luís Carlos Prestes (datelined "Barcelona"). After final speeches, aides planted in the audience hailed Prestes, the ANL, and the honored guests. The assemblage sang the ANL anthem and dispersed.[25]

The formal program of the National Liberation Alliance paralleled the anti-imperialist, antifascist, prosocial justice and economic reform programs of other contemporary popular front movements, especially the Chilean Popular Front, which was to be established a year later, and Peru's Popular Revolutionary American Alliance (Allianza Popular Revolucionária Americana, or APRA).[26] The ANL presented five basic demands, the last appended to the original program-manifesto at the insistence of Roberto Sissón:

1. Cancellation of all foreign imperialist-based debts.
2. Nationalization of foreign-controlled enterprises.
3. Full personal freedoms.
4. The right to popular government.
5. Ceding feudally held land to the peasantry, while protecting the property of the small and middle-sized proprietor.[27]

ANL demands embraced a variety of other points as well. Paulista cells stressed working conditions and called for a minimum wage for manual laborers; northeast spokesmen attacked government corruption, high railroad rates, and exploitation of agrarian labor; while the Rio de Janeiro chapters emphasized civil liberties and other issues considered relevant to their largely cosmopolitan membership.

In the economic sphere, the ANL stressed Brazil's semicolonial status in the international mercantile hierarchy. It demanded the cancellation of the weighty national debt as a declaration of fiscal independence. Domestically, it attacked the traditional land tenure system, whereby, according to the 1920 census, 70 per cent of the nation's 648,153 agricultural properties included only 9 per cent of its totally cultivated area. Lacking any explicit plan for national reorganization, the ANL nevertheless clearly identified the flaws in the existing system: latifundism, primitive agricultural methods, inadequate urban wages and workers' rights, illiteracy, and insufficient economic independence. The ANL view of the causes of Brazil's malaise did not differ markedly from that of the Integralist movement, although their views diverged radically as to required solutions. Both groups attacked foreign economic exploitation, the establishment's apathy to illiteracy and social abuses, and the feudal power of the landowners, although the AIB, drawing upon Brazil's traditional values, simply lamented the inefficiency of the agricultural elite, rather than challenge its role.

To secure broad support, the ANL emphasized the reformist, nonrevolutionary nature of its program. Prestes and ANL officials approached moderates, especially such anti-Vargas politicians as Virgílio de Mello Franco and João Neves da Fontoura. To Mello Franco's request for a personal statement outlining the movement's goals, Prestes affirmed that the ANL sought a "democratic government, revolutionary only in the face of imperialism." All individuals and groups, he added, would be welcomed to join a national ANL government, so long as they adhered to its principles and opposed the present "government of national treason."[28]

The ANL addressed itself to four principal sectors of the population: labor, students, the military, and urban intellectuals. In the labor sector, the ANL did not organize its own unions; rather, it preferred to work within the framework of its occupational cell structure. It also supported the Communist Party's national trade union congress and sent representatives to its clandestine conference held during the week of April 28, 1935. In Recife, the state ANL organized its own workers' federation and irregularly published a newspaper, *Solidariedade*.

ANL publicists frequently singled out individual capitalists for criticism, attacking their paternalistic condescension by which they often supplied meager social benefits (housing, chapels, clothing) but categorically denied adequate wages. *A Manhã* disclosed that Alceu Amoroso Lima, the respected Catholic lay spokesman, owned a considerable share of the Cometa textile mill, where fourteen-year-olds were paid 1$600 to 2$100 (ten to fifteen cents) for a day's work, and workingmen's families lived in quarters with one toilet for sixteen persons and one shower for three thousand. Workers were charged up to 50 per cent of their salaries for rent.[29] ANL members were encouraged to report such conditions where they found them, and cell campaigns were organized accordingly. Much of what success the ANL enjoyed among the urban working classes derived from this consciousness and the movement's efforts to unmask official claims regarding advances under Vargas' ambitious but largely ineffective social and working-class legislative program. The ANL advocated a true eight-hour work day, minimum salary scales, two months' severance pay, unemployment insurance, improved facilities for public health, lower consumption taxes for necessities, and equal salary for equal work, all conditions guaranteed for the most part by the 1934 and 1937 constitutions, but largely abused or ignored.[30]

In the university sphere, cells flourished within many of the faculties, notably the law and medical schools in Rio de Janeiro and the law school in São Paulo. The ANL sponsored a national students' movement, but it never functioned owing to police persecution. Federal District student cells published a brief-lived newsletter, *O Jovem Proletário,* which paid particular heed to the problem of poverty among those who worked while attending school. ANL university-oriented publications occasionally campaigned for equality for Negroes in Brazilian society, but attempts to organize a *Frente Negra* failed. An ANL newspaper series on the Negro João Cândido, the hero of the 1910 naval revolt, was seized by the police, but university students did not show unusual interest in the issue.[31]

Having drawn a portion of its leadership from the radical tenente wing of the armed forces, the ANL looked to the military ranks for widespread support. In São Paulo, General Miguel Costa, the creator of the briefly successful 1931 paulista Revolutionary Legion, virtually the only effort during Vargas' provisional government to organize workingmen behind it (and whose original manifesto had been written by the Integralists' Plínio Salgado, who subsequently departed over ideological differences), shared state ANL leadership with Caio Prado, Jr.; in Rio Grande do Sul, Captain Agildo Barata, another tenente compatriot of Prestes, organized the ANL before being transferred to Rio de Janeiro for disciplinary reasons. ANL president Captain Hercolino Cascardo visited military detachments in Minas Gerais, São Paulo, and Santa Catarina in behalf of the movement, and occupational cells were organized in barracks across the country.

But the ANL never won a mass following among the generally apathetic ranks. Cells published newsletters complaining about poor housing, low pay, and fascist influence among the officers. ANL leaders, aided by such anti-Vargas opposition deputies as Baptista Luzardo and Pedro Calmon, attacked the action of the minister of war for having expelled from the army a group of enlisted men who had attended an ANL rally in Rio's north zone, but nothing came of the protest.[32] Military authorities infiltrated ANL barracks cells and kept them under close surveillance, but in May, 1935, the movement was barred entirely from the armed forces and was forced underground. In July, a police report originating in São Paulo described clandestine ANL activity in the São Paulo region, citing conversations between Miguel Costa of the paulista ANL, Sissón, and emissaries from Cascardo during a meeting at a railroad station in Minas Gerais. An attached report, also dated July 22, warned that the ANL would carry out a civil insurrection in the northeast, later in the year.[33]

Among the urban middle classes, the ANL received its greatest support from professionals, intellectuals, and white-collar employees. The occupational cells for professors, writers, lawyers, and students assumed the same format as the working-class cells, and generally were the most dynamic of the ANL rank-and-file organizations. Like the Communist Party before it, the ANL established a variety of urban special-purpose front groups, ranging from its national women's auxiliary, the Brazilian Federation of Women (União Feminina Brasileira, or UFB), to the Popular Front Against Fascism and War and the National Front for Bread, Land, and Liberty, an electoral front. ANL leaders hoped that, by backing liberal and moderate candidates, the organization could entrench itself in public opinion and offer its own candidates later. But no elections occurred during the ANL's legal existence, and the idea collapsed. A cell for judiciary employees—solicitors, scribes, and minor court officials—demanded a minimum wage of 1:500$ monthly (about $83), a judiciary tax to pay for increased benefits, and recognition of professional standing. The ANL's Chauffeur's Beneficent Union led a parade of taxis to Rio de Janeiro's Praça Mauá, demanding reduction of gasoline prices by one hundred réis per liter, and using the occasion to document the presence of foreign petroleum interests in Brazil, including the Atlantic Refining Company of Brazil, the Texas Company, Standard Oil of Brazil, and Anglo-Mexican Petroleum.[34]

The success of the ANL in urban areas derived in good measure from its agitation for consumer rights, lower prices, and public services. ANL speakers attacked alien domination of public utilities—the mixed United States–Canadian Electric Light and Traction Company, the Leopoldina Railroad, foreign interests in navigation and coastal shipping, the Anderson Clayton Company and its share of the food-processing market—and demanded lower rents, increased salaries, and nationalized transport. The ANL press, anchored by PCB-oriented *A Manhã*, the financially unsuccessful *A Marcha* in Rio de Janeiro, *A Platéia* in São Paulo, and *Fôlha do Povo* in Recife, campaigned tirelessly against socioeconomic abuses. These papers frequently reprinted articles by such articulate social critics as northeasterners Gilberto Freyre and Josué de Castro, who were unaligned with the ANL but who were identified with the direction of its policy, to their later misfortune in the repressive aftermath of the ANL's extinction. In the initial period of the movement, the ANL press avoided irresponsible or inflammatory writing, although its journalists did take liberties with provocative headlines and features, much in the same way as the Integralist press. Sensationalism as a propaganda device increased noticeably after the police closed the ANL as a mass movement in July.[35]

Organizers employed the social club format to widen the ANL's membership base. In the armed forces, agents formed recreational clubs, providing ping-pong tables, card games, and free movies. Once attendance was established, speakers were brought in on topics related to social protest. ANL officials attempted to raise levels of cultural awareness among members of the movement At the Bank Employees' Social Center, such visitors as Arthur Ramos spoke on "Racial Problems in Brazil" and other themes.

ANL publications of cultural interest reprinted articles from the European antifascist press, offering a variety of reading matter on the fine arts, literature, and the dangers of anti-intellectualism. *Movimento,* edited by the ANL's Modern Culture Club in Rio de Janeiro, boasted socially conscious authors Jorge Amado and José Lins do Rêgo on its editorial board.

The UFB, the movement's women's auxiliary, endorsed the full ANL program, but stressed as well issues pertinent to its membership and general themes of feminine emancipation. A vocal, middle-class organization with chapters in the larger cities, the UFB criticized the docile role assigned to women by Brazilian society. As a result, it received heavy abuse from conservatives, who scored the reputation of the officials of the UFB for flamboyant and immoral behavior. While most members deviated in no way from accepted social behavior, some leaders, in fact, did provoke criticism by defending free love and by adopting such affectations as bobbed hair and Bahian cigars.

Financial support for the ANL came from two principal sources: dues and private contributions. Operating expenses were solicited from politicians and industrialists, many of whom gave secretly, some contributing simultaneously to the ANL and the Integralists. The Guinles and the governors of at least four states—Rio de Janeiro, Amazonas, Pernambuco, and the Federal District—contributed, according to Secretary-General Roberto Sissón, either directly or through personal aides.

The movement's total operating costs, however, were not high. What records survive show that the average cell contributed between only ten and thirty milréis per month to national headquarters, according to a formula by which 60 per cent of local revenue stayed with the cell, 30 per cent went to municipal and regional officials, and 10 per cent to Rio de Janeiro. But the ANL's brief legal existence precluded the development of an efficient collection network; most expenses probably were paid out of hand and from individual contributions. Daily expenses of the national directorate during July, 1935, ranged between seventy-five and one hundred eighty milréis—between five and thirteen dollars by exchange.[36] The largest contribution reported was 362$000, approximately twenty-six dollars. The meager budget of the national directorate was split between office rental and publicity costs. Any significantly larger contributions probably found their way into the treasury of the PCB.[37]

Only in the federal capital was the ANL strong enough to support a full range of organizational activities. In São Paulo it assumed less substantial proportions. Its president there, Caio Prado, was constantly attacked by the anticommunist press for his inherited wealth ("His riches," a leaflet proclaimed, "come by the sweat of the men he defends"), but he loyally steered the state movement according to the policies of the national directorate.

The inauguration of the local movement in São Paulo in early April coincided with a major strike in the Matarazzo textile complex, where a power struggle between family factions had thrown a portion of the work force at its Italo-Brasileira plant out of work. The ANL set up food lines and distributed clothing; it also registered members. At least fifteen industrial cells were initiated in the city of São Paulo, and, in the state's interior, fifty-three cells operated in mining areas and among railroad workers.[38]

Yet the progress of the São Paulo state organization did not satisfy either its organizers or the Rio de Janeiro directorate. The volatile Miguel Costa complained to the PCB that the state movement's trade union base was too narrow, hinting that he might like to organize a new statewide political party.[39] The state ANL emphasized labor activity, almost to the exclusion of other work. Its principal labor front organization, the São Paulo Common Anti-Integralist Front, included communists and anarchosyndicalists, as well as representatives from the small paulista socialist party, but police harassment curtailed its influence. Integralist strength, on the other hand, grew increasingly in the state, particularly in the small towns of the interior.

In southern Brazil the ANL was generally weak. A physician headed the state directorate in Rio Grande do Sul, but its vice-president, Captain Agildo Barata, effectively ran the movement, which in the state was overshadowed by strong Integralist influence.[40] Small cells functioned in the capital cities of Paraná and Santa Catarina, barely competing with local Integralist activity. ANL organization was weakest in the states of the central interior: Mato Grosso, Minas Gerais, and Goiás. Cells functioned in Cuiabá and Campo Grande in Mato Grosso, and in Belo Horizonte, Ouro Prêto, and Juiz de Fóra in Minas Gerais. Of these, only the group in the mineiro capital was especially active. An electoral front organization operated in Uberaba, as did the communist youth organization's modern culture club. The Santa Teresa *usina* (sugar refinery) boasted a sport club with the initials of the Soviet Union; ANL cells met in towns as remote as Araguarí, Monte Carmelo, Patricino, and Dôres (Minas Gerais), but they exercised little real influence.[41]

In northern Brazil the orientation of local ANL groups reflected more closely the economic and social tensions of the area. But organizational weakness, inadequate communications, and poor leadership slowed the movement. In Bahia three elements restricted the ANL's growth: active opposition from the governor (although ANL leaders thought that they could deal with him); divided communist cadres, especially in the labor sector; and constant pressure from Integralists, chiefly in the southern part of the state. But national ANL headquarters angrily accused state leaders of lack of initiative and failure to work with communist comrades, in spite of the local difficulties.[42]

The movement took hold in the large coastal cities from Recife to Belém, but lacked middle-class support. In the rural northeast, less sharp distinctions differentiated between the ANL and the Communist Party: high party officials visited the São Francisco region early in the year and established the groundwork for a peasant organization in the name of the ANL but to be directed by communist agents, including João Caetano Machado and Silo Meirelles, the brother of "Livio" [Ilvo Meirelles], a major PCB official on the national level.[43] Harassment by local officials and by factory and railroad foremen, within the already inflammable environment caused by sporadic labor violence and chronic unemployment, gave virtually a guerrilla flavor to ANL propaganda in the region. "If you must die of hunger," Recife's *Fôlha do Povo* warned the *sertanejo,* "you might as well die fighting."[44]

The speakers' caravan of the ANL national directorate departed for the northeast in mid-May, 1935. After a rally in Vitória, the capital of Espírito Santo, it sailed to Bahia, where, after a few minor rallies, government authorities expelled it from the state. On July 5 the caravan reached Recife, where Sissón addressed a mass gathering and demanded armed resistance to Integralism and foreign imperialism.[45] In Fortaleza, the capital of Ceará, an estimated six thousand bystanders gathered to hear Sissón and Ivan Pedro Martins attack the latifundian system.[46]

The ANL expedition brought to the festering northeast conceivably the most pointed social and economic protest in modern times. "The habitations of the poor around Recife are 40,000 *mocambos,* less than two meters tall, rented by their owners, rich *pernambucanos,*" the ANL manifesto declared; "there 40,000 families—200,000 human vermin—illustrate the depths of abandonment in which the Brazilian people live, in contrast to the ostentation of the landowners." In Bahia the caravan attacked foreign exploitation—the Estrada de Ferro Ilhéus a Conquista, the Spanish "bread and salt" trusts, the Port of Bahia Company—and misery in the *tugurios* of Maragogipe, the squalid shelters inhabited by industrial workers. Speakers denounced the light and power interests in Recife and Fortaleza; the powerful Ullen Management Company in São Luís; the foreign-owned Amazon River Company, Pará Electric, Manaus Tramway, and the Ford Motor Company in the Amazon region.[47] Yet, for all of its potential explosiveness, the caravan registered little visible impact among even those who, under threat of retaliation despite the legal status of the movement prior to mid-July, attended its fiery public gatherings. Its failure reflected in part the effectiveness of the national government's visible attention to the northeast—after decades of neglect—and, in equal measure, the basic apathy and lack of politicization among those to whom the ANL addressed its protests.

The expedition served an additional purpose: it allowed officials to oversee the general development of the movement and it camouflaged a private, secret mission of the national secretary-general, Roberto Sissón. On the orders of the Communist Party's executive committee, he delivered to all regional officials on the caravan's route contingency plans for armed insurrection, to be raised under the banner of popular revolution in the ANL's name.

Sissón's instructions outlined measures to arm the workers and peasants of the northeast and divide the region into revolutionary zones.[48] No specific date for the simultaneous uprisings was set, but recipients were told to remain alert, particularly after August 15. Whether the other members of the caravan, or the ANL national directorate, knew of these plans has not been determined.

Frequent harassment and the threat of government persecution of the ANL under the National Security Law undoubtedly encouraged Sissón to turn to the Communist Party for direction. By mid-May, recurrent attacks from its enemies, and the refusal of police officials to protect ANL meetings, demoralized the national directorate and forced Sissón to exercise increasing personal control. In early June, Integralists (allegedly with the complicity of the militia) attacked a rally in Petrópolis; several participants fell injured, and one died. In reprisal, the ANL forces regrouped, marched to AIB headquarters, and stormed the building, provoking further violence and raising demands that the popular front (but not the AIB) be outlawed. The publication on July 5 of Luís Carlos Prestes' revolutionary manifesto sealed the fate of the ANL, which federal authorities outlawed a week later. At the time of its suppression, the movement claimed 400,000 members. A more realistic estimate, based on surviving ANL records, probably would range between 70,000 and 100,000 persons at the height of its success.

During its legal phase from March to July, 1935, the ANL represented the Brazilian left's first attempt to articulate mass nationalistic activity by openly challenging the existing system. As well as frightening worried conservatives, the ANL embarrassed the Vargas administration by exposing its inconsequential revolutionary performance. The ANL identified the causes of social and economic adversity and offered unified action as the basis for progressive renovation.

To the intellectual, the ANL offered a nonconservative alternative to problems plaguing Brazilian society. If the left was fooled by communist intentions behind the ANL façade, then so were thousands who joined popular front movements in the 1930s. For many liberals, the ANL served primarily to combat the growing fascist threat within Brazil. The ANL cherished its role as watchdog over social affairs and civil liberties. It hammered repeatedly at specific abuses, formulating campaigns to protest the dismissal of factory workers and the deportation of nonnaturalized Brazilians. It portrayed itself as heir to the Brazilian revolutionary tradition, claiming such precursors as Antônio Conselheiro, the martyr of the federal assault on Canudos in the early days of the Old Republic, and Lampião, the *cangaceiro* bandit leader, in spite of his service against the Prestes Column in the pay of northeastern politicos.

The ANL hinted at issues normally avoided publicly: bias against Negroes, foreigners, and Jews; rural poverty and degradation; abuse of democratic institutions under the guise of antiextremism; and uneven ownership of the land. It avoided open warfare with the Church, although it attacked pro-Integralist clergymen and defended freedom of religious expression. It championed a free press, efficient postal service, and care for the aged. ANL spokesmen attacked the local recording industry (for nonpayment of royalties to *favela* songwriters), and the famous *samba* schools (for externalizing the misery of the working classes). But the ANL rarely attacked the evils of the top-heavy bureaucracy; indeed, it considered government jobs a panacea for unemployment.

ANL leaflets attacked inflation, corruption, and the failure of the federal government to reduce its financial deficit. The ANL offered few solutions, but it uncovered weaknesses when it saw them. It labeled the Chaco War in Bolivia "imperialist adventurism" and the government's continued support of coffee production through crop storage and destruction, "prejudicial and ineffective."[49] ANL newspapers attacked the concentration of landownership and the failure of local authorities to protect agricultural workers. The ANL contributed to the growing awareness in government circles of the potential use of nationalism as a political force. Yet it is unlikely that the ANL's members—or even its leaders—sensed the sudden turn which the movement would take in the face of repression or the fate it would suffer in the name of preservation of order at the end of 1935.

4

THE
INTEGRALISTS

Plínio Salgado's Integralist movement faced the popular front National Liberation Alliance from the opposite end of the ideological spectrum. To a degree, each movement resembled the other. Both utilized cellular formats; each attempted to attract the middle and working classes; each leveled attacks against the status quo, foreign economic domination, and the revolutionary failings of the Liberal Alliance. While both drew from foreign sources, each mirrored domestic conditions. In its own way, each was profoundly Brazilian. Both anticipated a nationalistic awareness ultimately embraced by the Vargas government.

Salgado borrowed Hitlerian trappings for his party and claimed to have been influenced by Charles Maurras, Gil Robles, Oliveira Salazar, Haya de la Torre, and a host of others.[1] But the primary model for his Ação Integralista Brasileira (AIB) was Italy. Admittedly confused and undirected prior to his European trip in 1930, Salgado returned to São Paulo a year later ecstatic over Mussolini's accomplishments. "The Italian man [today]," he wrote in Lourival Fontes' *Hierarchia,* "stands in the fullness of his integrity. He is a complete man." "The concept of fascism," he concluded, " . . . will be the light of the new age."[2]

The common theme underlying the movement's complex and often confused ideology—its advocacy of the substitution of organic unity and hierarchical national organization for liberal democracy—did not differ significantly from other demands for change which arose in Brazil in the post-World War I period. Integralism, Gustavo Barroso summarized in *What the Integralist Should Know,* sought truth raised to political principle, absolute faith, efficient and centralized government, an end to class struggle, controlled economic growth with the gradual nationalization of essential industries and services, inexpensive justice, education for literacy, moral vigor, and religious freedom "within the Christian [Catholic] ideal."[3] Integralists attacked international capitalism and its alleged links with the advocates of liberal democracy and laissez-faire constitutionalism in Brazil. Above all, Integralist doctrine sought synthesis—the integration of the individual into the "unity" of the state, nation, and universe.

Salgado emphasized Integralism's native roots to the point of caricature. In a manner suggesting the contemporary *indigenismo* movements of Spanish America, he identified a panoply of national heroes, including the early Jesuits, the *bandeirantes,* the Tupi civilization, statesman Rui Barbosa, the bellicose Duke of Caxias (the hero of the Paraguayan War), and the martyrs of the 1922 Copacabana Fort rebellion (the left embraced these young men as well).[4] Indebted to Brazil's Catholic heritage and the writings of Jackson de Figueiredo, the AIB characteristically adopted for its motto the pronouncement popularly attributed to Affonso Pena as his dying words: "For family, for country, and for God."

As articulated between 1932 and 1937, the program of the AIB demanded a sweeping overhaul of Brazilian political administration underscored by cultural and economic nationalism. The state, Salgado declared, rested on the three pillars of morality, economic organization, and corporate democracy. The specific proposals of the AIB seemed less radical (and less ideologically utopian) than those of the ANL. The Integralist movement called for a new Ministry of National Agriculture, to combine the existing Agriculture Ministry, the departments of Commerce and Industry from the Ministry of Labor, and the Department of Public Health from the Ministry of Education. It advocated a national banking system to aid manufacturers and to extend agrarian credit, as well as government control of transportation and communications networks in the interest of redressing regional imbalances. Other demands included a review of all contracts held by foreign businesses and of the external debt, a reform of the diplomatic service, more exclusive immigration laws, the nationalization of mines, water power, and petroleum, and the creation of a Ministry of Aviation. The AIB called for the creation of a National Ministry of Fine Arts to mobilize writers and artists to the nation's service and to offer subsidies for the study of Brazilian folklore. In sum, only its theoretical projection of a mechanistic totalitarian state stepped far beyond the boundaries of the solution preferred by other reform-minded Brazilians in the post-1930 world. Even so, the Integralist movement's unquestioned appeal to a wide cross section of Brazilians genuinely worried prodemocratic moderates and encouraged Vargas to deal with it with respect and even trepidation until his own power was firmly consolidated after November, 1937.

If the dual *raison d'être* of the ANL consisted of antifascist agitation and the awakening of the nation to the abuses of the capitalistic system, then the AIB simply substituted anticommunism and anti-Semitism for these goals. Both movements identified foreign penetration in Brazil and the government's lack of nationalistic initiative as the causes of domestic economic woes. The AIB attacked local constitutionalist politicians as the tool of foreign interests: New York and London (but not Berlin) bankers, the Rothschilds, and international communism, the last mysteriously linked with the capitalist world through the network of international Jewry. The writings of the left and right in Brazil on exploitation by nonnationals are virtually indistinguishable save for the left's added vehemence against the established order.[5]

As the AIB grew after 1932, it avoided direct political confrontation with Vargas, enjoying the government's tolerance and capitalizing on its links with several high civilian and military officials. Dozens of newspapers across Brazil were subsidized by or belonged to the Integralist movement, many of them (as well as a number of cultural and sportive journals and some radio stations, including Rio's Radio Mayrink de Veiga) wholly owned by the AIB. The Integralist press attacked conditions rather than personalities, trends rather than specific events. Its writers treated poverty, illiteracy, corruption, and disease as sources of patriotic shame. Salgado assailed the 1934 constitution, but he directed his attacks against the defenders of traditional states' rights. The document's retention of democratic forms, he wrote, provided "firm evidence of the incapacity of liberal democracy to organize itself for the national good."[6] He expressed shame at Brazilian underdevelopment, thus placing himself in the same camp with other intellectual critics, such as Affonso Arinos de Mello Franco, most of whom, however, never converted to Integralist ranks. In "The Country Which Does Not Read" Salgado charged: "Brazil is filled with superficial opinion. [Brazilians] are vain and empty."[7]

By the end of 1934 Integralism had become a significant force in the political arena, claiming 180,000 members. It reflected Nazi activities chiefly in its energetic anti-Semitic campaign, carried out largely by Gustavo Barroso, the director of the Integralist militia and the movement's leading intellectual. Salgado boasted of his acquaintance with individual Jews, including São Paulo's industrialist Horácio Lafer, but his press increasingly attacked Jews on both the domestic and international levels, frequently reprinting vicious Nazi propaganda materials. The AIB National Council maintained an Information Service, whose "Jewish Section" was charged with, among other functions, the compilation of statistics on the domestic Jewish community and the maintenance of a listing of prominent Jews in economic and political life.[8] *A Offensiva,* the principal newspaper among the nearly ninety published under the auspices of the AIB National Secretariat for Propaganda, in one issue offered photographs of alleged black African Jews gnawing raw meat. Barroso translated the *Protocols of the Elders of Zion* into Portuguese and asked that concentration camps be established for "Jewish communists." In addition to their anti-Semitic proclivities, Integralists also attacked freemasons, spiritists, advocates of sex education, liberal intellectuals, progressive educators, and campaigners for equal rights for women.

The October, 1932, Integralist manifesto, a verbose, pseudo-sociological treatise on man's place before God and universal order, gave formal birth to the movement. Annexing its doctrine to his circle of disciples in São Paulo and later in Rio de Janeiro, Salgado established the AIB with himself as its *führer.* It grew rapidly as thousands, including many second- and third-generation Germans and Italians, flocked to its uniformed ranks. Salgado, a small, frail man with a Hitler-like mustache, adopted the Greek letter sigma (the mathematical sign of the integral) as his substitute for the Nazi swastika. The militant, goose-stepping Integralists quickly caught the attention of the population and raised cries of alarm from moderates at home and abroad.

AIB cell organization linked each local group to higher authority in a progression through district, municipal, state, regional, and national levels. States were renamed Integralist provinces: there were twenty-one, including a Province of the Sea for sailors and nationals living outside Brazil. Cells in sparsely populated areas were organized under municipal units (*municípios*), each overseeing in theory at least one thousand members. In urban zones, cells were grouped into districts (*distritos*), units of fewer than a hundred adherents closely supervised by local officials. Urban cell activity for the most part dominated the national movement, with the exception of Integralist strongholds in the pastoral south among foreign-language settlers. At the height of the national movement's success in 1937, more than four thousand cells operated within a framework of nearly seven hundred municipalities and one hundred thirty urban districts.

On the highest organizational level sat the Integralist Chamber of the Four Hundred, and, above it, the Chamber of the Forty. The larger body performed chiefly honorary functions; membership was awarded to patrons of the movement and dignitaries from all parts of the country. It met infrequently, gathering in Rio de Janeiro to hear legislative proposals and to approve them ceremoniously.

Plínio Salgado personally chose the members of the Supreme Integralist Council, an administrative body which in turn selected the Chamber of the Forty. This prestigious chamber, presided over by its secretary-general, writer Olbiano de Mello, encompassed the innermost core of the movement. Many of its members, most of whom lived in the federal capital, held important positions in the AIB national hierarchy. The original Forty included a director of the Bank of Brazil, an official of the federal finance ministry, a former minister of education, and the director of the National School of Fine Arts. Of the thirty-nine members (in addition to Salgado, its president), twenty-one came from the professions, seven from the armed forces, two from government, and nine from industry, commerce, and finance.[9] At least one of them, Renato da Rocha Miranda, appears to have been a government agent who infiltrated the AIB at Vargas' request; he contributed money and helped organize meetings between Vargas and Salgado during 1937.[10]

Integralists thrived on ceremony and elaborate ritual. Their regular uniforms included green shirts and trousers, black or blue sigma arm bands, and black leather boots. Members wore uniforms to all meetings and were encouraged to use them on Sundays and holidays. Local merchants sold green shirts for 9$000 (sixty-three cents, somewhat more than the daily working-class wage in Rio de Janeiro, and three times the average wage in Pernambuco), and offered green cotton yard goods for women who preferred to sew their husbands' uniforms. Cells organized paramilitary "physical culture" squadrons which supplemented the independent national Integralist militia. All Integralists offered stiff armed salutes, hailing each other with an *anauê*, an oath of greeting Salgado created from the Tupi Indian dialect.

All Integralist meetings opened with the Brazilian national anthem, three anauês for the national chief, one or two for local dignitaries, and pledges of allegiance to the movement.[11] Headquarters distributed lengthy protocol manuals to all chapters: intergroup correspondence followed a uniform format, which included the date according to the Integralist calendar (1932 being the first year of the Integralist era). In addition, a secret subnetwork, unknown except to the highest Integralist officials, covered most of the national territory. Organized to gather military data, it used a full gamut of codes and conspiratorial safeguards, including hieroglyphic vocabularies with such symbols as ⊡ ("surprise attack") and ⟋⟍ ("shoot the officers").[12]

All Integralists received workbooks and catechisms. They memorized such dialogues as: "Do you love your country?" "Yes, because it is a geographic, historic, and moral unity; it lives in my heart and my soul."[13] Integralists were exhorted to improve their character. Punctuality received particular value: comrades guilty of tardiness were summoned for hearings and threatened with corrective action. Other disciplinary transgressions included improper performance of ritual, failure to execute orders, lying, or simulation of illness to avoid duty. Integralist conclaves frequently convened at eight in the morning and ran all day.[14]

The movement's statutes required Integralist chapters to display a portrait of Salgado draped with crossed flags, a map of Brazil, a movable sigma plaque, and appropriate green and blue bunting. "When there is a clock in the room," a manual ordered, "a sign should be placed next to it, reading 'Our hour will come.' "[15] All ritual was prescribed, standardizing ceremonies throughout Brazil. Expelled members were drummed out in a formal ceremony during which their membership cards were publicly burned to the chant, "Our Comrade ———— is dead; he has abandoned faith and his word of honor. . . . He is forgotten."[16] For the valiant, the movement offered numerous service awards, including the "Order of the Star of Guararapes" and the "Cross of Anchieta," a military honor.

But Salgado, the Integralist *führer,* was no fool. He admitted to Vargas at the height of his movement's success that the ritual and ceremony served the calculated function of intriguing the rank and file. "All sacrifices are compensated by things simple enough to understand—the uniform, the symbolic gesture," he wrote the President. "[Integralists] love these things to the point of delirium."[17]

Plínio Salgado's Christmas letter to the Brazilian people in 1935 warned against paganism, asserting that Christianity would always stand above the adoration of Caesars.[18] Yet the same national chief devised the Night of the Silent Drums ceremony in October, 1937, for which Integralist officials selected the "poorest and most humble" Integralist in every chapter across the country to play the part of Salgado in the midnight pageant."[19]

The supreme Integralist chief was born in the town of São Bento de Sapucaí, in the interior of São Paulo, in 1895. His father was a career army officer; his mother, of an old *bandeirante* family, was a schoolteacher. The father died when the boy was young, and Plínio, instructed by his mother in the classics, supported the family by teaching private classes while he still was in his teens. He took up journalism, although he continued to tutor, and worked occasionally on geological expeditions as a surveyor. He nearly succumbed to the influenza epidemic of 1918, and his wife died when their child was only sixteen days old. During this period Salgado read extensively, including the works of the Brazilian anti-Spencerian, Farias Brito, and the Catholic thinker, Jackson de Figueiredo. He also perused Soffici, Govoni, Apollinaire, Cocteau, Max Jacob, and Blaise Cendrars, the impulsive romanticist who once visited Brazil under the sponsorship of Paulo Prado.[20]

Migrating to the state capital, Salgado joined the modernist movement which had arisen after the tradition-shattering São Paulo Modern Art Week in February, 1922. He became a successful essayist and critic, contributing to such literary journals as Monteiro Lobato's *Revista do Brasil*. In order to pursue his commitment to native themes, he learned the Tupí language with a liberal colleague, Raul Bopp. This and other unorthodox scholarly interests earned him a reputation as an eccentric, and he withdrew further into self-examination. He now read Brazilian authors exclusively, especially Alberto Torres, Paulo Prado, and Euclides da Cunha, all of whom had searched as Salgado now did for the Brazilian identity.

By 1925 the brooding writer, now thirty years old, slowly drew a circle of young rebels around him: these included Bopp, the poet Augusto Frederico Schmidt, Plinio Mello, Araujo Lima, and Mario Pedrosa (the last three became Trotskyites in the early 1930s). During this stage in Salgado's career he published a novel, *The Stranger* (1926), and from 1927 to 1930 he served as an elected member of the São Paulo state Chamber of Deputies. Disillusioned by his legislative experience and unsettled by the death from poverty of his poet-friend Rodrígues de Abreu, he traveled to Europe and the Near East as the proctor for the dull son of a São Paulo businessman. Salgado came to life in Europe. He wrote a second novel in

Paris and devoured wide selections of communist and fascist literature. After meeting with Mussolini in July, 1930, he wrote his friends that a sacred fire had entered his existence.

Salgado returned to Brazil in 1932 and rejected Vargas' provisional government as "painfully mediocre." He organized the Political Study Society in São Paulo, out of which emerged the AIB. Joining the staff of Alfredo Egydio de Souza Aranha's *A Razão* in São Paulo, he used his daily column as a sounding board for his newly confirmed fascist ideology. His inner circle now included poet San Tiago Dantas, historians Hélio Vianna and Américo Lacombe, journalists Lourival Fontes and Gilson Amado, and jurist Miguel Reale.

Salgado took control of the new Integralist movement and ruled effectively, permitting only one challenge to his authority to reach public ears during his tenure. Only two men potentially rivaled his leadership: Gustavo Barroso and, after Salgado relinquished his active role in 1938, Belmiro Valverde. Barroso, one of the most brilliant and ruthless men in modern Brazil, nearly overshadowed Salgado during the AIB's growing years, but was successfully kept at bay until the movement declined after 1937.

More openly pro-Nazi than the other Integralist leaders, who generally favored Mussolini, Barroso commanded the AIB militia and at the same time acted as the movement's principal theoretician. As a journalist and a member of the Brazilian Academy of Letters, he dominated the Integralist movement's intellectual sphere, although his arrogance alienated an undetermined number of would-be adherents and caused Salgado frequent embarrassment. While his exaggerated anti-Semitism and exceptional drive made him stand as somewhat of an exception among Integralist leaders, his public exposure and intellectual stature gave him influence in the movement second probably only to Salgado.

Barroso was born in the northern state of Ceará in 1888. His father came from an old northeastern family, and his mother, a German by the name of Dodt, came from Württemberg. She died while her son was small, although he learned some German from her and received a good early education. Barroso studied medicine and wrote a series of essays for local newspapers under the pen name João do Norte. Throughout his life he suffered from extreme moodiness and an explosive temper. Frequently he would resign his job after unpleasantness, villify his former superiors publicly, and then use his connections to regain the post after feeling personally vindicated.[21]

Barroso's books, generally well written although inflammatory, sold well. He fancied himself a historian and, like Salgado, a folklorist. He wrote several works simplifying Integralist theory and scores of articles for the Integralist press, as well as a military history of Brazil. In spite of his election to the Academy of Letters and subsequently to its presidency in September, 1932, he published under his own name a triad of virulently anti-Semitic books—*Brazil, Colony of Bankers; The São Paulo Synagogue;* and *Roosevelt Is Jewish,* a book which enraged Ambassador Oswaldo Aranha in Washington.[22] But Barroso was not moved by protest; he proudly presented each new volume, usually autographed in the Brazilian custom, to local libraries.

Plínio Salgado quietly sanctioned the AIB's general anti-Semitic campaign, although for a brief time he backed the efforts of the editor of *A Offensiva* to exclude Barroso from its pages.[23] Julius Streicher's *Der Stürmer* praised Barroso's racist works, and he was well thought of throughout Germany. The *Deutsche La Plata Zeitung* of Buenos Aires called Barroso, not Salgado, the *"führer* of Brazilian Integralism."[24] Yet Barroso denied that he was a racist, claiming that he himself was descended from "diverse races."[25] A reported attempt by Barroso to edge Salgado out of the movement in early 1937 failed, even though João Dodt (as his enemies called him) allegedly attacked the national chief within Integralist circles for softness toward Jews and for being "false to his promises."[26]

Barroso's most controversial crusade was his attempt to introduce Integralism into the Brazilian Academy of Letters. He had been admitted in 1923, the youngest member in history, and was elected president in 1932 after a strenuous campaign. Two years later he told the press that the Academy would become a leading Integralist center; he wore his green militia uniform, complete with pith helmet, to Academy meetings. Even his attacks on refugees from Hitler as "human garbage" drew him no censure from his distinguished colleagues.[27]

Other prominent figures in the national movement included Raymundo Barbosa Lima and José Madeira de Freitas in the capital; Raymundo Padilha, chief of the Integralist province constituting the state of Rio de Janeiro; federal deputy Jehovah Motta and Ubirajara Indio, both of Ceará; Antônio Galloti, chief of the AIB's "foreign relations" office; historian Hélio Vianna; and Thiers Martins Moreira, of the Ministry of Education.

Others not formally associated with the AIB but publicly sympathetic to it lent prestige to the movement. These included General Pantaleão

Pessôa, chief of staff of the armed forces until 1935, and Newton Cavalcanti, ultimately Salgado's most active defender in high military circles. Police chief Felinto Müller maintained ties with Integralist leaders and the German Embassy. Intellectuals such as the Catholic lay-spokesman Alceu Amoroso Lima (Tristão de Athayde) and sociologist Artur Neiva were also considered friends of the movement.

White-collar workers, professionals, and career soldiers—usually non-commissioned officers—dominated urban rank-and-file membership, while rural and outlying cells generally attracted more modest sectors of the working-class population. The Cordeiro cell, of the state (Integralist province) of Rio de Janeiro's Cantagalo's municipality, presented the following occupational breakdown:[28]

Teachers	3
Clerks (commerce and banking)	9
Students	2
Artisans	11
Transportation workers	7
Factory workers	22
Domestics	15
Agricultural workers	9
Unemployed or no occupation	4
Minors	8

On local cell levels, leaders were usually young, between thirty and forty-five years of age. The firmest degree of allegiance to the Integralist cause came from city cells and from towns of medium size, particularly in regions settled by Italian and German immigrants. In rural Brazil, AIB officials frequently complained that adherents were illiterate and thereby difficult to indoctrinate.

Top military spokesmen so often praised the goal of the AIB that membership flourished in Brazil's armed forces, especially in the tradition-centered navy. General Meira de Vasconcellos lauded Barroso's *Brazil, Colony of Bankers,* and ordered copies placed in the library of the Military Academy.[29] The entire military contingent in Bahia, a correspondent told Ambassador Aranha, was under the domination of Integralist officers.[30] On one occasion sailors on the *Minas Gerais* allegedly were obliged to sing the Integralist hymn, "Avante," in place of the national anthem. Some observers reported that Integralist membership among Naval Academy cadets and among submarine crews approached 75 per cent. As late as 1941, the Navy Ministry complained that the crew of a training ship, the *Almirante Saldanha,* had left its scheduled course and visited with Plínio Salgado in his Portuguese exile for an extracurricular "picnic."[31] The AIB boasted of the membership of mulatto João Cândido, the tormented *marujo* hero of the 1910 naval revolt; but Cândido, not an articulate man, resisted an active role; later, he admitted that Integralism had deceived him, and that he had joined in deference to his friends.[32]

Academicians and intellectuals gravitated to the AIB more frequently than to the popular front of Roberto Sissón and Luís Carlos Prestes. This should not be surprising. The genteel educated elite, products of the conservative Brazilian intellectual environment, responded more warmly to Salgado's appeals to morality, traditionalism, and hierarchical order than to the left's promise of social upheaval. Many young men visited abroad after World War I, returning home somewhat ashamed of their country's backwardness.[33] Other Brazilians, unsure of their nation's future as a racially mixed tropical society, watched with interest what in the early 1930s seemed to be interesting experiments in national discipline in fascist Europe.

Yet despite the distinguished credentials of some of its sympathizers, the AIB maintained an arrogant posture in intellectual affairs. It attacked moderates and liberals crudely and ridiculed academic freedom. Puritanical, it opposed what it considered to be decadent influences in modern life: the cinema, athiestic secular education, and popular music.[34] As cultural czar, Gustavo Barroso addressed AIB audiences on various historical and intellectual themes; but during his speeches he wore his militia shoulder holster.

While the Integralist program embraced the Catholic faith and was frequently praised by Church officials, formal relations varied between warmth and caution. Many clergymen, particularly at the bishopric level, welcomed Integralism and considered the AIB a natural ally. "Nothing is more admirable than the unity of doctrine and the coherence of attitudes maintained by the Catholic Church through the centuries," an Integralist writer said in 1933.[35] "Integralism, in the social field, possesses for the most part the same adversaries as the Church," Alceu Amoroso Lima declared, although he tempered his endorsement by warning Catholics not to swear unconditional loyalty to any political chieftain.[36] The Integralist press proudly displayed favorable statements from more than twenty bishops and archbishops, one of whom, the pastoral father of Ilhéus in the state of Bahia, called the Integralists "soldiers of Christ."[37] Within the Church hierarchy, however, a determined minority resisted petitions for formal endorsement of the AIB, which was never given. A deliberate muffling of the Church debates on Integralism has obscured the identities of those involved.[38]

The AIB enjoyed only moderate influence among university students. Several private secondary school administrators supported the movement, but little observable pupil indoctrination took place. This was a far different condition from the Integralist-run primary schools, where the movement's catechism formed the core of the daily curriculum. Student Integralist cells at the universities were weak, except in the northeast; Integralist programs were frequently ridiculed. Most AIB student efforts concentrated upon attacking professors considered communists or fellow travelers.[39]

The AIB sponsored dozens of like-minded front groups, much in the same manner as the ANL. The Socôrro Verde, Salgado's version of the Red Cross, originated in the mid-1930s and survived through the next decade. Other Integralist fronts included the National Institute of Scouting, sport clubs such as the Apollo Club and the state of Rio's Aviation Association, social assistance groups, and a large number of German and Italian cultural societies, which received financial support from their respective embassies. In 1935 the AIB sponsored a labor front, the Frente Única Sindical, but it was not successful. In Belo Horizonte the Integralists operated the Minas Gerais Center of Anti-Jewish Studies.[40]

The Integralist women's federation began operation in 1935 and played a major role thereafter. The AIB "green blouses" imitated the zeal of their Integralist husbands; through their literacy and social work programs they reached into many areas otherwise untouched by the movement. The women's groups of the AIB distributed food during the Christmas season, ran *favela* health clinics, and established literacy schools for youngsters and night classes for adults, as well as sewing classes for indigent mothers and centers for undernourished infants.[41] Most of these activities centered in urban areas, but Integralists throughout Brazil demonstrated interest in the type of social problems local residents usually ignored. But the Integralists' own attitude toward the woman's role itself undermined any possible additional growth of volunteer social services. AIB dogma declared that the heart of national life was the home, and that the woman belonged in it. AIB-sponsored Pliniano and Pliniana societies for boys and girls also suffered from the Integralists' view that children should be seen and not heard—although the children were allowed to march in their green uniforms, and older boys were subjected to very rigorous physical training at the Integralist paramilitary sport camps.

The AIB's armed militia evoked the greatest fear from the public at large. By Integralist statute each local cell kept its own cache of large and small arms, and regular inventories were submitted to regional and national AIB headquarters.[42] Salgado formally abolished the militia after the government promulgated its National Security Law in April, 1935 (directed mainly, of course, against the left), but created in its place a "National Secretariat for Moral and Physical Education," also under Gustavo Barroso, and which amounted to the same thing.[43] Its regiments trained in public places or, where restricted by local authorities, at Integralist clubs. The philosopher Farias Brito, who a generation earlier had called for a holy army to lead Brazil to salvation, was claimed as the AIB's military patron. Yet the militia was never a truly national force: the problem of coordination alone precluded such organization in the few years of the AIB's existence. Apologizing for the ineffective organization of his troops, one militia official, writing to his superiors in early 1937, blamed government hostility, inadequate equipment, training facilities, and instructions, and the fact that the removal of the danger posed by the left's ANL had diminished interest in his force; local Integralists' attention, he said, had turned to Plínio Salgado's presidential campaign. Another commander agreed, declaring the necessity for a "restoration of a climate of struggle."[44]

From region to region, the Integralist movement varied slightly in composition. It flourished among the semirural populations of the south, which had heavy concentrations of German and Italian immigrants. Since the line between Integralist and Nazi activity in the south was often finely drawn, the federal government quietly approved restrictions on AIB activity by the governors of Paraná and Santa Catarina, to the anger of Integralist officials.[45] Foreign names dominated Integralism in these states: of thirty-two AIB officials in Santa Catarina, eight were clearly of Italian origin (e.g., Pelligrini, Margiotti); thirteen were Germanic (e.g., Stein, Malburg, Gruenwalt); and only nine were recognizably Portuguese.[46] In late 1935 more than 42,000 Integralists gathered for a provincial conference in Blumenau, a major Teuto-Brazilian center. At least four daily Integralist newspapers were printed in Santa Catarina and Paraná, one of which, the *Blumenau Zeitung,* appeared in German.

The state of São Paulo had the greatest number of Integralist municipalities (173), roughly divided between the interior and the state capital. Plínio Salgado led the first Integralist parade in April, 1933; the state movement grew rapidly afterward although its national administrative center shifted to Rio de Janeiro. The paulista Integralists faced opposition from the ANL and from a moderate bloc led by Paulo Duarte, a young intellectual and ally of Otávio Mangabeira and, later, Armando Salles de Oliveira, the paulista candidate for the presidency in 1937 before the coming of the Estado Nôvo.

Some São Paulo industrialists, on good terms with Salgado and fearing left-wing labor agitation, backed the movement financially. Count Francisco Matarazzo, who emigrated penniless from Italy in 1881 at the age of twenty-seven and who commanded an industrial empire by the time of his death in 1937, supposedly gave a million lire to Mussolini in exchange for a medal in 1927, and contributed a second million ($50,000) for the Ethiopian campaign in 1935. It is widely held that he contributed to the Integralists as well, although no amounts have ever been documented.[47] Other businessmen and industrialists in Minas Gerais, São Paulo, and the state of Rio de Janeiro contributed regularly. The Integralist movement in these states and in Espírito Santo fared reasonably well: Minas Gerais hosted 134 AIB *municípios,* the most active of which were located in the urban centers of Belo Horizonte, Teófilo Otoni, and Juiz de Fóra.

The movement in the state of Rio de Janeiro numbered 271 cells, most of them dynamic. It operated health posts, literacy courses, and social clubs in the larger *fluminense* cities of Niterói, Campos, and Friburgo. In 1935 Petrópolis was chosen for the AIB's second national congress. On the border between Espírito Santo and the state of Rio, Integralism flourished among railroad workers and small farmers of German origin.

Bahian Integralists pitted their strength against the prestige of the governor, Juracy Magalhães, who, in an effort to capitalize on his professed antiextremist posture, harassed Integralists and liberals alike. Police sporadically invaded cell meetings, and, in late 1936, the state AIB movement was ordered closed following the disclosure of an alleged antigovernment plot among state Integralist leaders. In late 1935 the national headquarters promoted a provincial conference in Salvador to coincide with Plínio

Salgado's visit to the region, but it was sabotaged by local left-wing unionists who refused to serve delegates in restaurants and bars, and who misrouted the baggage of Integralist officials arriving by railroad.[48]

Integralism prospered in the northeast, especially in Ceará, Gustavo Barroso's home state. In Rio Grande do Norte and Paraíba it attracted intellectuals; in Pernambuco, AIB strength centered among student groups in the faculties of law and medicine. But the movement in Pernambuco lacked a broad popular base, a factor which probably arose out of poor local leadership. Energetic Integralist officials in Alagôas built a strong local movement in that small coastal state.

The national Integralist body closely controlled the movement from its headquarters in the federal capital. As early as 1934, cells functioned in every residential district, and thereafter expanded into the industrial sections in the city's northern zone. AIB statistics show that the average cell in the Federal District numbered between 50 and 175 members, with between 15 and 40 per cent regularly participating in cell activities.[49] Rio de Janeiro's Ipanema cell, in the elegant beach-fronted southern zone, doubled its membership to 210 persons between 1934 and 1936 and petitioned to be allowed to acquire larger quarters, although its chief admitted that only 30 per cent of the rank and file attended regularly in spite of the fact that the cell maintained extensive facilities for sports, including gymnastic equipment and a beach house.[50] Total Integralist membership in the city numbered between ten and fifteen thousand. Most likely it totaled about four thousand activists. In November, 1937, Salgado claimed that 50,000 Integralists had participated in the parade which alarmed moderates and set the emotional stage for the proclamation of the Estado Nôvo a week later. But although the AIB imported dozens of busloads of Green Shirts from surrounding regions, Brazilian government sources estimated that only 17,000 persons had marched.[51]

By the end of 1937, Integralist leaders claimed between 300,000 and 400,000 adherents in 4,000 local cells. Based on the knowledge that most units inflated their rolls for reasons of prestige and that only one third of the rank and file attended meetings faithfully, a more accurate estimate of Integralist strength would fall between 100,000 and 200,000 activists. Nevertheless, the figures are impressive, considering their urban concentration and the generally low level of political mobilization in Brazilian society.[52]

Financial support for the movement came from dues, gifts from private contributors, and foreign sources. The Integralists denied that they received foreign help; probably it was minimal, contributed mostly to AIB German and Italian front groups. The Italian Foreign Ministry, through its Brazilian embassy, contributed approximately U.S.$ 2,500 per month.[53] German-controlled firms in Brazil such as Herman Stoltz Ltd. and Theodor Wille Ltd. reportedly contributed to the AIB, but in all probability German money went for the most part to Nazi organizations in the south. Nazi officials did, however, offer propaganda materials, maintaining frequent correspondence with Barroso and his aides.[54] In the early days of the movement, Salgado financed his organization himself.

According to Integralist records, the AIB National Council spent the equivalent of $5,000 per month in mid-1936 for publicity and office expenses. The individual cells operated on their own budgets, as did subsidiary and associated groups.[55] Provincial and regional committees shared responsibility for the operation of the nearly ninety Integralist newspapers.

In spite of its extensive fiscal machinery, the AIB often operated short of funds: one paulista cell regularly resorted to pleas for contributions from persons chosen at random from the local telephone directory. The AIB financial bureau often planned *ad hoc* fund-raising campaigns, usually administered by the movement's chief financial adviser, Belmiro Valverde. Valverde orchestrated such programs as a "Sigma Tax" and the "For the Welfare of Brazil" program to aid the militia. The Integralists' "Campaign of Gold" in 1936 sent representatives through Brazil seeking old jewelry and gold to pay for outstanding debts. After 80 per cent of all cells had reported, campaign leaders announced that the effort had yielded a total of less than $8,400.[56]

The AIB held its first national conference in the capital of Espírito Santo in the early part of 1934. Two months later its militia demonstrated publicly in Rio de Janeiro for the first time, marching up the city's main thoroughfare and impeding traffic. Three thousand Integralists attended the second national congress in Petrópolis in March, 1935, where fighting between Integralists and leftists provided exposure for the movement. Most newspapers decried the communist threat and portrayed the Integralists as victims of harassment and aggression.

New converts provided publicity for the movement. On March 30, 1935—the day of the first public ANL rally—banker Marcos de Souza Dantas returned from his financial mission to the United States and took the Integralist oath at dockside.[57] João Fairbanks, elected as an Integralist to the São Paulo state assembly, took his seat in April with a public proclamation of loyalty to Plínio Salgado, to shouts of *anauê!* from the galleries.[58] The ludicrous behavior of Integralist spokesmen amused onlookers, but the movement continued to draw adherents and to establish its influence nationally.

The AIB faced a major crisis in November, 1935, when it suddenly became embroiled in the conflict between Rio Grande do Sul and the federal government. Opponents of the Integralist movement, who since mid-year had demanded that it be restricted under the same provisions of the National Security Law that had closed the ANL in July, secured Vargas' temporary approval and support for a vote on the issue; their action was a strike at General Pantaleão Pessôa, Flôres da Cunha's close ally and, as chief of staff, the most influential friend of the Integralist movement within the military up to this time.

The Chamber of Deputies met to act on the matter on November 20, provoking near violence on the floor during the heated debate which preceded the vote. When the vote came, the anti-AIB forces mustered sufficient strength to side with the government against Flôres da Cunha, and the motion condemning the Integralists was carried, 80 to 73. An article in *O Imparcial* four days later warned that General Pessôa, stung by the result, had met with Gustavo Barroso and others to plan an Integralist coup d'état against Vargas.[59]

But the entire issue was swept aside in the jarring news of insurrection in the northeast which, by odd coincidence, reached Rio de Janeiro that same evening. Salgado, in Bahia on Integralist business, forgot his anger and wired the capital that one hundred thousand Green Shirts stood at the disposal of the federal government to preserve order. The message was not lost on Vargas. The promotion to general of the reactionary colonel Newton Cavalcanti on November 30 proved that the tide had turned again in favor of the Integralist movement.

As Integralist national chief, Plínio Salgado created an indigenous fascist movement within Brazilian political life. He permitted diversity within his AIB: the faction headed by Miguel Reale and others looked toward Italy and Portugal and advocated less violent solutions than the pro-Nazi wing led by Barroso.[60] But although Salgado commanded absolute authority from his subordinates, he lacked the charisma of Mussolini or even Vargas in his later years; few were prepared, as it turned out later, to fight for Integralism's survival.

It is doubtful that most Integralist adherents grasped the full ramifications of Salgado's "green nationalism," and, for all of his organizational ingenuity, it is unlikely that the AIB hierarchy could have reshaped society to the Integralist model had Salgado been given the opportunity. Long on elaborate ritual, Integralist doctrine only superficially treated social and economic conditions in Brazil, placing excessive faith on the practicality of its theoretical formulas. In the end, its proposed ideal revolutionary order stood on very traditional supports: oligarchic political organization, elitism, paternalistic social relations, and sluggish moral precepts.

The AIB is best viewed as an authoritarian, hierarchical movement borrowing from foreign fascist sources but rooted deeply in Brazilian nationalism and culture as well. Doctrinally, Salgado copied from the Latin fascist countries—Portugal, Italy, and Franco's Spain. From the German Reich, the Brazilian national chief took his movement's love of ritual and its preoccupation with anti-Semitism. But the Integralist militia failed to pose a serious threat; the AIB lacked genuine support in the armed forces. Brazil's economic recovery after 1930 and Vargas' ability to satisfy both planters and industrialists robbed Salgado of potential backers as the decade progressed.

Barroso's anti-Semitic drive made little impression in a culture unaccustomed to racist bombast: with only 42,000 Jews in Brazil in 1935 and few, if any, in visible positions of influence, the anti-Jewish campaign gained little credibility. The ANL and the government's subsequent anticommunist witch hunt provided the Integralists with vulnerable adversaries, but the suppression of the left after 1936 dulled the attraction of the AIB's calls for militant preparedness. The very failure of the left to entrench itself as a visible threat weakened potential Integralist appeal. Fatally for the AIB, virtually all politically conscious Brazilians identified themselves sufficiently with the acts of the federal government to render the AIB superfluous. After 1937, the imposition of order and the adoption of an authoritarian central government removed the two strongest bases of Integralist appeal: the communist threat and liberal democracy.[61]

To reassert national independence and liberate Brazil from external economic and cultural domination, Integralism prescribed discipline, self-pride, a revival of the traditional virtues, and the abandonment of divisive, class-conscious competition in favor of the organic unity of the Brazilian nation, a concept elevated to mystical proportions through intense patriotic indoctrination, ritual, and public declaration of loyalty.[62]

Organizationally, Integralism differed from contemporary fascist movements in Europe. While leaders tended to be young—Salgado was thirty-seven in 1932, and Barroso forty-four—the movement did not widely attract youth, as contrasted to the experience of Rumania, for example, where the average age of Codreanu's Legion of the Archangel Michael was twenty-seven, or Mussolini's Italy, where, a scholar notes, fascist methods made "the greatest impression on the young, who in turn developed and refined them."[63] Although Integralist doctrine promised the laboring classes the illusion of integration into an organic national society, urban workers and the marginally employed remained largely uninterested; white-collar workers, disgruntled bureaucrats and professionals, career military men of the lower ranks, and small-town tradesmen dominated Integralist cell membership.[64] In the south, Integralism faced strong competition from ethnic-based groups and from local Nazis. The AIB made little headway in rural zones, and, in return, devoted scant attention to rural problems. Individual businessmen and manufacturers offered the AIB some financial aid but most felt sufficiently at home with the status quo to resist Integralist appeals.

Had Vargas taken a left-of-center direction after 1930, or had liberal constitutionalists secured greater gains after 1934, Integralism probably would have encountered far more fertile soil in which to grow. What success it did enjoy can be attributed to its appeal to traditional values, its mystique, the desire among conservative intellectuals for imposed self-discipline and order, and its awareness of problems of economic nationalism and national reorganization.

5

THE
REVOLUTIONARY TURN

Restlessness on all sides increased through early 1935 as National Liberation Alliance and Integralist partisans clashed with growing frequency.[1] By May it was apparent that the government would not allow the left to mobilize without the closest surveillance. While the Integralists made vague and inconclusive legal motions to comply with the National Security Law and were not bothered, the ANL faced constant harassment, especially in regions where its activity encompassed labor agitation.

On May 13, ANL officials, during a mass gathering in Rio de Janeiro in commemoration of the abolition of slavery in Brazil, announced that Luís Carlos Prestes would issue a manifesto to the nation three weeks later, on July 5, the anniversary of the 1922 Copacabana Fort uprising and the 1924 tenente-inspired revolt in São Paulo. Plans for the simultaneous release of the document went to all ANL cells in the national organization. In the capital, Federal District police nearly sabotaged the event by canceling the ANL's July 5 permit for use of the *Estádio Brasil* (the forerunner of the modern *Maracanã*) on the eve of the scheduled rally, forcing it indoors, where Carlos Lacerda, the same law student who three months earlier had nominated Prestes for the movement's honorary presidency, read the manifesto to a token crowd.

The document launched the popular front into a frankly revolutionary phase. "The battle is joined," the text declared; "[on] one side there are those who would consolidate . . . the most brutal kind of fascist dictatorship. On the other . . . the national liberty of Brazil with bread, land, and liberty for its people."[2] Listing a drastic nine-point program which included immediate redistribution of the land, without compensation, to workers and peasants, nationalization of all public services and foreign enterprises, separation of church and state, and abrogation of all commercial accords, the manifesto demanded a popular, national, revolutionary government headed by Luís Carlos Prestes. It concluded on a radically new note for the Brazilian left: "All power to the National Liberation Alliance!"

The manifesto created confusion among noncommunist ANL officials, most of whom were totally unprepared for its militancy. The anticommunist press, which from the inception of the ANL had labeled it a Bolshevik front, unleashed renewed attacks, demanding its censure. Trapped, even some members of the ANL's national directorate backed away from the movement, including its administrative president, Hercolino Cascardo. Now the PCB, through Prestes and his advisers, gained full control of the popular front.[3]

The decision to alter the ANL within a revolutionary framework arose out of increasing police repression in the weeks before July 5, but the basic decision to so act probably was taken by the PCB as soon as the popular front was initiated. If a "legalist" wing of the Communist Party had resisted militancy prior to the elaboration of the July 5 manifesto, by April it had yielded to the "revolutionary" wing, which was undoubtedly fortified by the clandestine arrival of Prestes and at least four other Comintern agents— Harry Berger, Rodolfo Ghioldi, Leon Valée, and Victor Allan Baron, rumored to be the son of the *Daily Worker*'s Harrison George, from the United States.[4]

In the week following the release of the manifesto, the pro-ANL press, as if anticipating imminent repression, suddenly turned volatile and belligerent. On July 12, *A Manhã,* in banner headlines, threatened a general strike should the government suppress the popular front. That afternoon, federal police entered the main headquarters of the ANL, seized its archives, and padlocked its doors. Other ANL fronts, including the women's UFB, were closed as well. Yet few stirred in the popular front's defense; mass protest against the ANL's demise was limited to a march of five hundred workers in São Paulo led by Caio Prado, Jr. Some further acts of harassment occurred, including the kidnaping by police of São Paulo's *A Platéia* editor Brasil Gerson, and the unexplained murder in Recife of the editor of the ANL's *A Gazeta.*

But as quickly as it had heated up, the inflammatory format adopted by *A Manhã* and its sister publications abruptly cooled: in a clumsy attempt to forestall suppression, the papers sheepishly avoided direct attacks on the Vargas administration, instead blaming the British Intelligence Service and such "foreign agents" as the Guinles, Assis Chateaubriand, and Roberto

Simonsen for having exerted pressure on the Brazilian government to silence the ANL. Vargas, nonetheless, had acted on his own accord against the increasingly militant popular front. On the day of the release of the Prestes manifesto, he wrote to Governor Benedito Valladares of Minas Gerais that his government had been informed of Communist Party machinations through the ANL, and that it was ready to act at any moment. The July 5 revolutionary posture simply accelerated the inevitable.[5]

After July 12, the National Liberation Alliance expired as a legal mass organization. What remained of its organizational framework moved underground, kept alive by Roberto Sissón for the PCB. Admitting frustration and helplessness, Sissón claimed later that he so acted out of admiration for Prestes, still a figure of awe to young left-minded Brazilian intellectuals. But to the PCB, the turn of events was not unexpected. "The closing of the ANL came as no surprise," an undercover party newsletter disclosed in August. "Revolution provokes counterrevolution. It now becomes necessary . . . to adopt more aggressive forms of struggle."[6] While Prestes privately congratulated ANL leaders for having served well, party correspondents ridiculed the organization's efforts, blaming it for having failed to reach the masses.[7] Meanwhile, the government increased its pressure on the left, arresting liberal journalists (including Rubem Braga, a young writer for Recife's *Fôlha do Povo*) and initiating deportation proceedings against unwanted foreign nationals. One such case, involving the harassment of a fifteen-year-old girl, Geny Glaser, became a *cause célèbre* in the left-wing press until she foiled police officials by marrying a Brazilian newspaperman, thus preventing her automatic deportation.[8]

What were called ANL cells after July were simply Communist Party cells operating in the name of the ANL, mostly in the rural northeast where PCB regulars had generally maintained control. Sissón acted as liaison between Rio de Janeiro and the outlying regions. Working feverishly, he issued dozens of directives, inquiries, and letters in the name of "Lopes Chaves" and a largely fictional revolutionary ANL directorate. A second "directorate" issued instructions from São Paulo; this clearly was a PCB body.

Sissón reshaped the organization along revolutionary lines, following the instructions he had delivered during his trip to the northeast in May and June. In place of the original ANL local structures, Sissón created "compact and professional" sections, with responsibilities carefully divided among members.[9] He urged all units to stress propaganda activity, issuing to them model manifestoes and protests for adaptation to local circumstances. He encouraged the few antifascist front groups which continued to function, and attempted, unsuccessfully, to establish new ones.[10]

Prestes busied himself through August and September writing nostalgic letters to his old tenente comrades, appealing for their aid in the coming struggle.[11] They rejected him courteously. "Not having seen you for five years," João Alberto Lins de Barros replied, "this letter is a precarious means at understanding." The bases of radicalism had diminished since 1930, he warned Prestes. "It is much more comfortable to go along."[12]

Comfort of another type did not escape the top PCB leadership, particularly its Comintern advisers, who lived in different parts of Rio de Janeiro's best residential districts. According to later disclosures, the rents paid by Leon Valée, the Harry Bergers, and PCB Secretary Adalberto Fernandes ranged from 500$000 to 750$000 monthly, moderately expensive by 1935 terms. Prestes, in hiding, occupied more humble quarters in the city's working-class northern zone. But Prestes reportedly preferred taxis to streetcars and buses, even when he traveled from distant Jacarepaguá across the Federal District to Leblon.[13]

In early October, Berger set the machinery for revolutionary insurrection in motion through the national ANL-PCB network, and the regional committee of the Communist Party in Rio de Janeiro assumed firm control. Berger, in order to exclude Sissón from the final stages of planning, told him that the date for revolution had been postponed indefinitely. Meanwhile, Silo Meirelles stood ready in the São Francisco region; Agrícola Baptista, formerly of Pedro Ernesto's personal staff, proceeded to Mato Grosso; Costa Leite traveled south to Paraná; and preparatory work continued in São Paulo, Pôrto Alegre, Minas Gerais, and Pará.[14]

Party propaganda, issued in the name of the defunct ANL, continued to stress the principles of Prestes' July 5 manifesto: a popular, revolutionary government of all democrats and antifascists, with Prestes at its head; civil freedoms and racial and religious equality; extensive social legislation, including equal pay for equal work, minimum wages, and unemployment insurance; the elimination of the feudal power of landowners (although the party insisted that only freedom from economic slavery—not socialism or confiscation of private property—would result.[15] But, except for isolated instances, the PCB for the most part was speaking only to itself. No evidence testifies to any significant amount of public support for the left's position after the enforcement of the National Security Law against the

ANL. Political interest between July and November concentrated on Flôres da Cunha, the Congress, and the Vargas cabinet. A PCB-led strike against the arrival of Plínio Salgado in Bahia in mid-November received scant attention in the press. Prestes was presumed to be still in European exile; to most Brazilians, the ANL had disappeared from view.

From November 23 to November 27, 1935, three separate insurrections, raised at local military units in Natal, Recife, and Rio de Janeiro, challenged the established order in the name of popular revolution and the ANL. Each failed to garner popular support; each was subdued swiftly, affording Vargas a pretext to suspend the constitution under a prolonged state of siege and therefore temporarily obscuring the political difficulties which had neared their climax in November, 1935, behind a smoke screen of national unity. A further element should be noted: although the so-called Communist Revolution of 1935 had in fact been instigated fully by PCB planning, the individual revolts were nevertheless related closely to local conditions.

Immediately after his election as governor of Rio Grande do Norte, Rafael Fernandes moved to solidify the Popular Party's control of the state. Following the example set by his predecessor, he removed dozens of state officials loyal to the opposition. He suspended all of former Interventor Mário Câmara's public works projects, including the building of thirty elementary schools, and idled their construction crews. In an act which was to create extensive consequences, he dismissed without warning or compensation 420 members of the Civil Guard.[16] The Guard, he charged, could not be trusted. But he did not remove their arms. The guardsmen, unable to find jobs, roamed the streets of Natal aimlessly. In the western part of the state, a band of *cangaceiros* led by Colonel Balthazar Meirelles terrorized local towns in acts that were linked by the Popular Party's *A Razão* to the "political legacy" of Mário Câmara. Fernandes dispatched his police chief to the Ceará frontier and inaugurated a new security agency to deal with possible unrest, declaring through *A Razão* that "the government is equipped and strong enough to smother any attempt to disturb order."[17]

Of the opposing radical groups in Rio Grande do Norte, the Integralists commanded the greater influence. Folklorist and historian Luís da Câmara Cascudo, the state's leading intellectual celebrity, headed the Natal chapter. Other prominent Integralists included the director of the Catholic diocese's newspaper, *A Ordem;* academician Manoel Rodrigues de Mello; Padre Walfredo Gurgel, later governor; jurist Miguel Seabra Fagundes; and lawyer Hélio Galvão. Total membership amounted to perhaps a few hundred persons, chiefly businessmen, professionals, government employees, and students.[18]

The National Liberation Alliance cell, founded in April, 1935, probably did not attract more than several dozen adherents. It printed and distributed leaflets from a tiny headquarters above a store in downtown Natal, and promoted short-lived antifascist front groups. Bases were established in the rural interior of the state, where PCB agents agitated in favor of land reform and, after July, for the restoration of legal status for the ANL. An ANL cell among the soldiers of the Twenty-first Artillery Battalion (BC) claimed fifty-seven members, mostly privates and noncommissioned officers.[19] The soldiers, many of them angry at numerous transfers in recent months, were restless; a good portion resented their poor living conditions and the political activities of their officers.

During the state electoral campaign the ANL attacked both political factions, criticizing Câmara more harshly on the basis that his wider base of popular support made him a hypocrite in the light of his ingrown conservatism.[20] An ANL circular described both political blocs as "heterogeneous agglomerations . . . of the most reactionary elements, from the large feudal landowners to the . . . deceived workers and . . . petty bourgeoisie who are still convinced that it is possible to resolve prevailing misery and hunger with petty reforms." It concluded: "Only the force of the masses will guarantee the execution of our program."[21]

It was claimed later that communist influence had flourished in the state since the beginning of Mário Câmara's interventorship in 1933. Although the PCB took credit for labor agitation in the region, the degree of its participation in the sporadic strikes prior to 1935 cannot be ascertained.[22] Probably, the role of party agents did not reach major proportions. Even the conservative chronicler of the region admits that economic desperation rather than imported radicalism formed the basis for local unrest.[23]

Yet the Popular Party won mileage from claims that Câmara had turned the state into a "paradise for communism."[24] In general, anyone advocating reform was likely to earn the communist label. During the early 1930s such local bandits as Massilon and Chico Pereira, contemporaries of the still-at-large Lampião, were considered would-be revolutionaries, and authorities called the unrest in the Jaguaribe–Mirim valley perpetrated by Balthazar Meirelles and 300 *sertanejos* "communist adventurism," ignoring its possible social content.[25]

At 7:30 on Saturday evening, November 23, 1935, Governor Fernandes and his aides, in the company of many of the leading citizens of Natal, sat in the Carlos Gomes theater as guests at the graduation exercises of the Santo Antônio school. At that moment, shots rang out in the adjoining streets. The program faltered briefly and then continued; but when a group of armed men approached the theater and gathered outside, people in the rear of the audience started to leave their seats. To forestall panic, the governor rose and requested that the speeches cease and that the orchestra begin to play. But the audience continued to run from the theater, seeking refuge in nearby houses. Finally, the Fernandes party fled to the house of a close friend. They remained there during the night, while sporadic gunfire continued. In the morning, after learning about the developing insurrection, the group moved to the Chilean consulate, where it sought asylum, and, in so doing, ceded the government to the rebels.[26]

Shortly before the events at the theater, a small group of enlisted men and noncommissioned officers, led by Sergeant Eliziel Diniz Henriques and Musician Quintinho Clemente de Barros, took the barracks of the Twenty-first BC in the name of the National Liberation Alliance.[27] Many of the soldiers were absent from the barracks for the start of the weekend, and no resistance developed. The rebel leaders told the remaining men that the uprising was part of a larger movement to unseat Vargas and install General Góes Monteiro as military dictator. Other rumors asserted that the goal was to return Mário Câmara to power. Natal's most active labor body, the stevedores' union, had favored the Câmara–Café Filho Social Alliance, but dock workers did not participate in the revolt in significant numbers, despite Communist Party claims.[28]

The rebels, supported by approximately one fourth of the 450 men normally in residence in the barracks, moved into the streets, where they were joined at prearranged locations by armed members of the Civil Guard, some additional soldiers, and civilians. They shouted epithets against Vargas and the Fernandes government, and *vivas* for the army, the Twenty-first BC, the ANL, and Luís Carlos Prestes. The band stormed the military police headquarters and beseiged it for nineteen hours until its occupants surrendered. Meanwhile, rebel leaders took control of the city, broadcasting news of the revolt to neighboring states and severing rail connections into the city. With the arrest of police chief João Medeiros Filho in the early morning of November 24, no remaining authority stood in the way of the insurrection.

Through Sunday, looters thronged the commercial district and sacked the deserted buildings, including the Natal branch of the Bank of Brazil, the Bank of Rio Grande do Norte, the tax depository, and the local Ford and Chevrolet agencies. Men and boys invaded the military barracks and stole munitions and uniforms. Rebels commanded some of the roving bands; others formed at random, smashing windows and carrying off liquor, cigars, and merchandise. In all, perhaps three hundred persons joined the street anarchy while wealthy families barricaded their houses in terror or fled to foreign ships in the harbor.[29]

The insurgent leaders ignored the downtown government palace, but established themselves in the Vila Cincinato, today the Vila Potyguar, then the location of the auxiliary state government offices near the outskirts of the city. Soldiers under the command of Quintinho and Henriques left Natal and deposed local officials in neighboring towns—Ceará-Mirim, Baixa Verde, São José de Mipibu, and Canguaretama—extending rebel control to these areas. The only recorded resistance from forces loyal to the government came in the center of the state on November 25, in the form of a counter-march led by militia colonel Dinarte Mariz, a wealthy exporter from the town of Caicó, one of the founders of the Popular Party, and governor and federal senator in later years.[30]

Unchallenged in Natal, the rebels announced the formation of a revolutionary committee, or junta, on Monday morning, November 25. Although the immediate call to arms probably came from outside, it had gone directly to rebel leaders in the barracks rather than to local PCB officials. "Santa," a party agent, disclosed later to his superiors in Recife that he had been informed of the imminent uprising only four hours before its outbreak even though the PCB's regional committee had been in session since nine in the morning on that same day.[31] Thus the initial phase of the insurrection was purely an affair within the Twenty-first BC, the work of a handful of revolutionary activists. But by mid-Monday the junta took command. It claimed publicly that sympathetic revolts elsewhere had erupted and announced the formal dissolution of the Fernandes government and the state legislative assembly in the name of the ANL. It did not, as was subsequently charged, establish a Soviet Republic of Rio Grande do Norte, although rebel leader Agildo Barata later stated that this was the eventual goal of the insurrectionary movement.[32]

The junta issued a revolutionary newspaper, *A Liberdade,* on the requisitioned presses of the local diocesan journal, fabricating specific victories for rebel forces in João Pessôa (Paraíba), Recife, and São Paulo.[33] A junta member inexplicably cabled a compatriot in the town of Assú that Prestes' revolution had triumphed and that the Brazilian navy had joined the revolt.[34] But word from outside proved that the rebels were deluding themselves. Promised aid from the south never materialized. What was worse, most citizens of Natal showed little interest in the revolution. After the first waves of looting, the city returned to an uneasy calm; the population watched and waited, mostly behind locked doors.

The revolutionary junta, which took its orders from Henriques and Quintinho (who named himself minister of defense), was composed of an odd group for such a body. Of its four civilian members, only one, José (Zé) Praxedes de Andrade, a mulatto of slight stature and a shoemaker by trade, could claim a working-class background. Praxedes held the position of provisions minister in the short-lived insurrectionary government. He fled shortly after the revolt failed—never to be seen again.[35]

Lauro Cortês Lago, a well-educated former official of the state police and an ex-superintendent of the state prison, served as the revolutionary minister of the interior. When he was captured later, the thirty-six-year-old acquaintance of Mário Câmara admitted to complicity in the revolt, but he insisted that he should not be charged with radicalism since he came from a *potyguar* family whose devout Catholicism could not be questioned.[36]

José Macedo, postmaster of Rio Grande do Norte under both Mário Câmara and Rafael Fernandes, was the junta's minister of finance. Café Filho called him "the perfect type of innocent bourgeoisie," referring to Macedo's paunch, fashionable clothing, and affinity for expensive cigars.[37] João Baptista Galvão, a lawyer, journalist, former secretary of the elitist Rio Grande do Norte Academy, from a family active in the cotton textile trade, was the minister of public works. His friends called him *Papai Noel* (Santa Claus) because of his portliness. Galvão's wife was a niece of ex-governor Juvenal Lamartine, and thereby a relative, if distant, of José Augusto of the Popular Party. In spite of his ties to the oligarchy, Galvão reputedly helped establish the Communist Party's apparatus in the state. There is some possibility that he was no less than the "Santa" who corresponded with the central committee of the PCB in Recife in the days following the revolt.

In an effort to win public confidence, the revolutionary committee restored streetcar service and reduced fares. It ordered the price of bread lowered to one hundred réis. Tax collectors were apprehended and some of their records destroyed. The junta paid cash or issued scrip for all material requisitioned. The junta asked merchants to open their businesses on Monday, posting soldiers to guarantee against looting. No Integralists met harm, although their headquarters was demolished. The junta promised to leave Church property and personnel unmolested. Thousands of leaflets, some dropped from the air, pleaded for cooperation and promised order.

The revolution failed internally as well as externally. The junta exercised little control over the excesses committed in its name in the first hours of the insurrection; the population ignored it in its last hours. Many of the funds which were taken from local banks and government agencies were never recovered, indicating that not all of the money was turned over to the junta. Three murders, one of them to settle an old grudge, occurred among the bands of drunken looters who roamed the city in the early hours of the revolt.[38]

The junta never heard of the uprising in Rio de Janeiro, which occurred in the first hours of November 27 in belated response to the call to arms in the northeast. After confirmation arrived that the movement in Recife had collapsed and rumors spread that Natal would be bombarded by the air force, junta members hastily decided to flee Natal. About forty of the rebels seized a merchant ship in the harbor, the *Santos,* and escaped south down the coast where they were overtaken by two cruisers of the federal navy.[39] Lago, Macedo, and Galvão surrendered within a week in the interior of the state. Galvão's share of the junta's funds was found sewn into his trouser cuffs.[40]

Four days after his flight from the insurrection, the governor emerged from his place of refuge and reasserted his authority over a deserted city of shattered store fronts and hastily contrived revolutionary banners and wall inscriptions. By nightfall the city had returned to normal, and Fernandes was received with jubilation. Hundreds of congratulatory telegrams from all parts of the nation arrived in the weeks which followed. Newly confident, Fernandes ordered the arrest of all suspicious persons. Interestingly, although the uprising had largely confined itself to the Natal area, nearly half of the almost one thousand warrants were sworn elsewhere, in such places as Assú (5 warrants), Panellas (7), Santa Cruz (30), Curraes Novos (20), Macahyba (15), Arez (8), Areia Branca (5), Mipibú (50), Mossoró (45), Goyaninha (30), and Luís Gomes (30). Enlisted men, noncommissioned officers, and laborers constituted roughly one half of those implicated. Of those who did not flee from Rio Grande do Norte, many remained in prison two or more years before coming to trial; more than three quarters were absolved for lack of evidence when the federal tribunal finally met.[41]

Individuals with no role in the insurrection but considered dangerous to the state government also faced persecution. Police raided the homes of Câmara–Café Filho coalition deputies and ransacked them. A pro-Câmara landowner and his son were reputedly murdered by government agents on the grounds that they were communists.[42] A pro-Café Filho baker was arrested and jailed for having sold bread to the junta.[43] Abuses were so obvious that a federally appointed judge complained to the Justice Ministry in Rio de Janeiro, but no action was taken.[44]

Fernandes administration officials contributed to the growing myth of the revolutionary experience—that the state had been controlled by communists and the nation snatched from the jaws of domination by Moscow. The inevitable atrocity stories circulated: a Fortaleza newspaper claimed that girls of good families had been commanded to attend an "official dance," for purposes of being molested by communist soldiers.[45] A sensationalist account of the Vargas years published in English charged that the rebels had not spared Natalense women.[46] Café Filho complained to the federal Chamber of Deputies that state officials had invented the story that soldiers had violated ninety-six girls at the Escola Feminina de Commercio.[47]

The junta leaders received sentences of from eight to ten years' imprisonment (later reduced to six and a half years), the maximum penalty for civilians under the National Security Law. João Baptista Galvão was unexplainably released after ten months: before he could be reapprehended, he fled to the upper Amazon, where he became a rubber worker and ultimately contracted beriberi; he subsequently moved to the Venezuelan border, where he allegedly established himself in the contraband trade. Years later, he returned to Natal, where in the 1960s he opened a successful law practice. Other influential prisoners, in keeping with the flexible system of traditional northeast justice, arranged to serve their terms under house arrest, or in their own custody. Military prisoners fared worse: although Brazilian law did not (until later) provide for the death penalty, many received long sentences to fetid military camps where even short stays exposed inmates to tuberculosis and tropical diseases.

The restoration of stability in Natal released much of the anger fermenting among reactionaries since 1930. *A Ordem* attacked what it called "semicommunism" in the state's upper and middle classes, and "total communism elsewhere."[48] Its editors, grasping for the causes of discontent, blamed such inroads into modern northeastern society as academic freedom, freethinking and masonry, godless immorality, coeducation, sex education, dancing, and athletics for girls. The article concluded: "All this constitutes a waiting-room for communism. Who would prefer physical culture to the culture of the spirit?"[49]

Scores of persons fled the state fearing arrest following the revolt, although police pursued fugitives across state lines. The situation was not without pathos. The daughter of a state ANL official, ostensibly innocent of complicity in the late November events, although active in popular front organizations, wrote to her mother on January 3:

We took the train but had to disembark at the first station because we were recognized by investigators traveling on the same train. We then walked all the way to João Pessôa. We have suffered much, principally from lack of money. . . . Not feeling safe here, [father] left me in the house of a family whom we knew, and proceeded to Rio de Janeiro. . . . Here I am sewing to earn a living. . . . Your dear daughter misses you very much.[50]

What may be concluded about the revolutionary adventure is that it commenced under strained and unusual local circumstances. The political climate was abnormally tense on the eve of the outbreak. It is known that the defeated Café Filho–Câmara bloc had considered violence only weeks earlier; the hasty measures of the Fernandes administration to quell disloyalty and its inappropriate disbanding of the armed Civil Guard unquestionably added fuel to the volatile atmosphere. The governor's brother, Aldo Fernandes, later said that he thought the insurrection had been provoked by Câmara partisans. Opponents of the Popular Party, in turn, charged privately that Fernandes welcomed the revolt as soon as it proved impotent: the party knew that its electoral victory had been tenuous, and it feared imminent federal intervention. Certainly, either political faction could have benefited from unchecked civil disorder; in the end, the rebellion rescued the uncertain fortunes of the Popular Party.

The key to the insurrection itself lies with the men of the disgruntled Twenty-first Artillery Battalion, in the majority *pernambucanos,* who had fought in São Paulo in 1932 for three or four months, then were dispatched to the interior of Pernambuco, allegedly without being allowed to visit with their families in Recife. Six months later the BC was transferred to Natal, where barracks unrest and frequent changes of commanders in keeping with state political events during the angry electoral campaign set the stage for agitation by noncommissioned officers and caused morale to sink to new depths. During 1935, forty men and officers were cashiered from the unit; in November, most of them still resided in Natal. Six different men commanded the BC during little more than a year. Barracks housing, one of them wrote, resembled an "old hovel, lacking in comfort and hygiene." Instructional materials were so inadequate, he added, that the soldiers had neither rifle targets nor proper munitions.[51]

The readiness with which some of the troops joined the revolt and the lack of resistance among the others are more comprehensible in this light. Furthermore, the leaders of the revolt were a small minority: there is no evidence that their followers possessed a clear understanding of the nature of the revolt.

An incident occurred the day before the revolt which may have increased the proclivity for rebellion among the enlisted men. That morning, an unpopular lieutenant, one Santana, had been shot in the back by unidentified soldiers. A number of suspects were arrested and ordered to report for court-martial hearings on Monday. There were additional rumors in the barracks that mass transfers and disciplinary action would follow. There is reason to believe that the revolt owed as much to this atmosphere as to the soldiers' commitment to Prestes and the National Liberation Alliance.

Pernambuco had dominated the eight-state northeast (Pernambuco, Sergipe, Alagôas, Paraíba, Rio Grande do Norte, Ceará, Piauí, and Maranhão) for four centuries; in the middle 1930s the surviving social structure ignored the staggering evidences of human poverty. Recife, the state capital, served a region comprising one fourth of Brazil's population but which contributed less than a tenth to its national income in 1935.[52] Pernambuco's facilities for banking, commerce, and shipping linked the northeastern states with southern Brazil and, subsequently, with the outside world. In 1934-35 the state produced a third of Brazil's sugar cane and a tenth of its processed sugar, cotton, tobacco, and foodstuffs. Seventy-four *usinas* still operated in 1935, the oldest dating to 1874. Industrial products included textiles, glass, paper, ceramics, and alcoholic beverages.[53]

A gulf separated the state's urban minority from its impoverished rural masses, although rural migration to the cities created increasing problems after the turn of the century. Roughly a half-million of Pernambuco's three and a half millions lived in the Recife-Olinda area. Of the rest, almost one million languished in the arid *sertão,* still recovering from the great drought of 1931-32, the worst in a half-century. In 1935, only 1 per cent of the land in Pernambuco's interior was considered arable by agricultural officials.[54]

The ruling elite included the great sugar families (by the 1930s largely settled in Recife) and the more recently prosperous commercial and manufacturing groups, including the owners of the sugar *usinas.* In general, familial origin rather than absolute wealth determined one's final position in Pernambucan society. The older families occupied the elegant Dois Irmãos and Madalena sections, while the newly rich built their own fashionable neighborhoods and married into the landed aristocracy if they could.

The city's small middle class of tradesmen, professionals, and government officials occupied the next lower rung of the socioeconomic ladder. Far below them lay the lower classes, of two types. Employed working-class families, which averaged between 5 and 6 persons, earned between 100 and 200 milréis monthly ($7-14 U.S.), out of which they spent an average of 71 per cent for food and 18 per cent for shelter. A survey in late 1934 in Recife revealed that, out of 500 families, 78 could not afford to buy bread (16 per cent), 397 did not consume rice (80 per cent), 403 purchased no milk (81 per cent), and between 409 and 422 consumed neither fruit nor vegetables (82-85 per cent), the staple diet consisting solely of beans, manioc flour (*farinha*), coffee, and sugar. A kilo of bread cost the equivalent of five hours of work; a kilo of codfish, seven hours.[55]

Even in more dire straits were the urban squatters, for the most part unemployed *caboclo* refugees from the drought-ridden interior of the region. Numbering about 150,000 persons, they huddled in sprawling *mocambo* camps, acres of squalid wooden shacks near the waterfront, in the midst of mud, vermin, and excrement. Infant mortality reached 60 per cent or higher, when it could be measured. The mocambos spawned disease, crime, and misery in growing volume as new arrivals from the *sertão* swelled their population weekly and monthly. Only the presence of the crabs which burrowed in the filth-filled mud surrounding the mocambos kept its inhabitants from starving.[56] In August, 1935, General Manoel Rabello, commander of the northeast's Seventh Military District and a veteran of the Prestes Column and the 1930 Revolution, invited government and Church representatives to discuss the mocambo question. There were no results. With disgust, Rabello told the press: "In Pernambuco there is enthusiasm for nothing."[57]

The unsuccessful military conspiracy in early 1935 which had shaken the federal War Ministry implicated a number of local officers, one of whom, Captain Octacílio Alves de Lima, would play a major role in the November uprising in Recife. But the general political climate seemed quiet: in April the state legislative assembly elected Interventor Carlos de Lima Cavalcanti—a wealthy planter and the founder of Recife's *Diario da Manhã*—constitutional governor.[58] The state Integralist movement lacked extensive influence, except among university students. Prior to 1935, radical trade union organization was limited, hindered by an unwritten covenant among the press not to publicize such activity. The state ANL fared moderately well, but, after his arrival in the São Francisco region in May, Silo Meirelles of the PCB central committee took full control of the state popular front apparatus, although the Recife call was left to its own leadership and thus enjoyed a degree of autonomy. At the height of its membership, the ANL claimed two thousand adherents in the state capital, although official sources insisted later that a few hundred persons at the most participated actively.[59] Members included several parish priests, attracted by the movement's attention to workers' rights and wages. As a result, the Recife cells carefully avoided Church-related issues, in contrast with ANL policy elsewhere, in order to win additional support from the clergy. The PCB, however, was never satisfied with the degree to which the popular front attracted urban workers; shortly before the ANL was closed by federal authorities, its leaders were purged, after being reviled by communist agents as "fools, cowards, and reformers."[60]

The original state ANL directorate consisted almost entirely of lawyers and middle-class intellectuals, a fact that aggravated the communists' contempt. The police claimed that Gilberto Freyre belonged to the ANL's state cultural commission, but the journalist and academician denied membership in spite of the fact that his essays concerning social problems frequently appeared in the ANL's *Fôlha do Povo*.

A few of the ANL auxiliary groups, notably one briefly successful local electoral front, continued to operate after the closing of the national movement in July, but for the most part ANL influence vanished. Communist agents acting in the ANL's name claimed a role in the strikes on the Great Western of Brazil Railway in Pernambuco's Jaboatão region, where desperate wives of strikers camped on the tracks to impede rail traffic and were ordered fired upon by officers of the local Twenty-ninth BC. Communist sources insisted that, after the command was given, a lieutenant was shot in the back by the enlisted men, as a sign of solidarity with the strikers.[61] Although officials denied the story emphatically, agitation in the barracks increased measurably after the incident and as a result of other complaints affecting morale. The battalion was moved to new quarters in midyear, from its old downtown base in Recife to Socôrro on the outskirts of the city. Unfinished construction caused a large portion of the enlisted men to remain at the old barracks and commute daily, at their own expense. In addition, shortages of officers and equipment restricted training, leaving the troops to tedious work details. A number of men were accused of communist activity, but no action was taken and the PCB's clandestine barracks newsletter continued to circulate.

The barracks were virtually deserted when the news of the disturbances in Natal arrived at main military headquarters late in the evening of November 23, the beginning of the weekend. Neither General Rabello, Governor Lima Cavalcanti, nor the commander of the Military Brigade, Captain Jurandyr Mamede, were in the city: Rabello had left to visit the War Ministry in Rio de Janeiro, and the governor was traveling in Europe. At about midnight, a message cabled to the Twenty-ninth BC from the rebels in Natal was intercepted by military police officials who had been dispatched to the Socôrro base to alert its commanding officer. The interlopers narrowly escaped by motorcycle before conspirators on the base received their orders. Favored by their stroke of fortune, the police spent the night organizing their forces.[62]

The rebels made their move during the changing of the guard in the early hours of Sunday, November 24. Whether they had been expecting the signal to act cannot be determined; but they acted swiftly, taking control of the base after minor scuffles.[63] Returning officers, alerted by the military police, organized resistance, and the rebels could not move into the street until midmorning. By that time federal reinforcements from Paraíba and Maceió had departed for Recife.

Shouting slogans in the name of Prestes and the ANL, the rebel column of approximately four hundred soldiers was joined by bands of armed citizens as it marched through the industrial zone that separated Socôrro from the city. The civilians were armed from caches of weapons stored by PCB agents; their total number is not known, but probably not more than several dozen joined the column in the initial stage of the rebellion. At about eleven o'clock the rebel column met an advance police contingent, led by Captain Sidrack Corrêia, who asked by loudspeaker if its leaders would negotiate. The rebels declined. Shooting erupted; the column entrenched itself on the spot, at the entrance of the Largo da Paz, a broad public square perpendicular to the main artery entering Recife. The rebels constructed makeshift barricades and manned sniper positions in the taller buildings overlooking the square, including the church tower.

Captain Octacílio Alves de Lima commanded the rebels, aided by two lieutenants and a communist agent by the name of Gregório Bezerra. The hybrid force sent to meet them, commanded by police captain Malvino Reis in the absence of the governor, included military police units, Recife and Olinda's night guard, tramway motorists and conductors, maritime officials, and detectives normally assigned to the security police. Gradually, regular units from the Twenty-ninth BC which had remained loyal arrived at the scene and joined the resistance.

At the same time, isolated outbreaks in various parts of the city erupted under rebel leadership. At 8:30 in the morning, communist labor organizers seized the police barracks in Olinda, giving them temporary control of communications in Recife's sister city. Fighting took place near the Praça da Independência, the public market, the law school, and in residential areas of Santo Amaro, Torres, and Casa Amarela.[64] The rebels improvised trenches across the roadway joining Socôrro with Afogados, the site of the Largo da Paz. Streetcar and telephone service stopped; as word of the revolt spread, fear gripped the city; people remained indoors.

The battle on Largo da Paz continued through the day and night, but the arrival of federal reinforcements contained the rebel force and doomed the possibility for advancement. If the insurrectionists expected the city to rise in their support, their hopes failed to materialize. The police barricaded the bridges linking the suburbs with Recife, halting all traffic. The arrival of heavier arms at the line of siege early Monday climaxed the loyalist resistance; individual rebels began abandoning their positions and fleeing back through the rear lines.

Late on Monday the rebel commanders ordered a retreat; only one small force escaped, to be captured a few days later by local militia.[65] The others surrendered or were arrested immediately. Silo Meirelles, whose precise role during the fighting is unknown, was apprehended on the night of November 26.[66] Estimates of the total casualties during the two-day battle ranged from the official figure of 60 dead and 200 wounded to the exaggerated radical claim that 800 died, including 100 working-class civilians on the side of the revolt.[67]

Among the hundreds arrested before Lima Cavalcanti could speed back from Europe were the secretaries of justice and finance from the governor's cabinet. Both were accused of "communist sympathies," a charge arising from their reputed participation in a Recife ANL cell of government employees.[68] The exhausted resistance leaders received heroes' welcomes as Recife congratulated itself on its victory over communism. As in Rio Grande do Norte, the suppression of the revolt encouraged conservatives to exaggerate its potency and to excoriate liberalism and the pro-Vargas Lima Cavalcanti government. A torrent of abuse accompanied the to-be-expected stories of looting and deflowerings in rebel-held territory. While the state administration absorbed the abuse helplessly, Lima Cavalcanti's state political party neared dissolution three weeks after the insurrection.[69]

The PCB unwittingly added oil to the fire, misrepresenting the extent of its own role in the uprising. A still-at-large agent informed his superiors that entire proletarian neighborhoods had risen in general strike. "The masses," he wrote, "under our direction completely dominated the city and would have taken power if it had not been for the vacillation of our comrades."[70] Party propaganda hailed the revolt as the first example in Brazil of worker-soldier collaboration against the feudal order; the party did not admit that disgruntled soldiers composed the majority of the rebel force and that civilian recruits had failed to materialize in quantity either within the city or along the line of attack.

The single reasonable voice publicly raised in the aftermath of the insurrection was that of General Manoel Rabello, who told the press that brutal living conditions among the lower classes had contributed to the inflammatory atmosphere preceding the uprising. For this he was assailed vociferously, even though he disbanded the Twenty-ninth BC immediately upon learning of its role in the uprising.

Federal officials in Rio de Janeiro followed the developments in the northeast calmly. On Sunday morning, beginning before dawn, police arrested about 150 persons, including Sissón and most of the members of the former ANL national directorate.[71] The Communist Party secretariat met in emergency session through Saturday night to decide on its course of action. Counseled by Harry Berger and Rodolfo Ghioldi, Prestes ordered a second wave of revolts to begin after midnight Monday, in support of the risings in the northeast. It is probable that the party knew that the insurrections in Natal and Recife had been isolated, and that defeat was imminent. Nevertheless, messengers were sent hurriedly to Espírito Santo, Minas Gerais, and to the south; but each was apprehended by the police within hours.[72]

Prestes instructed confederates at Rio de Janeiro's Third Infantry Regiment (Regimento da Infantaria, or RI) at the Praia Vermelha to take control of their barracks after midnight on Tuesday and to march on the presidential palace about three miles away.[73] As in the plans for the northeast, party strategy depended upon the contingency that military rebellion would stimulate support from the civilian population in the form of paralyzing strikes, leading to the downfall of the government and the formation of the national, popular revolutionary regime envisioned by the ANL's July manifesto.

On Monday and Tuesday, clandestine radio transmitters appealed for a general strike, but few, if any, heard the broadcasts or paid heed. Additional directives for revolt were sent to various military bodies in the city. At the Second RI, authorities intercepted the orders for revolt sent there from the PCB; the commander of the regiment, the same Newton Cavalcanti reviled by moderates for his relentless persecution of the left, arrested suspected officers and alerted the commander of the First Military District, General Eurico Dutra. Yet government officials took few precautions in the light of the revolutionary threats in the north, save for ordering a general alert of armed forces personnel and dispatching the military police to guard electric power and gas utilities from sabotage.[74] The federal administration stood firm in its confidence.

A handful of young officers executed the uprising at the Third RI, led by captains Álvaro de Souza and Agildo Barata. Barata, a combatant at the side of Juarez Távora in the northern campaign in 1930, had joined the radical Prestes–Miguel Costa wing of the tenente movement and, still on active duty, was the principal spokesman for the ANL in Rio Grande do Sul before he was transferred to the federal capital for disciplinary action in mid-1935. As accorded to officers by the Brazilian military code, he was allowed to remain at liberty while serving his punishment at the Praia Vermelha base; he commuted daily from a Copacabana apartment, his movements unrestricted. Captain Barata directed the small ANL cell within the Third RI, a cadre of thirty men, one third of them undercover PCB agents. These men reportedly received their instructions for revolt jubilantly, although Barata himself claimed that he knew that chances for success were practically nil.[75]

The small band of insurgents rose at two in the morning on November 27, arresting all available officers and shooting their way into barracks headquarters. Some loyalist soldiers tried to flee across the avenue to the Urca casino, but it was taken by the rebels and turned into a makeshift stockade. Approximately two thirds of the regiment's 1,700 troops—almost all of them newly enlisted recruits—joined the rebellion, but the remainder resisted. As a result, the ramshackle barracks, built in 1908 for the temporary use of a trade exposition, did not fall into rebel hands until after dawn.

Barata dispatched appeals for aid, including a cable to his old tenente comrade, Juracy Magalhães, but his pleas went unanswered. By morning government troops commanded by General Dutra, transported from the outskirts of the city in buses requisitioned from the Light and Power Company, moved up the thoroughfare which linked Urca with the remainder of Rio de Janeiro, in so doing effectively precluding any rebel move to escape by land. Barata was asked to surrender, but he refused; in his response, he insisted that his rebellion was not communist but nationalist in character.[76] Dutra then ordered the shelling of the base with heavy guns and the use of aerial bombs, resulting in the deaths, according to reports, of nineteen cadets and a civilian.[77]

A separate uprising, among about seventy cadets at the outlying Aviation School at the Campo dos Affonsos, broke out in the early morning. Initially successful, the rebels took the school's headquarters and attempted to invade the nearby First Aviation Regiment, but they were confronted by forces led by Colonel Eduardo Gomes (who received a flesh wound on his hand) and were subdued by daybreak.[78]

The popular support hoped for by the insurrection's strategists never materialized, neither from military nor from civilian sources. The PCB's *A Manhã* issued a revolutionary edition inciting mass rebellion—Prestes reportedly spent the night in the pressroom—but it was seized by police before it could be distributed. Communist agents elaborated plans for strikes on November 27 at the Malvillis and Bonfim textile factories, by maritime workers and metallurgists, and at the Light and Power Company, but the insurrection collapsed before they could be carried out. Unable to initiate a strike on the Central do Brasil Railroad, party agents resorted to the destruction of a strategic switch point on the Rio–São Paulo–Minas line at the Barra do Piraí and attempted to derail passing trains by placing railroad ties on the tracks.[79]

By early afternoon, President Vargas personally visited the line of fire to comfort the wounded; the danger had passed. By the time Barata capitulated, about fifty men, mostly young rebel cadets, had died in the Praia Vermelha battle. The Third RI lay in ruins. The rebels were marched into Botafogo while large crowds cheered the government victory.[80] About 1,100 insurgents were shipped directly from the docks to island prison camps in Guanabara Bay; the leaders of the uprising, as well as the suspects arrested three days before, were placed on the newly resurrected prison ship, the *Pedro I,* which had not seen like service since 1932.

Just as in the case of insurrection in the northeast, no evidence exists that the rebel soldiers knew what they were fighting for. Low morale among the Aviation School cadets and in the Third RI contributed to the willingness to join the revolt. The cadets, earlier in the year, had complained bitterly about martinet discipline, inadequate facilities, ill-treatment, and "imbecilic officers."[81] The rebellion, in the end, proved tragically futile. It has been alleged that authorities knew almost exactly the hour of the scheduled uprising—although Agildo Barata temporarily gained the upper hand by advancing his timetable one-half hour during the early hours of November 27.

Various sources suggest that government officials anticipated the successive revolutionary uprisings.[82] All that is certain, however, is that radical noncommissioned officers in Natal, acting on November 23 according to established plans but probably ahead of schedule, raised a briefly successful barracks revolt which was inseparable from local issues; this in turn triggered a second, coordinated uprising in Recife, which yielded a final, delayed revolt in the federal capital sanctioned by the Communist Party in response to the original call to arms.

Preliminary instructions had been distributed in midyear by ANL secretary-general Roberto Sissón, although he personally was excluded from the final stage of the revolutionary adventure. In fact, his last communiqué to Rio Grande do Norte warned against premature revolt, pointing out the necessity for additional preparatory work in rural areas and for further cultivation of the political unrest in the state. Sissón wrote, on October 31, 1935:

[It is too early to] attempt an extensive national movement, or even to precipitate events in the other states of the northeast. Without simultaneous activity elsewhere, we believe that any call for the immediate seizure of power would be neither opportune nor viable. In the light of present conditions in Brazil, it would be reckless to attempt to initiate the armed struggle independently of the rest of the country. We are marching rapidly to the moment of national insurrection; we do not possess the right, as we wait for that time, to sacrifice the advantage which we already have won.[83]

One may only speculate on the immediate causes for the revolt in Natal, particularly in recognition of its seemingly erroneous timing. It is known that the PCB had planned the uprisings for early December, probably on the fifth. Quintinho and Henriques may have acted according to instructions; they may have misread them, or, as is most likely in view of the evidence, they may have received false instructions from police agents who had infiltrated the Communist Party leadership. On December 23, Ilvo Meirelles wrote clandestinely to Luís Carlos Prestes in Rio de Janeiro, lamenting that the Natal and Recife uprisings had taken place "by surprise" and that many comrades had been caught unprepared, although earlier in the month the same correspondent had simply maintained that the events had been caused by an "error of impatience."[84] According to Leoncio Basbaum, Vargas' *agent provocateur* was a Paul Gruber, an ex-member of the German Communist Party who in 1935 was sent to Brazil by the Gestapo with the full knowledge of Itamaratí.[85]

Of the various aspects of the revolutionary drama, the role of Luís Carlos Prestes, believed publicly to be in continued European exile but known to PCB leaders (and to federal authorities) to have arrived secretly earlier in the year to assume personal leadership of the party of which he was titular head, holds particular significance. Prestes, who had been rebuked by the PCB's Leninist leaders in 1930 as a bourgeois, would-be *caudilho* opportunist, had been imposed upon the party by the Comintern in recognition of his reputation as the popular hero of the 1924-27 Long March; as a result, he was resented by the party's older leaders for his vanity, his theoretical obstinacy, and his stubborn loyalty to his Stalinist Comintern advisers. Prestes' tragedy lies in his docility: absent from Brazil for nearly a decade, he was unable to perceive the inadequacy of his revolutionary preparations, believing, instead, his propagandists' inflated assertions of popular support. But although he lived faithfully by the taut rules of party discipline, his correspondence with former tenente associates reveals a softer, nostalgic side to the man who coldly ordered the strangulation of sixteen-year-old Elza Fernandes. In 1937 he wrote to a friend that he had objected to Moscow's orders for a popular-front insurrectionary organization, but that his revolutionary duty had forced him to comply.[86] When Berger and others wrote directives during the ANL period in his name (including the critical July 5 manifesto), Prestes did not complain. He allowed party propagandists to exploit the deportation of his German-born wife:

although she probably died in a Swiss hospital of tuberculosis in 1938, two years after she had given birth to their daughter Anita, the communist press asserted that she had been liquidated in a Nazi extermination camp, an allegation never satisfactorily documented. In 1945, when circumstance wed the fortunes of Vargas and the Brazilian Communist Party, Prestes publicly embraced the man who had imprisoned him for nine years under conditions of despair.

The part played by the PCB's Comintern advisers is more readily understood, although no less curious in its folly. Berger, after personally visiting the São Francisco region, failed to appreciate, at least visibly, the impotent state of preparedness. What is most likely is that the PCB central committee was ordered directly to organize a popular front-based insurrection—conceivably as a test case to contrast the experience with the alternative policy of electoral popular front belligerency being followed by the Chilean Communist Party at the same time—and that the Comintern agents in Brazil simply followed their instructions as best they could. For Berger, the premature call to arms in an already doubtful revolutionary atmosphere meant arrest, brutal treatment at the hands of the police, and years of crippling imprisonment. Meekly PCB leaders labeled the ill-fated adventures "rousing forerunners" of the coming national revolution, worthy successors to the two July 5 revolts and the heroic Prestes Column.[87]

The federal government, embarrassingly vulnerable at the outset of the month in the face of the nearing threat to its congressional majority, now immediately took the offensive, reestablishing a firm grip on the reins of national power as it moved swiftly to restore order. Vargas, in a personal appeal to the legislature, asked for (and received with virtually no opposition) a thirty-day state of siege, a condition which, rather than being permitted to expire, would be renewed repeatedly during the following twenty-four months in response to an inflated communist threat largely fabricated by administration officials.

In the aftermath of the outbreak of violence, the President received the authority to discipline any military officer or public functionary charged with subversive behavior. Censorship, an instrument of the administration since 1930, was now tightened although it remained a process selectively applied by government officials. The military purged its ranks; and police sealed state borders, requiring safe-conduct passes from all travelers. In

spite of the general impotence of the attempted rebellions, the new measures seemed harsh and unjustified; but under the wave of emotion fostered
by the patriotic, anticommunist campaign in the name of national unity,
no opposition could be raised. Vargas clearly moved to take the upper hand.
Waxing eloquent, he declared to the nation in his 1936 New Year's Day
address that "the forces of hate and evil oppress our land and our people."[88]
To personal correspondents he repeated the undocumented charge that
rebels at the Aviation School had murdered sleeping officers in their beds,
as he assumed privately and publicly the air of a leader deeply shocked by
the radical uprisings.[89]

Given perspective, the exaggerated anticommunist campaign of repression
which followed November, 1935, revealed the President's deeper intent: to
use the rebellion as a vehicle to enlarge federal power, to establish the unquestioned supremacy of the national armed forces, and to silence the voices
of moderates as well as of all potential opponents, however politically directed. The trend to consolidation of national power—visible as early as 1932
in the provisional government's victory over rebellious São Paulo—after 1935
assumed harsh and irreversible proportions. "Brazil," a Rio de Janeiro daily
observed, "is on the road to military dictatorship."[90]

A minor international incident occurred when the New York *Times*
published an article by its South American correspondent, J. W. White,
filed from Buenos Aires in order to avoid Brazilian censorship. The November revolt, White asserted, was "not communistic, as reported by the
federal authorities. It was socialistic and strongly nationalistic." Citing the
progress of the National Liberation Alliance prior to its closing, White
termed the demands of the revolutionaries "mild": an effective eight-hour
workday, free Sundays, minimum wages, and adequate working conditions. He added that Vargas himself had promised these reforms, and that
they had been written into the constitution of 1934 but had not been enforced. "It has become popular in all South American governments to de-
nounce all opposition as communist," White concluded.[91] Ambassador
Aranha complained bitterly to the *Times,* but its publisher stood fast, even
though the article's allegations that 162 antigovernment Brazilians had
been executed later proved false.

The Western powers acclaimed Vargas for his victorious defense, although *The Times* of London repeated White's theme, reporting that dis-
affection over presidential interference (in Rio Grande do Sul) and consti-

tutional weaknesses had contributed to the troubled atmosphere. It issued a final warning about Brazilian politics under the state of siege: "[There is no] give and take; it is too easy to override the minority."[92] Assis Chateaubriand, czar of the *Diários Associados* newspaper chain, stated a similar conclusion in like terms: "The recipient of all that Luís Carlos Prestes has lost is Getúlio Vargas."[93]

6

REACTION
AND REPRESSION

An ominous pattern of reaction and repression followed the defeat of the November insurrections. Once Vargas received emergency powers, he did not relinquish them. The new atmosphere, hotly antiliberal, gave expression precisely to those groups most openly committed to the suspension of the forms of liberal constitutionalism. The federal government entered a new, transitional phase after November, 1935, which ended in the fascistic Estado Nôvo twenty-three months later.

The military showed its hand quickly by treating the feeble barracks uprisings as a major threat to national security. War Minister João Gomes convened his general staff on December 3 and demanded amendment of the federal constitution to provide stronger penalties for treason than the existing six-year maximum sentence. Góes Monteiro, again regularly appearing in military councils, circulated a draft manifesto advocating major constitutional revision in the face of what he called Brazil's "most terrible crisis in its history," one that threatened the armed forces ("which should be the backbone of the nation") with ruin.[1]

The cabinet supported the generals' demands at a special session nine days later, which was dominated by the ministers of war and justice. Góes reminded his colleagues that the insurrections had been directed from Moscow; public opinion, therefore, expected the repression to be harsh.[2] Police chief Felinto Müller, in agreement, dispatched a confidential report to Vargas asking for an investigation of the armed forces, a review of extradition statutes to facilitate the expulsion of undesirable aliens, and other repressive measures.[3] But Vargas remained noncommittal: he accepted the continuation of discretionary powers under a ninety-day extension of the state of national emergency granted on December 18, but he stalled and finally cast aside proposals to alter the constitution.[4]

Yet opposition to the new restrictions lay submerged beneath the wave of anticommunism raised by reactionaries. Vargas himself was not disturbed; he seemed rejuvenated by the restoration of stability. He addressed the public with increasing frequency and an air of renewed authority. Although nothing materialized, he cleared his desk for several new projects, including the possible formation of an official party with nationalistic underpinnings.[5] Through the good offices of a mediator, he negotiated a temporary truce with Flôres da Cunha, who had been angered when his request to exempt Rio Grande do Sul from the national state of siege was ignored. "The government has received manifestations of solidarity from even the working classes," Vargas wrote Aranha on the initial success of the anticommunist campaign. "It seems that the circumstances [of the] moment will facilitate the work which is to be realized."[6]

On January 24, 1936, Justice Minister Ráo announced the formation of the National Commission for the Repression of Communism, an autonomous investigatory agency whose powers included the right to hold star-chamberlike hearings. An admiral from the Naval Ministry headed the commission, but its effective director was Adalberto Corrêia, a reactionary Rio Grande do Sul deputy called by his enemies the "trombone-voiced pseudo number-one enemy of communism" and a "burlesque Robespierre." Summarizing the attitude which gripped Brazil under his commission, he wrote boastingly to Vargas: "It is better to make one or more unjust arrests than to permit Brazil to be bloodied again."[7] A warning from police captain Affonso Corrêia that such matters should be left to existing police authorities was summarily ignored.[8]

Prestes and his comrades remained in hiding during the first weeks after the collapse of the November uprisings. On the prison ship *Pedro I,* Cascardo, Sissón, Barata, and the others—a total of nearly four hundred—lived as best they could under the crowded conditions. They played chess, argued politics, and promoted various protest strikes, one of which moved them to abandon their clothing to call attention to the lack of provisions for those among them whose vestments were in rags.[9] The pugnacious Agildo Barata resisted all authority; on one occasion he dived into the bay in an attempt to swim to the mainland, but was fished out by a police launch. Cascardo sent strenuous pleas to his old friends asserting his innocence, but most of the others accepted their fate stoically.[10] Still, the rebel officers of the Third RI issued a prisoner's manifesto, affirming their revolutionary effort in the name of liberty and antireactionary nationalism.[11]

On January 6 a police dragnet located Harry Berger and his wife in their rented house in fashionable Ipanema. The raid netted a considerable portion of the Communist Party archives, and led to further arrests and additional seizures of material. Police in Recife, São Paulo, and other cities held similar raids within their own jurisdictions.

Luís Carlos Prestes was arrested at seven in the morning on March 5, 1935, a week after Carnival, by a contingent of fifty-three policemen, who surrounded his small, stucco frame house in the working-class district of Meier, in the northern zone of the city. He had not been seen in Brazil since 1926; he had been sought by military and police authorities since 1924.

Prestes' arrest followed the capture of Berger, Rodolfo Ghioldi, Leon Valée, and Victor Allan Baron in previous weeks. Berger, appearing with his wife before a judge at the House of Detention, had admitted that his real name was Arthur Ernest Ewert and that he had entered Brazil by ship from Buenos Aires with a forged United States passport. He admonished the court because he and his wife Elisa had been treated brutally during their two-month imprisonment: their food and water had been withheld frequently and they had been systematically tortured. Speaking first in German and later in English through interpreters, Berger claimed that each had been forced to watch the other's sufferings; they had been burned with cigar butts and electrodes, and Elisa had been stripped, dragged across the floor by her hair and breasts, and raped repeatedly.[12] But the prison warden disclaimed mistreatment; the judge denied Berger's appeal and called him a shallow-minded faker and a "type of low social extraction."[13]

On the day that Prestes was taken, the police announced the death, by suicide, of the American Victor Allan Baron. Opponents of the government protested that he had been tortured until he revealed Prestes' hiding place, and that his body had been thrown from an upper-story window to simulate suicide. Baron's mother in the United States demanded an investigation, which was led by New York's volatile Representative Vito Marcantonio. The American Communist Party charged Ambassador to Brazil Hugh S. Gibson with complicity because he had refused to protect Baron, but both Cordell Hull and Aranha defended Gibson and denied the allegations.[14]

Most public attention centered on Prestes and his German-born wife

Olga, whom he had married in the Soviet Union. The press described Olga as a charming woman, known in social circles as Yvone Vilar, a dashing agent for the party's secret missions.[15] Whatever such missions were, Olga was pregnant with her first child at the time of her arrest. She was a dedicated party worker, poised but not elegant. Born Maria Bergner (or Bregner) in 1908 to a poor Jewish family in Munich, she worked for the Russian Commercial Legation in Berlin while in her teens; later she went to France and finally to the Soviet Union. Throughout 1936 the anticommunist Brazilian press documented with relish the deportation proceedings initiated against her by federal officials. She was dispatched to Germany where she died two years later.

Prestes himself was not mistreated during the long months of his confinement, although he was kept isolated, allowed no exercise, and was refused reading matter. Brooding, he made no statements either to his court-appointed lawyers or to reporters prior to his public trial. The international communist press protested his arrest, establishing an anti-Vargas campaign which reverberated around the world in succeeding years.[16]

An ominous warning to proponents of civil liberties was given in March when police invaded the federal legislature and arrested five Congressmen: deputies Abguar Bastos, Domingos Velasco, João Mangabeira, Octávio da Silveira, and senator Abel Chermont. Bastos and Velasco had spoken openly in praise of the ANL, and all five had been sympathetic to it. Chermont, an outspoken defender of civil liberties, had offered to serve as counsel for Harry Berger, as did David Levinson, a lawyer who said that he represented the International Red Cross, but who was quickly deported to the United States by Brazilian authorities. Silveira was a founder of the ANL in Paraná and had replaced Cascardo as titular president in July when Cascardo was transferred by the navy away from Rio de Janeiro. Each belonged to the so-called pro-popular liberties bloc of the legislative opposition, but their colleagues were helpless to defend them. The police charged that Velasco and Chermont had defended the Communist Party's A Manhã, suspended after November, 1935, and that Bastos had been proposed as its editor should publication begin anew. To remove any legal barriers to the five's arrest, the Chamber of Deputies sheepishly waived their constitutional immunity as legislators, in a 190-to-59 vote taken on July 7.

Bastos, Velasco, Mangabeira, Silveira, and Chermont languished in prison for more than fourteen months before coming to trial. Their arrest dealt a demoralizing blow to the moderate camp. Oswaldo Aranha, following events closely from his Washington post, became increasingly morose, particularly over the fate of his friend João Mangabeira, whose health had declined dangerously through his ordeal. When Mangabeira was finally sentenced to a term of three years and four months, Aranha sent his condolences, expressing to Mangabeira's family his "bitterness and shock beyond imagination."[17]

Two days following his release in May, 1937, Domingos Velasco returned to the Chamber of Deputies and, in one of the last acts of open protest against the repression, attacked Felinto Müller and the federal government. Chermont addressed the Senate a few days later, attacking the "cannibalism" and the tyranny of the authorities. He had been arrested, he told the legislature, by sixteen detectives; they had forced him, his wife, and two small children to ride to the police station, where he had been beaten with a rubber hose and held prisoner. When he tried to resist, he said, he was removed by the throat to the police garage and beaten senseless by twelve men. In prison, the five legislators were held in solitary confinement for the first two months and were refused even the fresh-air privileges given to regular prisoners.[18] The legislature's incapacity to protect its own members from police brutality shattered its resolution and cast a pall over its remaining affairs.

The administration's National Security Tribunal (Tribunal de Segurança Nacional, or TSN), established in 1936 under the provisions of the state of national emergency, sat in judgment on the alleged acts of treason against the state and the Brazilian people. It functioned continuously until 1945, although many political prisoners refused to testify before it, calling it unconstitutional and a tool of reactionaries. Prestes and Barata forced guards to drag them, bloodied, before the tribunal in early 1937 when their cases came to trial.[19] TSN judges normally accepted state's evidence and sentenced defendants as the prosecution requested, although a goodly number of accused were acquitted for lack of evidence. No restitution was offered for the two or three years spent in prison awaiting trial. Of the twenty men who at one time served on the ANL's national directorate, thirteen were released without trial, two were acquitted, and only five were sentenced for treason.[20]

Nevertheless, penalties were usually harsh, averaging between four and six years at hard labor; and most persons were sentenced not for revolutionary acts but for membership in the various antifascist fronts which thrived during 1934 and 1935, or simply for "extremist tendencies." In mid-1936, Oswaldo Aranha bitterly protested to Vargas that the TSN hearings had transformed the simple barracks revolts into a "civil war of ideas." Vargas answered him only with friendly clichés, as if he did not see the problem.[21]

The total number of persons arrested during the post-1935 period of repression has not been established accurately. The domestic communist press claimed that 20,000 Brazilians had been imprisoned; the French communist journal, *L'Humanité,* offered the figure of 17,000. In October, 1937, the New York *Times* claimed that Felinto Müller had acknowledged 7,000 arrests by federal authorities, not counting those carried out on state and local levels.[22] The exact number of all arrests may have totaled anywhere between five and fifteen thousand persons. After mid-1937, about one hundred arrests monthly were still being made in and around Rio de Janeiro of persons accused of complicity in radical activities outlawed two years earlier.[23] The continued antileftist campaign also included mass deportations of supposed agitators, most of whom had Central or Eastern European sounding names.[24]

Prison conditions universally ranged from uncomfortable to oppressive. The nonmilitary jails were administered by the individual states, most of which considered prison administration a patronage plum, thereby opening prison budgets to indeterminable graft and subjecting prisoners to wanton neglect and, in some cases, exploitation. Jails were helplessly overcrowded, particularly in urban areas, where four or five prisoners were often crowded into cells constructed for one or two. Military prisoners, who were generally sent to camps in the north or in the Amazon region, fared the worst. Their fate remains largely undocumented, although conditions at military prisons are legendary in Brazil.

São Paulo's Maria Zélia stockade typified the treatment afforded to accused sympathizers with the left. Called Zé Maria by its inmates, the abandoned textile-factory complex held approximately four hundred prisoners, mostly from São Paulo. Officials constructed low wooden barracks in the factory courtyard to house half of the inmates. The others were confined indoors, subject to the cold dampness of the paulista winters. The latrines reeked and the only running water came from a dirty stream which ran through the courtyard. Prisoners complained that the hospital staff rarely reported to work, and that drugs and supplies were sold for private profit. Chronic tuberculosis and a host of other infirmities plagued inhabitants and guards alike.[25] Ironically, São Paulo achieved worldwide recognition in the 1930s for a new, model prison organized according to the most advanced principles of penal science.[26] Such facilities were not afforded to political prisoners.

Inmates joked that the best educational curriculum in São Paulo operated within Maria Zélia's walls. Volunteers offered an elaborate classroom schedule, holding classes in subjects ranging from basic literacy to philosophy, Russian, and Esperanto. Some of the best authorities in their fields taught fellow prisoners, including Professor Danton Dampre of the University of São Paulo and Dr. Mário Gomes, a widely known specialist in leprosy. The courses did not exclude ideology, leading the PCB to boast later that Brazil's prisons were "the best revolutionary schools" in the country.[27] In almost all prisons, inmates laboriously hand-lettered their own newspapers, which were then circulated by hand from cell to cell. Articles usually expressed the prisoners' view of the world, but none incited disobedience or rebellion, since this would surely provoke cancellation of the privilege.[28]

Some sporadic resistance did occur. Agildo Barata led approximately two hundred prisoners transferred from the *Pedro I* to an overcrowded prison in Rio de Janeiro in revolt; their subsequent hunger strike was crushed by the arrival of Brazilian army troops.[29] In Belém, guards threw bombs of tear gas into a peaceful demonstration for better medical treatment; prisoners' arms were broken, and leaders were removed by agents of the political police. In Maranhão, ten imprisoned students between the ages of fifteen and nineteen petitioned state officials in protest against conditions at the correctional colony to which they had been sent. They charged that prisoners' heads were shaved, that they were given zebra-striped clothing, and that they were forced to walk with their arms folded and to perform heavy labor in total silence. A second letter from physicians who had been imprisoned there corroborated the charges, citing conditions of malnutrition and diseases ranging from dysentery to bubonic plague among inmates.[30] Stories of youths forced to perform homosexual acts by prison guards were also reported.

Few of those arrested for political subversion had been involved directly in the November uprisings. Of those that were, the leading principals in the PCB's revolutionary adventure received terms ranging from four years' imprisonment (Rodolfo Ghioldi) to thirteen years and four months (Berger) to sixteen years and eight months (Prestes, who received an

additional term of thirty years for his alleged part in the murder of Elza
Fernandes). Many of the members of the party's rank and file who were
seized in early 1936 were dispatched to prison on desolate Fernando de
Noronha Island, off the northeastern coast. Agildo Barata, like Prestes and
some of the others released in Vargas' general amnesty in 1945, left prison
in broken health. Twenty-two years later, in 1967, Barata was formally
stripped of his military rank by the Brazilian Supreme Court as he sat,
semiparalyzed, confined to his residence.[31] Less than a year later he died.

Stricken by the arrest of its most prominent activists, the PCB virtually
ceased to exist as an effective political force for nearly a decade after 1935,
although its skeletal organization remained largely intact and some party
activity continued. The central committee moved its headquarters to São
Paulo to build anew, but the effort proved unsuccessful. After the arrest
of Leon Valée, the so-called financier of the 1935 revolution, Ilvo Meirelles
became the party's treasurer, but no evidence exists that he received significant monetary aid from either foreign or domestic sources. In some states,
such as Amazonas, Piauí, and Pará, the PCB disappeared altogether during the war years. The party was weakened further by relentless attacks
from the Trotskyites, who blamed Prestes and the Stalinist Comintern for
what they labeled the "fiasco of 1935."[32] Trotskyites established their own
Leninist Workers' Party (Partido Operário Leninista, or POL), but its
membership never grew significantly.[33] Some POL leaders, including
São Paulo art critic Mário Pedrosa, were arrested in the indiscriminate
roundup of left-wing activists carried out by regime officials during 1936
and 1937.

Within the PCB, still-at-large cadre officials raised a contradictory screen
of simultaneous self-criticism and self-aggrandizement. On one hand, the
party blamed itself for its sorry fate, but on the other hand, it rationalized
its defeat, citing the insurrections as heroic and nearly successful first efforts at revolutionary organization in Brazil, which was on the road to a
"higher, decisive stage of national emancipation."[34] Party ideologists retreated increasingly into a world of illusion, clearly bewildered by events
and dogged by the necessity to follow the Comintern line. Some remnants
of the national executive council fled north, establishing small training bases
in Pernambuco and preparing to aid local authorities in the case of a
rumored Integralist *putsch*. A few comrades in the Federal District—in-

cluding Bangú [Lauro Reginaldo da Rocha], the highest party official still at large—planned a raid on the House of Detention to liberate its prisoners, but desisted. A new wave of arrests in late 1936 removed Bangú as well.[35]

By the end of 1936, most of those sought had fled the country or been captured, and the anticommunist drive showed evidence of tiring. But privately, officials expressed fears that underground radical elements might unite with opportunistic antigovernment politicians—a farfetched possibility but indicative of the irrational lengths to which the anticommunist campaign had led. Party agents writing idly to one another mentioned such would-be allies as General Manoel Rabello, Carlos de Lima Cavalcanti, Juracy Magalhães, and Flôres da Cunha. This moved the police to increase their surveillance and added fuel to conspiracy stories circulating among the radical right.[36]

Even the armed forces prepared themselves for a supposed communist *golpe* in April, 1936, which was to involve the Fourth RI in São Paulo, the state's Republican Party, the navy, the state militia, and additional forces from southern states. Although the revolt never materialized, the army stood on the verge of national mobilization. "The country is like an automobile, hanging off a cliff on the edge of an abyss, held only by its brakes," a police informer wrote to Felinto Müller in mid-July.[37] Dubious statements from Trotskyites were produced to show links between the PCB and the faction in the state of Rio de Janeiro identified with Flôres da Cunha. Police followed suspected agents across the Uruguayan border in the hope that they might lead to antigovernment activities among exiles.

These scares probably amounted to little more than the readiness of officials to construct elaborate designs from uncritically gathered intelligence. In reality, there was little danger from the emasculated left. Opposition to Vargas after 1936 would come from regional political factions chafing at the growing consolidation of federal control, or from the still-not-satisfied radical right.

Typical of the atmosphere of the repression period were the cases of Pedro Ernesto Baptista, the Federal District's interventor, and his secretary of education, Anísio S. Teixeira. A professional educator, Teixeira had never ventured into the political arena, but his identification with reform made him easy prey for his enemies. Pedro Ernesto, no longer backed by the federal administration from motives of jealousy—Vargas apparently was irked by the colorful prefect's popularity—stood defenseless by virtue of his links with the National Liberation Alliance and his generally progressive administration.

Teixeira was the leading educator of his day and the only Brazilian to have studied with John Dewey. He was born in Caitité, in the interior of Bahia, in 1900; his father was a *fazendeiro* who had been educated by French tutors and trained in medicine. When he sent his son to school in Salvador, it took the boy and two servants a week on horseback to cross the several *municípios* under his father's influence.[38] He went on to law school in Rio de Janeiro; then, developing an interest in primary education, he was named director of public instruction of the state of Bahia at the age of twenty-four. After inaugurating plans for a sweeping reform of the state's meager educational system, he was sent to France and Belgium in 1925, and, in 1929, was awarded a fellowship by Columbia University Teachers College, where he spent ten months under the influence of John Dewey, receiving a Master's degree in that same year.

Abandoning an earlier calling to become a Jesuit, Teixeira was named secretary of education in the Federal District by Interventor Pedro Ernesto in 1932. Some pedagogical reforms in local areas had been undertaken after 1927, by Fernando de Azevedo in Rio de Janeiro, by Teixeira himself in Bahia, and in some other states—Minas Gerais (1927-30), São Paulo (1931-33), and Pernambuco (1932-34). All were attempts at modifying the traditional antidemocratic educational system, and none, save perhaps in São Paulo, had been visibly effective. Teixeira's own plans for reform included the establishment of an educational research center, state-sponsored rural schools, the construction of neighborhood schools and training centers, and the creation of a central university out of several previously autonomous local *faculdades,* a concept novel for Brazil although anticipated by Francisco Campos in the federal Ministry of Education in 1931 and first instituted in São Paulo in 1934.[39] Teixeira wrote dozens of articles on educational theory, planned vocational schools, imported foreign teaching materials, and talked of eliminating the mediocre normal schools which prepared primary and secondary teachers.

He was approaching his goals when the ANL raised its banners in 1935. Never politically motivated, Teixeira did not join the movement, and, for its part, the ANL did not publicly recognize his work. While the young administrator issued free textbooks and fought for a broad-based system of public education, ANL spokesmen demanded vaguely defined educational reforms and a war on illiteracy—and remained oblivious to Teixeira's presence. But his opposition to religious training in the public schools won him the enmity of conservatives and the Catholic Church, both fighting for the institution of religious instruction in Rio de Janeiro as permitted by the 1934 constitution.

Almost immediately after the suppression of the November insurrections, the "bolshevik educator" became the prime scapegoat for the Pedro Ernesto administration. He and all of his aides were dismissed on December 1 at the climax of a vocal campaign led by Catholic lay-spokesman Alceu Amoroso Lima. With Teixeira were released the rector of the university, Afrânio Peixoto; eight *faculdade* directors; and numerous professors. Others, including Heitor Villa-Lobos, the titular director of musical and artistic education in the Federal District, resigned in protest.[40]

In an act reflecting the humiliation of his administration, Pedro Ernesto replaced Teixeira with Francisco Campos, Vargas' first minister of education and the co-founder of the mineiro "black shirts" in 1931, and the subsequent author of the corporatist Estado Nôvo constitution in 1937 and the repressive Institutional Act of April, 1964. For his part, Teixeira sought exile in France, where he remained until 1946, serving as one of the founders of UNESCO. Campos personified the elitist view of education which Teixeira had worked to destroy. Taking office on December 27, he promised to purge the schools of bolshevism and to uphold "traditional, humanistic, and Christian Brazil."[41] Although Campos argued for such measures as new school construction and a consolidated, university-structured reorganization based upon the integration of classical programs with technical and professional training, in reality education in the Federal District returned to its pre-1930 framework, not to be challenged until the late 1960s by critics in the face of growing percentages of illiterates and hopeless inadequacies inherent in the educational system.[42]

With Teixeira, their prime target, gone, conservatives intensified their attacks on Pedro Ernesto, who was called a latent communist for his opposition to religious education in the schools and his reported dealings with the ANL. Many resented the manner in which he championed programs of social welfare—including the provision of 11,000 new hospital beds and the renewal of the old Department of Public Assistance—as a challenge to the popularity and prestige of the Vargas administration.[43] Sensing his vulnerability, his political coalition, the Autonomous Bloc (Partido Autonomista), collapsed shortly after Teixeira's removal. A faction headed by vice-prefect Cônego Olímpio de Mello, a Pernambuco-born priest known as the "working-class padre" despite his strong support from business interests and Catholic lay spokesmen, ascended to power when Pedro Ernesto was subsequently deposed.[44]

The degree to which Pedro Ernesto's enemies reviled him was startling. "It is an infamy for me to tell you that I am associated with [him]," Carlos de Lima Cavalcanti wrote from Recife; "it is shameful that the capital of the Republic must have as its governor a type of this species, dishonest, treasonous, and illiterate."[45] Bewildered by the intensified accusations, Pedro Ernesto lost his usual confidence. Prominent figures such as Afrânio de Mello Franco, Levy Carneiro, and Oswaldo Aranha rose to his defense, but the fact that his son (Odilón Baptista) had actively participated in radical causes and had collaborated personally with the ANL, even contributing money through intermediaries, sealed his fate, despite his rejection of Prestes' requests for open support.

While Vargas, his former close friend, refused to intervene, the National Security Tribunal accepted the charge of the Commission for the Repression of Communism and found Pedro Ernesto guilty of subversion. He received a prison term of three years and four months. He was released in late 1936 because of ill-health, but after he was received by jubilant crowds, military officials reconsidered their generosity: without warning, he was returned to jail in early 1937.[46] His physical condition worsened and he died shortly after his final release in the early 1940s. His populist tendencies and his political naïveté, exemplified by his clumsy relations with the ANL, marked him for political destruction in spite of his personal popularity and the fact that his medical treatment had saved the life of Vargas' wife Darcy after an automobile accident in April, 1933.

Virtually no public opposition to the reckless anticommunist campaign manifested itself through 1936 and 1937. A brief exception was a student protest against the arrest of four popular law professors in Rio de Janeiro on grounds of suspected communist ties. One of the demonstrators was Alzira Vargas, the President's daughter and a student at the law school. According to Alzira, her father admitted to her that he was aware of occasional injustices, but that he was no longer Supreme National Chief, only constitutional President, and that the military had demanded the purge of the academic sector.[47]

Artists, journalists, academicians, and intellectuals of all callings suffered as the climate of events took on anti-intellectual overtones and fear of creative expression mounted. Among those attacked as subversive were writers Jorge Amado, Raquel de Queiroz, and Graciliano Ramos, sociologist Gilberto Freyre, artist Cândido Portinari, architect Oscar Niemeyer, dramatist Joracy Camargo, musician Eleazar de Carvalho (who was detained in 1937 for possessing "communist books"), and André Carrazoni, ex-director of *A Hora* and *Diario de Notícias* of Pôrto Alegre and Vargas' biographer, accused of ties with Pedro Ernesto and of having carried clandestine letters from political prisoners. To be sure, some cultural figures (Niemeyer, for example) allowed themselves to be identified with communist causes; but most were attacked simply out of fear and distrust. The poignant, almost Kafkaesque experiences of novelist Graciliano Ramos, director of public education of the state of Alagôas, who was imprisoned for alleged sympathies with that state's small ANL cell, testify to the anguish of those persons intimidated for political purposes.[48]

To the nation, Vargas justified the work of the repressive campaign with images of unity, patriotism, and common interest against bolshevism. On May 10, 1936, he addressed all Brazilians over the *Hora do Brasil*:

The destructive activities of Russian communism are varied and multifaceted. In the light of the insidious nature of its work, ordinary means to guarantee the security of the state show themselves to be . . . weak and ineffective. . . . The struggle . . . against our internal enemies . . . must be hard, dedicated, and relentless.

"Confident in the patriotism and devoted example of the armed forces," he concluded, ". . . I affirm to you that order will be maintained and that our institutions will be defended."[49]

7

THE
ESTADO NÔVO

Although Vargas regularly confirmed his intention to leave office at the conclusion of his four-year term, his administration marched uncompromisingly in the direction of authoritarianism. While the President's public restraint kindled hopes among some, the outline of the future showed clearly in the declaration of a ninety-day period of national emergency decreed in December, 1935, and renewed five additional times. The revolutionary promise of the Liberal Alliance slowly ebbed away. On November 10, 1937, Vargas, with strong military backing, announced a corporatist-style constitution (the Estado Nôvo), canceled the scheduled presidential elections, and assumed dictatorial powers.

By early 1936 Vargas had probably made his decision to ease out the federal system and what he termed its "Franciscan poverty of ideas."[1] He was undoubtedly encouraged by leaders of the armed forces, to whom he increasingly drew close. Those most influential around him included Góes Monteiro, who, as chief of staff, dominated the military command; Eurico Dutra, the minister of war; Felinto Müller, the pro-Nazi police chief; and Francisco Campos, the government's chief ideological spokesman, who wrote in 1937: "Corporatism kills communism just as liberalism breeds [it]."[2] Few knowledgeable observers believed privately that Vargas would retire from public life. In April, 1936, Aranha wrote prophetically to a friend: "I do not believe any more in election. We will have either civil or military dictatorship first."[3] But in mid-1937 Vargas arranged to enlarge his São Borja ranch and for his belongings to be shipped from the federal capital at the end of the year.[4]

More ominous signs appeared. Virgílio de Mello Franco, since 1933 leader of the opposition bloc in Minas Gerais, faced the financial ruin of his newspaper *Fôlha de Minas* because continued harassment by government censors crippled its circulation. Ambassador Aranha complained to Vargas that police agents regularly opened his correspondence.[5] Newton Cavalcanti, outspoken reactionary and defender of the AIB, continued to rise in the armed forces command although elected civil officials warned against him.[6] Vargas dismissed War Minister João Gomes after a police report noted that his fellow generals were losing confidence in him because he was considered "soft" toward Flôres da Cunha. His replacement, Eurico Dutra, was appointed on the recommendation that he was closest to General Góes Monteiro.[7]

Nonetheless, the air cleared briefly in late 1936 as speculation about potential presidential candidates filled the press and the anticommunist crusade seemed to wane. A number of names were advanced, even that of Antônio Carlos, the embodiment of the old system of state politics and parliamentary oratory—as if the course of events since 1935 could be turned back. Others included J. C. de Macedo Soares of São Paulo, who resigned as foreign minister so that he might become eligible, and Armando de Salles Oliveira, São Paulo's popular governor, backed by would-be candidate Flôres da Cunha, whose reported 20,000 *provisórios* and 6,000 state troops continued to provoke the anger of the federal military command. In early 1936 Vargas paid a special visit to Pôrto Alegre to test conditions for a reconciliation with da Cunha, but it failed. On his return the President complained bitterly to his brother that Flôres' staff had opened his personal correspondence even while he was a guest at the governor's residence.[8] A similar effort at peacemaking attempted in April by Oswaldo Aranha came to the same end.

Sensing Vargas' reluctance to relinquish control, Governor Juracy Magalhães of Bahia attempted to form a covert alliance among the states of São Paulo, Minas Gerais, Rio Grande do Sul, Bahia, and Pernambuco. Although the plan failed, Pernambuco's Lima Cavalcanti tacitly agreed to it, thereby dooming his own political future as well as Juracy's. Vargas also knew that the Bahian governor had considered giving support to São Paulo's Armando Salles (as had Benedito Valladares).[9] While Valladares became the only governor to be allied closely with Vargas during the planning for the Estado Nôvo, even he raged in private at Góes Monteiro's attempts to strip his state's militia of its independent command, but political exigencies precluded disloyalty to Vargas. Valladares' strongest enemies within Minas Gerais supported Armando Salles; he, therefore, had no choice but to remain in the administration's camp or be ousted from power.

Armando de Salles Oliveira resigned his governorship on the last day of 1936 to proclaim his candidacy. He represented his state's commercial and industrial interests, the cause of liberal constitutionalism as a spokesman for São Paulo, and, tacitly, resistance to increased centralized power in the hands of the national government. He was born in 1887 to an old paulista family of coffee exporters. As a young man he established a successful electric power corporation, but in 1927 sold out to the foreign-controlled Bond and Share Corporation and moved on to other enterprises. He married the sister of the *Estado de São Paulo*'s publisher, Júlio de Mesquita Filho, and he became its editor in 1929; in 1931 he was elected president of a leading paulista industrialists' association.

After the unsuccessful constitutionalist revolt, with which he sympathized, he was named interventor by Vargas. The President was applauded for his choice. When he made his decision to become a candidate, Salles paid a formal call on Vargas, who reportedly begged him to change his mind, promising the Constitutionalist Party the federal Finance Ministry, the directorship of the Bank of Brazil, and fiscal concessions, and threatening to favor the opposition Republicans should he refuse. Salles remained unshaken and returned to São Paulo.[10]

Vargas attempted at the last minute to delay the selection of a candidate but then desisted. On May 25 a convention of state governors acting for the administration nominated José Américo de Almeida of the small state of Paraíba. José Américo, a protégé of the late João Pessôa, was closely identified with the Liberal Alliance as its minister of transport and public works, and was the choice of tenente Juarez Távora. Deeply involved in their own preparations for political action, Góes Monteiro and his fellow staff officers did not object. José Américo was an honest bureaucrat with a reputation for toughness, an effective cabinet minister who appealed to advocates of national economic and technological planning. Some expressed surprise at Vargas' failure to name his ambassador to Washington as his successor, but Aranha's enemies were too numerous (he had never accepted party discipline in Rio Grande do Sul, and his cosmopolitanism earned him distrust); moreover, the military suspected him of possible sympathy for Flôres da Cunha. José Américo seemed safer; anyway, Aranha was too far away to maneuver, although he continued to be unhappy in Washington and certainly would have accepted the nomination had it been offered to him. Rio's monthly *O Observador Econômico e Financeiro* noted the importance of the selection: in the absence of national political parties "capable of acting as restraints," the power concentrated in the hands of the Brazilian president could only be called "formidable."[11]

The "official" candidate drew the support of most of the tenentes, including João Alberto Lins de Barros. Governor Valladares organized his campaign. Most of José Américo's strength came from the north, from the Federal District, and from pro-Vargas groups in hostile São Paulo and Rio Grande do Sul. Armando Salles' Brazilian Democratic Union (União Democrática Brasileira) attracted supporters who viewed with suspicion Vargas' experimentation with working-class legislation and who feared his growing reliance on executive authority. The smaller states of the north and northeast favored José Américo, fearing lest a paulista assume the presidency, as did middle-class groups identified with the expansion of the powers of the federal government.

But events threw the campaign into disarray. José Américo startled his political advisers by forcefully and unexplainedly shifting to the left, as if he were trying to appeal to a working-class electorate apprehensive that Salles Oliveira would turn the clock back to 1929. The entry into the presidential race of Integralist chieftain Plínio Salgado in June, 1937, clouded the matter even further. Vargas noted both developments without public comment. Privately, he expressed shock at José Américo's attacks. He did not seem to object to Salgado's candidacy: it would serve to remind moderates of the still-unsettled political climate.

The President's 1937 New Year's address declared his administration's intention to expand the railroad network, increase agricultural production, and aid public health and education. Of the political situation, Vargas said only that the presidential campaign would proceed in a "free and healthy atmosphere."[12] But potential obstacles to the elections remained. These included the renewed difficulties in the states, increasing pressure from the military for intervention, the gathering threat of war in Europe, and the continued militancy of the far right. To reduce tension, the new justice minister, J. C. de Macedo Soares, ordered on his return to the cabinet that several hundred political prisoners still awaiting trial before the TSN be released. Macedo Soares visited Prestes and Berger in prison and assured the press of their good treatment. But a month later Prestes was removed to poorer quarters; the warden declared that his prisoner had complained too much.[13]

Vargas seemed to act more swiftly and with more resolution during 1937 than he had done before. He ordered interventions frequently—in Mato Grosso, twice in the Federal District, and in Maranhão, where the opposition successfully impeached the pro-Vargas governor.[14] Federal troops invaded the Ceará village of Caldeirão and destroyed a semireligious communal sect on the probably spurious grounds that it harbored refugees from the Natal and Recife uprisings.[15] In other states, Vargas waited. A political conflict rent Alagôas into two factions, each led by one of Góes Monteiro's brothers. The departure of paulista Vicente Ráo from the Justice Ministry increased anti-Vargas feeling in São Paulo, but Armando Salles' successor as governor calmed the situation.

Above all else in the sphere of domestic politics, pressure to resolve the Flôres da Cunha question mounted. In March, hostilities led by Flôres-bloc state deputies in the state of Rio de Janeiro upset the precarious political balance by violently attacking the interventor, who finally departed to France for medical treatment. The interim governor proved even less able to maintain order, and federal military authorities demanded decisive action.[16]

Vargas tested his strength in April by successfully unseating Antônio Carlos from the presidency of the Chamber of Deputies, albeit by a small margin, aided by the loyalty of the "class" deputies and representatives from the northeast.[17] He moved on several fronts to counter Flôres da Cunha's armed strength: by increasing the authority of the federal military commander in Rio Grande do Sul, by preparing for the incorporation of the state forces into the federal command, by authorizing troop reinforcements and shoreline patrols against contraband smuggling of weapons, and by decreeing a state of siege in April.[18] Góes Monteiro personally visited Curitiba to reorganize the military region, and the War Ministry drew up contingency plans in the case of armed conflict.[19] The list of formal accusations compiled by the army included charges that Flôres had disguised militia forces as railroad workers along the São Paulo–Rio Grande do Sul line and on the border with Santa Catarina. The army accused the governor of a campaign of persecution against state legislative opposition, of having exploited regionalist sentiment for political purposes, and of harboring communist fugitives, including Trifino Corrêia, Prestes' envoy to Minas Gerais, who had escaped from a prison hospital in 1936. Finally, it warned that he was preparing secret military alliances with other states.[20] In August, Góes sent General Manoel Daltro Filho, a trusted aide, to supervise the military region and to carry out further orders.

The army's vow to strip Flôres da Cunha of military power set the stage, by early 1937, for the planning of a new constitution and the cancellation of elections, and, with them, the federal system. Publicly, Vargas belied his decision by ostensibly heeding requests for moderation from Aranha and Macedo Soares and hinting at still another attempt at reconciliation, leaking word to the press that gaúcho Lindolfo Collor, his first minister of labor who had backed São Paulo in 1932, might return to the cabinet as part of a settlement.[21] At the same time, the authors of the *golpe* elaborated their strategy: rather than move singularly in the south and possibly provoke civil war, they would complement the federal program of interventions in anti-Vargas states with the isolation of Flôres' potential allies in Bahia and Pernambuco. Then Flôres would be removed and the Estado Nôvo could be imposed. The elevation of Góes Monteiro to Army Chief of Staff in July and his efforts to remove recalcitrant officers from military commands increased pressure on Vargas to act or be deposed.

The campaign against Pernambuco's governor, Lima Cavalcanti, began in April, although at first he did not seem to understand what was happening.[22] The governor's strained relations with the federal capital began in the aftermath of the Pernambuco insurrection, when federal officials refused to intervene in his behalf after the arrest of his cabinet ministers for subversion. Lima Cavalcanti's discussions with Juracy Magalhães in late 1936 on a possible anti-Vargas state alliance increased the distance between Recife and Rio de Janeiro. Finally, during the struggle over the presidency in the Chamber of Deputies, Pernambuco had allied itself with Flôres da Cunha in favor of Antônio Carlos. According to a letter to Oswaldo Aranha, only Agamemnon Magalhães' efforts to retain members of the Pernambucan delegation at the door of the Chamber during the roll-call vote had prevented an opposition victory.[23] In retaliation, federal authorities withheld patronage from Lima Cavalcanti's state. Later, they issued statements alleging that he was soft on communism, charges that the governor—for the time being—successfully refuted through public denials.[24]

The presidential campaign opened formally in July. Armando Salles campaigned widely, but avoided direct attacks on the federal government. Speaking largely to business and professional groups, he advocated honest constitutional government and economic responsibility—clearly not issues calculated to incite the electorate. According to João Alberto Lins de Barros, Salles' financial backing came from the São Paulo Commercial

Association, a claim doubted by few.[25] José Américo's candidacy, however, suddenly took an unexpected turn. Ostensibly, the "official" candidate represented the tenente-nationalist position, favoring Vargas' achievements and his exercise of authority in the national interest. But in his public appearances José Américo declared himself the "candidate of the people," assaulting the status quo and, in effect, biting the hand that offered to feed him. In May, a newspaper poll forecast his probable victory, predicting that he would carry every state but São Paulo, Rio de Janeiro, and Rio Grande do Sul, and thereby adding to his self-confidence.[26] Overestimating the security of his candidacy, he grew increasingly belligerent, angering his sponsors by declaring mysteriously, "I know where the money is."[27] Police officials responded by closing a number of pro-José Américo electoral groups, including the Democratic Student Union. Never enthusiastic about the succession and now greatly annoyed, Vargas ordered the selection of a third candidate, but a gathering for this purpose (which included Góes Monteiro, Benedito Valladares, and others) at the Mello Franco residence in Copacabana failed to reach an agreement.[28] The candidate's managers virtually abandoned him, and Francisco Negrão de Lima, his campaign director, made preparations for a trip to the north in order to sound out the state governors on a possible suspension of the elections.

José Américo's own rationale for embracing radical antigovernment slogans must rest with his egoism, a naïve failure to understand the precarious nature of the presidential campaign, and the belief that he could win support from the literate urban middle class by identifying Armando Salles with the traditional conservative elite. He probably sensed the insincerity and lack of genuine concern for his candidacy among his backers; he did not know where his *own* money was coming from, and his campaign suffered badly from lack of funds. As it progressed, he stated his fears publicly: "If the politicians abandon me," he declared, "I will not remain alone; I will go with the people to the polls and forward to the revolution."[29]

Police officials frequently warned him of communist infiltration into his ranks, a doubtful allegation deeply resented by the candidate. The self-appointed "people's candidate" turned to populism in the naïve belief that his was the role of the successor to the Liberal Alliance revolution. Rumors that Vargas would cancel elections (never forcibly denied by José Américo's backers) drove him further to the left as the campaign developed. The climate was summarized by Maciel Filho in mid-September: "Getúlio's strength," he advised Aranha, "merits a *golpe* to end this foolishness. The navy is firm and dictatorial-minded; the army is the same. There are no more constitutional solutions for Brazil."[30]

On September 28, Chief of Staff Góes Monteiro assured the press that rumors of a coming coup d'état were groundless. But on the following day War Minister Dutra addressed the nation on the *Hora do Brasil* radio program, urgently requesting a new declaration of a state of war, in response to a sensational 10,000-word document reportedly apprehended from clandestine communist sources that revealed plans for violent revolution. A blatant forgery, the so-called Cohen Plan had been fabricated by Integralist agents and passed on to Góes Monteiro by Captain Olympio Mourão Filho, the chief of the AIB's propaganda service.[31] The frightened Congress approved Dutra's request overwhelmingly at a special joint night session, with only Rio Grande do Sul, São Paulo, and a small group of civil libertarians demurring. Twenty sections of the article of the 1934 constitution dealing with personal rights were suspended by executive decree. If Vargas knew of the falsity of the document, a reasonable assumption, he maintained his expressionless façade.

The military had acted to accelerate the move to the right. A newly enlarged campaign to isolate and suppress all opposition was revealed shortly with the creation in every state of executive commissions for the execution of the state of war. In all but two states—São Paulo and Rio Grande do Sul—the respective governors were named to head their state commissions.[32] To oversee the program on the national level, Vargas selected two reactionaries, Admiral Paes Leme (of the National Commission for the Repression of Communism) and Newton Cavalcanti. Taking office, Leme told newsmen that anyone not publicly anticommunist was, by definition, a communist himself.[33]

The commission's first act was to order the reimprisonment of Pedro Ernesto. Federal District Education Secretary Francisco Campos, still privately at work on a new Brazilian constitution, pledged to cooperate with the commission and to expand his efforts to uproot communist infiltration.[34] In the Chamber of Deputies, Adalberto Corrêia attacked Justice Minister Macedo Soares, and the executive state of war commission outlawed Masonry as inherently bolshevist.[35] A new wave of repression seemed poised on the horizon.

Reactionary state commission military officers in Bahia and Recife accelerated the administration's public campaign against communism. In Bahia, the military commander, Colonel A. F. Dantas, attacked the governor furiously, not neglecting to report his progress to the War Ministry.[36] In Pernambuco, Colonel Amaro Villanova (like Dantas an Integralist sympathizer) barred Lima Cavalcanti from the meetings of the state of war commission and acted as if he, Villanova, were the commander of an occupying force. He censored the governor's mail, persecuted pro-Lima Cavalcanti editors, and arrested several of Lima Cavalcanti's staff members for undisclosed acts of subversion. The governor pleaded with federal officials for help, but they refused.[37] In late October he wired Vargas that Villanova had removed the guards from the gubernatorial palace and had threatened to storm it during the night. The state of war commission, he declared, "seeks my exile from the government and my personal humiliation."[38] Villanova responded calmly: "Communism is 50 per cent stronger in Pernambuco now than in 1936."[39]

In Rio Grande do Sul, Flôres da Cunha remained passive before his own state of war commission, unable to do anything else for the time being. Fugitives Trifino Corrêia and Silo Meirelles were arrested in Pôrto Alegre forty-eight hours after the declaration of a state of war became federal law. Military authorities gave their attention to the exposure of stored caches of arms and to the transfer of state militia units to federal control. The state opposition group, the Gaúcho United Front, nearly succeeded in impeaching the governor; its efforts fell short by a single vote.[40]

Church leaders spoke in every major city on the renewed communist threat. In the capital of Paraná, students formed an anticommunist league at the university.[41] Authorities closed all *faculdades* and secondary schools in Belém (Pará), pending investigations for communist subversion.[42] All spiritist societies in Rio de Janeiro—always an annoyance to the local branch of the Church—were closed by police. On November 8, a joint statement from the Ministry of Education and Culture and the executive state of war commission named a ten-man watchdog committee for the defense of national culture against bolshevism. Members included Alceu Amoroso Lima, Raul Leitão da Cunha of the foreign service, Affonso Arinos de Mello Franco, and Carolina Nabuco, the daughter of the Brazilian statesman.[43] In a small sense, this move confirmed the conservative elite's acceptance of the conditions preceding the final step in the march to the right.

When the state of war commission in Rio Grande do Sul demanded that the state militia be integrated into the federal forces, Flôres stood chastened;

on October 17 his personal militia commander surrendered his command to federal headquarters. Archbishop Dom João Becker carried the news personally to Flôres, who left on a commercial flight to Montevideo to avoid public confrontation. Vargas swiftly named the commander of the state of war commission as interventor, providing an anticlimactic end to the three-year struggle between Flôres and the federal government.

Flôres' manifesto on departing offered hope that the constitutional authority of his state would not be destroyed by the federal assertion of power.[44] Not to be denied the last word, the state of war commission in the capital demanded the removal of Flôres' honorary generalship.[45] On October 20 Benjamin Vargas wired the President that things in the state had gone very well.[46]

As the administration initiated its eighth year four days after the beginning of November, Vargas now held near-absolute control. His combined use of federal pressure and an inflammatory anticommunism campaign had created the conditions which drove Flôres into exile, pushed Bahia and Pernambuco to the edge of federal takeover, and reduced significantly the possibility of resistance from the announced candidates for the presidency.

The army, holding the upper hand, stood clearly behind the President. A vote among the active generals taken by the war minister yielded a nearly three-to-one ratio favoring revision of the 1934 constitution and a change of government.[47] The Integralists, briefed by Francisco Campos, awaited events which they believed would catapult them into coalition status in the national administration. To display his strength, Salgado marched thousands of Integralists on November 1 from Praça Mauá to the presidential palace, where Vargas and General Newton Cavalcanti reviewed the paraders. Satisfied, the Integralist national chief withdrew from the presidential race.[48] A War Ministry report advised the President that over one quarter of the active army officers could be classified as Integralist or Integralist sympathizers, as well as about half of their navy counterparts.[49]

During the first week of November, word leaked out of Negrão de Lima's mission to the north. To allay rumors, Vargas told the press on an off-the-record basis that Negrão had been sent in order to sound out opinion for a substitute presidential candidate.[50] The die was now cast. Valladares made additional contacts in the south with São Paulo's interventor and progovernment forces in Rio Grande do Sul.[51] Totally isolated, José Américo angrily pointed out that he had not authorized anyone to negotiate his withdrawal from the race.[52]

Justice Minister Macedo Soares, the cabinet's last moderate voice, resigned on November 8. Vargas replaced him with Francisco Campos; by this time, rumors were flying that there would be no elections and that a *golpe* was close at hand. In Minas Gerais, the Bernardes–Mello Franco bloc attacked the government and the Integralists, moving Valladares to wire Vargas that the state legislature should be closed.[53] On November 6 the opposition had attacked the to-be-imposed "constitution written by Francisco Campos"; and on the eighth, Armando Salles sent a manifesto to the Congress forewarning an imminent coup. Now, to retain the element of surprise, Dutra, Campos, and Müller persuaded the others to advance their timetable for action from November 15, the anniversary of the proclamation of the Republic, to the tenth.

On the day Campos entered the cabinet, Vargas informed Oswaldo Aranha in Washington of the precarious national situation. He was less than specific, considering Aranha's close relationship to him and the ambassador's strategic diplomatic position. He did not disclose the full scope of the changes that would be imposed. Describing the political environment, Vargas cited general apathy, the failure of the José Américo campaign, and uneasiness in the armed forces. The authority of the federal administration, he wrote—at a time when it probably stood at its seven-year apex— was "anemic." The Congress was demoralized, he added; the government was unable to check communist infiltration.

From this [situation] rose the idea for the government to revise the Constitution . . . to execute an extensive administrative program capable of opening new economic directions . . . and [to] permit broadly relevant initiatives.

"I count on your collaboration," he concluded, "as a friend and patriot."[54]

On the afternoon of the ninth, Valladares sent a final telegram to Vargas, assuring him that São Paulo would not resist and that the "solution" would be "tranquil."[55] Viriato Vargas promised full support from Rio Grande do Sul "when the H-hour comes."[56] No potential opposition stood between the President and what now proved to be his efficient and well-elaborated plans for a coup d'état.

At dawn on the tenth, cavalry troops surrounded the congressional palace and barred access to its entrance.[57] Copies of Francisco Campos' new constitution, secretly printed earlier, were distributed after the cabinet affirmed its near-unanimous approval. Only the minister of agriculture, Odilón Braga, objected; he was immediately replaced by paulista Fernando Costa, significantly the head of the National Coffee Institute and a member of the anti-Armando Salles São Paulo Republican Party. War Minister Dutra read a brief statement to the press, praising the "lofty mission entrusted to the national armed forces."[58] A handful of military men resigned, the most important of them being Colonel Eduardo Gomes, one of the two survivors of the 1922 Copacabana Fort uprising and a hero in the defense against the ANL-inspired military insurrection in Rio de Janeiro in November, 1935. General Newton Cavalcanti, responsible in part for the pressure which had been applied on Gomes, was promoted to the rank of marshal although he had only become a colonel in February, 1933, and had stood forty-eighth on the list for promotion to general as late as November, 1935. Interventors were named in every state except Minas Gerais, where Valladares, the politician most deeply involved in the pre-November planning, retained his status; Vargas thus kept alive the tradition that Minas had never had an interventor. In most cases, state governors succeeded themselves, but new interventors were appointed in Rio Grande do Sul, São Paulo, the state of Rio de Janeiro, Bahia, and Pernambuco, where Dantas and Villanova respectively assumed office. After thirteen days, São Paulo's interventor, Cardoso de Mello, was reinstated when military authorities saw that no resistance was likely. On November 13 a delegation of eighty members of the suspended Congress visited Catete in support of the new government, in spite of the fact that a number of their colleagues had been arrested two days earlier. But the remaining three hundred fifty stayed away, ostensibly embittered. Constitutional government under the traditional federal formula was dead. The Chamber of Deputies' penultimate session had been spent debating the nature of a quorum; in their last debate, the deputies, having been warned of the coming *golpe,* argued whether or not the body should discuss the creation of a national Institute of Nutrition.

The change came with little fanfare and without visible protest, as if it had been expected for a very long time. In the evening, Vargas addressed the nation by radio from a studio in the Guanabara Palace. He explained that the coup had been executed in order to rescue the nation from demagogic and opportunistic presidential candidates who were acting to legitimize their "personal caudillistic ambitions," and demanded firm governmental authority in order to meet the nation's economic needs and to end the divisiveness of partisan politics. The foreign debt would have to be suspended; the armed forces would be reequipped; and the government would inaugurate a broad program of public works and railway and highway construction. He had been compelled to act, he said, by the pleas of patriotic Brazilians:

Buoyed up by the confidence of the armed forces and responding to the requests of my co-citizens, I agreed to sacrifice the just rest to which I was entitled, with the firm intent to continue to serve the nation.[59]

From his office in Rio de Janeiro, United States Ambassador Jefferson Caffery wired Secretary of State Hull that the Brazilian foreign minister had sought him out "before any other ambassador" and had explained the situation to him. The electoral campaign, Caffery said, had threatened chaos; the President failed to receive the consent of the governors of Bahia and Pernambuco for a third candidate. A plebiscite would be held at "an early date" for the new constitution, which replaced its weak predecessor. The Brazilian government, he added, would follow a "very liberal policy with respect to foreign capital and foreigners who have legitimate interests in Brazil." Off the record, Caffery added some personal observations about his friend, Getúlio Vargas. Noting that the coup obviously had been in preparation for a considerable time, he indicated his skepticism about the "effective preservation of democratic institutions under the new constitution."[60] The ambassador's premonitions proved accurate.

Juracy Magalhães, now thirty-two years of age and presumably far wiser in political matters, resigned without formal protest when Vargas elevated Colonel Dantas to the interventorship. In a final, emotional address to the Bahian people, he assured Rio de Janeiro that his government had behaved honorably; he eschewed acrimony and announced his return to active military duty. "I remain not bitter, but firm in my thinking," he wrote to a cabinet minister on the day prior to his departure from office.[61]

Lima Cavalcanti departed angrily but without incident. Dozens of state officials considered loyal to him were dismissed. Friends secured for him the post of ambassador to Mexico, and he left the country, still publicly loyal to Vargas.[62] After two weeks in the interventorship, Colonel Villanova was replaced by Agamemnon Magalhães, the former protégé of the ex-governor, and the man personally responsible for his political execution.[63] In Rio Grande do Sul, Flôres da Cunha having since left the state, officials arrested his brother Francisco, an ex-senator, for complicity in the murder of a local newspaperman four years earlier.

The new corporatist Estado Nôvo constitution took its name from Salazar's Portuguese government imposed in 1933; it also drew from the fascist constitutions of Italy and Poland. The Estado Nôvo canceled individual civil rights, although it offered lip service to individual liberties. The press presented the change as the final victory for national stability over the forces of dissension and subversion. The November 10 constitution extended Vargas' term six years, leaving the door open as well for reelection. On December 2 a decree outlawed all political parties. Armando de Salles Oliveira was escorted to Minas Gerais, where he was held for six months under house arrest and then removed to the interior of São Paulo. In November, 1938, he was placed on the French ship *Lipardi* and dispatched into exile. Restless, he took up various residences in France, New York, Buenos Aires, and Santiago, before he finally returned to Brazil, gravely ill, to die in May, 1945.[64]

For the first time in recent Brazilian history, the states were decisively removed from the realm of effective political power. The designation of the state governors as interventors illustrated their reduction to the status of federally appointed administrators. Regional army commands absorbed all state militia forces. But Vargas saw no necessity to establish a monolithic Estado Nôvo party, although he might have imitated a variety of foreign models. Neither would he spend the effort required to compose an all-inclusive ideological program. Vargas, in spite of his tough *caudilho* ability to deal with the personalities around him, held little talent for totalitarian dictatorship in the strict sense of the word. The fact that his government eschewed political mobilization and that it may be characterized by a "distinctive mentality" rather than any elaborate ideology earns it an "authoritarian" label.[65]

The authors of the Estado Nôvo sought to reform Brazil by eliminating its traditional weaknesses. As conservatives, they viewed the roots of inefficiency and unproductivity as lying in the excesses of traditional liberal constitutionalism: faith in parliamentarism, lack of discipline, lack of unified leadership, inadequate national pride. The new government outlawed strikes as well as lockouts, subjugating the interests of labor to the national economic interest according to the corporatist formula. The rationale behind the Estado Nôvo shared elements of the fascist's reliance on national planning and state authority, the positivist's faith in a disinterested, bureaucratic elite, and the Brazilian conservative's distrust of open expression and fear of potential subversion. Yet the Estado Nôvo was not, and did not pretend to be, a vehicle for sweeping revolution; rather, it drew heavily from the existing system. The political and social climate of 1939-40 probably bore a closer resemblance to the Brazil of the period between 1934 and 1937 than to the atmosphere prevailing at the end of World War II, by which time Vargas had abandoned the Estado Nôvo in an attempt to win the support of a new political base.

A host of new appointments gradually transformed the upper levels of government leadership in the months after the November 10 *golpe*. Some of the faces were familiar—Campos, Müller, Agamemnon Magalhães. Others were not. For the most part, the new men possessed a singular loyalty to Vargas and the federal government, a feature paralleled in Brazil only by earlier developments within the structure of the armed forces through the middle 1930s, when the national military command developed a professional pride jealous of state military power and committed to the cause of national unity.

The Estado Nôvo intensified the police-state atmosphere present since the repression of the uprisings of November, 1935. Internal security measures trebled under the auspices of the new Justice Ministry. Francisco Campos and Felinto Müller—the latter still federal police chief—did not report to the cabinet but answered directly to the President.[66] Vargas delegated wide powers to his new National Department of Propaganda (Departamento Nacional de Propaganda, or DNP), whose Press Information Service (Departamento de Imprensa e Propaganda, or DIP), directed by young pro-Hitler Lourival Fontes, assumed monolithic control of all public communications.

Although some liberals exiled themselves from the Estado Nôvo, public comment within Brazil remained mild, intimidated by government pressure and the general sense of national relief. Many welcomed the change and its appeal to Brazilian unity. Newspaper columns, bolstered by official handouts, lauded Vargas, showering the President with publicity for the first time in his national political career.[67]

But foreign views were less quiescent. Argentine military circles lauded the Estado Nôvo, but most Argentine newspapers attacked it, apprehensive lest the Justo administration move even further to the right. Chilean reaction was hostile. In Uruguay, the press and radio—generally favorable to Flôres da Cunha during the course of the decade—reacted even more violently.[68] In the United States and Great Britain, most commentators paused short of outright condemnation, but warned bluntly that Brazil teetered on the brink of fascist dictatorship. A statement attributed to Francisco Campos in the New York *Times* in late November, 1937, affirming Brazil's fascist organization and defending it on the basis of the ignorance of the Brazilian people provoked additional reaction.[69] The New York *Post* and the *Daily Worker* led a barrage from the left attacking the neutral position of the State Department and taunting the hasty explanations offered by Oswaldo Aranha in Washington. Aranha, upset by the harsh attacks, wrote to Vargas that "Communists and American Jews" were responsible for the anti-Brazilian press campaign.[70]

Favorable public comment came only from the European fascists. Although the German press was directed to restrain its enthusiasm by the Reich Foreign Office, Propaganda Minister Goebbels publicly praised Vargas' political realism and his ability to act at the correct moment. The German press—as well as the German-language press throughout the Southern Hemisphere—lauded the assertion of authoritarian control as a victory against bolshevism. Clippings from these sources were freely translated and distributed to Brazilian editors by the official Brazilian propaganda outlets.[71] In private, the Germans showed less enthusiasm, aware of Vargas' growing efforts to suppress Nazi activity in Brazil. Italian reaction was openly exuberant.[72]

In Washington, Oswaldo Aranha took the news badly despite his public defense of the new government, although he had been forewarned for months by his Brazilian friends. Vargas' failure to confide in him adequately undoubtedly angered him, and the five-day acceleration of the Estado Nôvo's timetable in November probably accounted for the fact that Aranha received Vargas' bland communication only after he first learned of events in the press. Aranha's health in recent years had been poor, although his dedication and his personal ambition had sustained him in his work. Intrinsically sensitive, he was torn between his sympathy for the victims of antiliberal persecution and his feeling that only severe measures could resolve Brazil's national dilemma. Aranha's popularity in Washington and his close relationship with Sumner Welles influenced the latter to temper his criticism; in fact, on November 11 Welles assured the press that the coup was an internal Brazilian matter and would not be judged by the United States. Three weeks later, in a speech at George Washington University, he praised Vargas and, in the spirit of the Good Neighbor Policy, chastized those who had attacked Brazil "before the facts were known."[73]

But after acquitting himself in defense of Vargas, Aranha wired his resignation on November 13, citing Lincoln's "You can fool some of the people some of the time" parable to the man whom he considered a close personal friend.[74] Three days later, his brother Luís and Finance Minister Souza Costa telephoned him long-distance. The twenty-five minute conversation, transcribed at presidential request—probably without the knowledge of the speakers—reached Vargas' desk on the same day. It included the following exchanges:

Souza Costa: How are you, Oswaldo?
Oswaldo Aranha: Good—and you, with your Estado Nôvo?
SC: Everything is well here.
OA: I received the news from [the foreign minister]. I don't agree with what you are doing, and I am leaving.
SC: [Exhorts patience]. Without you it would be a disaster.
OA: [Referring to his resignation] . . . I am calmly defending what you are doing. . . .
SC: You cannot leave us at this time.
OA: I cannot agree with a constitution written by an abnormal person, without norms, without rules. . . .
SC: [Pleads again].
OA: . . . I have defended with all of my energy the name of Brazil in this country. . . . But this constitution is an affront against freedom.
SC: I agree with you . . . [hands phone to Luis Aranha, who pleads in the same vein].
OA: I approve of a *golpe* of the government, but not of the constitution. . . . You know that I consider any matter with Getúlio a family matter, but I cannot agree to receive a writ of slavery.
Luís Aranha: Yes, but it was the only solution. . . .
OA: Do you know that I received a deriding telegram from Flôres in Montevideo?
LA: Well, this is logical. Now we are discovering various things in the south which he and others did.
OA: Have you arrested many people there?
LA: No. . . .
OA: And Juracy?
LA: Nothing, he resigned. He who said he was as courageous as a *cearense* and not as a *gaúcho* left his post shamelessly.
OA: And Lima [Cavalcanti]?
LA: Also, the same way.
SC: We need you. . . .[75]

On November 18 Vargas wired Aranha that he would not accept his resignation, at least not until normal conditions could be established.[76] Other friends implored Aranha to remain at his post. Even Virgílio de Mello Franco, estranged from the Vargas administration since 1933, wrote in defense of the Estado Nôvo.[77] Under this pressure Aranha capitulated, turning to defend Brazil against exaggerated claims of fascist takeover.[78] He finally returned in March, 1938, to become Vargas' minister of foreign affairs and the leading spokesman for strong economic and military ties with the United States.

A complex variety of factors culminated in the coming of the Estado Nôvo. On the one hand, Vargas looked with pride at his accomplishments in the areas of social reform legislation and the steady transformation of the economy to the point where, by late 1936, Brazil consumed 80 per cent of its total agricultural and industrial production. On the other hand, the failure of the 1934 constitution to restore effective legislative activity convinced many of the obsolescence of the constitutional system, which was rent by state and regional intransigence and was symbolized by the continued presence in Congress of such holdovers from the Old Republic as Artur Bernardes and J. J. Seabra. Seabra, the Bahian deputy, the only active survivor of the Old Republic's 1890-91 Constituent Assembly, crocheted as he sat in the Chamber of Deputies month after month.[79]

The 1937 constitution incorporated all major social and nationalistic legislation decreed or ratified since 1930: immigration restriction; national claims to subsoil resources, water power, and shipping rights; the "two-thirds" law; and the federal government's welfare measures. In addition, it provided for the nationalization of banks, insurance companies, and essential industries. Many reacted favorably to the promise of national progress. "The future of our nationality will be preserved," the editor of the usually hostile *A Pátria* wrote, following the coup. "What all Brazilians recognize is the sincerity of the gesture . . . determined by the action of the government and the armed forces, closing ranks . . . in this hour in which a new sun blazes forth on the national horizon."[80]

The Estado Nôvo was not welcomed openly by commercial and manufacturing groups, which viewed it with suspicion, particularly in the light of the cancellation of the presidential elections and the transfer of fiscal and industrial policy-making to the state and its National Security Council, strongly influenced by the military. But businessmen quickly warmed to the Estado Nôvo's consolidation of authority, its corporatist framework, and its nationalistic plans for the acquisition of facilities for domestic iron and steel production. New policies in marketing, taxation, banking, and revenue distribution, facilitated by the removal of effective power from the states, aided growth toward a genuine national market.[81] Twenty-one months before November, 1937, the first issues of Valentim F. Bouças' *O Observador Econômico e Financeiro* anticipated the future changes, advocating banking and monetary reform, new foreign debt policies, and an expanded federal role in national industrial development.[82]

Persistent international fiscal instability through the 1930s and decreasing faith among Brazilians in orthodox liberal economic policy groomed receptiveness to strong federal initiative. Estado Nôvo policy encompassed both "managing of stimulants" (exchange and credit controls, taxes, banking, import quotas, wages) and direct intervention (public investment, government-sponsored cartels, and natural resource development by official agencies).[83] As the relative domestic influence of coffee continued to decline (prices were lower in 1938 than in 1930), federal officials devoted close attention to the stimulation of other sectors, such as cotton manufacture.[84] Beginning in October, 1937, Vargas drastically relaxed coffee supports approximately 30 per cent, claiming that the lower prices which would result would encourage increased world consumption.[85] Even so, the federal government maintained its policy of destroying coffee surpluses for seven additional years.

Measures terminating the exchange tax paid by agricultural exporters were initiated immediately; as a result, the drop in revenue necessitated the suspension of payments on the national debt. The emergence of Germany (by a slight margin) as the chief supplier of imports after 1937 (25 per cent for Germany in 1938 as opposed to 12.7 per cent in 1929; 24.2 per cent for the United States as opposed to 30.1 per cent; 10.4 per cent for Great Britain as opposed to 19.2 per cent) capped three years of pressure from Germany to increase bilateral trade. Vargas had experimented with the German scheme of compensation marks, which allowed trade to bypass the international exchange market through the use of nonconvertible currency.[86] Yet the scheme was suspended on July 31, 1936, at the request of the Brazilians, whose officials complained, according to the United States Embassy, that the plan forced them to buy only what Germany wanted to sell, and to provide only what Germany wanted to buy, products marketable elsewhere.[87] After July, 1936, trade with Germany returned to a regular basis.

The military, clearly the strongest influence behind the establishment of the Estado Nôvo, evolved its own aggressive nationalism in response to conditions throughout the Vargas decade, its relatively weak position vis-à-vis Argentine military strength, and the survival of divisive local and regional political jealousies. Contemptuous of liberal constitutionalism, the faction within the military command headed by Góes Monteiro became dominant by 1933. Calling for centralized planning, the development of national steel production, and, later, technological aid to manufacturing, transportation, and heavy industry, this faction represented a convergence of ideological influences from *tenentismo* and a general demand within the Brazilian military for professionalization, increased military strength, and absolute superiority over autonomous state forces. Even Oswaldo Aranha advised Vargas to renew the country's antiquated stock of arms and supplies, some of which predated World War I. The successful effort of the Argentine Foreign Office to block the sale of three obsolete destroyers from the United States to Brazil in early 1937 deeply angered the Brazilian military command and contributed to its unwillingness to accept the status quo.[88]

Administration policy favoring military growth and, ultimately, disarming the potential for independent state action contributed importantly to the emergence of the armed forces as the decisive political power after the middle 1930s. Table 2 shows the relative strength of federal military forces in contrast to combined state police and militia personnel from 1909 to 1937.

TABLE 2

APPROXIMATE NUMERICAL STRENGTH OF FEDERAL AND STATE ARMED FORCES, 1909-1937
(in thousands of men)

	1909	*1917*	*1921*	*1927*	*1932*	*1937*
Federal	19	22	29	38	58	75
All states	18	28	29	28	33	38

Sources: Joseph Leroy Love, Jr., "Rio Grande do Sul as a Source of Potential Instability in the Old Republic, 1909-1932" (Ph.D. dissertation, Columbia University, 1967), p. 307, figure 9.1, based on *Anuário estatístico 1939/1940*, p. 1279; Directoria Geral de Estatística, *Annuaire statistique du Brésil* (1908-1912) and succeeding volumes.

Now a national power, the army played an increased role in foreign affairs under Vargas; between 1932 and 1934, the War Ministry actively pressed for the creation of a Ministry of National Defense, to give it greater leverage in political matters. Spurred by heightened consciousness about military preparedness caused by the Chaco War between Bolivia and Paraguay, Brazil intensified its arms race with Argentina, its traditional foe to the south, and a threat to the balance of power in South America in the minds of many Brazilian military officials.[89] In 1936 Argentina rejected a Brazilian offer for a "collective security pact" to meet any threatened invasion. Navy officers were particularly concerned about their service's antiquated equipment; collapse of the negotiations for the purchase of surplus destroyers from the United States angered the Brazilian naval command and added to its resolve to purchase arms from any source.[90]

By 1937 the armed forces command could no longer tolerate Flôres da Cunha's maintenance of well-armed independent state forces, and, acting in what it firmly considered to be the national interest, it claimed its traditional right to intervene. To some observers, in fact, the military exaggerated the threat posed by Flôres da Cunha simply to provoke a confrontation with the national government that seemed unavoidable.[91] With the Estado Nôvo, the military finally achieved its objective of a strong nationalistic military-backed central government.

Many armed forces leaders saw their role in the imposition of the Estado Nôvo as a natural reflection of the worldwide growth of military power. As a sign of its new aggressive orientation, the Brazilian army scrutinized its ranks, significantly toughened military justice, and moved to screen with rigor any undesirable candidates (allegedly including blacks, Jews, sons from broken homes, and the poor) from entrance to the military academies.[92]

Other supporters of the new order shared the military's optimism. One, Plínio Salgado, waited expectantly in the wings during the first days of the new administration. Most observers fully expected the Integralists to take their place in the new order. The refusal of the armed forces to move in Salgado's favor following the November *golpe* represented one of the greatest surprises of the post-1935 political drama.

8

NATIONALISM
OVER INTEGRALISM

Plínio Salgado—no less than many of his enemies—fully believed that his movement stood on the threshold of victory with the establishment of the Estado Nôvo. Brazil now embraced corporatism and abandoned the forms of liberal democracy. Francisco Campos had shown Salgado his draft constitution in October, and it was well known that Vargas had met with the Integralist chief and promised a cabinet seat for the AIB. On November 1, Salgado paraded thousands of armed Green Shirts through the downtown streets of Rio de Janeiro to the presidential palace in Laranjeiras, where Vargas and pro-Integralist Newton Cavalcanti admiringly reviewed the marchers from a balcony. After this, the AIB national chief waited patiently to be admitted to the inner circles of the new government.

But Vargas, ignoring earlier promises, abandoned the AIB no sooner than the *golpe* was accomplished. Suddenly, Salgado stood naked, powerless to act. Brazil remained unified behind the Estado Nôvo; tradition-minded nationalists welcomed it and abandoned the AIB as excess baggage. The military, supposedly a repository of Integralist support, stood unmoved, united behind the new dictatorship.

Vargas' acute sense of timing had caught the AIB off balance and exposed its vulnerability at the very time that Integralist leaders were prepared to assume political legitimacy for the first time in the movement's brief history. Integralism's weakness lay in its failure to develop an effective mass base. Its officials, like their former ANL counterparts, gave excessive credence to their inflated statistics. While Salgado claimed that 50,000 Integralists had marched before Guanabara Palace, government agents privately estimated that only 17,000 persons, including women and children, had participated. The AIB had grown steadily since its inception but it had become top-heavy. Middle- and local-level leadership ranged from uneven to unreliable, in spite of the movement's elaborate and carefully organized hierarchy of command. Its greatest military strength lay in the navy, as fate would have it, the least politically active of the Brazilian armed forces.

Repression of Integralist activity on the state level, in fact, had been sanctioned by the national government at least since 1935. Anti-Integralist measures had been taken in Minas Gerais, Alagôas, Paraná, and Santa Catarina, where the governor banned the Integralist militia in July, 1935, from marching publicly. In 1936 Governor Juracy Magalhães wrote to Vargas of an Integralist plot to overthrow the state government, adding that he would not tolerate further activity of the movement in Bahia. In September, police invaded AIB headquarters in Salvador and arrested Integralist leaders for alleged conspiracy, even though the National Security Tribunal threw out the charges and the movement resumed its activities in Bahia in early 1937.[1] In Rio de Janeiro Felinto Müller had quietly banned two Integralist parades scheduled for Army Day, August 27, and Independence Day, September 7, 1937, in order to prevent possible "violence."

Such antiextremist measures as the 1935 National Security Law forced the Integralists to modify their statutes and frequently caused the movement difficulty. Nevertheless morale soared during the period of repression which followed the left's abortive November, 1935, uprisings. In mid-1936 several hundred Integralist municipal councilmen and nearly two dozen mayors won elective office as the AIB capitalized on the antiliberal, anticommunist atmosphere fostered by government policy.

Salgado's nationwide campaign for the presidency in 1937 gained valuable publicity for the AIB and helped recruit members. National headquarters decreed the obligation of every Integralist to register to vote; local cells organized special literacy courses to prepare those ineligible. As a presidential candidate Salgado spoke earnestly of the need for national control of natural resources and advocated the eradication of such obstacles to national unity as political parties and regional interest groups. Before he personally withdrew from the race in September, 1937, Salgado predicted that he would win a half-million votes and lead thirty Integralist congressional candidates to victory. On the eve of the Estado Nôvo coup he boasted to a radio audience that his movement had penetrated the armed forces and that it had achieved major political stature.[2]

When Vargas failed to reward the AIB or even to praise it publicly after November 10, Integralist newspapers mirrored the confusion and embarrassment which suddenly enveloped the movement. Without explanation, *A Offensiva* abruptly abandoned national coverage, printing instead pages of Integralist organizational filler. On November 12 Salgado announced in a small insert in *A Offensiva* that the movement would not be affected adversely by the newly imposed constitution, but the announcement carried no further comment. Thirteen days later Salgado led the last public show of Integralist strength, a parade through the federal district which again was reviewed by Vargas. On December 2 the President decreed the abolition of all political parties, including the AIB. The announcement of the abrupt resignation of Newton Cavalcanti from active military service on the same day did not appear in the Integralist press.[3]

Salgado meekly reconstituted the AIB as the Brazilian Cultural Association (Associação Brasileira de Cultura), with himself as president, Miguel Reale as director of research, and Gustavo Barroso as director of physical education. Integralist paraphernalia, including the sigma symbol, the uniform, and attendant ritual, disappeared. The abrupt changes shattered the movement's prestige. Out of frustration, Barroso intensified his anti-Semitic campaign in the otherwise morose Integralist press.

Clearly, the President had outmaneuvered and humbled the Integralists. In early January, Salgado expressed his bitterness in a letter to Getúlio Vargas, in which he described his pre-November meetings with Campos, Müller, and Dutra, and the praise which had been heaped upon his movement by them as well as by the President himself.

The first warning, Plínio wrote, had come when Francisco Campos had informed him about the coup only during the early morning hours of November 10, considerably after Salgado had learned of it from his own private informants. When Vargas ignored the AIB during his first public statements, Salgado realized that he had been betrayed. The press began to ridicule Integralism, Salgado charged, at the request of the government. In a number of cities Integralist leaders had been arrested. After a frustrating second meeting with Vargas, Salgado—despite reassurances from Góes Monteiro—refused the post of education minister which had been offered to the AIB earlier.[4] Later, after he reconsidered and asked that it be given to Barroso, Vargas had ignored him. The Integralist national chief retreated sullenly to São Paulo.

After November, Vargas faced many of the same problems that had bothered his government prior to the coup. What is not often realized is that the Estado Nôvo took form gradually. Announcements and explanations of new programs and decrees often appeared weeks apart; the total impact of the change wrought by the adoption of corporatist dictatorship probably did not become apparent until late 1938 or 1939.

Vargas' attention focused to the south of Brazil in the first few months of 1938. Previously strained relations with Argentina were alleviated to some degree by a presidential visit to Buenos Aires in late 1937 and by growing tension between Argentina and Chile, which relieved pressure on Argentina's other diplomatic fronts. Vargas sent João Alberto Lins de Barros as special minister to Buenos Aires, and Góes Monteiro toured South America on a good-will tour.[5] Flôres da Cunha, still in Montevideo, was kept under close surveillance by agents of the Brazilian police.[6]

Vargas visited his home state of Rio Grande do Sul early in the new year, after first taking elaborate security precautions against a rumored plot by partisans of Flôres and Armando Salles in the region. Ties between Rio de Janeiro and Pôrto Alegre were strengthened by the nomination to the state's interventorship of Prestes Column–veteran Colonel Oswaldo Cordeiro de Farias, a gaúcho and a personal friend of Dutra and Góes Monteiro.

Very likely embarrassed by foreign charges of fascism against his new regime (critics labeled Campos' Estado Nôvo draft *a polaca,* in reference to its more than passing resemblance to Pilsudski's Polish constitution), Vargas now hinted at a national campaign to suppress the remnants of the Integralist movement. His statement received wide attention abroad. In the state of Rio de Janeiro, the federal interventor, Vargas' future son-in-law Ernani do Amaral Peixoto, ordered all Integralist headquarters searched and drove Integralist activists out of the state. Caches of arms were uncovered, confiscated, and displayed publicly. In mid-March, 1938, federal police announced that a conspiracy involving Integralists and others had been unmasked, sending Integralist officials into hiding and breeding rumors that Salgado had sought refuge in the German Embassy.

The plan to overthrow the new government had been elaborated by Belmiro Valverde, the Bahian physician who had taken effective control of the Integralist machinery following Salgado's semiretirement after the start of the year. Participants included Integralists, nonfascist political allies of Flôres da Cunha and Armando Salles, and some dissident military officers, including General Euclides Figueiredo, the officer who had declined the command of the Liberal Alliance in 1930 and who had led the paulistas in 1932. Exposed, the liberal constitutionalist members of the conspiracy, including ex-Senator Otávio Mangabeira and the owner of the *Estado de São Paulo,* Júlio de Mesquita Filho, were arrested and ultimately permitted to leave Brazil. Mangabeira went to New York where he took a job translating articles for the Brazilian edition of the *Reader's Digest,* and Mesquita Filho sailed into exile on the same ship as his brother-in-law, Armando Salles. Still at liberty himself, Valverde continued to oversee Integralist activities, most of which now took clandestine forms. Valverde, General Castro Júnior, and Belmiro Lima, chief of the Integralists' Guanabara province, planned for a second uprising tentatively scheduled for April or May. Like the first, this conspiracy was supported by Flôres da Cunha money, which was used to rent an operational headquarters on Avenida Niemeyer, more than an hour's drive from the center of the city. An attempt to recruit both Newton Cavalcanti and former tenente hero Eduardo Gomes for the coming *putsch* proved unsuccessful.[7]

The national government functioned quietly through March and April. Oswaldo Aranha, who had returned angrily from Washington during Christmas week, agreed after long deliberations with his friends and family to be sworn in as the Estado Nôvo's foreign minister out of personal loyalty to Vargas and to protect the amicability of United States–Brazilian relations. Vargas issued his first economic manifesto in April, in which he pledged to open internal markets and to initiate a sweeping program of industrial consolidation and working-class legislation. Vargas left the capital in April for his first vacation since the coup, indicating to observers his confidence in the stability of his government.[8]

On the evening of May 10, Vargas had returned and was working in his private office; Aranha was traveling in Rio Grande do Sul; Francisco Campos was receiving friends; Felinto Müller was at the movies; and the capital seemed normally tranquil. But shortly after midnight a band of armed rebels attacked the presidential palace. The strange effort to kidnap the President and unseat the government by an *Anschluss*-like *putsch,* which collapsed within hours, electrified public attention and briefly made Vargas a national hero.[9]

Under orders not to storm Vargas' Guanabara Palace but to wait for reinforcements, the attackers exchanged pistol fire with the residents of the building, including Vargas and his daughter Alzira, but did not fire their heavier weapons. They managed to cut off exits and sever electric lines but failed to cut telephone connections, through which members of the President's family called for help. Incredibly, no assistance arrived for several hours—and that a contingent of a dozen soldiers rounded up personally by War Minister Dutra. The bizarre sequence of events gave the adventure an air of unreality and, to some, the scent of fakery. Full government reinforcements led by Cordeiro de Farias did not arrive until 5:00 A.M., at which time they assumed control immediately. The defenders lost only one man, a palace guard.

Belmiro Valverde was taken prisoner by the police as he drove wildly through the city looking for "points of action." Smaller Integralist assault groups had taken the Navy Ministry, attacked two radio stations, the homes of two generals, the residence of police chief Felinto Müller, and Góes Monteiro's apartment house; but plans to kidnap other officials and to seize government buildings and communications facilities collapsed. Rebels overran one radio station and broadcast news of the uprising, which reportedly was heard by Plínio Salgado, who was nearly overcome with excitement. On the following day, seven hundred men were arrested for complicity, seventy-eight of them noncommissioned military officers. By the end of the month, fifteen hundred fugitives, a third of them enlisted men, had been arrested by embarrassed authorities. In anger, Vargas decreed an amendment to the constitution to allow for the death penalty for attempts against the life of the President, but it was not made retroactive.[10] Among those wounded in the hapless would-be *putsch* was reserve navy lieutenant Dom João Orleans e Bragança, the son of the royal pretender to the Brazilian monarchy. The young officer denied vehemently any connection with the affair, claiming that he had been passing by the area, had stopped to investigate, and that Integralists had placed small arms in his car, which was apprehended later. Most critics failed to believe his story, but the affair was generally not publicized.

The complete explanation of the absurd affair unfolded with the arrest of Valverde and Lieutenant Severo Fournier, the leader of the attack force and not an Integralist himself. They had plotted against the Estado Nôvo since November, they disclosed, but they avowed that Salgado had not known of the plans, a doubtful assertion. One of the captured rebels confessed that the Banco Germânico had aided the plot; as a result, several of the bank's officers were held and a brief wave of anti-German feeling ensued. The *Ibero-Amerikanische Rundschau* of Hamburg acidly remarked that, had Germans actually participated in the ill-fated *putsch,* it certainly would not have been confined to Rio de Janeiro.[11]

But no sweeping repression of the far right occurred in the aftermath of the attack, as might have been expected in the light of the left's experience after November, 1935. The guilty conspirators received sentences from the TSN which ranged from one to ten years in prison, but most won release before the expiration of their terms. Former AIB chieftain Plínio Salgado was not arrested, but was allowed to enter voluntary exile; in 1939 he sailed for Portugal. When high Integralist officials called on Vargas on May 13 to affirm their personal loyalty they were received cordially. Although the national Integralist organization lay dormant after 1938, many former activists continued to publicize Integralist doctrine, eulogizing the role of their movement as a patriotic watchdog against communism during the dangerous middle years of the 1930s.

One minor related incident threatened to disrupt the government after the collapse of the plot, although it did not receive wide public attention. In June, 1938, Severo Fournier, who had become disgusted at the behavior of his Integralist comrades for their last-minute indecision and blundering, broke from his hiding place and took refuge in the Italian Embassy with the aid of several friends, one of whom was Captain Manoel Aranha, the foreign minister's brother. War Minister Dutra dismissed the guilty parties from the army without a hearing, invoking the anger of the Aranha family and leading to a number of threatened resignations by Aranha, Góes, and Dutra himself. Vargas finally worked out a compromise by which Fournier, to the relief of the Italian government, voluntarily entered custody to stand trial. The episode demonstrated that family politics had not been erased from the inner workings of the Estado Nôvo.[12]

Vargas received worldwide acclaim for his heroic self-defense, but the commotion raised by the pathetic attack subsided rapidly. Only the Valverde wing of the old AIB remained active, directing a variety of front groups and operating an underground network similar in structure to the skeletal organization maintained by the communists through the late 1930s. Integralist ideology allegedly permeated the Red Cross-like Socôrro Verde, the National Institute of Scouting, which provided physical training for youths, and Rio de Janeiro's fashionable Colégio Andrade.[13]

Vargas consolidated his power during the time that it eliminated the Integralist fringe from its right flank. On May 16 he amended the constitution to permit the immediate dismissal by the President of any civilian or military official. Censorship and government propaganda intensified. By 1939 few vestiges of the once-free press remained, and every month saw newspapers suspend publication. Increased repression of civil liberties, police brutality, and a steady but small stream of voluntary exiles occurred. The federal government moved to curb Nazi and Integralist influence in the country, especially in the south among the German and Italian immigrant groups, where in late 1938 a pro-Armando Salles, pro-Reich insurrection linked to Flôres da Cunha was exposed by agents posing as Nazi employees of the Mannesman Company but actually in the employ of the Brazilian ambassador in Montevideo.[14]

Domestically, the Estado Nôvo propaganda machine set out to portray Vargas as the father of the working classes, even though many of his reforms had dubious impact. The rule forbidding businessmen to fire salaried workers after nine years on the job was flouted by the practice of firing those approaching tenure and immediately rehiring them (if the employers so desired). The various minimum wage and pension statutes were not enforced any more frequently after 1937 than they had been before, although the lower classes rallied to Vargas' side, a credit to his publicists and their patriotic campaign for civic responsibility and cultural nationalism (*brasilidade*). Neither were some of the more ostensibly corporatist provisions of the constitution enacted, such as the mandate to establish a National Economic Council, to be composed of representatives elected by employers' groups and workers' syndicates.[15] Yet Vargas instilled a national sense of purpose and contributed to Brazilian development. By 1945 the presence of an urban electorate expanded by the electoral reforms of the Vargas era promised, for better or worse, to restructure political life.

Although his government after 1937 can be said to have behaved dictatorially, Vargas himself did not covet the trappings of a dictator. Conscious of the significance of such an act, he refused to permit the Estado Nôvo-sponsored youth movement, the *Juventude Brasileira,* to adopt a paramilitary format, a suggestion of Education Minister Gustavo Capanema. The threat of intervention by the armed forces always remained present, a fact which limited Vargas' options, particularly after the imposition of the Estado Nôvo.[16] While in office through the 1930s, he allowed changing circumstances to influence his political posture—a device which, when successful, was viewed as a sign of strength, but, when less so, was proof to some of political opportunism.

Brazil found itself plagued in 1938 and 1939 by troubles which were rooted in the pre-Estado Nôvo period. Even with Flôres da Cunha still in Uruguay, the Rio Grande do Sul question remained open. Armando de Salles Oliveira continued to attack Vargas in Europe, causing embarrassment to Brazil in diplomatic circles. Comintern agencies demanded publicly that Prestes be released and that federal officials restore civil liberties. Plínio Salgado corresponded freely with his former aides from his Portuguese exile, and ex-Integralist officials lived peacefully at home; for example, Gustavo Barroso resumed the directorship of Rio de Janeiro's Historical Museum and remained an active member of the national Academy of Letters.

The Estado Nôvo affected life in many ways. It formalized the stifling of intellectual creativity, which had been on the wane since the institution of censorship in the early 1930s and Vargas' acceptance of repressive tactics against dissent.[17] His *brasilidade* campaign fostered national unity but also restricted cultural expression by banning foreign-language clubs, newspapers and schools. European Jews, who had fled to Brazil in large numbers before 1937, were excluded by government policy, although many Brazilian consular officials welcomed bribes. Fear shadowed the lives of intellectuals and liberals through the years of World War II.

Vargas' officials attempted to influence youth through required school programs stressing physical fitness, morality, and national pride. The administration banned as contrary to the public interest such films as Chaplin's *The Great Dictator*. Police confiscated books and periodicals considered offensive to the government. The political police's information service, created under federal auspices in 1930 and given wider power as the decade progressed, was reorganized under the Estado Nôvo as the Serviço de Divulgação by a November 10 decree. Between 1937 and 1939, it oversaw the publication of forty-five official documents in editions between 10,000 and 75,000 each. In addition, it distributed articles attacking communism and liberal democracy to all Brazilian newspapers.[18] The dictatorship's Press Information Service was installed in the old Chamber of Deputies building under the direction of Lourival Fontes; Vargas granted it an annual budget of approximately U.S.$ 300,000. Its nightly one-hour radio program, the *Hora do Brasil,* was broadcast over all commercial stations. The carefully planned patriotic mixture of speeches, music, and dramatic presentations soon became popular among the national audience drawn from the nearly 1,000,000 owners of radio receivers by the year 1941.[19] In

1937 Vargas established the National Book Institute for the purpose of promoting interest in native authors and national culture. The government sponsored an orthographic reform of the Portuguese language, and in 1937 consolidated a number of independent faculties into the Federal University of Rio de Janeiro, an act in the spirit, if not admitted as such, of the reforms of Anísio Teixeira.

The Estado Nôvo's quiet anti-Nazi campaign attests to its effective independence from the Axis bloc. Despite friendly contact with Reich officials by Francisco Campos and Felinto Müller, relations with Nazi Germany cooled significantly after the November coup despite pro-Nazi sympathies among many high military officers. In late 1937 Justice Minister Campos requested and received Nazi cooperation in helping to import an anti-Comintern exhibition and police chief Felinto Müller visited Heinrich Himmler in Berlin. But Vargas, alarmed by Nazi activities in southern Brazil, countered by taking steps to suppress Nazi groups under the national ban on political parties and by ordering the arrest of top Nazi agents in Brazil, including Ernst Dorsch, the leader of the Nazi Party in Rio Grande do Sul. Ambassador Karl Ritter warned Berlin in March, 1938, that the Estado Nôvo's antiforeign culture campaign threatened to turn Brazil permanently against "everything German and all German activities."[20] Vargas' prohibition of foreign cultural societies and foreign-language newspapers as part of his *brasilidade* campaign angered the Nazis, a situation which was exacerbated by charges that Germans possibly had been linked to the May, 1938, *putsch*. As a result, Brazilian-German relations declined sharply, although Ritter himself confessed to his foreign office that he did not personally know whether the Brazilian charges were accurate.[21] Investigation by the local police produced evidence of complicity which led to the arrest of nine German nationals and the removal of Ambassador Ritter, who was declared *persona non grata* by Itamaratí and whose departure prompted Berlin to expel the Brazilian ambassador in retribution. Relations improved within a year when Vargas, fearful of German power, restored diplomatic ties, arranging to send his son to the University of Berlin for six months. Through 1941 Vargas negotiated privately with the new German ambassador, without the knowledge of his cabinet or Itamaratí.

Urban Brazilians, who had identified themselves with the federal government as soon as it came to power in 1930, voiced no opposition to the Estado Nôvo. The middle classes responded warmly to government attention and welcomed the creation of thousands of new bureaucratic jobs made particularly attractive by regulations governing salaries, work security, and social benefits—in all, a process termed by one Brazilian observer "the political counterpart of import-substitution."[22]

Vargas established the federal Administrative Department of Public Service (DASP) in 1938, the first president of which, gaúcho Luís Simões Lopes, had elaborated plans for federal civil service reform four years earlier. Although the civil service agency was widely acclaimed, within a decade the system became corrupt, creating a staggering drain on the resources of future administrations. Even as originally conceived, the system functioned on merit only in so far as competitive examinations determined initial entrance. But for the time being, Vargas successfully protected the stability of his own government, offering civil servants security in exchange for their loyalty as administrators.[23] For the select few who could rise to the highest bureaucratic levels, moreover, Vargas provided access into the elite; they were principally fiscal planners and officials of such new technically oriented agencies as the National Petroleum Board (Conselho Nacional de Petróleo), created in 1938 to supervise all facets of petroleum policy.

The broad appeal of developmental nationalism muted potential protest against the authoritarian centralization of the Estado Nôvo. Furthermore, to literate urban Brazilians, liberal constitutionalism evoked not democracy but the surviving rural oligarchy and its narrow self-interest. No longer obstructed by legislative opposition, the government adopted a nationally oriented approach to problems of transportation and natural resources. Yet economic nationalism as an ideology of development remained limited in over-all effectiveness. Obstacles included the undependability of the world market, Brazil's need to reserve exchange funds to permit arms purchases, the basic unwillingness of the entrepreneurial sector to undertake radical changes in the economic system, and unresolved discussion over national policy toward the role of foreign capital in national investment. As a result, many of the corporatist provisions of the Estado Nôvo constitution were never enforced by government officials. In the early 1940s Vargas relaxed the strict Water and Mining Code and his decree requiring a nationalized banking system, to the applause of foreign investors. In spite of experimentation with production boards and mixed public-private corporations, the 1942 industrial census showed that almost half of all shares in Brazilian firms were still owned by foreigners.[24]

Yet the Estado Nôvo did attempt major economic initiatives. As early as January, 1937, Vargas had proposed a military arms agreement with the United States, but efforts had come to naught when the Brazilian armed forces command rejected Washington's prices as too high, ordering arms instead from Europe. The 1939 Hull-Aranha agreements on debt payments and technical assistance provoked anger among the Brazilian military command, since they curtailed domestic, and hence military, spending; relations were smoothed over by the visit to Brazil of United States Chief of Staff General George C. Marshall and by Góes Monteiro's return visit to Washington. Further negotiations led to the United States commitment to extend sufficient credit through the Export-Import Bank to permit the beginning of the construction of Volta Redonda in 1941, the national iron and steel complex in the state of Rio de Janeiro linked by a railroad network with the southern states, in exchange for Brazilian permission for the construction of United States air bases along the northeastern coast from Amapá to Santa Cruz in Bahia.[25]

Of the legacies of the first (1930-45) Vargas administration, two can be considered the most lasting: the consolidation of the power of the federal armed forces and the transformation of the federal government into a vehicle for national integration. Increased federal budgets made possible by redistributed sources of taxation gave the national government 55.5 per cent of all revenue in 1940, contrasted with 51.2 per cent ten years earlier. More importantly, federal ministries spent four billion cruzeiros in 1940 as opposed to only one and a half billion in 1930, a considerable increase in spite of wartime inflation.[26]

After 1937 the President grasped initiative in such areas as municipal government and administrative reform. While officials had long called for a census to update the venerable 1920 document, no action was taken until Vargas created the Brazilian Institute of Geography and Statistics (Instituto Brasileiro de Geografia e Estatística, or IBGE) in January, 1938, a government-sponsored agency which played a major role in national planning in the 1940s. Before its post-Vargas decline in influence, the IBGE served as a center for debates over such programs as João Alberto's "Rubber Army," an ambitious but technically unsound blueprint to relocate thousands of destitute refugees from the northeastern drought of 1941 in the Amazon region to produce rubber for the war effort.[27]

The administration of the more than 1,400 municipalities continued to suffer from the inconsistencies of the broad federalism of the Old Republic, in which, for example, in Ceará, Bahia, and Paraíba, the governor had named the local *prefeitos,* while in other states, including Minas Gerais, they were generally elected locally. In all states, municipal governing bodies were frequently dominated by local *coronéis* who acted in collusion with the dominant state political party.[28] Vargas first acted to reform municipal affairs with a decree in August, 1931, which established state advisory commissions and set standardized norms for public administration. Through supplementary legislation local affairs were placed under the authority of the federal interventors. Officials attempted to join low-income municipalities into regional groupings. The 1934 constitution forbade states and municipalities to contract foreign loans, issue bonds, or enter into mining or investment contracts without the permission of the federally dominated advisory commissions.

The constitutional interlude between 1934 and 1937 saw efforts for further centralization slowed. At the Constituent Assembly, the states' rights bloc secured a compromise by which the states received broader authority in local affairs in exchange for promises to create state offices, on the model of São Paulo's Municipal Administration Department (Departamento de Administração Municipal) established in 1931. What the states called municipal autonomy, however, simply meant the right to dominate local affairs, a condition sanctioned constitutionally in 1934 by a provision authorizing intervention by authorities in cases of fiscal insolvency or alleged irregularity. But the new attention to local affairs encouraged the growth of local services; technical commissions introduced uniform accounting and budgetary methods in the dynamic states, generally improving administrative procedures.

The Estado Nôvo restored the authority of the national government, which received the right to appoint municipal officials. Some sources of tax revenue previously reserved to the municipalities passed to the union. Centralization firmly replaced traditional pretenses to local autonomy, and control of state and local administration passed to the federal interventors and a hierarchy of bureaucratic organs, including the Federal Commission on State Affairs and the individual state public service agencies. Vargas accomplished in 1939 by administrative reorganization what his administration had fought to impose politically between 1930 and 1937.

Was the Estado Nôvo truly a fascist state? Examining *Peronismo,* Kalman H. Silvert finds the Argentine case significantly different from European fascist models.[29] The following consideration of post-1937 Brazil utilizes Silvert's basic categories.

1. *Political support*. Although the authoritarian Estado Nôvo cannot accurately be called "popular," it touched virtually all possible bases for its support: the urban middle classes, the military, industrialists, landowners, and urban workers. Many Brazilian intellectuals, heirs to an introspective, conservative tradition, viewed the pre-World War II fascist movements as reasonable experiments in national discipline. A broad spectrum of Brazilian businessmen, officials, and journalists spoke favorably of fascism after visiting Europe in the 1930s.[30]

Whereas Vargas created neither an official party nor an official movement (indeed, tenente efforts to form revolutionary legions in the early 1930s had proved singularly unsuccessful), few supporters of the Estado Nôvo seemed to object to the omission.[31] A "no-party" rather than a "one-party" state, the 1937-45 regime cannot be compared with the European fascists on equal terms.[32] The Vargas government attracted no particular sort of "adherent," although the fascist Integralists recruited followers with backgrounds similar to Mussolini's Fascists and the Nazis: shopkeepers, artisans, civil servants, teachers, and members of lower military ranks.[33] In both prewar Brazil and Italy members of the middle and upper classes can be said to have offered their support to the government to preserve their personal security lest newer forces achieve political mobilization.[34]

2. *Police-state technology*. Totalitarian Nazi Germany, and to a much lesser degree fascist Italy, reached hitherto unseen heights of refinement in the area of police-state technology, whereas authoritarian Spain, Portugal, Hungary, Rumania—and Vargas' Brazil—relied on traditional forms of political control.[35] The Brazilian police utilized crude but selective forms of repression against a tiny percentage of the population, spying, as well, on other branches of the government and the armed forces. Resident aliens (including German Jewish refugees from Nazism) were harassed by the police after Brazil's entry into the war. But Vargas' network of propaganda and censorship paled in comparison to German efforts at thought control. In all, the Estado Nôvo shared few of the monolithic trappings of totalitarianism.

3. *Charisma*. Vargas, who practiced deliberate personal restraint, cannot be said to have been a charismatic leader. Jokingly, Brazilian journalists labeled the Estado Nôvo a "dictablanda," not a "dictadura."[36] Nonetheless, the working classes generally responded favorably to Vargas' paternalism

and his attempt—especially after 1943—to win labor support. In spite of the events of the 1930s, Vargas possessed few bitter enemies. Thomas E. Skidmore has attributed this fact to his "chameleon-like ability to embody the [Brazilian] national character."[37]

4. *Ideology.* The Estado Nôvo did not attempt to elaborate a formal ideology, although individuals justified its creation on ideological grounds. Azevedo Amaral rationalized Vargas' centralization of authority by declaring the function of the state to be the prevention of abuse of authority by individual parties, a common theme of fascist thought as well as a principle of the Mexican Revolution.[38] Oliveira Tôrres and others claimed that the Estado Nôvo met democratic criteria because of its defense of the collective interest, a situation, they pointed out, which was not to be found in Italy, where corporative agencies had been made mere appendages of the state.[39] Francisco Campos repeatedly attacked the liberal democratic past, referring to the 1934 constitution as "monstrous" and unharmonic. "We must work to construct the spirit of our economy and national power," he first wrote in 1938, ". . . against the spirit of our inherent indolence."[40] A bridge from an earlier intellectual generation, Oliveira Vianna emphasized the need for collective action to create new structures and build the nation. There were two kinds of democracies, Vianna averred: the old liberal variety of England, France, Belgium, and the United States, and the "new social type" developed by Portugal, Italy and Germany, fitting for Brazil's inarticulateness.[41]

Racism, successfully used by Hitler as a device to mobilize the German nation behind the Nazi Party, was used by other fascists as well (e.g., Codreanu's Rumanian *Credo* of February, 1920), although Italian (and other Latin) fascists took it far less seriously.[42] Racism did not haunt the Estado Nôvo save for faint reminders of xenophobia and survivals of anti-Japanese and anti-Semitic attitudes among a small minority.

5. *Militarism.* Mussolini and Hitler dominated their own armed forces and used military activity as a basic element of foreign policy. Brazilian armed forces leaders exerted significant influence on Vargas' political decisions but they did not pursue expansionist ends. The advocacy by the Brazilian military during the 1930s of national economic planning and centralized authority cast it in a progressive, reformist role. The survival of tenente attitudes in the armed forces contributed to rising military disgust at inept and passive civilian politics. The Brazilian officer corps, recruited from the middle class, shared that group's opposition to the preeminence

of the oligarchy. In consequence it adopted largely domestic priorities, including national integration, administrative efficiency, and disinterested political participation.[43]

6. *Economic control.* The 1937 constitution included such explicitly corporatist provisions as its Article 138 (modeled after the 1927 Italian Labor Code), which organized labor on seven horizontally ascending levels but which offered no vertical machinery for redress of grievances, and Article 61a, which created a National Economic Council with powers to reorganize the economy on corporative lines. But save for its labor structure—designed in keeping with Vargas' earlier assertion of government control over labor organization—Estado Nôvo corporatism in practice more closely approximated the spirit of Franklin D. Roosevelt's National Recovery Administration than Mussolini's Italy of the 1920s and 1930s.

The enlargement of government responsibility between 1937 and 1945 did not significantly restructure the economic system. Brazilian planners did not desire the complete nationalization of the economy in spite of the Estado Nôvo constitution. The National Economic Council never functioned. Some members of the political elite sought more sweeping change, but the entrepreneurial sector took no aggressive stance; Vargas, influenced by Oswaldo Aranha, continued to look to the United States for aid, and attuned his policies accordingly.[44] His relationship with industrialists never approached Hitler's methodical efforts to protect independent firms in order to "liberate" creative industrial capital from loan capital and other restrictions.[45] Paternalism, although strained after 1943, continued to color Brazilian labor-management relations, unlike Spain, where Franco's industrial allies assumed aggressively reactionary stances after the Civil War.[46]

Vargas' government can be termed fascist only in so far as it adopted authoritarianism, antiliberalism, national planning, and systematic police repression, attributes present under fascism but also identifiable in such conservative authoritarian governments as Miklós Horthy's Hungarian regency, Pilsudski's Poland, and even Greece in the late 1960s and post-1964 Brazil. The Estado Nôvo, to borrow Ernst Nolte's category, stood on the periphery of fascism alongside Mustafa Kemal Pasha's "national defense dictatorship," Spain's Falange Española Tradicionalista, and Salazar's "artificial" civilian-led military government from which Vargas borrowed the name of his own administration after 1937.[47]

The Estado Nôvo must be considered on its own terms, as a logical consequence of such domestic trends during the 1930s as centralization and impatience with liberal democracy. Vargas' unwillingness to assume totalitarian powers testifies to his personality as well as to the absence of a serious challenge from the left after 1935. His ability to delegate unsavory assignments to others enabled him to remove himself from direct association with the police-state violence practiced selectively during the decade. Nonideological, he avoided permanent identification with either the radical left or the radical right. His carefully maintained diplomatic neutrality between 1938 and the attack on Pearl Harbor, despite strong domestic pressure to take sides, attested to this skill.

Perceiving the realities of the Brazilian system, he chose to preserve the traditional social outlook while he assumed sufficient power to smother the political machines of the state oligarchies and guarantee the supremacy of the armed forces, particularly the army. Vargas truly believed what he declared publicly on the evening of November 10, 1937: "[Up to now] there have been no appropriate organs by which the country could express its thoughts and wisdom."[48]

After 1937, Vargas' tacitly corporatist government played a modernizing role within a conservative framework. It spoke for the new urban middle class and for industrial sectors against the traditionally centrifugal interests of the pre-1930 rural political and economic elite. Vargas neither challenged the basic pattern of economic distribution nor permanently destroyed faith in representative democracy. Protest against the dictatorship appeared openly in early 1943 with the lengthy mineiro manifesto, signed by nearly one hundred public figures from Minas Gerais including Virgílio de Mello Franco and ex-President Artur Bernardes.[49] Blueprints for expanded police surveillance of private activity in local areas were abandoned.[50] Only near the end of the Estado Nôvo did Vargas, faced with rising worker demands, offer concessions to the labor sector by increasing real wages and initiating plans for a national Labor Party.[51] The threat by labor precipitated Vargas' unceremonious ouster by the military in late October, 1945.

CONCLUSION

The most telling characteristic of the transformation which Brazil underwent between 1930 and the establishment of the Estado Nôvo was the fact that the change came from above, administered through official channels, and was carefully planned. Those who viewed Vargas as a tool of his political and military advisers failed to understand the manipulative skill of the man who had preserved national unity, isolated and crushed his potential enemies, and presided over the Brazilian recovery in the face of economic dislocation, rising nationalism, and clashing aspirations. A product of the violent environment of Rio Grande do Sul, Vargas cultivated his image of blandness and taciturnity and thus belied his ability to act with swift bluntness, even when he was forced to turn against his close friends, such as Pedro Ernesto and Oswaldo Aranha, when that became expedient.

Vargas' masterful technique by which he gathered information from a variety of independent and often mutually hostile sources allowed him to play one interest group against another. By showing favor to pro-Integralist General Newton Cavalcanti and by affording Plínio Salgado reason to expect quick promotion into the government's inner circle after the Estado Nôvo coup, Vargas lulled the Integralists into false self-confidence while at the same time he used their presence to fan the winds of anticommunism (and thereby prepare the atmosphere for the *golpe*) and to spy on anti-Integralist officers inside the armed forces. Similarly, he dealt with each of his cabinet ministers independently, delegating complete authority to none of them. Police chief Felinto Müller reported exclusively to Vargas although in theory he was responsible to the Justice Ministry: the police kept the entire administration under surveillance, even the highest levels of the diplomatic corps. While Vargas refused to heed the warnings of many of his correspondents that both Müller and Francisco Campos enjoyed close ties with the Reich, he quietly ordered local officials in the south to suppress Nazi activities, and in late 1938 asked Sumner Welles to send an agent of the FBI to help organize a Brazilian secret service.[1] Vargas' broad private intelligence network (which included phone tapping and interception of civil and military correspondence by the police) utilized the services of his father, brothers, daughter, and personal friends, keeping him consistently informed on all matters ranging from local politics to would-be national conspiracies.

If not welcomed, the imposition of the Estado Nôvo was at least tolerated by virtually every element in Brazilian society. Business and industrial interests agreed in principle with expanded economic planning, the suspension of debt payments, and efforts to restrict foreign investment and reform banking and currency policies. Landowners did not object to the new government so long as it continued to aid agriculture and left the rural political structure intact, preserving planter hegemony at the local level.[2] The Ministry of War carefully dismantled the formerly independent state military units, placing them under federal command. Military leaders took their seats on the new National Security Council and, with the approval of the government, ordered large amounts of foreign arms, which included $55,000,000 worth of artillery from Krupp, naval vessels from Great Britain and Italy, infantry weapons from Czechoslovakia, and aircraft from the United States.[3] Oswaldo Aranha, sworn in as foreign minister in March, 1938, embarked in the following year for Washington to negotiate for military aid and to exchange credit in return for United States air bases in the northeast. In 1931, the share of the federal budget taken by the war and navy ministries totaled 19.4 per cent. By 1938 it had risen to 30.4 per cent.[4]

If the military provided a route for upward mobility for the middle classes following the Paraguayan War and the fall of the Empire, the enlargement of the bureaucracy under Vargas and the emergence of the political system into what Hélio Jaguaribe has called the Brazilian "cartorial state" assured the loyalty of the middle classes and offered nominal public jobs to *bacharéis,* coopting them in exchange for their acceptance of the cancellation of legislative democracy, which, at any rate, had threatened to restore the traditional oligarchy to power after 1934.[5]

The anger which had been provoked by the cancellation of the electoral campaign and the exile of Armando Salles and his closest supporters quickly subsided behind the campaign of patriotic unity elaborated by the new Estado Nôvo propaganda agencies. Dispatches to Washington from the United States Embassy in Rio de Janeiro frequently described existing political apathy, noting that even immediately following the alarming siege of the Catete Palace in May, 1938, the local press soon turned to news of Brazil's unexpected soccer victories over Poland and Czechoslovakia. Neither the intensification of censorship nor the continued use of repression by the police was publicly protested. Newspapers that would not accede to DIP management, or, as the war approached, that had received subsidies from Axis sources, quietly suspended publication.

The coming of the Estado Nôvo did not take place in an ideological vacuum. The admonitions of such critics as Paulo Prado, Oliveira Vianna, and Azevedo Amaral linked the anguished self-examination of earlier intellectual generations with the ideological assumptions of Francisco Campos, the author of the 1937 constitution. In defense of corporatism the new apologists for the Estado Nôvo stressed the necessity for national unity, ascribing to the state the injunction to prevent the monopoly of power by any single interest or group.[6]

Some forms of traditionalism not only survived but were renewed during the 1930s. The Brazilian Church recruited powerful allies, most notably during the Constituent Assembly debates in defense of the family. As a result, the 1934 constitution preserved the illegality of divorce but permitted religious instruction in the public schools and Church work in hospitals, prisons, and in the armed forces. For a time following the 1937 coup, relations between the Church and Rio de Janeiro cooled, a situation provoked (according to Felinto Müller in a private report to Vargas) by the unhappiness of Dom Helder Câmara and Cardinal Leme at the suppression of the Integralist movement. Relations were gradually restored through the aid of intermediaries.[7] Vargas soothed the Church in one area by decreeing a law in 1937 (rewritten and clarified in 1941) granting civil recognition to religious marriage ceremonies under certain conditions. Other efforts by the Church to exercise influence were limited by its relative weakness in numbers: in 1939 the clergy included only 4,700 priests, a ratio of about one priest per 10,000 inhabitants.[8]

Careful examination of Brazil's social welfare programs of the 1930s indicates their limited scope and impact. Child labor persisted in São Paulo until at least 1941. Government-sponsored unionism was never extended to agricultural workers; strikes, rural or urban, were suppressed with armed force. Although the Electoral Code of 1932 introduced the secret ballot and expanded the electorate to include women and persons over eighteen, its ultimate impact was, at best, delayed, since no national elections occurred between 1933 and 1945. But the urban working classes remained satisfied with their lot. The reasons for this docility include Vargas' intentionally cultivated image as the father-to-the-poor, industrial progress and the simultaneous growth of the internal market, and the limited aspirations of workingmen owing to their low level of political mobilization.

The number of those who could be identified as industrial workers doubled in the two decades after 1920, yet, in spite of the statistical increase, most industrial enterprises by 1940 still employed fewer than two dozen workers. Wages remained hopelessly low, and owners were reluctant to train their employees or to introduce new technological processes. The middle classes avoided skilled labor as beneath their dignity, taking refuge in the white-collar trades and the civil service (which on the state level remained dominated by the patronage relationships of traditional *coronelismo*).[9]

Even among the more progressive sectors of the industrial economy, Fernando Henrique Cardoso notes, the sociocultural limitations of the old precapitalist order prevailed. Paulista industrialists, he observes, were generally men "whose stable view of life represented a highly imperfect adjustment to a capitalist industrial order."[10] As a result, although 1930 ended the political primacy of the planter elite, industrialization carried with it the attitudes and prejudices of the environment from which it emerged. Agricultural producers responded favorably to Vargas and his efforts to aid them, yet the degradation and apathy of life on the rural *fazenda* remained. The chief impact of the federal system in the interior lay in advances in transportation and the curtailment of banditry. According to the census of 1940, nearly 1,500,000 Brazilians still lived on plantations owned by absentee landlords.

Industrial growth in the 1930s was buoyed by the pump-priming effect of the collapse of the coffee exporting sector, the resulting lack of hard currency, a growing domestic market, and successive currency devaluation, which had the effect of pricing foreign goods out of competition and allowing import substitution. Agricultural and industrial production rose by 50 per cent during the decade, while imports fell by 23 per cent. Although manufacturers disliked Vargas at the outset of his provisional government for his opposition to protection for so-called artificial industries and his creation of the Ministry of Labor, relations warmed markedly by 1934 as employers recognized that Vargas shared their interests. Government policy for the remainder of the decade aided manufacturing and catered to the demands of employers.

Vargas, whom officials of the United States Embassy in 1931 had dismissed as a pawn of the tenente Third of October Club, convincingly proved his political mettle with his handling of the São Paulo revolt. To Góes Monteiro, the paulista defeat assured the supremacy of the union and restored discipline and order in the armed forces.[11] In 1933 Vargas imposed his formula for class representation, guaranteeing him majority control of the Constituent Assembly. Although the ephemeral 1934 constitution represented a major victory for advocates of strong centralized government, the survival of legislative autonomy and the results of the state elections in 1934 and 1935 challenged the administration's congressional majority and threatened to restore the power of local interests antipathetic to the national administration. Aided by the naïveté of the left, Vargas swiftly asserted his personal supremacy behind the façade of the threat to national security thrown up after the ill-fated insurrections of November, 1935, which were probably triggered prematurely by government agents. Vargas proceeded methodically to suppress further political intransigence, aided by the nearly continuous states of siege during 1936 and 1937.

Despite rising nationalistic sentiment after 1930, Vargas, who seemed to prefer to remain out of the spotlight, provided little public ideological leadership before 1937. Rather, he fostered the impression that his government was run by his cabinet ministers and by advisers. In 1935 the communist-dominated left futilely challenged the Liberal Alliance's revolutionary role. On the right, the Integralists multiplied in influence between 1932 and 1937, but Vargas abruptly turned upon them as soon as he became certain of the loyalty of the armed forces.

Both the ANL and the Integralists reflected the anxiety for nationalistic change expressed in some segments of public opinion. Both movements displayed sensitivity to urban social ills, most successfully the AIB, which mobilized Integralist wives as *favela* social workers and teachers of literacy. Each movement employed strikingly similar methods of publicity and recruitment, although the popular front ANL lacked the Integralists' concern with paramilitary preparedness and their dependence upon ritual and discipline. Neither group achieved meaningful contact with the urban and rural poor although each saw its role in similar fashion: to challenge the status quo, awaken Brazilians to the realities of national life, and restructure society along revolutionary utopian lines.

The middle class rejected the ANL on several grounds, among them that group's positive identification with Vargas, its fear of the dormant masses below, and its general political apathy. ANL speakers achieved their greatest degree of success when they dealt with specific nonideological issues, such as the dismissal of workers from a factory, or the absence of public health facilities in working-class neighborhoods. But public opinion did not share the movement's visceral fear of fascism and seemed unmoved by cries against foreign imperialism and economic exploitation. The ANL, suppressed during its earliest stages of development, quickly disintegrated as a national movement, falling under the absolute control of the Communist Party, which led it to its revolutionary adventure.

The Integralists lingered longer and achieved broader support than the ANL but in the end did not fare significantly better. Salgado's fascist experiment, while consciously grounded in indigenous themes and domestic nationalism, never seriously penetrated the minds of the Green Shirt rank and file. Although Integralist allegiance was occasionally strong, the reputed influence of Integralism in influential circles deserted it after November, 1937. By 1939, much of the Integralists' patriotic emphasis had been borrowed by the Estado Nôvo's *brasilidade* campaign for patriotism, national unity, and cultural integration.

As the decade progressed, Vargas responded to the demands of nationalists in his midst. The 1934 constitution incorporated the provisional government's Water and Mining Code, and imposed guarantees for national control of coastal and maritime shipping and for the exclusion of undesirable immigrants. Nationalism served Vargas' efforts to assert national supremacy over state and regional obstructionism. The 1934 constitution removed many of the traditional sources of revenue from the states, principally the authority to tax exported goods; by undermining state domination of municipal affairs, it encouraged, in the process, the standardization and reform of public administrative practices. The President delegated strong authority to the Bank of Brazil and decreed federal regulation of monetary exchange. After 1937 the government turned to direct public investment and developmental nationalism, the former illustrated by the creation of such mixed public-private agencies as the Companhia do Vale do Rio Doce, and the latter by the wartime Volta Redonda steel complex.

Vargas' political use of nationalism and his goal of national unity were not unique to the Brazil of the 1930s, but occurred at the same time in several other Latin American nations, notably in neighboring Argentina. Opportunity for free intellectual and cultural expression declined sharply after 1935, when scores of persons considered enemies of the government were silenced or arrested for subversion. *Ex post facto* censorship of the theater, radio, and cinema dominated Brazilian cultural life between 1937 and 1945.

The uncompromising action of November, 1937, silenced political opposition, most of which had taken the form of legislative oratory from the *ad hoc* coalition which united the surviving voices of the Old Republic (Otávio Mangabeira, Artur Bernardes, Borges de Medeiros) with the small bloc of radical congressmen (Abguar Bastos, Abel Chermont, João Café Filho). But while authoritarian rule was imposed, the Estado Nôvo lacked either ideological unity or totalitarian perseverance. In a sense, it simply institutionalized Vargas' personal rule. Although many moderates fell from political influence in its wake, others remained publicly loyal, even Oswaldo Aranha, out of his personal ties with Vargas, his own ambitions, and his commitment to the cause of United States–Brazilian relations.

Vargas' ability to forge and maintain effective support from diverse elements within the civilian and military elite, yet at the same time cultivate and strengthen his popularity among the larger population, kept him in power during the difficult period between 1930 and 1945.

The government's public works policy and its program of federal relief to the northeastern area affected by drought, as Albert O. Hirschman has pointed out, illustrate its search for new areas of economic development as well as its attempt to repay past political debts.[12] Many of the socioeconomic goals of the Vargas era, another observer has noted, later became unchallenged national aspirations.[13] Construction of dams and public reservoirs quadrupled existing water storage capacity in the drought polygon; road building, employing refugees from stricken areas, accounted for three thousand kilometers of new highways in the northeast in the 1930s.

But drought victims continued to flee south, particularly to the new *favelas* of Rio de Janeiro and São Paulo and to the smaller cities of the center-south. Rising internal migration and continuing urbanization transformed the demographic face of the nation even before industrial output rose sharply in the early 1940s. Federal largess, however, generally favored established population centers. The government rarely faced the social needs of the most destitute.

The political history of the Vargas years through the end of the 1930s reveals carefully applied forces of restraint: elitism, paternalism, police repression, and government-imposed nationalism. As chief of state, Vargas skillfully dominated threats from the left, the right, and surviving spokesmen for the old pre-1930 order. He supervised the deliberate expansion of the social and geographic base of political influence and thereby set the stage for the events of postwar Brazil. He assumed dictatorial powers at a time when dictatorships controlled seventeen of the twenty-seven countries of Europe[14] and most Latin American states. But the impact of accelerated industrialization, military growth, and the consequences of urbanization transformed Brazil under Vargas and anticipated his removal in late 1945 in the face of a new threat to the political elite, this time from below.

APPENDIX A: LATIN AMERICAN ECHOES

Brazil's experience during the 1930s with nationalism and political unrest was by no means unique to it. Virtually every Latin American country struggled under the impact of rising nationalism, their depression-ravaged economies, and interference in political affairs by local armed forces. The year 1930 saw governments replaced in Argentina, Brazil, Bolivia, Peru, and the Dominican Republic. The peaceful election of a civilian president in Colombia in 1931 seemed to be the exception, not the rule. Where it existed, stability more often arose from the presence of United States troops (Nicaragua and Haiti), dictatorship (Cuba and Venezuela), or one-party control (Mexico). In 1931 the Ibañez government in Chile was overthrown; governments fell also in Panama, Guatemala, Ecuador, and El Salvador. Between 1931 and 1940 fourteen different presidents held office in Ecuador. A new generation of Latin American strongmen assumed power during the 1930s: Fulgencio Batista in Cuba, Anastacio Somoza in Nicaragua, Rafael Trujillo in the Dominican Republic, the leaders of the United States-trained black *Garde* in Haiti, and Jorge Ubico in Guatemala. Military nationalists dominated Paraguay, leading that country into its wasteful and tragic Chaco War with Bolivia between 1932 and 1935.

Hemispheric contemporaries of the Brazilian Integralists included the anti-Semitic Mexican Gold Shirts, local Nazi groups in Argentina, Bolivia, Chile, Uruguay, and elsewhere, and the Silver Shirts and the German-American Bund in the United States. Activity on the left flourished also. Under the direction of the Comintern's South American and Caribbean Bureau in Montevideo, communists from Mexico to Argentina worked to create successful antifascist popular fronts. Activity on the left ranged from the anticlerical Red Shirts of Tomás Garrido Canabal in Mexico to the Chilean Popular Front (Frente Popular), which, like the Brazilian PCB, was guided by a diverse cadre of communists including Peruvian Eudocio Ravines, Marcucci, the director of Italy's Communist Youth, and a Russian, Kazanov, whose revolutionary pseudonym was "Casanova." In Peru, the reformist Popular Revolutionary American Alliance (APRA) remained on the verge of political power for more than a generation: under Haya de la Torre in the 1930s and 1940s its nationalistic programs won the praise of foreign communists and fascists alike, both identifying themselves with the *Aprista* program.[1]

Small communist parties emerged in the aftermath of the Russian Revolution in virtually every Latin American country, with the strongest movements arising in areas affected by early forms of industrialization, urban concentrations of European immigrants, or both. The Profitern's Latin American Syndical Confederation oversaw communist labor union activity: the PCB's Brazilian General Workers' Federation (CGTB) joined it when the CGTB was founded in Rio de Janeiro in 1929.[2] In all cases, the parties remained insignificant, reflecting the experience of the PCB in Brazil, although they may have contributed in some small measure to the beginnings of public social consciousness visible after World War I. The first recorded attempt by a Latin American communist party at armed revolt came in 1932 in El Salvador, where an insurrection of impoverished peasants led by party agents won brief control in the name of a military-peasant national revolution, at the expense of as many as twenty-five thousand lives and brutal repression of the left in every country in Central America.[3]

Argentina, whose Communist Party was headed by Victor Codovilla— alleged!ʏ the Comintern's most trusted lieutenant in Latin America, although in the end, like Prestes, a failure as a revolutionist—served as host for the first Latin American Communist Party Congress in June, 1929, a fifteen-day meeting in Buenos Aires at which such themes as labor union organization, racism, and anti-imperialism were discussed.[4] Kept under close surveillance by the post-1930 right-leaning governments which followed the successful Uriburu coup against the Radical government backed by the middle class, the Argentine Communist Party concentrated its efforts on antifascist propaganda clandestinely produced. In 1935 and 1936 it attempted to form an antifascist front with the Socialist and Progressive Democratic parties, but it was doomed by the refusal of the Radicals to join.[5]

Fascist influence in Argentina grew steadily under Presidents Justo and Castillo, although the failure of individual right-wing groups to unite weakened their over-all impact. The first major profascist group was Juan P. Ramos' ADUNA Legion, anticommunist and procorporatist, which reached its peak of 15,000 members in 1933 but declined subsequently.

Eight profascist groups formed the Argentine Guard in late 1933 under Leopoldo Lugones; he, too, proved unable to lead effectively, and he committed suicide in 1938. Most successful was the Alliance of Nationalist Youth, which inaugurated right-wing May First rallies and which grew in prominence during the early war years under an antiliberal, corporatist, anti-Semitic, and militant program. But the Nationalists could not successfully attack the conservative regimes of the oligarchy (who were too close to them ideologically) and still combat their mortal enemies, the Communists and Socialists on the left: their thunder was stolen by the harsh governments which dominated Argentina from 1930 to 1943 and after.[6] Argentine officials, for example, applauded the Brazilian Estado Nôvo in 1937 in spite of their government's frequently bitter rivalry with Brazil, and the two countries promulgated an agreement by which they would exchange police officials and expedite arrangements for the bilateral extradition of political prisoners.

Uruguay, generally hospitable to Brazilian exiles from the earliest revolts and factional disputes within Rio Grande do Sul, was directly affected by the events of November, 1935, when, sensitive to the fact that the Comintern had used Montevideo as the base for its South American activities, the Terra government accused the local Soviet legation of having helped finance the Brazilian revolutionary movement; as a result, diplomatic relations between Uruguay and the Soviet Union were severed in December, 1935, and the Iuyamtorg Corporation was liquidated.[7]

The arrival of Eudocio Ravines in Chile in 1935 inaugurated the Communist Party's efforts to implement the new Comintern popular front strategy. It declared its opposition both to Arturo Allesandri's coalition government, the small Nazi Party (Partido Nacional Socialista) headed by González von Marées, and the so-called Falange de Portales, a paramilitary organization named for the nineteenth-century dictator.[8] In December, 1935, partially to show sympathy for the unsuccessful Brazilian revolt, it distributed plans for a nationwide general strike as a possible prelude to a movement to overthrow the government, but word leaked out and the plot evaporated. After 1936 the party dedicated itself to the electoral work of the socialist- and communist-backed popular front, which finally won at the polls in 1938. Ironically, popular outrage at the murder by police of Nazi youths who had unsuccessfully attempted an antigovernment *putsch* in September, 1938, contributed to the opposition victory. The communists refused to participate in the elected government, preferring to stand outside and reserve the right of free criticism.[9]

In Paraguay, the Communist Party fared badly under the dictatorial regimes during the period of the Chaco War (1932-36). In Bolivia, isolation precluded contact of the tiny Communist Party with Moscow, and it remained nearly inoperative until the late 1940s. In some ways, the government of Colonel Germán Busch paralleled the Vargas administration, with the Bolivian constitution of 1938 guaranteeing the rights of labor and asserting government responsibility in the area of social welfare.[10] Nonetheless, fascist influence persisted in the armed forces through the period of "military socialism."

The Venezuelan Communist Party was formally established in early 1931, but it never exerted significant influence, particularly before the death of the repressive dictator Juan Vicente Gómez in December, 1935, after twenty-six years as head of state. Interestingly, under Gómez, Venezuela was the only Latin American country during the early years of the depression to show no foreign debt and to maintain a surplus in its treasury, probably a consequence of the nation's flourishing petroleum industry.[11] In 1937 the new military dictator, Eleazar López Contreras, cracked down on his opponents and expelled nearly fifty of them for alleged communist sympathies. In Colombia, liberal democracy survived after peaceful elections in 1930. But in Peru the early communists broke with Haya de la Torre's APRA movement in 1928 and, led by the brilliant young Marxist theorist José Carlos Mariátegui, formed the Peruvian Socialist Party, which remained independent of the Comintern. The APRA reflected the sensitivity of the Peruvian left to the latifundia problem, Indian misery, and the hemispheric role of the United States and other foreign capitalist powers. It attacked Peru's subservient economic role as supplier of raw agricultural products; like the Mexican Partido Nacional Revolucionário (PNR) it represented domestically rooted nationalism, only minimally based upon foreign models. Following a probable APRA electoral victory in 1931, the party was suppressed; from 1933 to 1939 a strongman, Marshal Oscar Benavides, ruled Peru.

The Cuban Communist Party's hostility to the noncommunist rebels who secured power in mid-1933 and who constituted the opposition to the Batista government after early 1934 led to an odd alliance between the communists and Batista, resulting in the award of legal status to the party in September, 1938, under Secretary-General Blás Roca and its domination of Cuban organized labor through the war years.[12]

In Mexico, the Communist Party organized a Worker's and Peasant's Bloc in 1929, along the same lines as its sister bloc sponsored by the PCB. Suppressed by Portes Gil, the party reemerged publicly in later 1935 when it proposed the formation of an antifascist alliance with Lázaro Cárdenas, wooing the President by calling the 1910-20 Mexican Revolution the fore-runner of the national liberation spirit; in 1937 it endorsed the reformist program of the federal administration.[13] Mexican fascism took the form of the Acción Revolucionaria Mexicana, headed by a former Pancho Villa general, Nicolás Rodríguez. The movement, whose members wore gold shirts, attacked Cárdenas, the small Mexican Jewish colony, and left-looking government reforms. Like the Brazilian Integralists, the *Dorados* organized themselves into paramilitary regiments and expended much of their energy marching. Clashes between Dorados and Mexican Communists occurred during 1935; in November a band of Communists using automobiles engaged a reported five thousand Dorados on horseback. Among the casualties was the Dorados' General Rodríguez. Other Mexican fascist movements included the Associación Española, the Anti-Communista y Anti-Judia, founded in 1937, and the Falange Español Tradicionalista, led by pro-Franco Spanish residents in Mexico.[14]

The most powerful antirevolutionary group in Mexico in the prewar period was the Unión Nacional Sinarquista, established in 1937; by 1940 Sinarquismo, a nationalistic, prosyletizing movement seeking to restore Catholicism, to divide the land among the peasants, and to expel all foreign ideas, required its adherents to travel among the impoverished poor, on foot, as humble missionaries of the faith. Although the movement did not copy a European fascist form, like Integralism its leadership was drawn from the well-educated middle class and it linked nationalism with anti-liberalism, anti-Semitism, the Catholic religion, and the mystical Spanish heritage.[15]

The volatile and anticlerical Red Shirt movement was created by Tomás Garrido Canabal in 1932 as the militant arm of his dictatorship in the state of Tabasco. All men between the ages of fifteen and thirty were legally required to serve, although youths of eighteen and nineteen dominated its ranks. Garrido's bizarre puritanism took the form of a prohibition on liquor, a ban on cosmetics and short hair for women, and a law, enforced by police patrols, that all children under eight must be in bed before eight in the evening. Like the Brazilian Integralists, the Red Shirts stressed morality and discipline. The group was sustained by obligatory contributions from private citizens, and followed Garrido to Mexico City when he was named agriculture minister at the end of 1934. Obsessively anticlerical, the Red Shirts rooted out all traces of Catholic survivals in Tabasco. Claiming thirty thousand adherents, the Red Shirts clashed frequently with Dorado partisans. Cárdenas maintained an uneasy neutrality, although he was publicly accused of favoring the left, just as critics of Vargas assailed his tacit approval of Integralist activities prior to 1938. Like Vargas, the Mexican President managed to assert his own authority by sending Garrido back to Tabasco in his red and black airplane, and arresting Gold Shirt chieftain Rodríguez in 1936 for alleged labor union agitation.[16] Relations with the Communist Party were eased as Victorio Lombardo Toledano, acceptable to the communists, rose to the leadership of the Mexican Labor Federation.

Throughout Latin America, ideologically inspired movements on the far left or right ultimately secured political power during the 1930s. Of those that did, none managed to modify substantially the structure of social and economic organization in their respective countries. The period between World Wars I and II saw the emergence of Latin American nationalism and, in many cases, the first active challenges to traditional life. During this time, some national administrations experimented with political and social welfare reform; others struggled to preserve liberal democratic institutions. Change did occur, in some cases dramatically: in 1934, for example, Brazil, Chile, and Uruguay all granted women the right to vote for the first time.

But liberal fortunes declined during the period between 1930 and the conclusion of World War II. Throughout Latin America persons unsympathetic to the new order found themselves caught in its web and were subject to persecution. The international depression staggered the export economies of the Latin American republics and strengthened nationalists in general and enemies of democracy in particular. Events reflected the frustation of the times, as the world marched to war and beyond.

APPENDIX B

POPULATION OF BRAZIL: ESTIMATED, 1935-1936

State	Population[a]	Capital	Population[b]
Alagôas	1,205,204	Maceió	133,858
Amazonas	438,691	Manaus	90,317
Bahia	4,203,033	Salvador	369,692
Ceará	1,650,991	Fortaleza	146,852
Federal District	1,711,466	Rio de Janeiro	1,756,080
Espírito Santo	691,169	Vitória	36,369
Goiás	756,030	Goiás	30,948
Maranhão	1,168,176	São Luís	71,583
Mato Grosso	364,070	Cuiabá	47,819
Minas Gerais	7,583,673	Belo Horizonte	180,241
Pará	1,499,213	Belém	298,340
Paraíba	1,367,172	João Pessoa	104,936
Paraná	1,014,077	Curitiba	119,635
Pernambuco	2,949,634	Recife	491,078
Piauí	831,737	Teresina	61,413
Rio de Janeiro	2,038,943	Niterói	128,333
Rio Grande do Norte	764,070	Natal	52,582
Rio Grande do Sul	3,052,009	Pôrto Alegre	336,504
Santa Catarina	986,855	Florianópolis	50,829
São Paulo	6,634,389	São Paulo	1,167,862
Sergipe	551,887	Aracajú	60,203
Territory of Acre	115,451	Rio Branco	29,220
Fernando de Noronha	n.a.		n.a.
Brazil	41,560,147		

Source: Brazil, Ministry of Foreign Affairs, Commercial Service, *Brazil: 1937* (Rio, 1937), pp. 34-35.

[a] Estimated, December 31, 1935.

[b] Estimated, December 31, 1936.

n.a. = not available.

APPENDIX C

COMPARATIVE ASPECTS OF AIB AND ANL PROGRAMS

	AIB	ANL
Civil liberties	individual dignity protected by state; rapid justice	complete individual liberties; rapid justice
Economic policy	federal regulation of economy; control of essential production; nationalization of exploitative foreign-owned firms	expropriation of exploitative foreign-owned firms; cancellation of debts to imperialist interests
Education	free on all levels; moral and civic instruction	free on all levels; aid to university students
Property rights	respect for private property	protection of small and medium-sized landholdings; expropriation of unproductive and feudally held land for redistribution to poor
Rights of labor	adequate wages according to need; child labor regulation; labor organization within occupational structure	right to organize; minimum wages; 8-hour day; child labor regulation; social security and pensions; equal pay for equal work
Social philosophy	solidarity based upon God, family, and country	solidarity for all classes
Taxation	gradual elimination of oppressive taxes; no internal barriers to economic exchange	progressive taxation; taxation of unused land and property
Welfare goals	free public health care; aid to *favela* dwellers	free public health care; aid to the poor
Dissimilarities:	Church-state relations; concept of the state; concept of popular representation; relationship of individual to the society; class analysis	

Source: Based upon Abguar Bastos, *Prestes e a revolução social* (Rio, 1946); Gustavo Barroso, *O que o Integralista deve saber*, 3d ed. (Rio, 1935).

APPENDIX D

DOLLAR EQUIVALENTS OF BRAZILIAN CURRENCY, 1920-1944
(YEARLY AVERAGE RATE)

Year	Contos (1:000$000)	Dollars	Milréis (1$000)	Dollars
1920	1	225.00	1	0.225
1921		131.00		0.131
1922		129.00		0.129
1923		102.00		0.102
1924		109.00		0.109
1925		122.00		0.122
1926		144.00		0.144
1927		118.00		0.118
1928		119.00		0.119
1929		118.00		0.118
1930		107.00		0.107
1931		70.00		0.070
1932		71.00		0.071
1933 (official rate begins)		79.00		0.079
1934		84.00		0.084
1935		82.00		0.082
1936		85.00		0.085
1937 (free rate)		61.00		0.061
1938		58.00		0.058
1939 (free rate)		52.00		0.052
1940 (free rate)		50.00		0.050
1941 (free rate)		50.00		0.050
1942 (free rate)[a]			Cruzeiro	0.051
1943 (free rate)			Cruzeiro	0.051
1944 (free rate)			Cruzeiro	0.051

Source: United States Department of Commerce, Bureau of Foreign and Domestic Commerce, *Statistical Abstract of the United States*, cited in John D. Wirth, "Brazilian Economic Nationalism: Trade and Steel under Vargas" (Ph.D. dissertation, Stanford University, 1966), p. 173.

[a] On November 1, 1942, the milréis was replaced by the cruzeiro, one milréis (1$000) being equivalent to one cruzeiro ($1.00). From 1942 to 1967, one thousand cruzeiros equaled one conto. New cruzeiros (NC$1.00) were adopted in 1967, the value of 1000 cruzeiros.

NOTES

Introduction

1. João Cruz Costa, "Nationalism and the Evolution of Brazilian Thought in the Twentieth Century," mimeographed (Mexico City, 1962), p. 9, in Arthur P. Whitaker and David C. Jordan, *Nationalism in Contemporary Latin America* (New York, 1966), p. 79. For the dynamics of the 1930 revolutionary movement and the conditions leading to it, see Virgínio Santa Rosa, *O sentido do tenentismo* (Rio de Janeiro [hereafter cited as Rio], 1933); Virgílio de Mello Franco, *Outubro, 1930*, 2d ed. (Rio, 1931); John D. Wirth, *"Tenentismo* in the Brazilian Revolution of 1930," *Hispanic American Historical Review* [hereafter cited as *HAHR*], XLIV, No. 2 (May, 1964), 161-79; Nelson Werneck Sodré, *História da burguesia brasileira*, 2d ed. (Rio, 1967); and other sources indicated in such works as John W. F. Dulles, *Vargas of Brazil* (Austin, 1967).
2. The *panelinha* is analyzed by Anthony Leeds in his "Brazilian Careers and Social Structure: An Evolutionary Model and Case History," *American Anthropologist*, LXVI, No. 6 (Dec., 1964), 1321-47.
3. See Joseph Leroy Love, Jr., "Rio Grande do Sul as a Source of Potential Instability in Brazil's Old Republic, 1909-1932" (Ph.D. dissertation, Columbia University, 1967), *passim*. The term *paulista* refers to an inhabitant of the state of São Paulo; other such examples are *mineiro* (Minas Gerais), *gaúcho* (Rio Grande do Sul), *fluminense* (the state of Rio de Janeiro,), *carioca* (Rio de Janeiro, the Federal District), and *potyguar* (Rio Grande do Norte).
4. Courtesy of Neil Macauley. The most detailed printed treatment of the Prestes Column to date is Hélio Silva's *1926: A grande marcha* (Rio, 1966). See also João Cabanas, *A coluna da morte* (Rio, n.d.); João Alberto Lins de Barros, *Memórias de um revolucionário* (Rio, 1953); Nelson Werneck Sodré, *História militar do Brasil* (Rio, 1965); Nelson Tabajara de Oliveira, *1924: A revolução de Isidoro* (São Paulo, 1956); Italo Landucci, *Cenas e episódios da Coluna Prestes e da revolução de 1924* (São Paulo, 1952); and the classic Lourenço Moreira Lima, *A coluna Prestes (marchas e combates)*, 2d ed. (São Paulo, 1945).
5. Love, "Rio Grande do Sul," pp. 264-65.
6. Dulles, *Vargas of Brazil*, pp. 56-57. For the 1930 election and its consequences see Franco, *Outubro, 1930*; Barbosa Lima Sobrinho, *A verdade sôbre a revolução de outubro* (São Paulo, 1933); Rubens do Amaral, *A campanha liberal* (São Paulo, 1930); and Hélio Silva, *1930: A Revolução traída* (Rio, 1966). Ricardo J. Montalvo, *Getúlio Vargas y la unidad brasileña* (Buenos Aires, 1939), describes Vargas'

platform. See also Jordan M. Young, *The Brazilian Revolution of 1930 and the Aftermath* (New Brunswick, 1967), especially ch. III.

7. Love, "Rio Grande do Sul," pp. 245-46.

8. Thomas E. Skidmore, *Politics in Brazil, 1930-1964: An Experiment in Democracy* (New York, 1967), pp. 12-19; Love, "Rio Grande do Sul," pp. 262-76.

9. See Edgard Carone, "Coleção Azul: Crítica pequeno-burguêsa à crise brasileira depois de 1930," *Revista Brasileira de Estudos Políticos,* XXV-XXVI (July, 1968-Jan., 1969), 249-51. See also Hélio Silva, *1931: Os tenentes no poder* (Rio, 1966), pp. 74-77. Miguel Costa's Revolutionary Legion is discussed in Dulles, *Vargas of Brazil;* Paulo Nogueira Filho, *Idéias e lutas de um burguês progressista: A guerra cívica, 1932,* Vol. I (Rio, 1965); and Paulo Duarte, *Que é que há?* (São Paulo, 1931).

10. See Charles A. Gauld, *The Last Titan: Percival Farquar, American Entrepreneur in Latin America* (Stanford, 1964).

11. U.S. Embassy, Rio de Janeiro, report to Washington, March 11, 1932, cited in Dulles, *Vargas of Brazil,* pp. 96-97.

12. See Stanley J. Stein, *The Brazilian Cotton Manufacture: Textile Enterprise in an Underdeveloped Area, 1850-1950* (Cambridge, Mass., 1957), ch. X; Sodré, *História da burguesia brasileira,* pp. 266 ff.; Victor Nunes Leal, *Coronelismo, enxada e voto: O município e o regime representativo no Brasil,* p. 187, cited in Stein, *Brazilian Cotton Manufacture,* p. 135; Warren Dean, "The Planter as Entrepreneur: The Case of São Paulo," *HAHR,* XLVI, No. 2 (May, 1966), 138-52.

13. Love, "Rio Grande do Sul," pp. 282-85; Dulles, *Vargas of Brazil,* pp. 97-103.

14. Skidmore, *Politics in Brazil,* p. 17, São Paulo's lower classes did not participate spontaneously in the revolt, a middle-class affair. See Dulles, *Vargas of Brazil,* pp. 37-116; Hélio Silva, *1932: A guerra paulista* (Rio, 1967); Glauco Carneiro, *História das revoluções brasileiras,* II (Rio, 1965), 396-413; and memoir accounts by João Alberto Lins de Barros, *Memórias de um revolucionário,* 2d ed. (Rio, 1954); Nogueira Filho, *Idéias e lutas,* Vols. I, II (Rio, 1965-66); Leoncio Basbaum, *História sincera da República,* Vol. III (São Paulo, 1962); Aureliano Leite, "Causas e objetivos da Revolução de 1932," *Revista de História,* XXV, No. 51 (July-Sept., 1962), 139-66. Peter Flynn is preparing an important study of the São Paulo rebellion.

15. Love, "Rio Grande do Sul," pp. 294-95.

16. Opening address to Constituent Assembly, Getúlio Vargas, Nov. 15, 1933, in *A nova política do Brasil,* III (Rio, 1938), 15-158. See Hélio Silva, *1934: A constituinte* (Rio, 1969); Affonso Arinos de Mello Franco, *Curso de direito constitucional brasileiro,* II (Rio, 1960), 186-201; Karl Loewenstein, *Brazil under Vargas* (New York, 1942), pp. 21-25; Dulles, *Vargas of Brazil,* pp. 119-37; Araujo Castro, *A nova constituição brasileira* (São Paulo, 1936); Whitaker and Jordan, *Nationalism,* p. 81; Castro Nunes, in *Revista Forense,* LXXII (1938), 629-30, an unfavorable account, cited in Pedro Luis, *Militarismo e República (crítica e história)* (São Paulo, n.d.), p. 146; Hamilton Leal, *História das instituições políticas do Brasil* (Rio, 1962), pp. 469-505; Pedro Calmon, *Curso de direito constitucional brasileiro* (Rio, 1937). The program and tactics of the São Paulo

delegation are described in *A ação da bancada paulista por São Paulo unido na Assembléia Constituinte* (São Paulo, 1935). Vargas' hostility to the work of the *constituinte* is cited in Alzira Vargas do Amaral Peixoto, *Getúlio Vargas, meu pai* (Pôrto Alegre, 1960), pp. 153-54, and Paul Frischauer, *Presidente Vargas: Biografia* (São Paulo, 1943), pp. 313-15.

17. See *A Pátria* (Rio), Aug. 11, 1934, p. 1; Aug. 21, 1934, p. 1.

18. George Wythe *et al., Brazil: An Expanding Economy* (New York, 1949), p. 69; Sodré, *História da burguesia brasileira*, p. 285; Caio Prado, Jr., *História econômica do Brasil*, 9th ed. (São Paulo, 1965), p. 297.

19. Celso Furtado, *The Economic Growth of Brazil* (Berkeley, 1963), p. 212. Vargas' coffee program was financed by a fixed tax on each bag exported, first ten shillings, later, in 1937, fifteen. L. C. Bresser Pereira, *Desenvolvimento e crise no Brasil entre 1930 e 1967* (Rio, 1968); Skidmore, *Politics in Brazil*, p. 46. The Furtado thesis, it should be noted, is currently undergoing careful scrutiny by economists, including Nathaniel Leff of Columbia University and Carlos Manoel Paláez. See the latter's "A balança comercial, a grande depressão e a industrialização brasileira," *Revista Brasileira de Economia*, March, 1968.

20. See Stein, *Brazilian Cotton Manufacture*, p. 140; Donald W. Giffen, "The Normal Years: Brazilian-American Relations, 1930-1939" (Ph.D. dissertation, Vanderbilt University, 1962), pp. 68-71.

21. A description of mid-1930 politics in a rural state (Rio Grande do Norte) appears in ch. 2. See David H. P. Maybury-Lewis, "Growth and Change in Brazil since 1930: An Anthropological View," in Raymond S. Sayers, ed., *Portugal and Brazil in Transition* (Minneapolis, 1968), pp. 168-69.

22. In terms of total months served in office, the figures are: Rio Grande do Sul (216), Minas Gerais, (151), São Paulo (85), Federal District (83), Pernambuco (52), Paraíba (44), Bahia (40), Alagôas (35), Mato Grosso (27), Rio de Janeiro (25), and Ceará (20). In the Old Republic, Minas Gerais dominated, followed by São Paulo, Rio Grande do Sul, Bahia, Santa Catarina, Pernambuco, Rio Grande do Norte, Pará, and Piauí. See Love, "Rio Grande do Sul," Table 1.2, p. 22.

23. *Coronelismo* is best described in Nunes Leal, *Coronelismo, enxada e voto*. See note 9, p. 232 below.

24. Hélio Jaguaribe, "The Dynamics of Brazilian Nationalism," in Claudio Veliz, ed., *Obstacles to Change in Latin America* (New York, 1965), p. 170.

25. Lawrence S. Graham, *Civil Service Reform in Brazil* (Austin, 1968), p. 27.

Chapter 1. The Social and Ideological Setting

1. Brazil, Ministry of Foreign Affairs, Commercial Service, *Brazil: 1937* (Rio, 1938), pp. 34-35. See also Appendix B above. Agnes Waddell offers a physical description in "The Revolution in Brazil," *Foreign Policy Association Information Service*, VI, No. 26 (New York, 1931), 489 ff.

2. Horace B. Davis, "Brazil's Political and Economic Problems," *Foreign Policy Reports,* XI, No. 1 (New York, March 13, 1935), 2-3; Serviço Nacional de

Recenseamento, "População presente no Brasil de 15 anos e mais, segundo a instrução, 1920-1940," courtesy of Centro Latinamericano de Pesquisas em Ciências Sociais, Rio de Janeiro.

3. The 1940 census classified 22.2 per cent as urban and 9.0 per cent as suburban. Statistics courtesy of Instituto Brasileiro de Geografia e Estatística (IBGE), Conselho Nacional de Estatística, Serviço de documentação e informação.

4. Rural Brazil is treated in a social context by Josué de Castro in *A alimentação brasileira à luz da geografia humana* (Pôrto Alegre, 1937), and in his *Geografia da fome*, 9th ed. (São Paulo, 1965). See also Cleto Seabra Velloso, "A alimentação do povo brasileiro," *Boletim do Ministério do Trabalho, Indústria e Commércio* (April, 1937), pp. 578-90; Hernani de Carvalho, *Sociologia de vida rural brasileira* (Rio, 1951).

5. Joseph L. Love, Jr., "Rio Grande do Sul as a Source of Potential Instability in Brazil's Old Republic, 1909-1932" (Ph.D. dissertation, Columbia University, 1967), pp. 10-12.

6. Robert J. Havighurst and J. Roberto Moreira, *Society and Education in Brazil* (Pittsburgh, 1965), p. 92.

7. See Florestan Fernandes, "Pattern and Rate of Development in Latin America," in Egbert De Vries and José M. Echevarría, eds., *Social Aspects of Economic Development in Latin America*, II (Paris, 1963), 196-97; Jacques Lambert, "Requirements for Rapid Economic and Social Development: The View of the Historian and Sociologist," *ibid.*, p. 64; Bertram Hutchinson, "A origem socio-econômica dos estudantes universitários," in B. Hutchinson, ed., *Mobilidade e trabalho* (Rio, 1960), p. 145, cited in Seymour Martin Lipset and Aldo Solari, eds., *Elites in Latin America* (New York, 1967), pp. 25-26.

8. Davis, "Brazil's Political and Economic Problems," p. 4. This was confirmed by the Niemeyer Report (*Report Submitted to the Brazilian Government by Sir Otto Niemeyer, K.C.S., G.B.E.* [London, July 4, 1931]), cited in Davis. The Brazilian elite paid neither inheritance nor income taxes. See also Emilio Willems, "Immigrants and Their Assimilation in Brazil," in T. Lynn Smith and Alexander Marchant, eds., *Brazil: Portrait of Half a Continent* (New York, 1951), esp. p. 224.

9. See Thales de Azevedo, *Social Change in Brazil* (Gainesville, 1963), p. 7.

10. Compiled from *O Globo* (Rio), 1918-65.

11. *A Offensiva* (Rio), Oct. 5, 1935, p. 4; see *O Malho* (Rio), April 4, 1935; *O Cruzeiro* (Rio), Dec. 28, 1935.

12. See *Jornal de Polícia* (Rio), April, 1935, p. 1.

13. See João Camilo de Oliveira Tôrres, *Estratificação social no Brasil* (São Paulo, 1965), pp. 215-22. Tôrres bases his study largely on the work of an American sociologist, Donald Pierson, who worked in Bahia in the early 1930s. See Pierson's *Negroes in Brazil: A Study in Race Contact at Bahia* (Chicago, 1942).

14. Oswaldo Aranha to Eugênio Gudim Filho, Washington, July 23, 1935, Oswaldo Aranha papers, Rio de Janeiro; hereafter cited as OA.

15. Commander Rivera Fuentes, air aide of Chile, letter to subsecretary of aviation, Santiago, from Rio de Janeiro, mid-1934, OA. The letter warned against the use of the public mails "because the pigs censor [them]."

16. Getúlio Vargas to Oswaldo Aranha, Oct. 18, 1934; Aranha to Vargas, March 6, 1935, Sept. 21, 1937; OA and Getúlio Vargas papers, hereafter cited as GV.

17. Elias Lipiner, *A nova imigração judáica no Brasil* (Rio, 1962), p. 114. See Robert M. Levine, "Brazil's Jews During the Vargas Era and After," *Luso-Brazilian Review*, V, No. 1 (Summer, 1968), 45-58.

18. See João Alberto Lins de Barros to Luis Carlos Prestes, Rio, June 8, 1935, GV; Oswaldo Aranha to Getúlio Vargas, Washington, May 19, 1937, GV; Aranha to Vargas, Washington, Dec. 7, 1939, OA.

19. Affonso Arinos de Mello Franco, *Preparação ao nacionalismo* (Rio, 1934), p. 42.

20. Sociedade Nacional de Agricultura, *Immigração: Inquérito promovido pela Sociedade Nacional de Agricultura* (Rio, 1926). On Japanese immigration, see Waldyr Niemeyer, *O japonez no Brasil*, 2d ed. (Rio, 1932); Areobaldo E. de Oliveira Lima, *A imigração japoneza para O Estado da Parahyba do Norte* (São Paulo, 1936); Miguel Couto, *Selecção social* (Rio, 1930); *idem, Para o futuro da pátria evitemos a niponização do Brasil* (Rio, 1946); Bruno Lobo, *De japonez a brasileiro* (Rio, 1932). See also the extensive Constituent Assembly debates; Brasil, Assembléia Constituinte, *Annais*, Vols. I-XXVI (Rio, 1934-36). The best sociological analyses are Hiroshi Saito, *O japonês no Brasil* (São Paulo, 1961), and Yukio Fujii and T. Lynn Smith, *The Acculturation of the Japanese Immigrants in Brazil* (Gainesville, 1959).

21. Alberto Guerreiro Ramos, *A crise do poder no Brasil* (Rio, 1961), pp. 152-77. The intellectual history of the Old Republic is reviewed in Thomas E. Skidmore's perceptive "Brazil's Search for Identity in the Old Republic," in Raymond S. Sayers, ed., *Portugal and Brazil in Transition* (Minneapolis, 1968), pp. 127-41.

22. Hélio Jaguaribe, "The Dynamics of Brazilian Nationalism," in Claudio Veliz, ed., *Obstacles to Change in Latin America* (New York, 1965), pp. 162-64.

23. Affonso Arinos de Mello Franco, *Conceito da civilização brasileira* (São Paulo, 1936), pp. 135-43, 159-62, 234-35. See also Oswaldo Aranha to General Pedro Góes Monteiro, Washington, March 9, 1935, OA, a letter in which like feelings are expressed, if less explicitly.

24. See Euclides da Cunha, *Os sertões*, 2d ed. (Rio, 1903); Francisco José Oliveira Vianna, *Populações meridionais do Brasil*, Vol. I: *Populações do centro-sul* (São Paulo, 1920); *idem, Pequenos estudos de psicologia social* (São Paulo, 1921).

25. Martins de Almeida, *Brasil errado* (Rio, 1932), pp. 127-30, 170. See Edgard Carone, "Coleção Azul: Crítica pequeno-burguêsa à crise brasileira depois de 1930," *Revista Brasileira de Estudos Políticos*, XXV-XXVI (July, 1968–Jan., 1969), 249-95. The series included *Brasil errado*, Affonso Arinos de Mello Franco's *Introdução à realidade brasileira*, Virgínio Santa Rosa's *O sentido do tenentismo*, Alcindo Sodré's *A gênese da desordem*, and Plínio Salgado's *Psicologia da revolução* (all but Almeida's published in Rio in 1933).

26. Mello Franco, *Introdução à realidade*, n.p., discussed in Carone, "Coleção Azul," pp. 260-69.

27. Santa Rosa, *O sentido do tenentismo*, p. 42, cited in Ramos, *A crise do poder*, p. 173.

28. Azevedo Amaral, *A aventura política do Brasil* (Rio, 1935), pp. 235-36.

29. Octavio Ianni, *Estado e capitalismo: Estrutura social e industrialização no Brasil* (Rio, 1965), p. 137.
30. See Fernando H. Cardoso, "The Industrial Elite," in Lipset and Solari, *Elites in Latin America,* pp. 101-2. See also Keiros [Queiroz], "The Eve of Revolution in Brazil," *Communist International,* XII, No. 10 (May 20, 1935), 584.
31. Roberto C. Simonsen, *Brazil's Industrial Evolution* (São Paulo, 1939), p. 31. The figures are approximate.
32. Davis, "Brazil's Political and Economic Problems," p. 7. Of 1,494 unions existing before 1931, 364 were recognized by the Labor Ministry. See Leoncio Martins Rodrigues, *Conflito industrial e sindicalismo no Brasil* (São Paulo, 1966), pp. 157-62.
33. Kenneth P. Erickson, "Labor in the Political Process in Brazil," MS, 1968, pp. A21-A24.
34. Simonsen, *Brazil's Industrial Evolution,* p. 27. See also Horace B. Davis and Marian Rubins Davis, "Scale of Living of the Working Class in São Paulo, Brazil," *Monthly Labor Review,* Jan., 1937, pp. 245-53. The Davises note (p. 247) that in 1934, while the official exchange rate listed 12 milréir to the dollar, the "free" market paid only 7, which will be the figure used in this study. For a glimpse of the burden of the laboring classes, see Frederico Heller, "A carreira profissional de um pedreiro de subúrbio," *Sociologia,* IV, No. 2 (1942), 151-56.
35. Júlio Paternostro, *Viagem ao Tocantins* (São Paulo, 1945), cited in Florestan Fernandes, *Mudanças Sociais no Brasil* (São Paulo, 1960), pp. 137-38.
36. As reported in U.S. War Department, *Survey of the Rio de Janeiro Region of Brazil,* Vol. I (530-772), Aug. 6, 1942, pp. 24, 144. Claimed circulation statistics for the five Rio papers were, in order, 210,000, 90,000, 55,000, 35,000, and 10,000.
37. Emílio Willems, "Assimilation of German Immigrants in Brazil," *Sociology and Social Research,* XXV, No. 2 (1940), 125. Reinhard Maack, "The Germans of South Brazil: A German View," *Quarterly Journal of Inter-American Relations,* I, No. 3 (July, 1938), 5-9, cites somewhat lower numbers.
38. Saito, *O japonês no Brasil,* pp. 36-47.
39. See William Newton Simonson, "Nazi Infiltration in South America, 1933-1945" (Ph.D. dissertation, Fletcher School of Law and Diplomacy, 1964), pp. 70-290 *passim;* Alton Frye, *Nazi Germany and the American Hemisphere; 1933-1941* (New Haven, 1967), pp. 65-70. See also police files on Nazi activities, Departamento Federal de Segurança Pública de Polícia Política e Social, Rio de Janeiro, hereafter cited as RP; Delegacia de Ordem Política e Social, Pôrto Alegre, *Boletim informativo,* May 9, 1939, pp. 2-8, RP; Pedro Motta Lima and João Barbosa de Mello, *El Nazismo en el Brasil* (Buenos Aires, 1938); Maack, "Germans of South Brazil," p. 15.
40. United States observers in 1942 commented harshly on Müller's Federal District police, calling them "untrained and underpaid . . . notorious for their low morale and their proclivity to solicit and accept bribes." U.S. War Department, *Survey,* p. 143.
41. "O atentado militar da Polônia contra o Brasil," RP. This curious document, dating probably from 1935, is fairly detailed and lists dozens of names associated

with specific activities; nevertheless, it is sensationalistic and must be weighed carefully. It claims that, according to intercepted Polish sources in Brazil, the Polish government under Pilsudski had been preparing to invade the state of Paraná by air from an African base once Germany had conquered the Southern Hemisphere. The new state ceded to Poland would be renamed Nova Polônia (New Poland). The document asserts Polish youths from Brazil were training with the Polish air force for the coming invasion.

42. Donald Warren, Jr. has undertaken extensive research on spiritism; see, for example, his "Portuguese Roots of Brazilian Spiritism," *Luso-Brazilian Review*, V, No. 2 (Winter, 1968), 3-33.

43. See Alceu Amoroso Lima, *Da revolução à constituição* (Rio, 1936). The best biography of Leme is by a Brazilian sister, Laurita P. R. Gabaglia, *O Cardeal Leme* (Rio, 1962).

44. Tristão de Athayde [Alceu Amoroso Lima], "A igreja e o momento político," *A Ordem* (Rio), July, 1935, p. 8. The influence of the French military mission is described in Lourival Coutinho, *O General Góes depõe* . . . , 3d ed. (Rio, 1956), pp. 3-6; Nelson Werneck Sodré, *Memórias de um soldado* (Rio, 1967), pp. 61 ff.

45. Warren Kempton Dean, "São Paulo's Industrial Elite, 1890-1960" (Ph.D. dissertation, University of Florida, 1964), pp. 129-30.

46. See Davis, "Brazil's Political and Economic Problems," pp. 2, 4; Charles A. Gauld, *The Last Titan: Percival Farquar, American Entrepreneur in Latin America* (Stanford, 1964), p. 320.

47. See Simonsen, *Brazil's Industrial Evolution;* Donald W. Giffen, "The Normal Years: Brazilian-American Relations, 1930-1939" (Ph.D. dissertation, Vanderbilt University, 1962); John D. Wirth, "A German View of Brazilian Trade and Development, 1935," *HAHR*, XLVII, No. 2 (May, 1967), 225-35.

48. See "Dependência do imperialismo: Dívidas do país, estados, e municípios" (author unknown), Aug. 20, 1935; U.S. War Department, *Survey*, p. 126.

49. Wanderley Guilherme, *Introdução ao estudo das contradições sociais no Brasil* (Rio, 1963), p. 41. Investment statistics are compiled from "Dependência do imperialismo." See also Davis, "Brazil's Political and Economic Problems," p. 4; U.S. Department of Commerce, "Trade Information Bulletin No. 767" (Washington, 1931), p. 16. The American colony in Brazil in 1941 numbered approximately 70 in Santos, 500 in Rio, and 800 in São Paulo (U.S. War Department, *Survey*, p. 19).

50. Stanley J. Stein, *The Brazilian Cotton Manufacture: Textile Enterprise in an Underdeveloped Area, 1850-1950* (Cambridge, Mass., 1957), pp. 136-37.

51. See João Neves da Fontoura, *A voz das opposições brasileiras* (São Paulo, 1935), for the position of the legislative opposition.

52. For the history of the PCB, see Astrojildo Pereira, *A formação do PCB: 1922-1928* (Rio, 1962); Hermínio Linhares, "O comunismo no Brasil," *Revista Brasiliense* (São Paulo), XXV (Sept.-Oct., 1959), 146-66; XXVI (Nov.-Dec., 1959), 178-97; XXVIII (March-April, 1960), 122-42; Robert J. Alexander, *Communism in Latin America* (New Brunswick, 1957), pp. 93-134; and Leoncio Basbaum, *História sincera da República*, III (São Paulo, 1962), 301-52. Basbaum was the secretary

of the Brazilian Communist Youth, founded in 1927. He was purged from the PCB Central Committee in 1934.

53. *Jornal do Povo* (Rio), Oct. 16, 1934, p. 10, cited in Davis, "Brazil's Political and Economic Problems," p. 8. Two strikes, among telegraph workers and Brazilian Lloyd employees, are documented in Everardo Dias, *História das lutas sociais no Brasil* (São Paulo, 1962), pp. 314-15.

54. Letter, Oswaldo Aranha to João Mangabeira, Washington, June 11, 1935, OA. Aranha frequently complained of his personal depression at the isolation of his diplomatic post. See letter, Aranha to José Fernandez Alcázar, Washington, Oct. 4, 1935, OA; letter, Aranha to Luís Simões Lopes, Washington, May 21, 1935, OA.

55. Letter, Oswaldo Aranha to Pedro Góes Monteiro, Washington, March 9, 1935, OA.

56. Letter, Pedro Góes Monteiro to Oswaldo Aranha, Caxambú, June 5, 1935, OA.

57. Letter, Viriato Vargas to Getúlio Vargas, Pôrto Alegre, March 10, 1936, GV.

Chapter 2. The Vargas Administration

1. Alzira Vargas do Amaral Peixoto, *Getúlio Vargas, meu pai* (Pôrto Alegre, 1960), p. 1; see also ch. I. The *provisórios* were local forces, generally under the command of partisan political chieftains. The official state force, the *Brigada*, comprised only several thousand troops, in contrast to the *provisórios,* which reportedly totaled 20,000 men in the early 1930s. See also Joseph Leroy Love, Jr., "Rio Grande do Sul as a Source of Potential Instability in Brazil's Old Republic, 1909-1932" (Ph.D. dissertation, Columbia University, 1967), pp. 223-27. Vargas' early career is treated in biographies by Paul Frischauer, *Presidente Vargas: Biografia* (São Paulo, 1943), an authorized work; Affonso Henriques' hostile *Vargas, o maquiavélico* (São Paulo, 1961); José Maria Bello, *História da república*, 4th ed. (São Paulo, 1959); John W. F. Dulles, *Vargas of Brazil* (Austin, 1967); Affonso Arinos de Mello Franco, "The Tide of Government: From Colony to Constitutional Democracy," *The Atlantic Monthly,* CXCVII, No. 2 (Feb., 1956), 152-56; Barros Vidal, *Um destino a serviço do Brasil* (Rio, 1945).

2. *Time* magazine, according to its fashion, consistently ridiculed the Brazilians and their baggy clothes and penchant for nicknames. See *Time,* May 23, 1938, pp. 17-18.

3. Calvino later changed his name legally to Manoel. Courtesy of Hélio Vianna.

4. Letter, Oswaldo Aranha to Luís Simões Lopes, Washington, May 21, 1935, OA.

5. Compiled from appendix charts in Peixoto, *Getúlio Vargas,* pp. 265-85.

6. Courtesy of Alzira Vargas do Amaral Peixoto, Rio, Sept. 14, 1965. His daughter says that his favorite newspaper was the *Jornal do Commercio,* which largely ignored national politics.

7. See Florestan Fernandes' review of Jacques Lambert's *Le Brésil, Structure Sociale et Institutions Politiques* (Paris, 1953), in *Revista Brasileira de Estudos Políticos,* VII (Nov., 1959), 144-45. See also Affonso Arinos de Mello Franco, *Evolução da crise brasileira* (São Paulo, 1965), p. 80.

8. Letter, J. S. Maciel Filho to Oswaldo Aranha, n.d., Maciel Filho papers. Maciel

soon joined Vargas' camp. On Jan. 1, 1938, the President, whom Maciel had called a "trapeze artist" in 1935, was hailed as Brazil's savior by a special edition of *O Imparcial.*

9. Letter, Getúlio Vargas to Oswaldo Aranha, Rio, Dec. 31, 1934, OA.

10. São Paulo, *A ação da bancada paulista por São Paulo unido na Assembléia Constituinte* (São Paulo, 1935), p. xvi.

11. Report of Samuel H. Lowrie, cited in Oscar Egidio de Araujo, "Uma pesquisa de padrão de vida," *Revista do Arquivo Municipal*, Vol. LXXX, Supplement (1941), in Warren Kempton Dean, "São Paulo's Industrial Elite, 1890-1960" (Ph.D. dissertation, University of Florida, 1964), p. 110.

12. Asiz Simão, *Sindicato e estado* (Rio, n.d.), pp. 89-96; Orlando de Carvalho, *Política de município (ensaio histórico)* (Rio, 1946), pp. 100-27.

13. See letter, Artur de Souza Costa to Getúlio Vargas, London (?), March 2, 1935, GV.

14. Letter, José Bento de Monteiro Lobato to Getúlio Vargas, São Paulo, Feb. 15, 1935, GV.

15. See Stanley J. Stein, *The Brazilian Cotton Manufacture: Textile Enterprise in an Underdeveloped Area, 1850-1950* (Cambridge, Mass., 1957), pp. 136-40; Nathaniel H. Leff, *The Brazilian Capital Goods Industry, 1929-1964* (Cambridge, Mass., 1968), pp. 9-12.

16. Dean, "São Paulo's Industrial Elite," pp. 97-110.

17. Nelson Werneck Sodré attended the Military Academy during this time. His account is basically sympathetic to Pessôa's efforts to reform the school. See Sodré, *Memórias de um soldado* (Rio, 1967), pp. 53-93.

18. The brigade commander was General João Guedes da Fontoura. See letter, Getúlio Vargas to Oswaldo Aranha, May 10, 1935, GV; telegram, Getúlio Vargas to Governor Flôres da Cunha, Rio, March 12, 1935, GV; letter, General Pantaleão Pessôa to Getúlio Vargas, Rio, March 13, 1935, GV; Lourival Coutinho, *O General Góes depõe . . .* (Rio, 1956), p. 258; *O Globo* (Rio), April 22, 1935, pp. 1, 3.

19. Letter, Góes Monteiro to Oswaldo Aranha, Rio, June 5, 1935, OA; Coutinho, *O General Góes depõe . . .*, p. 260.

20. General Pedro Góes Monteiro, circular to all active generals, Rio, April 9, 1935, GV.

21. Letter, José Pessôa to Góes Monteiro, Rio, April 11, 1935, GV; letter, Góes Monteiro to José Pessôa, Rio, April 13, 1935, GV.

22. Telegram, Flôres da Cunha to Getúlio Vargas, Pôrto Alegre, Feb. 24, 1935, and replies, Vargas to Flôres, Feb. 24 and March 12, 1935, GV; telegram, General Pantaleão Pessôa to Getúlio Vargas, Recife, Feb. 24, 1935, GV. Apparently the plot involved military officials in several northeastern states, including Sergipe and Pernambuco.

23. Letter, Getúlio Vargas to Oswaldo Aranha, Rio, May 10, 1935, GV.

24. *Ibid.*

25. Letter, Luís Simões Lopes to Oswaldo Aranha, Rio, April 26, 1935, GV.

26. J. S. Maciel Filho, editorial, in *O Imparcial* (Rio), Nov. 13, 1935, p. 4; *A Pátria* (Rio), Oct. 31, 1935, p. 1.

27. There is no satisfactory history of Rio Grande do Norte. The best is Luís da

Câmara Cascudo's *História do Rio Grande do Norte* (Rio, 1955). See also Cascudo's *História da cidade de Natal* (Natal, 1947); Stefan Robock, *Brazil's Developing Northeast* (Washington, 1963), pp. 14-15; Juvenal Lamartine, *O meu govêrno* (Rio, 1933).

28. Brazil, *Anuário estatístico do Brasil,* Ano III (1937), p. 140; Anfiloquio Câmara, *Cenários municipais (1941-1942)* (Natal, 1943), pp. 60, 234; Josué de Castro, *Death in the Northeast* (New York, 1966), p. 49.

29. Raimundo Nonato, in *Bacharéis de Olinda e Recife (Norte-Riograndenses formados de 1832 a 1932)* (Rio, 1960), lists 289 *Norte-Riograndenses* graduated in Recife between 1832 and 1932, including most of the members of the state political elite during the 1920s and 1930s.

30. Lamartine, *O meu govêrno,* pp. 7-29; interviews with José Augusto Bezerra de Medeiros, Rio, August, 1965 and June, 1968.

31. Edgar Barbosa, *História de uma campanha* (Natal, 1936), pp. iv-vi, 15-20. This book is a documentary history of the Popular Party by one of its founders. The platform did not specify how the land should be redistributed or how private property should be maintained. Like the majority of its fellow Brazilian political parties, particularly in rural areas, the Popular Party fit Emílio Willems' definition of "ephemeral groups centered on persons rather than programs." See Willems, "Brazil," in Arnold M. Rose, ed., *The Institutions of Advanced Societies* (Minneapolis, 1958), esp. p. 534. Mário Câmara, in a letter to Vargas on Aug. 6, 1934 (Natal), GV, attests to the hostility of the PP.

32. See João Café Filho, *Do sindicato ao Catete,* 2 vols. (Rio, 1966); João Café Filho, written statement to author, Sept. 30, 1965.

33. See letters, Mário Câmara to Getúlio Vargas, Natal, May 10, June 29, and Aug. 6, 1934. GV. See also Barbosa, *História,* pp. 31-35.

34. Letter, Mário Câmara to Getúlio Vargas, Natal, Aug. 6, 1934, GV. Câmara's own faction had called itself the Social Democratic Party (Partido Social Democrático).

35. Barbosa claims that 47,000 voters were registered in the state and that 70 per cent favored the Popular Party. See Barbosa, *História,* p. 68.

36. See letter, Armando de Alencar to Getúlio Vargas, Rio, Aug. 28, 1935, GV, blaming the Popular Party. The Social Alliance is blamed in Barbosa, *História,* pp. 102-46, in which he lists hundreds of documented, if minor, abuses. See also *A Razão* (Natal), May-Oct., 1935; *A Pátria* (Rio), Oct. 22, 1935, p. 3; speeches by Borges de Medeiros, João Neves da Fontoura, and others in the federal Chamber of Deputies, Oct. 18, 1935.

37. Protásio de Mello, written statement to author, Natal, April 24, 1966; Barbosa, *História,* p. 57.

38. Letter, Carlos de Lima Cavalcanti to Getúlio Vargas, Recife, Aug. 26, 1935, GV; letter, Francisco Antunes Maciel to Getúlio Vargas, Rio, Sept. 11, 1935, GV.

39. Letter, Paulo Câmara to Getúlio Vargas, Natal, Oct. 7, 1935, GV. Electors for the selection of the proposed compromise candidate did replace those for Câmara on the ballot, indicating that some political maneuvering took place. In a letter to Vargas on October 8, in GV, Armando de Alencar told the President that the "cause [is] not lost" although the situation looked less than good.

40. Café Filho suggests that Vargas could have influenced the federal Electoral Tribunal had he so desired. To placate Câmara after his defeat, he was named to the Brazilian Foreign Trade Delegation. See Café Filho, *Do sindicato ao Catete,* I, 82-83.
41. Telegram, Mário Câmara to Getúlio Vargas, Natal, Oct. 20, 1935, GV.
42. Barbosa, *História,* pp. 214-15; Café Filho, *Do sindicato ao Catete,* p. 83.
43. Telegram, Magalhães Barata to Getúlio Vargas, Belém, April 4, 1935, GV. The full record of the Pará crisis is documented among the Getúlio Vargas papers, Rio de Janeiro.
44. Góes Monteiro, cited in *O Globo* (Rio), April 6, 1935, p. 1; see letters, Getúlio Vargas to Magalhães Barata and to Abel Chermont, Petrópolis, April 4, 1935, GV.
45. Telegram, Abel Chermont and others to Getúlio Vargas, Belém, April 5, 1935, GV.
46. Letter, Magalhães Barata to Getúlio Vargas, Belém, April 5, 1935, GV.
47. New York *Times,* March 10, 1935, p. 32. The incident, conceivably part of Góes Monteiro's reason for resigning, was not reported in the Brazilian press.
48. Letter, Carlos de Lima Cavalcanti to Getúlio Vargas, Recife, Feb. 28, 1935, GV.
49. Letter, Juracy Magalhães to Getúlio Vargas, Salvador, Jan. 30, 1935, GV; *O Globo* (Rio), April 25, 1935, p. 1.
50. Telegram, Gen. Pantaleão Pessôa to Getúlio Vargas, Recife, Feb. 24, 1935, GV. The pro-Vargas governor, Carlos de Lima Cavalcanti, had defeated tenente José Alberto Lins de Barros in late 1934. See Dulles, *Vargas of Brazil,* pp. 141-42.
51. Telegram, Juracy Magalhães to Getúlio Vargas, Salvador, Feb. 12, 1935, GV.
52. Interview with Odilón Baptista, Rio, Feb. 8, 1965; Tad Szulc, *Twilight of the Tyrants* (New York, 1959), p. 76.
53. See Affonso Arinos de Mello Franco, *A alma do tempo* (Rio, 1961), p. 303; *idem, Um estadista da república* (Rio, 1955), III, 1529-33; Benedicto Valladares, *Tempos idos e vividos* (Rio, 1966), p. 34; Carolina Nabuco, *A vida de Virgílio de Mello Franco* (Rio, 1962), pp. 92-96.
54. Note, however, the excellent recent doctoral dissertation by Joseph Love, "Rio Grande do Sul," and the projected doctoral study of Carlos Cortés, University of New Mexico.
55. Erico Veríssimo, written statement to author, Jan. 19, 1967; interview with J. S. Maciel Filho, Rio, March 15, 1965. Maciel points out that the greatest number of belligerents came from the towns closest to the borders with Argentina and Uruguay: São Borja (Vargas); Itaquí (Aranha); and Santa Ana do Livramento (Flôres).
56. Love, "Rio Grande do Sul," pp. 50-74.
57. See Coutinho, *O General Góes depõe . . . ,* pp. 237-39.
58. Telegrams, Flôres da Cunha to Getúlio Vargas, Pôrto Alegre, March 2, April 18, 1935, GV; letter, Góes Monteiro to Oswaldo Aranha, Caxambú, June 5, 1935, OA.
59. Letter, Ary Parreiras to Getúlio Vargas, Niterói, Jan. 5, 1935, GV.
60. Letter, Flôres da Cunha to Getúlio Vargas, Pôrto Alegre, Oct. 8, 1935, GV.
61. Letter, Getúlio Vargas to Protásio Vargas, Rio, Oct. 8, 1935, GV. Getúlio mentioned unspecified attempts by Flôres to "direct federal policy from Pôrto Alegre."

62. Letter, Getúlio Vargas to Oswaldo Aranha, Rio, Nov. 25, 1935, GV; *O Imparcial* (Rio), Nov. 21, 1935, pp. 3, 5.

63. *O Radical* (Rio), Nov. 16, 1935, p. 1; *O Imparcial* (Rio), Nov. 16, 1935, p. 1.

64. J. S. Maciel Filho, editorial in *O Imparcial* (Rio), Nov. 19, 1935, p. 4; *A Pátria* (Rio), Nov. 23, 1935, p. 1.

65. See letter, Pantaléao Pessôa to Flôres da Cunha, Rio, Nov. 13, 1935, GV, on the deteriorating political atmosphere, and expressing fears of an imminent disruptive move by "communists or other political enemies."

66. See Henri van Deurson, "L'Émancipation industrielle du Brésil . . . ," *Revue Économique Internationale*, Aug., 1934, cited in Richard M. Morse, *From Community to Metropolis: A Biography of São Paulo, Brazil* (Gainesville, 1958), p. 232; Dean, "São Paulo's Industrial Elite," pp. 80-117. The Polytechnical School is mentioned in Leff, *Brazilian Capital Goods Industry*, pp. 16-19.

67. Octavio Ianni, *Industrialização e desenvolvimento social no Brasil* (Rio, 1963), p. 120; *Brazil: 1935* (Rio, 1936), pp. 13-14; Dean, "São Paulo's Industrial Elite," pp. 1-10.

68. See letter, Monteiro Lobato to Getúlio Vargas, Feb. 15, 1935, Rio, GV; Dean, "São Paulo's Industrial Elite," *passim.*

69. Carlos Lacerda, "Rosas e pedras do meu caminho," *Manchete* (Rio), Part VI (May 20, 1967), p. 25.

70. See *Fôlha da Noite* (São Paulo), June 22, 1935, p. 1; *O Imparcial* (Salvador) [an Integralist newspaper], Dec. 10, 1935, p. 1; *Fôlha do Povo* (Recife), Sept. 3-4, 1935; *O Globo* (Rio), April 22, 1935, 2d ed., p. 3; *A Manhã* (Rio), June 25, 1935, pp. 1, 3.

Chapter 3. The Left and the National Liberation Alliance

1. Information on the growth of the PCB courtesy of Ronald H. Chilcote. See Departamento de Pesquisa, *Jornal do Brasil* (Rio), "Comunismo de norte a sul," Nov. 7, 1967, Caderno B, pp. 2-4; Rollie Poppino, *International Communism in Latin America* (New York, 1964), pp. 70-76, 84-157; Oswaldo Peralva, "O Marxismo no Brasil," *Jornal do Brasil* (Rio), Nov. 5-6, 1967, Caderno Especial, p. 5. For more extensive treatment of the history of the PCB, see Astrojildo Pereira, *A formação do PCB* (Rio, 1962); Supremo Tribunal Federal, *Apelação criminal No. 1563* (July, 1948), archive of the Palácio da Justiça, Rio; Augusto Machado [Leoncio Basbaum], *O caminho da revolução operária e camponeza* (Rio, 1934); Hermínio Linhares, series of articles in *Revista Brasiliense* (São Paulo, 1959-60); Jorge Amado, *A vida de Luís Carlos Prestes* (São Paulo, 1945); Abguar Bastos, *Prestes e a revolução social* (Rio, 1946); Robert J. Alexander, *Communism in Latin America* (New Brunswick, 1957). The discussion of the ANL and of PCB activities in this chapter is based in part upon interviews with Astrojildo Pereira, Roberto H. Sissón, Hercolino Cascardo, Agildo Barata, Mario Pedrosa, João Costa Leite, Silo Meirelles, Ivan Pedro Martins, Caio Prado, Jr.,

Nelson Werneck Sodré, João Echeverri, Leoncio Basbaum, Eurico Bellens Pôrto, Heraclito Sobral Pinto, and João Café Filho. Carlos Lacerda and Oswaldo Peralva denied permission for interviews.

2. Eudocio Ravines, *The Yenan Way* (New York, 1951), p. 79; "D-48" report to Captain Baptista Teixeira, Delegado de Segurança Política e Social, Rio, July 28, 1939, RP.

3. Untitled document 00155, mimeographed, n.d., RP.

4. Editorial, *A Classe Operária*, n.d., cited in "Comunismo de norte a sul," p. 3; Machado, *Caminho*, pp. 52-55, 136-42; police document 00493, "Comité dirigente da União Operária e Camponeza até 1933," RP, no additional information furnished.

5. Kermit E. McKenzie, *Comintern and World Revolution, 1928-1943: The Shaping of Doctrine* (New York, 1964), pp. 143-55.

6. See Álvaro Soares Ventura, in *Novos Rumos* (Rio), April 14, 1961, cited in "Comunismo de norte a sul," p. 3; Keiros [Queiroz], "The Eve of Revolution in Brazil," *Communist International*, XII, No. 10 (May 20, 1935), 577-87, a speech given in mid-1934 at the Third Communist Party Conference for South and Caribbean America, Montevideo.

7. Keiros, "Eve of Revolution," p. 581.

8. *Ibid.*, p. 585. See also V. Myro, "The Struggle to Establish Inner Soviet Regions in the Semi-Colonial Countries," *Communist International*, XII, No. 4 (Feb. 20, 1935), 151-59.

9. Bangú [Lauro Reginaldo Teixeira], "Programma do curso para activistas," Bureau de Agit-prop Nacional do PCB, Rio, May, 1935, RP.

10. Honório de Freitas Guimarães, handwritten autobiography, MS, c. 1938, RP.

11. "Elza Fernandes" dossier, RP. Adalberto Fernandes was suspected of having informed on the PCB to the police, although he denied any guilt; Elza, the daughter of a factory worker, was held hostage and strangled by members of the central committee. See Luís Carlos Prestes to "Companheiros do Secretariado Nacional," n.d., cited in *O Imparcial* (Rio), Dec. 4, 1936, p. 15; Apelação 4899, Series A, Vol. II, TSN records, Supremo Tribunal Militar, Rio, on the Elza Fernandes (*garôta*) case.

12. See published letter from Romain Rolland, president of the World Committee Against War and Fascism; news from Spain and France in *A Marcha* (Rio), Ano 1, No. 1, Oct. 26, 1935, RP; dossiers on PCB popular front groups, RP; *Solidariedade* (Rio), Ano 1, No. 1, March, 1935; *A Pátria* (Rio), July 25, 1934, pp. 2-3; July 26, 1934, p. 3.

13. Roberto H. Sissón, *Carta aberta à marinha de guerra* (Rio, 1936), *passim*.

14. ANL national directorate (provisional), minutes of first meeting, RP; interview with Roberto Sissón, Aug. 20, 1964, and later dates.

15. The spontaneity of Lacerda's nomination of Prestes remains in question. The ANL Secretary-General believes that Lacerda, under orders from the Communist Party, acted without the prior knowledge of ANL officials. This is denied by Lacerda himself, who says that the ANL's João Costa Leite proposed the nomi-

nation to him. (Carlos Lacerda, *Rosas e pedras do meu caminho,* serialized in *Manchete* [Rio], Part VI, May 20, 1967, p. 23.)

16. Letter, May 3, 1935, cited in Luís Carlos Prestes, *The Struggle for Liberation in Brazil* (New York, 1936), pp. 31-32.

17. *A Manhã* (Rio), May 16, 1935, p. 2. The ANL national directorate issued organizational instructions through this daily newspaper, which was owned by the PCB and edited by Pedro Motta Lima, a friend of Roberto Sissón.

18. *A Manhã* (Rio), May 30, 1935, p. 6.

19. Compiled from ANL membership lists in the possession of Rio de Janeiro police officials. Courtesy of Dr. Hélio Silva.

20. Leoncio Basbaum, *História sincera da república,* III (São Paulo, 1962), 86. Basbaum used and wrote under the name Augusto Machado during his active PCB membership in the late 1920s and early 1930s.

21. "Santa Catarina" dossier, RP.

22. "Bahia" dossier, RP.

23. Compiled from lists written by Caio Prado, Jr., president of the São Paulo state ANL, São Paulo, late 1936. Caio Prado papers, São Paulo; hereafter cited as CP.

24. Caio Prado, Jr., "Circular de instruções aos directorios municipais," early 1935, CP, privately circulated to ANL officials.

25. Summarized from ANL state directorate report, "São Paulo" dossier, RP.

26. See Ernst Halperin, *Nationalism and Communism in Chile* (Cambridge, Mass., 1965), and John Reese Stevenson, *The Chilean Popular Front* (Philadelphia, 1942); "Open Letter to Haya de la Torre," *International Press Correspondence* [hereafter cited as *IPC*], XV, No. 22 (May 25, 1935), 593-94, an appeal to APRA to ally with the Peruvian Communist Party, on most occasions its rival and enemy. See also Ravines, *The Yenan Way,* and his *América Latina: Un continente en erupción* (Buenos Aires [?], 1956).

27. ANL programs, March, 1935, courtesy of Roberto Sissón, Sissón papers; hereafter cited as RS. See *Terceira República* (Rio), Ano 1, No. 1, July 5, 1935, RP, in which PCB analysts compare the ANL program to the 1934 constitution.

28. Letter, Luís Carlos Prestes to Virgílio de Mello Franco, and reply, "Barcelona" [Prestes was in Rio], June, 1935, RP.

29. *A Manhã* (Rio), May 31, 1935, p. 2. The Cometa factory did provide a chapel, the article pointedly indicated.

30. In 1941, a study of working-class districts in São Paulo showed that 13 per cent of the children under fourteen years of age were still employed in industry, despite categorical legal prohibitions. See Warren Kempton Dean, "São Paulo's Industrial Elite, 1890-1960" (Ph.D. dissertation), University of Florida, 1964), p. 110.

31. See letter, Luís Carlos Prestes to ANL directorate, n.d., cited in minutes, ANL national directorate, May 10, 1935, RP; Lopes Chaves [Roberto Sissón], ANL Circular No. 31, Rio, Oct. 13, 1935, RP; Edmar Morel, *A revolta da Chibata,* 2d ed. (Rio, 1963), p. 13.

32. *A Manhã* (Rio), June 4, 1935, p. 8; "Um grupo de patriotas," ANL leaflet addressed to military personnel, mid-1935, in Apelação 4899, Vol. XX, Série C,

apenso 2, TSN archive; *União de Ferro* (Rio), RP; *O Soldado Vermelho* (Rio), RP.

33. Unsigned police report, São Paulo, to Delegado da Ordem Política e Social, Rio, July 22, 1935, RP.

34. *A Manhã* (Rio), June 27, 1935, p. 8.

35. See *A Manhã* (Rio), July 5-12, 1935; *ibid.*, Oct. 15, 1935, p. 2 ("Seduced by Integralist Chief!"), an article relating the tragic story of a working-class mother, allegedly driven to prostitution and finally murdered by her enraged husband after she was mistreated by a local fascist.

36. ANL national directorate, financial ledger for March-July, 1935, RS; miscellaneous financial records, São Paulo state ANL, CP and RP. Affonso Henriques (see his *Vargas, o maquiavélico* [São Paulo, 1961]), acted for a time as treasurer for the ANL national directorate. The ANL paid 1,200$000 (U.S. $66) monthly rent for its Federal District headquarters.

37. Many contributions, obviously, were not registered in ANL records. The Communist Party, which still had some of the money given to Prestes in 1930 by Oswaldo Aranha, maintained its own sources of support. But the PCB probably contributed little to the ANL during the latter's short legal existence. See John W. F. Dulles, *Vargas of Brazil* (Austin, 1967), p. 148.

38. *Correio Popular* (Campinas), Dec. 12, 1935, p. 1; interviews with Caio Prado, Jr., São Paulo, Oct. 26, 1965, and Edgar Leunroth, São Paulo, Oct. 24, 1965; *A Platéia* (São Paulo), clipping file, CP.

39. See letter, Luís Carlos Prestes to General Miguel Costa, Rio, Oct. 10, 1935, in response to earlier correspondence, RP. In 1933 Costa had founded the Socialist Party of São Paulo. See Dulles, *Vargas of Brazil*, p. 122.

40. Agildo Barata, written statement to author, Rio, Dec. 8, 1964; see statement by Borges de Medeiros concerning the ANL, reprinted in *A Manhã* (Rio), July 5, 1935, p. 2.

41. See PCB document, "Relatório de triângulo mineiro," n.d., RP.

42. ANL national directorate, Circular No. 39, Nov. 4, 1935, RS. See also *A Manhã* (Rio), June 6, 1935, p. 3, concerning Integralist pressure on the movement.

43. See letter, Harry Berger to Luís Carlos Prestes, June 21, 1935, TSN archive, following his northeast visit; Bastos, *Prestes*, p. 316 *et passim.*

44. "Carta pra [*sic*] o vaqueiro do nordeste," *Fólha do Povo* (Recife), July 17, 1935, p. 2.

45. *A Manhã* (Rio), July 6, 1935, p. 7.

46. *Fólha do Povo* (Recife), July 9, 1935, p. 1; *A Manhã* (Rio), July 11, 1935, p. 2. Sissón acted as the self-appointed "President of the Caravan."

47. "Manifesto da Caravana ANL," July, 1935, RS.

48. See, for example, Lopes Chaves [Roberto Sissón], Circular No. 1, Manaus, July 20, 1935, RS; Circular No. 2, *ibid.*

49. See letter, Luís Carlos Prestes to Henri Barbusse, n.d., cited in *A Manhã* (Rio), May 24, 1935, p. 1 (on the Chaco War); ANL program announcing public rally on the coffee issue, June 2, 1935, for the Estádio Brasil, Rio, RP.

Chapter 4. The Integralists

1. See Plínio Salgado, *Despertemos a nação!* (Rio, 1935), ch. I.
2. Plínio Salgado, "Como eu vi a Itália," *Hierarchia* (Rio), March-April, 1932, pp. 203, 205. See also Miguel Reale, *Perspectivas Integralistas,* 2d ed. (Rio, 1936), pp. 143 ff.; Tasso de Oliveira, "O Estado Nôvo em Portugal," *A Offensiva* (Rio), Oct. 17, 1935, pp. 10-11; Heinz H. F. Eulau, "The Ideas Behind Brazilian Integralism," *Inter-American Quarterly,* III, No. 4 (Oct., 1941), 36-43.
3. Gustavo Barroso, *O que o integralista deve saber,* 3d ed. (Rio, 1935), pp. 4, 57-61.
4. Plínio Salgado, *Psicologia da revolução,* 4th ed. (São Paulo, 1953), p. 159; Olbiano de Mello, *Razões do Integralismo* (Rio, 1935); Comandante Victor Pujol, *Rumo ao Sigma* (Rio, 1935), p. 25; *A Offensiva* (Rio), July 6, 1935, p. 1; Aug. 10, 1935, p. 1.
5. Affonso de Carvalho, *O Brasil não é dos brasileiros* (São Paulo, 1937), pp. 29, 38-61. See also *O Imparcial* (Salvador), Nov. 10, 1935, p. 1; *A Offensiva* (Rio), Jan. 30, 1936, p. 1; Nov. 2, 1937, p. 2; *Doutrina* (Rio), July, 1937, pp. 1-3.
6. *A Offensiva* (Rio), July 19, 1934, p. 1.
7. Plínio Salgado, "O país que não lê," in *Despertemos,* pp. 174-80. See also Salgado, "O crepúsculo nacional," reprinted from *A Razão* (São Paulo), Nov. 24, 1931; Salgado, editorial, "Dois annos de marcha," *A Offensiva* (Rio), July 13, 1935, p. 1.
8. Francisco de Paula Queiroz Ribeiro, Directivo No. 1, n.d., AIB, Departmento Nacional da Polícia, RP. The Service's five divisions covered Jews, Communists, Liberal Democrats, Integralists, and special groups (including Freemasons).
9. Compiled from Olbiano de Mello, *A marcha da revolução social no Brasil* (Rio, 1957), pp. 91-92.
10. Report, Ambassador Jefferson Caffery to Secretary of State Cordell Hull, Dispatch 658, June 10, 1936, Rio de Janeiro, State Department Archive, Washington, 832.00 (Revolutions/607).
11. Guanabara (Rio de Janeiro) AIB, *Boletim provincial,* No. 2, March 23, 1934, RP.
12. Code sheet in police file, n.d. (c. 1937), RP.
13. Integralist catechism, n.d., in police files, RP.
14. AIB, *Boletim,* No. 34, "Para conhecimento e execução faço público," Sept. 18, 1934, RP. In all, 64 items were listed. The Integralist, the catechism proclaimed, is "attentive, studious, enthusiastic, religious, courageous, loyal, disinterested, strong, tenacious, punctual, and disciplined." See *Boletim,* No. 1, Primeiro Conclave Parlamentar da AIB, Rio, Oct. 16, 1936, RP.
15. Oswaldo Robinson, Chefe de Gabinete, Chefia Provincial da Provincia da Guanabara, Circular No. 1, July 20, 1935, RP.
16. Memorandum, Chefia Provincial da Provincia da Guanabara, n.d., RP.
17. Letter, Plínio Salgado to Getúlio Vargas, Rio, Jan. 28, 1938, GV.
18. Plínio Salgado, "Carta de natal," *A Offensiva* (Rio), Dec. 25, 1935, p. 1.
19. *A Offensiva* (Rio), Oct. 2, 1937, p. 3.
20. Salgado, *Despertemos,* pp. 6-7.

21. For example, he resigned from the directorate of the National Historical Museum in 1930 (he later became its president) and from the Academy of Letters in 1933. See Gustavo Barroso archive, Museu Histórico, Rio, clipping file, Vol. 1 (1932-35). Archive hereafter cited as GB.

22. Letter, Oswaldo Aranha to Getúlio Vargas, Washington, Nov. 30, 1937, OA.

23. The boycott lasted six months, after which time Barroso's articles reappeared. During his absence from *A Offensiva*, he published regularly in *Fon Fon* and *Século XX*, other Integralist journals. Courtesy of Aron Neumann, Rio, Feb. 16, 1965.

24. *Deutsche La Plata Zeitung* (Buenos Aires), April 25, 1935, GB.

25. Gustavo Barroso, "Judaismo Internacional," *A Offensiva* (Rio), Aug. 3, 1935, n.p., GB.

26. *Diário da Noite* (Rio), March 27, 1937, p. 1.

27. See *O Carioca* (Rio), Aug. 29, 1933, n.p., Academy of Letters archive, Rio.

28. Dossier, "Provincia de Rio de Janeiro," membership listing, Cordeiro cell, RP.

29. *Diário da Noite* (Rio), July 4, 1935, p. 1.

30. Letter, F[rancisco?] Ribeiro to Oswaldo Aranha, São Paulo, Nov. 3, 1937, OA.

31. Dossier, "Almirante Saldanha," AIB files, RP.

32. Edmar Morel, *A revolta da Chibata*, 2d ed. (Rio, 1963), pp. 193-94.

33. Among the young Brazilians who traveled abroad in the 1920s and 1930s were J. S. Maciel Filho, who studied under Croce in Italy; Sérgio Buarque de Holanda, who lived in Germany between 1928 and 1931, reading literature and earning expenses by adding Portuguese subtitles to German films earmarked for Brazilian distribution; Raul Bopp, Adhemar de Barros, and Mário Pedrosa, who traveled in Central Europe; Caio Prado, Jr., who lived in England; and Sérgio Millet and Rubens Borba de Moraes, who lived in Switzerland. Luís Carlos Prestes, of course, took up residence in the Soviet Union at the invitation of the Executive Committee of the Third International.

34. Oswaldo Gouvea, essay for AIB Serviço Cultural; Renato Paula, "Sentimentalismo," *ibid.*

35. Josephat Linhares, *O Integralismo à luz da doutrina social catholica* (Rio, 1933), p. 9.

36. Alceu Amoroso Lima [Tristão de Athayde], "Catholicismo e Integralismo," *A Ordem* (Rio), Feb., 1935, pp. 84-85.

37. Eduardo, bishop of Ilhéus, in Salgado, *Despertemos*, p. 102.

38. See D. Alexandre do Amaral, "Apreciação das 'Impressões sôbre a orthodoxia da doutrina integralista perante a Egreja Catholica,' por S. Excia. Revma. D. Gastão Liberal Pinto," MS, 1937; courtesy of Padre Ponciano Stenzel dos Santos, Rio de Janeiro.

39. See Otto Guerra, Álvaro Lins, *et al.*, "Manifesto," Recife, Nov., 1932, courtesy of Dr. Otto Guerra, Natal; letter from "Estudantes nacionalistas" to Getúlio Vargas, in *A Offensiva* (Rio), Dec. 12, 1935, p. 4.

40. *Diário de Minas* (Belo Horizonte), Oct. 23, 1937, GB.

41. Mary Galeno, report to the AIB on the projected organization of a district sub-

cell on the Morro dos Cabritos (a Rio de Janeiro *favela*), Nov. 26, 1936. AIB file, RP. See also *A Offensiva* (Rio), Jan. 6, 1937, p. 1.

42. "Armamento pertencente ao Integralismo," 1936, AIB dossier, RP; Province of Guanabara file, RP. The cell inventory listed 8 large guns, 15 rifles, 3 pistols, 3 grenades, and 1,500 rounds of ammunition.

43. A second, lesser-known Integralist, a gaúcho by the name of Manoel Hasslocher, reportedly helped organize militia activities. Courtesy of J. S. Maciel Filho, Rio de Janeiro.

44. Memorandum, Everardo Dias da Motta, Chief of Third Militia Region, to AIB Chefe Provincial da Guanabara, March 6, 1937, RP; letter, "Liberalli," Chief of Fourth Militia Region, to Chefe Provincial da Guanabara, March 1, 1937, RP.

45. See report, Claribalde Vilarim de Vasconcellos Galvão, chief of police, Florian-ópolis, to Governor Nereu Ramos, Aug. 10, 1935, RP.

46. See "Santa Catarina" dossier, RP; Reinhold Maack, in a pro-Nazi article some-what hostile to the Integralists ("The Germans of South Brazil: A German View," *Quarterly Journal of Inter-American Relations* I, No. 3 [July, 1938], 5-23) claims that 55 per cent of the Integralist leaders in Rio Grande do Sul were of German extraction (p. 19).

47. Samuel Putnam, "Vargas Dictatorship in Brazil," *Science and Society*, V, No. 2 (Spring, 1941), 101. Matarazzo's affinity for Italian fascism is described in Warren Kempton Dean, "São Paulo's Industrial Elite, 1890-1960" (Ph.D. dissertation, University of Florida, 1966), pp. 120-26.

48. *A Offensiva* (Rio), Nov. 23, 1935, *passim*.

49. AIB, Guanabara province, *Boletim provincial*, No. 2, May 23, 1934; *A Offensiva* (Rio), July 27, 1935, p. 1.

50. Report, M. Bandeira, Ipanema cell, to Chefe Provincial, May 16, 1936, RP.

51. Report, Ambassador Jefferson Caffery to Secretary of State Cordell Hull, Rio, March 28, 1938 (?), cited in John W. F. Dulles, *Vargas of Brazil* (Austin, 1967), p. 166.

52. Membership records of the Irajá and Cascadura cells (Federal District) list numerous infants as regular members. Frequently entire families were listed individually in Integralist records, then listed again as members of the "green blouses," Pliniano, or Pliniana auxiliaries. The ANL also practiced similar infla-tionary statistical tactics. See dossier, "Municípios onde há núcleos Integralistas," RP.

53. [Galeazzo Ciano], *Ciano's Hidden Diary, 1937-1938*, tr. Andreas Mayor (New York, 1953), p. 30. The payments were initiated in late 1936 and ran for some-what more than a year. Left-wing sources have claimed that foreign support was far more extensive. See F. Lacerda, "The Fascist Coup d'État in Brazil," *Communist International* (London), May 20, 1935, pp. 577-87; Samuel Putnam, "Fascist Penetration in Latin America," *Communist*, XVII, No. 5 (n.d.), 458-67. Putnam cites financial backing from such German industrialists as Renner, Von Hartt, Hassencliver, Henning, and Stoltz. These sources, however, do not differentiate between money given to the Integralists and aid for Nazi activity in southern Brazil.

54. See letter, Thiele Kessemeirer, Deutsche Fitchtebund Union für Weltwahrheit, Hamburg, to Raimundo Martins Filho, Feb. 11, 1937, RP. Allegations about financial support from the German government and private sources in Germany have heretofore not been documented. See, for example, Morel, *A revolta da Chibata,* p. 193.

55. Secretaria Nacional de Finanças (AIB), financial statements, 1936-37, RP. Individuals were required to pay at least 2$000 per month (fourteen cents) to their local cells.

56. AIB financial records, "Campanha do Ouro" dossier and others, RP; *A Offensiva* (Rio), Jan. 3, 1937, p. 9. The telephone-directory mailing campaign is described in a letter from A. Pompêa to Belmiro Valverde, São Paulo, Dec. 17, 1935, RP.

57. *O Globo* (Rio), April 5, 1935, p. 1, 2d daily edition.

58. *A Noite* (Rio), April 24, 1935, p. 1. Fairbanks, who wore his Integralist uniform to the legislative session, claimed in a prepared statement that Jesus Christ had been an Integralist; the session, at that point, was gaveled to a close by its chairman.

59. *O Imparcial* (Rio), Nov. 24, 1935, p. 3, also p. 2; see also *A Pátria* (Rio), Nov. 21, 1935, p. 1. Treatment of the Chamber of Deputies' vote appears in *O Imparcial,* Nov. 21, 1935, p. 5. A coalition of moderates and radicals, including João Café Filho and Domingos Velasco, championed the anti-AIB measure; Vargas government officials, however, for whatever undisclosed purpose, initiated the final strategy that resulted in the November 20 vote.

60. For Barroso's pro-Nazi position, see Gustavo Barroso to European Racist Alliance [Berlin], Rio, May 25, 1934, RP.

61. Cf. Edward R. Tannenbaum, "The Goals of Italian Fascism," *American Historical Review,* LXXIV, No. 4 (April, 1969), 1183-1204, esp. p. 1204.

62. See George L. Mosse, "The Genesis of Fascism," in Walter Laqueur and George L. Mosse, eds., *International Fascism, 1920-1945* (New York, 1966), pp. 14-15.

63. Ernst Nolte, *Three Faces of Fascism* (New York, 1966), p. 201; Eugen Weber, "The Men of the Archangel," in Laqueur and Mosse, *International Fascism,* p. 108.

64. See Tannenbaum, "The Goals of Italian Fascism," p. 1204.

Chapter 5. The Revolutionary Turn

1. Each side accused the other of violence and provocation. In October, 1934, rooftop machine-gun fire sprayed a crowd of nearly 10,000 Integralists in São Paulo's Praça da Sé, wounding forty-two and killing six. AIB officials blamed communist agents; the assassins were never apprehended. Scores of minor incidents took place in the following months, especially after the establishment of the ANL. See *A Manhã* (Rio), June 2, 1935, p. 8; June 11, p. 1; *A Offensiva* (Rio), Feb. 23, 1935, pp. 4-5; Dec. 21, 1935, p. 3; *Jornal de Petrópolis,* June 11-21, 1935 (on the so-called Cantú murder); *A Classe Operária* (Rio), May 1, 1935, pp. 6-11.

2. Luís Carlos Prestes, Manifesto of July 5, 1935, in *A Manhã* (Rio), July 6, 1935, pp. 1-2.

3. Interviews with Hercolino Cascardo and Roberto Sissón. Cascardo returned to semiactive military duty, during which time he was watched carefully by the authorities. He was transferred to the Santa Catarina–Paraná military region. Other former ANL officials in the armed forces, including Captain Henrique Oest, Moesias Rollim, Costa Leite, Amorety Osório, and Antônio Rollemberg, were similarly sent away from areas of potential political activity. See *A Manhã* (Rio), July 28, 1935; Aug. 7, 1935, p. 1.

4. Thomas E. Skidmore (*Politics in Brazil, 1930-1964* [New York, 1967], p. 340, n. 43) points out this distinction between the two wings of the party, citing Leoncio Basbaum (*História sincera da república*, III [São Paulo, 1962], 77-103). By April, 1935, however, the "legalists" were silent. See also Timbaúba, "A ANL," *Diário Carioca*, Nov. 29, 1963, p. 4. The precise reasons for the decision to adopt a revolutionary program still remain cloudy, although they must have reflected the overly optimistic reports of PCB agents throughout Brazil and the frustration among PCB leaders over Integralist attacks and general police repression.

5. Getúlio Vargas to Benedito Valladares, Rio, July 5, 1935, GV. See *A Manhã* (Rio), July 3, 1935, p. 1; July 8, 1935, p. 1; July 27, 1935, p. 1; Aug. 7, 1935, p. 1.

6. PCB agitprop memorandum, printed in *Revista Proletária* (Rio), Aug., 1935, RP.

7. Luís Carlos Prestes to Roberto Sissón, Sept., 1935, RS; miscellaneous PCB correspondence, Sept.-Dec., 1935, RP.

8. *A Manhã* (Rio), Sept. 7, 1935, p. 1; Sept. 12, 1935, p. 1; Oct. 19, 1935, p. 1.

9. "Lopes Chaves" [Sissón], Circular No. 6, Sept. 7, 1935, RS.

10. S-2 police report, Nov. 11, 1935, RP. Sissón attempted to open an electoral front along ANL lines. The "Popular Front Against War and Fascism," headed by Maurício de Lacerda and Francisco Mangabeira, operated until at least the end of the year.

11. See Luís Carlos Prestes to Virgílio de Mello Franco, "Barcelona" [Prestes was in Rio] (June, 1935); to Oswaldo Pereira de Carvalho (Sept. 8); to Agildo Barata (Aug. 2); to Trifino Corrêia (July 17); to Estillac Leal (Oct. 16); to Alberto Guerin (Aug. 5); to Ary Salgado Freire (July 20); to Pedro Ernesto Baptista (Oct. 16); to Agricola Baptista (n.d.); and to others, RP.

12. Letter, João Alberto Lins de Barros to Luís Carlos Prestes, Rio (?), June 8, 1935, GV.

13. Taxi drivers claimed that Prestes tipped generously. See *O Imparcial* (Rio), Dec. 16, 1936, pp. 14, 16 (based on the TSN hearings in progress).

14. Letter, Luís Carlos Prestes to Agildo Barata, Aug. 2, 1935; letter, Maurício de Lacerda to Prestes, Nov. 15, 1935; letter, anonymous to federal police chief, Rio, Aug. 23, 1935 (regarding Pará); letter, Grassi e Castro to central committee of PCB, São Paulo, Aug. 14, 1935, RP; *Diário Carioca* (Rio), Nov. 29, 1963, p. 1; Honório de Freitas Guimarães, handwritten autobiography, MS, c. 1938, RP.

15. Lopes Chaves, "O govêrno Popular Nacional Revolucionário e o seu programma," Oct. 10, 1935, RS.

16. Col. Aloísio de Andrade Moura. *Relatório das actividades comunistas no Rio*

Grande do Norte (Natal, July 8, 1947), Departamento Federal de Segurança Pública, archive, Natal, hereafter cited as RA; *O Radical* (Rio), Dec. 14, 1935, p. 1; interviews with Aldo Fernandes, João Café Filho, João Medeiros Filho, Col. Bilac de Farias, João Baptista Galvão, and José Augusto Bezerra.

17. *A Razão* (Natal), n.d., cited in João Medeiros, *Meu Depoimento* (Natal, 1937), pp. 34-35.

18. Otto Guerra, written statement to author, Natal, Oct. 22, 1965; interviews with Cascudo, Rodrigues de Mello, and Hélio Galvão.

19. Information on the barracks cell is cited in General Antônio Carlos da Silva Muricy, *A guerra revolucionária no Brasil e o episódio de novembro de 1935* (Natal, 1966), p. 31. This source is not well documented, although it seems to be roughly correct.

20. Directoria Nacional da ANL, Rio de Janeiro [Sissón], "Confidencial: A ANL e a situação política do estado do Rio Grande do Norte," mid-1935, RS.

21. *Ibid.*

22. See PCB, *Boletim Sindical*, Sept., 1935, in Polícia Civil do Distrito Federal, *Arquivos da delegacia especial de segurança*, III (Rio, 1938), 135; Basbaum, *História*, III, 189-90.

23. Manoel Rodrigues de Mello, *Várzea do Assú* (São Paulo, 1940), *passim*. The author of this description of *sertanejo* life in the interior of the state attributed communist influence to Protestantism and freethinking.

24. Medeiros, *Meu Depoimento*, pp. 45-46. This charge also appears in a letter, author unidentified, to Pedro Rocha, Mossoró (Rio Grande do Norte), Nov. 29, 1935, RA.

25. Medeiros, *Meu Depoimento,* p. 46; Abguar Bastos, *Prestes e a revolução social* (Rio, 1946), p. 322; interview with João Baptista Galvão.

26. See the speech of João Café Filho to the Chamber of Deputies, Dec. 13, 1935, cited in *O Radical* (Rio), Dec. 14, 1935, p. 1. See also Medeiros, *Meu Depoimento*, pp. 51-71; *A República* (Natal), Nov. 28, 1935, p. 1; letter, "Santa" to central committee of the PCB, Recife, Jan. 16, 1936, in *Arquivos*, pp. 29-33; João Café Filho, *Do sindicato ao Catete* (Rio, 1966), I, 88. Each of the accounts varies slightly. No two agree, for example, on the place of refuge taken by the governor: other places cited are the Italian consulate and an "Air France oil tanker."

27. Most of the leaders had participated in the barracks' ANL cell. Henriques, according to some, had belonged to the Communist Party for a number of years; this allegation is not proven.

28. Moura, *Relatório*; Departamento de Pesquisa, "Comunismo de norte a sul," *Jornal do Brasil* (Rio), Nov. 7, 1967, caderno B, p. 3; telegram, União Operários Estivadores de Natal to Deputy Martins Silva, Constituent Assembly, 1934; in Brasil, Assembléia Constituinte, *Anaes*, Vol. III, annexos.

29. The various sources do not agree on the total strength of the rebel forces. The police observer, Moura, and the PCB agent, "Santa," both exaggerated the number for different reasons. Moura would show that the government forces were overwhelmed and therefore could not have been expected to offer resistance; "Santa" sought to establish that the rebellion quickly won mass support. Neither is

accurate. See Moura, *Relatório,* pp. 1-6; "Santa," *Arquivos,* pp. 29-33; Muricy, *Guerra revolucionária,* pp. 30 ff. Many of the records pertinent to the revolt were burned during the mid-1950s by Natal police authorities.

30. Café Filho, *Do sindicato,* I, 89; Glauco Carneiro, *História das revoluções brasileiras* (Rio, 1965), II, 419-20.
31. "Santa," *Arquivos,* p. 29. Musician Quintinho finally informed "Santa" at three in the afternoon.
32. Agildo Barata, written statement to author, Rio, Dec. 8, 1964.
33. *A Liberdade* (Natal), dated Nov. 27, 1935, RA. The paper, which actually appeared on November 25, never published again.
34. Letter, João Baptista Galvão to Amélia Santa Rosa, Natal, Nov. 24, 1935, RA.
35. Natal police archive; Café Filho speech, Dec. 13, 1935, cited in *O Radical* (Rio), Dec. 14, 1935, p. 1; Márcio Moreira Alves, "Um govêrno comunista no Brasil: Natal, 1935," *Correio da Manhã* (Rio), July 11-12, 1959, pp. 8, 16; Luiz Machado, "Revolution in Brazil," *IPC,* XVI, No. 2 (Jan. 11, 1936), 32 (asserting that Praxedes fled to the interior with 500 rebels to organize the *sertanejos*). Jorge Amado used Praxedes as the model for Luís, the shoemaker, in his novel of the northeast, *Seara vermelha,* 8th ed. (Rio, 1961). A possible fifth member of the junta, Mário Paiva, known only as a "popular representative," is mentioned in Samuel Putnam, "Vargas Dictatorship in Brazil," *Science and Society,* V, No. 2 (Spring, 1941), 107.
36. Lauro Lago, transcript of testimony to police, n.d., RA.
37. Café Filho speech, Dec. 13, 1935, cited in *O Radical* (Rio), Dec. 14, 1935, p. 1; "Comunismo de norte a sul," *Jornal do Brasil* (Rio), Nov. 7, 1967, p. 3.
38. Moura, *Relatório,* p. 5; Café Filho, *Do sindicato,* I, 89.
39. *Jornal Pequeno* (Recife), Nov. 27, 1935, p. 1; *The Times* (London), Nov. 28, 1935, p. 14. Communist sources exaggerated the number of rebels who had commandeered the *Santos,* which was not a large vessel, and claimed that it managed to unload its rebel crew along the coast before it was taken. See *Partisan Review and Anvil,* III, No. 1 (Feb., 1936), 6.
40. *A República* (Natal), Nov. 30, 1935, p. 1. About $10,000 was taken from the three junta officials; an additional $90,000 was ultimately recovered, approximately one half of the total claimed by officials to have been stolen. See Medeiros, *Meu Depoimento,* p. 102.
41. Police registries (*Lista dos indivíduos implicados no movimento comunista de novembro de 1935* [Natal, 1938] and other documents), RA; Hermínio Linhares, "Levante comunista em 1935," unpublished MS, 1965.
42. *O Radical* (Rio), Dec. 14, 1935, p. 6.
43. Interview with João Fagundes de Almeida. For his deed he was called "the Luís Carlos Prestes of Rio Grande do Norte" by the press.
44. Judge Floriano Cavalcanti de Albuquerque, *Relatório* (Natal, 1936), Part I of summary presented to the Ministry of Justice. The judge alleged that many private citizens had been arrested for their connections with Mário Câmara or João Café Filho. That over half of the arrests were made outside Natal, through-

out the entire state, adds credence to the judge's allegation that not all those arrested had participated in the insurrections.

45. *O Nordeste* (Fortaleza), Dec. 11, 1935, p. 4.
46. Anthony Patric, *Toward the Winning Goal* (Rio, 1940), p. 251.
47. João Café Filho, cited in *O Radical* (Rio), Dec. 17, 1935, p. 2.
48. *A Ordem* (Natal), Dec. 1, 1935, p. 1.
49. *Ibid.*, Dec. 3, 1935, p. 1.
50. Letter, Amélia Gomes Reginaldo to her mother, João Pessôa, RA.
51. Muricy, *Guerra revolucionária*, p. 6; Café Filho, *Do sindicato*, I, 83-84.
52. Alexandre Barbosa Lima Sobrinho, *Interêsses e problemas do sertão pernambucano* (Rio, 1937), p. 37. The northeast contributed approximately 8 per cent to the G.N.P.
53. Apollônio Pires and Manoel Machado Cavalcanti, *Indústrias de Pernambuco* (Recife, 1935), pp. 29-84.
54. Lima Sobrinho, *Interêsses e problemas*, p. 21; *Brazil: 1935* (Rio, 1936), p. 14.
55. Departamento de Saúde Pública, Estado de Pernambuco, "Questionário sôbre o custo da vida," *Revista do Arquivo Municipal de São Paulo*, XVIII (Nov.-Dec., 1935), 171-74. See also Manoel Correia de Andrade, *A terra e o homen no nordeste*, 2d ed. (São Paulo, 1964), p. 114.
56. See Josué de Castro's "The Crab Cycle," in his *Death in the Northeast* (New York, 1966), pp. 128-29; see also letter, Hermogenes Bezerra de Menezes, Gamelleira, Pernambuco, to "Sr. Banker Johann Davidson Rockefeller, Standard Oil of New York," Aug. 31, 1936, OA, a plea for financial relief for his region.
57. General Manoel Rabello, in *Fôlha do Povo* (Recife), Aug. 20, 1935, p. 1. The local PCB was not unaware of Rabello's humane concern; see letter, Ilvo Meirelles to Luís Carlos Prestes, n.d., in *O Imparcial* (Rio), Dec. 22, 1936, p. 3; letter, "Lívio" [Ilvo Meirelles] to "Léo" [Luís Carlos Prestes], Dec. 9, 1935, Rio, RP.
58. See Carlos de Lima Cavalcanti, *Manifesto ao povo pernambucano* (Recife, 1935).
59. Testimony by Harry Berger, "As declarações prestadas por Arthur Ernest Ewert," 1936, TSN archive, Rio; *O Globo* (Rio), Dec. 4, 1935, p. 1.
60. Letter, "Alencar" [João Caetano Machado] to PCB headquarters, Recife, April 11, 1935, Secretaria de Segurança Pública, Recife (hereafter cited as RC).
61. The official version is presented in Mensário de Cultura Militar, *Guerra revolucionária* (Recife, 1962), p. 9. The Communist Party view is summarized in "Tenente X," "Os acontecimentos no Recife," *Novos Rumos* (Rio), Nov. 22-28, 1963, p. 5.
62. Interviews with Captain Sidrack Corrêia, Wandenkolk Wanderley, and Malvino Reis Neto; Captain Everardo de Barros e Vasconcellos, eyewitness report, n.d., RP.
63. *Diário da Manhã* (Recife), Nov. 26, 1935, p. 1; "Tenente X," "Os acontecimentos no Recife"; *Diário de Pernambuco* (Recife), Nov. 27, 1935, p. 1.
64. See *Diário de Pernambuco* (Recife), Nov. 27, 1935, p. 1; *Diário da Manhã* (Recife), Nov. 27, 1935, p. 1; "Cópia do informe da secretaria técnica do comitê revolucionario de Pernambuco," in *Arquivos da delegacia especial*, III, 199-201. The communist view of the various insurrectionary outbreaks is given in "G.,"

"The National Revolutionary Uprising in Brazil," *IPC*, XV, No. 70 (Dec. 21, 1935), 1718-19.

65. "Tenente X," "Os acontecimentos no Recife," p. 5; untitled police document, n.d., RP. The communists charged later that local Integralists had aided the militia to make the arrests.

66. See J. W. F. Dulles, *Vargas of Brazil* (Austin, 1967), p. 149. Dulles overestimates the extent of Meirelles' role; he does not mention the parts played in the revolt by other communist agents, and fails to discuss the case of Octacílio Lima, who may not have been allied with the communists at all. Meirelles later escaped.

67. *Diário de Pernambuco* (Recife), Nov. 27, 1935, p. 2 (claiming 150 deaths); *A Pátria* (Rio), Nov. 29, 1935, p. 1; *The Times* (London), Nov. 28, 1935, p. 14; Lourival Fontes and Glauco Carneiro, *A face final de Vargas* (Rio, 1966), p. 23, n. 1.

68. See "Movimento comunista," police document, n.d., RC; *O Imparcial* (Rio), Nov. 26, 1935, p. 1; *A Offensiva* (Rio), Feb. 19, 1936, p. 8; AIB, *O Integralismo em poucas palavras* (Fortaleza, 1936), p. 69.

69. Letter, Carlos de Lima Cavalcanti to Agamemnon Magalhães, Recife, Dec. 18, 1935, GV.

70. Letter, A. Serrano to PCB regional committee, Recife, n.d., RP. Serrano, a near-illiterate Negro, according to police, died of tuberculosis shortly after his capture in 1936.

71. See Felinto Müller, "Golpe de vista retrospectivo," report to Getúlio Vargas, early 1936, GV.

72. Guimarães, statement, RP; Müller, report, GV; police report, "Relatório do secretariado nacional do PCB . . . ," n.d., RP.

73. Agildo Barata, written statement to author, Rio, Dec. 8, 1964; Barata, *Vida de um revolucionário* (Rio, 1957), pp. 226-300.

74. *O Globo* (Rio), Nov. 28, 1935, p. 1.

75. Barata, *Vida*, pp. 189, 264-65. A more cynical view of the proceedings is provided by Affonso Henriques, *Vargas, o maquiavélico* (São Paulo, 1961), ch. XVII.

76. Agildo Barata to General Eurico Dutra, reply to surrender request, Nov. 27, 1935, TSN archive, Vol. XII, Series B.

77. New York *Times* (AP dispatch), Nov. 29, 1935, p. 13.

78. *A Noite* (Rio), Nov. 27, 1935, p. 1; Hermínio Linhares, "Levante comunista em 1935," pp. 6-7; Dulles, *Vargas of Brazil*, p. 151; Bastos, *Prestes*, p. 320.

79. Courtesy of Timothy Harding. See also Guimarães, statement, RP; letter, José Medina Filho to Secretariado Nacional, early Dec., 1935, in *O Imparcial* (Rio), Dec. 22, 1936, p. 3.

80. Ministério da Guerra, "Como cessou o fogo no 3° R.I.," Nov. 27, 1935, memorandum, RP; Patric, *Toward the Winning Goal*, pp. 253-54; "G.," "The National Revolutionary Uprising," p. 1714 (who claims that the captured troops, not Vargas and the loyalists, were acclaimed by the people, a rather dubious proposition).

81. See Anonymous, "Palestra sôbre o levante da Escola de Aviação Militar," typed report, c. Jan., 1936, RP.

82. See copy of telegram from Souza Leão of the Brazilian Embassy in London, sent

by Getúlio Vargas to the Ministry of Justice, Rio, Document No. 1556, Jan. 1, 1940, Ministry of Justice Archive, Rio. See also letter, Getúlio Vargas to Oswaldo Aranha, Rio, Dec. 14, 1935, GV; letter, Virgílio Alfredo Dolabella to Oswaldo Aranha, Rio, Dec. 19, 1935, OA. A paulista contemporary of the uprisings, Aureliano Leite, points out that the PCB itself described the general outlines of the would-be postrevolutionary order, citing *Terceira República* (Rio), Oct. 31, 1935 (*Páginas de uma longa vida* [São Paulo, 1967 (?)], p. 259).

83. Lopes Chaves, ANL Circular No. 38, for Rio Grande do Norte, Oct. 31, 1935, RS.
84. Letter, "Lívio" [Ilvo Meirelles] to "Léo" [Luís Carlos Prestes], Rio, Dec. 23, 1935, RP; letter, "Lívio" to "Léo," Dec. 7, 1935, RP. See also "G.," "The National Revolutionary Uprising," p. 1719; Fernando Lacerda, "The Recent Uprising in Brazil," *IPC*, XVI, No. 9 (Feb. 15, 1936), 237-38.
85. Interview with Leoncio Basbaum; Basbaum, *História*, III, 91-98. Gruber's "services rendered" in 1935 were recalled in Souza Leão's telegram (note 82 above). Natal's police chief, João Medeiros, also alleges that Vargas or his agents triggered the revolt prematurely (*Meu Depoimento*, pp. 47-48).
86. Letter, Luís Carlos Prestes to unnamed correspondent, Rio, mid-1937, RP.
87. Letter, "Lívio" [Meirelles] to "Léo" [Prestes], Rio, Dec. 4, 1935, RP.
88. Getúlio Vargas, *Hora do Brasil* transcript, Jan. 1, 1936, in *A nova política do Brasil*, IV (Rio, 1938), 139.
89. Letter, Getúlio Vargas to Oswaldo Aranha, Rio, Dec. 14, 1935, GV. Virtually no contemporary sources clearly identified the murdered officers or attempted to investigate the authenticity of the charge, which was widely repeated in the sensationalist press. Captain Agilberto Vieira de Azevedo, one of the two accused rebels, did receive twenty-seven years in prison for the act, while Agildo Barata received a much lighter sentence, ten years. See *O Imparcial* (Rio), May 9, 1937, p. 1; Carneiro, *História*, Vol. II. The PCB position, denying the charge, is stated in Astrogildo Pereira, "Calúnia a moda nazista," *Novos Rumos* (Rio), Nov. 22-26, 1963, p. 5. See also letter, Rubem Rosa to Oswaldo Aranha, Rio, Dec. 19, 1935, OA; memorandum, Estado Maior, Quartel General [*sic*] do Distrito Federal, "Rebelião de 27 de novembro," n.d., OA.
90. *O Imparcial* (Rio), Dec. 18, 1935, p. 4; Dec. 17, 1935, p. 1. Maciel Filho added, however: "Perhaps this [anticommunism] is the only form of salvation."
91. J. W. White, in New York *Times*, Nov. 29, 1935, p. 13; see letter, Oswaldo Aranha to Arthur Hays Sulzberger, Washington, Jan. 7 (?), 1936, and reply, OA.
92. *The Times* (London), "Destinies of Brazil," Nov. 29, 1935, pp. 15-16.
93. Assis Chateaubriand, "A revolução hyperbólica," *Diário de Pernambuco* (Recife), Dec. 8, 1935, p. 4.

Chapter 6. Reaction and Repression

1. Minutes, General Staff Meeting, Rio, Dec. 3, 1935, including manifesto and statements by General Góes Monteiro, GV.

2. Stenographic notes taken by Getúlio Vargas at special cabinet meeting, Dec. 12, 1935, GV.

3. Felinto Müller, "Golpe de vista retrospectivo," report to Getúlio Vargas, early 1936, GV. See letter, Oswaldo Aranha to Getúlio Vargas, Washington, May 3, 1937, on the effects of the censorship of foreign dispatches upon press opinion in the United States.

4. The Congress voted 210 to 59 for the ninety-day state of emergency. The legislative opposition, led by João Neves da Fontoura, unsuccessfully opposed the measure as unnecessary.

5. Memorandum, "Devolvendo projeto fundação partido e dando sua impressão," Vicente Ráo to Getúlio Vargas, Jan. 18, 1936, GV.

6. Letter, Getúlio Vargas to Oswaldo Aranha, Rio, Dec. 14, 1935, OA.

7. *A Pátria* (Rio), Sept. 17, 1936, p. 1; letter, Juracy Magalhães to Getúlio Vargas, Salvador, March 10, 1936, GV; letter, Adalberto Corrêia to Getúlio Vargas, Rio, April 2, 1936, GV.

8. Letter, Capt. Affonso Corrêia to Chefe da Polícia, Rio, Aug. 12, 1936, RP; see also letter, Gustavo Capanema to Getúlio Vargas, June 13, 1936, with covering letter from Vicente Ráo, GV.

9. *O Imparcial* (Rio), Dec. 7, 1935, p. 5; Dec. 13, 1935, p. 5. See also Affonso Henriques, *Vargas, o maquiavélico* (São Paulo, 1961), ch. XVII.

10. Letter, Hercolino Cascardo to Augusto do Amaral Peixoto, Rio, Dec. 25, 1935, from the *Pedro I*, GV; earlier, undated penciled note, *ibid.*; see letter, João Neves da Fontoura to Getúlio Vargas, Rio, c. March, 1937, asking mercy for Cascardo, GV.

11. Cited in Glauco Carneiro, *História das revoluções brasileiras* (Rio, 1965), II, 433.

12. See *O Imparcial* (Rio), March 7, 1936, p. 3; March 10, 1936, p. 1; New York *Times*, Jan. 8, 1936, p. 7; Richard Freeman, "Arthur Ewert Is Being Tortured," *IPC*, XVI, No. 20 (April 25, 1936), 556-57.

13. Judge Ribas Carneiro, in *O Imparcial* (Rio), March 14, 1936, p. 1. The New York *Times* (Jan. 8, 1936, p. 7), on the other hand, called the Bergers "two of the smartest members of Rio de Janeiro's fashionable circles." Elisa Berger was deported to Europe, where she ultimately escaped to France before the outbreak of the war. Berger left Brazil in 1947 for the Soviet zone of Germany, where he died in 1959. See Günther Nollau, *International Communism and World Revolution* (New York, 1961), p. 124.

14. New York *Times*, March 27, 1936, p. 14; *O Imparcial* (Rio), March 7, 1936, p. 5; letter, Joseph Gilders, secretary of the National Committee for the Defense of Political Prisoners, New York, "Statement of the Joint Committee for Brazil . . . ," to Oswaldo Aranha, March 19, 1936, OA.

15. Américo Dias Leite, in *O Imparcial* (Rio), March 17, 1936, p. 16.

16. See Richard Freeman, "A Peep into Vargas' Dungeons," *IPC*, Vol. XVI, No. 23 (May 16, 1936); Red Aid of Brazil, "A Call for Help for Brazil," *ibid.*, Vol. XVI, No. 16 (March 28, 1936); Octávio Brandão, "Luís Carlos Prestes, the Champion of National Liberation of the Brazilian People," *ibid.*, Vol. XVI, No. 15 (March 21, 1936), and continuing articles in *IPC* through 1944. See also Jorge Amado,

A vida de Luís Carlos Prestes: O cavalheiro da esperança (São Paulo, 1945), pp. 261-90.

17. Letter, Oswaldo Aranha to Dona Yayá [Mangabeira], Washington, May 28, 1937, OA; see reply, Rio, July 17, 1936, OA.

18. Speeches, Domingos Velasco and Abel Chermont, reported in *O Imparcial* (Rio), May 15-19, 1937; João Mangabeira and others, letter of protest to Police Commander, Rio, May 20, 1936, GV; letter, João Neves da Fontoura to Getúlio Vargas, Rio, March, 1937, GV.

19. *A Pátria* (Rio), Jan. 9, 1937, p. 1; Jan. 15, 1937, p. 1.

20. Testimony in behalf of Hercolino Cascardo, TSN proceedings, Vol. XX, Revisão 59, p. 5, STM archive, Rio.

21. Letter, Oswaldo Aranha to Getúlio Vargas, July 29, 1936, Washington. See also Aranha to Vargas, Washington, Aug. 14, 1936, OA; Vargas to Aranha, Rio, May 28, 1936, GV.

22. New York *Times*, Oct. 1, 1937, p. 3; untitled records and newspaper clippings, "PCB" dossier, RP; *Communist*, XV, No. 4 (1937 [?]), 352.

23. See report, Felinto Müller to Getúlio Vargas, Rio, June 18, 1937, GV.

24. *A Nação* (Rio), Dec. 17, 1935, p. 5; *A Offensiva* (Rio), Feb. 12, 1936, p. 8; Feb. 14, 1936, p. 7. For example, Anatole Podoroski, Rubens Goldberg, Cesar Zibemberg, Moyses Garbas, among dozens more. Jewish spokesmen blamed Felinto Müller personally for the anti-Semitic dimension of the arrests, although there were no public protests from Jewish community leaders, who were either too frightened to complain or who agreed with the policy of deporting subversives.

25. Letter, Augusto Machado [Leoncio Basbaum] to unnamed correspondent, São Paulo (from Maria Zélia), RP; interview with Caio Prado, Jr., São Paulo. See Capt. Davino Francisco dos Santos, *A marcha vermelha* (São Paulo, 1948), pp. 148-49.

26. See letter, Stefan Zweig to Frederike Zweig, São Paulo, Sept. 3, 1936, in Henry G. Alsberg, ed. and tr., *Stefan and Frederike Zweig: Their Correspondence, 1912-1942* (New York, 1954), p. 291.

27. PCB, "Informes sôbre as actividades políticas e culturaes dos presos políticos do Rio de Janeiro," n.d., RP.

28. See, for example, *Boletim de Informações* (Maria Zélia stockade), No. 1, July 14, 1936, Caio Prado papers.

29. New York *Times*, June 19, 1936, p. 2; Marini, "Revolt of the Political Prisoners in Rio de Janeiro," *IPC*, XVI, No. 32 (July 11, 1936), 860. The event was not reported in the Brazilian press.

30. Letter, "Vários médicos prêsos," Casa de Detenção, Rio, to unnamed authorities, Dec. 3, 1936, RP. See also letter, José Reynaldo Serra Costa and nine others, to Sen. Clodomir Cardoso and others in the Maranhão state legislative delegation, mid-1937, RP.

31. *Jornal do Brasil* (Rio), May 30, 1967, p. 3. See *Relação de comunistas fichados D.E.S.P.S.* (Rio, May, 1940), courtesy of Hélio Silva. See also Octávio Brandão, "Important Events Are Developing in Brazil," *IPC*, XVII, No. 23 (May 29, 1937), 536-37.

32. Various Trotskyite newspapers, RP files.

33. Police records (RP files) list about 130 activists in the Leninist Workers' Party in 1936-37.

34. Luiz Machado, "Revolution in Brazil," *IPC*, XVI, No. 2 (Jan. 11, 1936), 32. See also *Novos Rumos* (Rio) series, Nov. 22-28, 1963; Octávio Brandão, "The First Skirmishes in the Battle for Democracy," *IPC*, XVII, No. 24 (June 5, 1937), 655.

35. Honório de Freitas Guimarães, statement, RP.

36. Police report, "Estrictamente confidencial. Archivo apprehendido em casa do Antonio Vilar, aliás Luís Carlos Prestes," Rio, March 25, 1936.

37. S-2 report to Felinto Müller, Rio, July 17, 1936; see also S-2 report to Müller, July 11, 1936, RP.

38. Courtesy of Anísio S. Teixeira. Bibliographical information also courtesy of Dr. Teixeira.

39. Fernando de Azevedo, *Brazilian Culture* (New York, 1950), pp. 451-52; Richard M. Morse, *From Community to Metropolis: A Biography of São Paulo, Brazil* (Gainesville, 1958), p. 250.

40. *A Nação* (Rio), Dec. 5, 1935, p. 3; *O Globo* (Rio), Dec. 2, 1935, 2d ed., p. 1; see Padre Helder Câmara, "Educação progressiva," *A Ordem* (Rio), X (April, 1933), 544-49, an attack on the "seductive and erroneous philosophy of progressive education." Teixeira's career is outlined in a volume organized in his honor, Jaime Abreu *et al., Anísio Teixeira: Pensamento e ação* (Rio, 1960).

41. Francisco Campos, inaugural address as Federal District secretary of education, in *Correio da Manhã* (Rio), Dec. 25, 1936, p. 2; see *A Offensiva* (Rio), Dec. 28, 1935, p. 1, stating the AIB's satisfaction with the change.

42. Francisco Campos' attitude on education is described in his *Educação e cultura*, 2d ed. (Rio, 1941). For an indictment of the backward and faltering educational system in the 1960s, see *O Cruzeiro* (Rio), July 13, 1968, pp. 39-43; Maria José Garcia Werebe, *Grandezas e misérias do ensino no Brasil*, 3d ed. (São Paulo, 1968).

43. See *O Globo* (Rio), May 11, 1935, p. 1; June 15, 1935, p. 1; June 17, 1935, p. 1; *A Nação* (Rio), Jan. 16, 1936, p. 11.

44. See Laurita Pessôa Raja Gabaglia, *O Cardeal Leme* (Rio, 1962), pp. 350-52.

45. Letter, Carlos de Lima Cavalcanti to Agamemnon Magalhães, Recife, Dec. 18, 1935, GV.

46. Pedro Ernesto Baptista, *Defesa prévia* (Rio, 1937); testimony of Eliezer Magalhães, TSN archive. See Virgílio Alfredo Dolabella to Oswaldo Aranha, Rio, Nov. 20, 1937, OA; Martin Guilayan to Oswaldo Aranha, Rio, April 2, 1936, OA; letter from "Sá" [Ilvo Meirelles] to Luís Carlos Prestes, Dec. 9, 1935 (implicating Pedro Ernesto's son, Odilón Baptista), cited in *O Imparcial* (Rio), Dec. 4, 1936, p. 15.

47. Alzira Vargas do Amaral Peixoto, *Getúlio Vargas, meu pai* (Pôrto Alegre, 1960), pp. 138-44; *O Imparcial* (Rio), Dec. 4, 1936, p. 15. Vargas' reputed impassivity to repression has been attributed variously to a personal lack of emotion, an underlying machiavellianism, or the tough gaúcho *guerrilheiro* environment out

of which he came. See Affonso Arinos de Mello Franco, "The Tide of Government: From Colony to Constitutional Democracy," *The Atlantic Monthly*, CXCVII, No. 2 (Feb., 1956), 143-47.

48. See Graciliano Ramos, *Memórias do cárcere* (Rio, 1953) 4 vols., published posthumously. Information on accused subversives is provided briefly in *Relação de comunistas fichados D.E.S.P.S.* (Rio, May, 1940).

49. Getúlio Vargas, "Necessidade e dever de repressão ao comunismo," speech given May 10, 1936, in *A nova política do Brasil*, IV, (Rio, 1941), 151-56.

Chapter 7. The Estado Nôvo

1. Letter, Getúlio Vargas to Oswaldo Aranha, Rio, Jan. 11, 1936, GV.

2. Francisco Campos, *O estado nacional: Sua estrutura, seu conteúdo ideológico,* 3d ed. (Rio, 1937), p. 61.

3. Letter, Oswaldo Aranha to Ricardo Xavier [of the Caixa Econômica], Washington, April 21, 1936, OA. See also Nelson Werneck Sodré, *Memórias de um soldado* (Rio, 1967), p. 139.

4. Alzira Vargas do Amaral Peixoto, *Getúlio Vargas, meu pai* (Pôrto Alegre, 1960), p. 180.

5. Carolina Nabuco, *A vida de Virgílio de Mello Franco* (Rio, 1962), pp. 92-93; letter, Oswaldo Aranha to Getúlio Vargas, Washington, Aug. 14, 1936, GV.

6. Carlos de Lima Cavalcanti, exchange with General Newton Cavalcanti, cited in *O Imparcial* (Rio), Aug. 14, 1936, p. 3.

7. Police *Relatório* No. 163, "O ambiente de hostilidades em tôrno do Ministro da Guerra," Rio, July 7, 1936, GV; Peixoto, *Getúlio Vargas*, p. 150; Lourival Coutinho, *O General Góes depõe . . .*, 3d ed. (Rio, 1956), p. 283.

8. Letter, Getúlio Vargas to Protásio Vargas, Petrópolis, April 29, 1936, GV.

9. See letter, Virgílio de Mello Franco to Juracy Magalhães, Oct. 10, 1936, cited in Nabuco, *Vida*, p. 96; Hélio Silva, "Lembrai-vos de 1937," *Tribuna da Imprensa* (Rio), Oct. 3-4, 1959, cited in John W. F. Dulles, *Vargas of Brazil* (Austin, 1967), pp. 156-57.

10. Aureliano Leite, *Páginas de uma longa vida* (São Paulo, 1967 [?]), pp. 267-68; A. C. Pacheco e Silva, *Armando de Salles Oliveira* (São Paulo, 1966), *passim*.

11. *O Observador Econômico e Financeiro* (Rio), I, No. 11 (Dec., 1936), 9.

12. Getúlio Vargas, radio broadcast, Jan. 1, 1937, in *A nova política do Brasil*, IV (Rio, 1938), 209-17.

13. See letter, Adalberto Aranha to Oswaldo Aranha, Rio, June 12, 1937, OA; letter, Felinto Müller to Getúlio Vargas, Rio, June 18, 1937, GV; *O Imparcial* (Rio), July 9, 1937, p. 1.

14. Telegram, Paulo Ramos (governor of Maranhão) to Getúlio Vargas, São Luís, Sept. 1, 1937, GV.

15. New York *Times*, Sept. 16, 1936, p. 14. Raids continued through 1937. The Brazilian press did not report the story.

16. See letter, J. E. Macedo Soares (the brother of the justice minister) to Getúlio Vargas, Rio, May 17, 1937, GV.

17. See telegram, Benedito Valladares to Getúlio Vargas, Rio, May 17, 1937, GV.

18. Coded telegram, General Emílio Esteves, Commandant, Third Military Zone, to Getúlio Vargas, Pôrto Alegre (?), April 25, 1937, GV; Benjamin Vargas to Getúlio Vargas, March 5, 1937, two telegrams dispatched the same day, GV.

19. Memorandum, General Eurico Dutra to Getúlio Vargas, "Instruções pessoais e secretas," May 6, 1937, GV; telegram, General Góes Monteiro to Eurico Dutra, Curitiba, May 25, 1937, GV; letter, João Alberto Lins de Barros to Oswaldo Aranha, Rio, May 29, 1937, OA.

20. Ministério da Guerra, "Actividades subversivas do governador do Rio Grande do Sul," April 7, 1937, initialed by War Minister Dutra, GV.

21. See letter, Augusto Souza e Silva to Getúlio Vargas, Rio, Aug. 7, 1937, GV.

22. See telegram, Carlos de Lima Cavalcanti to Getúlio Vargas, Recife, May 11, 1937, GV; telegram, Lima Cavalcanti to Vargas, Teresina, Piauí, May 12, 1937, GV.

23. Letter, Adalberto Aranha to Oswaldo Aranha, Rio, May 5, 1937, OA.

24. See telegram, Jurandyr Mamede to Major Carneiro Mendonça, Recife, May 13, 1937, GV.

25. Letter, João Alberto Lins de Barros to Oswaldo Aranha, Rio, May 29, 1937, OA. Some observers criticized the candidate's restraint. See letter, Adalberto Aranha to Oswaldo Aranha, Rio, Sept. 22, 1937, OA.

26. *O Imparcial* (Rio), May 23, 1937, p. 1.

27. See letter, Virgílio Dolabella to Oswaldo Aranha, Rio, Nov. 20, 1937, OA.

28. Letter, Raul Pilla to Getúlio Vargas, Rio (?), Nov. 8, 1937, GV; letter, Getúlio Vargas to Oswaldo Aranha, Rio, Nov. 9, 1937, GV; interview with Affonso Arinos de Mello Franco, Rio. A reference to police repression is made in the letter of Adalberto Aranha to Oswaldo Aranha, Rio, Oct. 15, 1937, OA.

29. José Américo de Almeida, quoted in letter, Adalberto Aranha to Oswaldo Aranha, Rio, Sept. 4, 1937, OA. See José Américo's *A palavra e o tempo (1937-1945-1950)* (Rio, 1965), an anthology of selected campaign addresses.

30. Letter, J. S. Maciel Filho to Oswaldo Aranha, Rio, mid-Sept., 1937, Maciel Filho archive; see similar statement by Otávio Mangabeira, *A Pátria* (Rio), Oct. 12, 1937, p. 2.

31. See Olbiano de Mello, *A marcha da revolução social no Brasil* (Rio, 1957), pp. 103-5; Ministro Olympio Mourão Filho, statement, in *Jornal do Brasil* (Rio), Nov. 10, 1967, p. 4.

32. Decreto Lei No. 2020, Oct. 7, 1937. Dulles' statement that the governors in Bahia and Pernambuco were also excluded from commission presidencies is incorrect. See Dulles, *Vargas of Brazil*, p. 163.

33. Admiral Paes Leme, quoted in *O Radical* (Rio), Oct. 10, 1937, p. 1.

34. *O Imparcial* (Rio), Oct. 15, 1937, p. 5.

35. *Ibid.*, Oct. 24, 1937, p. 1.

36. See letter, Col. A. F. Dantas to Eurico Dutra, Salvador, Oct., 1936 (no exact date), GV.

37. Telegram, Carlos de Lima Cavalcanti to Getúlio Vargas, Recife, Oct. 6, 1937, GV;

printed notes, Lima Cavalcanti to Oswaldo Aranha and others, Sept. 2, 1937, OA.

38. Telegram, Carlos de Lima Cavalcanti to Getúlio Vargas, Recife, Oct. 29, 1937, GV.

39. Telegram, Col. Amaro Villanova to Gen. Eurico Dutra, Recife, Nov. 3, 1937, GV.

40. See Dulles, *Vargas of Brazil*, p. 164.

41. *A Nação* (Rio), Nov. 10, 1937, p. 4.

42. *O Imparcial* (Rio), Oct. 21, 1937, p. 3.

43. *Ibid.*, Oct. 30, 1937, p. 1.

44. Flôres da Cunha, "Ao Rio Grande do Sul," Oct. 18, 1937, copy in GV.

45. *O Imparcial* (Rio), Oct. 26, 1937, pp. 1, 4; Oct. 29, 1937, p. 1.

46. Telegram, Benjamin Vargas to Getúlio Vargas, Pôrto Alegre, Oct. 20, 1937, GV. See also João Neves da Fontoura to Manoel Cardoso (intercepted telegram), Oct. 19, 1937, GV.

47. The votes are listed in Hamilton Leal, *História das instituições políticas do Brasil* (Rio, 1962), pp. 525-28. About a third of the generals and military commanders polled indicated indifference. Dulles points out that the exact nature of what they were voting about may not have been particularly clear to the generals (*Vargas of Brazil*, p. 164).

48. Speaking via radio on the evening of November 1, he declared that he would rather be his country's adviser "than its president." Francis D. McCann, Jr., "Brazil and the United States and the Coming of World War II, 1937-1942" (Ph.D. dissertation, Indiana University, 1967), p. 22.

49. Dispatch, United States Embassy, Rio, to Secretary of State, Nov. 6, 1937, cited in Dulles, *Vargas of Brazil*, p. 166.

50. Getúlio Vargas, notes for a telegram to Benedito Valladares, Rio, Nov. 5, 1937, GV.

51. Telegrams, Benedito Valladares to Getúlio Vargas, Belo Horizonte, Nov. 5 and Nov. 9, 1937, GV.

52. *Vanguarda* (Rio), Oct. 28, 1937, p. 1; Oct. 30, 1937, p. 1.

53. Telegram, Benedito Valladares to Getúlio Vargas, Belo Horizonte, Nov. 4, 1937, GV.

54. Telegram, Getúlio Vargas to Oswaldo Aranha, Rio, Nov. 8, 1937, OA.

55. Telegram, Benedito Valladares to Getúlio Vargas, Belo Horizonte, Nov. 9, 1937, GV.

56. Telegram, Viriato Vargas to Getúlio Vargas, Pôrto Alegre, Nov. 8, 1937, GV.

57. They were Federal District troops, not from the federal army. See Dulles, *Vargas of Brazil*, p. 172.

58. *A Pátria* (Rio), Nov. 11, 1937, p. 1.

59. Getúlio Vargas, *Hora do Brasil* broadcast, Nov. 10, 1937, transcript, GV.

60. Telegram, Ambassador Jefferson Caffery to Secretary of State Cordell Hull, Rio, Nov. 19, 1937, 832.00/1077, in U.S. Department of State, *Foreign Relations of the United States*, V (Washington, 1937), 312-13; see also letter, Oswaldo Aranha to Sumner Welles, Rio, Sept. 14, 1938, OA.

61. Letter, Juracy Magalhães to Marques dos Reis, Minister of Public Works, Salvador, Nov. 9, 1937, in Juracy Magalhães, *Minha vida pública na Bahia* (Rio, 1957), pp. 68-69.

62. Barbosa Lima Sobrinho, "Carlos de Lima Cavalcanti" (obituary), *Jornal do Brasil* (Rio), Sept. 24, 1967, p. 6.
63. See telegram, Col. Amaro Villanova to Getúlio Vargas, Recife, Nov. 18, 1937, GV.
64. Pacheco e Silva, *Salles Oliveira,* p. 147. While in exile, Salles spoke bitterly against Vargas and the Estado Nôvo. See his open letter to Góes Monteiro, Paris, Feb. 25, 1939, RP; also, "Mensagem dos exilados ao Presidente Roosevelt," Paris, Jan. 7, 1939, RP.
65. See Juan Linz, "An Authoritarian Regime: Spain," in Erik Allardt and Yrjö Littunen, eds., *Cleavages, Ideologies, and Party Systems* (Helsinki, 1964), p. 297.
66. Heron P. Pinto, *Nos subterráneos do Estado Nôvo* (Rio, 1950), and David Nasser, *Falta alguém em Nuremberg: Torturas da polícia brasileira* (Rio, 1947). Both document in vivid language the accusations against the federal police during the period between 1935 and 1945.
67. Newspapers were required by law to print all press releases given to them by government agencies. See New York *Times,* Nov. 13, 1937, p. 9.
68. See letter, João Alberto Lins de Barros to Felinto Müller, Buenos Aires, Nov. 13, 1937, GV; José Bernadino da Câmara Canto to Getúlio Vargas, Montevideo, Nov. 17, 1937, GV; clippings from *El Dia* and *El Plata* (Montevideo), GV.
69. New York *Times,* Nov. 29, 1937. See telegram, Oswaldo Aranha to Getúlio Vargas, Washington, Nov. 29, 1937, OA.
70. Letter, Oswaldo Aranha to Getúlio Vargas, Washington, Dec. 7, 1937, OA. The official United States government position on the Estado Nôvo is summarized in a memorandum from Green H. Hackworth, legal adviser to the Chief of the Division of the American Republics, Washington, Jan. 7, 1938, in United States National Archives. See also memorandum, Cordell Hull to Jefferson Caffery, "Personal," 832.00/1089a, in *Foreign Relations of the United States,* p. 313.
71. Reich Minister Goebbels, in *Politische Korrespondenz,* cited in *O Imparcial* (Rio), Dec. 12, 1937, p. 11; *Il Messagere* (Rome), cited in *A Pátria* (Rio), Nov. 17, 1937, p. 1.
72. William Newton Simonson, "Nazi Infiltration in South America, 1933-1945" (Ph.D. dissertation, Fletcher School of Law and Diplomacy, 1964), p. 465 (citing telegram from U.S. Embassy [Rome] to Department of State, Nov. 12, 1937–Nov. 18, 1937); Alton Frye, *Nazi Germany and the American Hemisphere* (New Haven, 1967), p. 101.
73. See letter, Oswaldo Aranha to Luís Simões Lopes, Washington, May 21, 1935 (regarding his health); letter, Oswaldo Aranha to João Mangabeira, Washington, June 11, 1935, OA; McCann, "Brazil and the United States," pp. 34-48.
74. Cable, Oswaldo Aranha to Getúlio Vargas, Washington, Nov. 13, 1937, GV.
75. Transcript of telephone conversation between Artur Souza Costa, Luís Aranha, and Oswaldo Aranha, Washington–Rio de Janeiro, Nov. 16, 1937, 17:14 P.M., copy signed by Oswaldo de Carvalho Lemgruber, GV.
76. Vargas' penciled notes for reply to telegram from Oswaldo Aranha, Nov. 18, 1937, GV.
77. Letter, Virgílio de Mello Franco to Oswaldo Aranha, Rio, Nov. 20, 1937. GV.
78. His defense of the Estado Nôvo stressed its constitutional legitimacy. See letter, Oswaldo Aranha to Getúlio Vargas, Washington, Nov. 20, 1937, OA.

79. *O Imparcial* (Rio), Nov. 4, 1936, p. 4; Leite, *Páginas,* p. 266; *O Observador Econômico e Financeiro* (Rio), Dec. 1936, p. 3.

80. Antenor Novaes, "Brasil Nôvo!" editorial, *A Pátria* (Rio), Nov. 11, 1937, p. 2.

81. See George Wythe *et al., Brazil: An Expanding Economy* (New York, 1949), pp. 34, 263-66, cited in Thomas E. Skidmore, *Politics in Brazil, 1930-1964* (New York, 1967), p. 34. As early as 1935 textile industrialist and editor J. S. Maciel Filho had advocated a nationalistic economic policy, although he also had warned against authoritarian excesses. See, for example, *O Imparcial* (Rio), Dec. 17, 1935, p. 4. See also John D. Wirth, "Brazilian Economic Nationalism: Trade and Steel under Vargas" (Ph.D. dissertation, Stanford University, 1966), p. 26.

82. Valentim F. Bouças, "O nosso programma," *O Observador Econômico e Financeiro* (Rio), Feb., 1936, inaugural issue, p. 4.

83. Skidmore, *Politics in Brazil,* pp. 43-44, 34.

84. Wirth, "Brazilian Economic Nationalism," p. 33; Stanley J. Stein, *The Brazilian Cotton Manufacture: Textile Enterprise in an Underdeveloped Area, 1850-1950* (Cambridge, Mass., 1957), pp. 135-36.

85. Oswaldo Aranha–Luís Aranha–Artur Souza Costa telephone conversation transcript, Nov. 16, 1937, GV; *O Diário de Minas* (Belo Horizonte), Nov. 5, 1937, p. 4; *A Nação* (Rio), Nov. 16, 1937, p. 2; Skidmore, *Politics in Brazil,* p. 29; Adhemar de Barros, *Discursos (1938-1939)* (São Paulo, 1940), p. 207.

86. See United States Tariff Commission, *Foreign Trade of Latin America,* Part II, Report No. 146, 2d series (Washington, 1942), Table 7, p. 88, cited in Wirth, "Brazilian Economic Nationalism," p. 33. See also John D. Wirth, "A German View of Brazilian Trade and Development, 1935," *HAHR,* XLVII, No. 2 (May, 1967), 225; Donald W. Giffen, "The Normal Years: Brazilian-American Relations, 1930-1939" (Ph.D. dissertation, Vanderbilt University, 1962), esp. pp. 69-71.

87. Frye, *Nazi Germany,* p. 75, citing U.S. Embassy to Cordell Hull, April 24, 1936, Rio, in *Foreign Relations of the United States,* V (1936 volume), 249.

88. See McCann, "Brazil and the United States," pp. 21-28; letter, Oswaldo Aranha to Getúlio Vargas, Washington, June 4, 1937, OA; Wirth, "Brazilian Economic Nationalism," pp. 4, 19-20, 107-8, 170. See report, Góes Monteiro to Getúlio Vargas, Jan. (?) 1934, cited *ibid.,* p. 5. Nelson Werneck Sodré, *História militar do Brasil* (Rio, 1965), p. 281.

89. See letter, Virgílio de Mello Franco to Oswaldo Aranha, Rio, Nov. 20, 1937, GV; letters, Getúlio Vargas to Oswaldo Aranha, Rio, Dec. 24, 1934, and June 17, 1937, OA; letter, Sumner Welles to Oswaldo Aranha, Washington, Sept. 9, 1937, OA. Further diplomatic correspondence can be found in the Aranha archive.

90. McCann, "Brazil and the United States," pp. 66, 72. In his memoirs, Góes Monteiro relates the shock felt by the military command in May, 1938, when it was disclosed that Brazil possessed only enough petroleum reserves to fight an eight-day war. (Coutinho, *O General Góes depõe . . . ,* pp. 340-41, 348-49.)

91. This is hinted in a letter from Adalberto Aranha to Oswaldo Aranha, Rio, Oct. 15, 1937, OA.

92. Sodré, *História militar,* p. 282-83.

Chapter 8. Nationalism over Integralism

1. Telegram, Juracy Magalhães to Getúlio Vargas, Salvador, Aug. 25, 1936, GV; telegram, Benedito Valladares to Juracy Magalhães, Belo Horizonte, Sept. 18, 1936, copy also sent to Vargas, GV.
2. Plínio Salgado, radio address, Nov. 1, 1937, in *A Offensiva* (Rio), Nov. 2, 1937, p. 2. See Olbiano de Mello, *A marcha da revolução social no Brasil* (Rio, 1957), for a description of the Integralist presidential campaign and later developments through the coup d'état.
3. Cavalcanti's letter of resignation, in which he attacks Vargas for having betrayed his agreements with the Integralist movement, is cited in Mello, *Marcha*, p. 119.
4. Letter, Plínio Salgado to Getúlio Vargas, Rio, Jan. 28, 1938, GV. The twelve-page, single-spaced typed letter summarized the history of the AIB and its relations with Vargas through mid-1937. Of the matter of the post of minister of education, Salgado admitted privately that he had not rejected it but had proposed Gustavo Barroso's name to Vargas, only to have been ignored (Mello, *Marcha*, p. 124).
5. Letters, João Alberto Lins de Barros to Getúlio Vargas, Buenos Aires, Feb. 28, 1938, and March 20, 1938, from Lima, Peru, describing Góes' South American visit, GV.
6. See letters, Baptista Luzardo to Getúlio Vargas, Montevideo, Feb. 26, 1938, and March 26, 1938, GV; letter, José Bernardino da Câmara Canto to Alzira Vargas, Pôrto Alegre, March 13, 1938, GV.
7. John W. F. Dulles, *Vargas of Brazil* (Austin, 1967), p. 182.
8. See dispatch No. 468, Scotten to Secretary of State, Rio, April 1, 1938, 832.00/1186.
9. The best synthesis to date is in Dulles, *Vargas of Brazil*, pp. 181-88, which is based on Hélio Silva's manuscript, "Rhapsódia verde em 5 atos," 1965, which will be published in his *Ciclo de Vargas* series. See also Alzira Vargas do Amaral Peixoto, *Getúlio Vargas, meu pai* (Pôrto Alegre, 1960), pp. 117-33; David Nasser, *A revolução dos covardes*, 2d ed. (Rio, 1947); TSN Apelação No. 182, Processo 600, Aug. 9, 1938, National Archives, Rio.
10. Dispatch No. 581, Jefferson Caffery to Secretary of State Cordell Hull, Rio, May 12, 1938, 832.00/0604.
11. *Ibero-Amerikanische Rundschau* (Hamburg), IV, No. 4 (June, 1938), 86; courtesy of Dan Perlmutter.
12. David Nasser discusses Severo Fournier's role (in *A revolução dos covardes*). See also letter, Getúlio Vargas to Oswaldo Aranha, Rio, July 1, 1938, OA; [Galeazzo Ciano], *Ciano's Hidden Diary*, tr. Andreas Mayor (New York, 1953), pp. 132, 153, 199, for the Italian government's role. Ambassador Lojacano's decision to grant asylum to Fournier led ultimately to his recall from Brazil. Nelson Werneck Sodré (*Memórias de um soldado* [Rio, 1967], p. 142) points out that Fournier contracted tuberculosis while in prison, and that he died shortly following his release.
13. See letter, Plínio Salgado to Joaquim Secco, Lisbon, June 20, 1939, RP;

Manifesto Diretivo do Integralismo (Rio, July, 1945), RP. These and other documents boast that the Integralist movement strongly influenced the Estado Nôvo and express Salgado's desire to return to the political arena. A modified form of Integralism headed by Salgado, then federal Senator, continued to exist into the 1960s, although with minimal public support.

14. Letter, Baptista Luzardo to Getúlio Vargas, Montevideo, Nov. 15, 1938, GV; police dossier on "Armandista golpe," c. 1939, RP. For Nazi activities in Latin America see William Newton Simonson, "Nazi Infiltration in South America, 1933-1945" (Ph.D. dissertation, Fletcher School of Law and Diplomacy, 1964), and Alton Frye, *Nazi Germany and the American Hemisphere, 1933-1941* (New Haven, 1967), although Frye is not entirely reliable.

15. Karl Loewenstein, *Brazil under Vargas* (New York, 1942), p. 343; New York *Times*, Nov. 13, 1937, p. 9.

16. José Américo de Almeida noted, on the occasion of his seating in the Brazilian Academy of Letters at the age of eighty in 1967, that Vargas had never been a particularly strong or stable president. *O Globo* (Rio), June 19, 1967, p. 11.

17. See the letter from J. S. Maciel Filho to Getúlio Vargas, Rio, March, 1942, Maciel Filho papers, listing the reasons for the closing of *O Imparcial*. The letter does not disclose that the newspaper, staunchly pro-Mussolini through the 1930s, had been receiving Axis subsidies. On the matter of censorship David Nasser provides a day-to-day list of articles vetoed by government officials between January, 1943, and February, 1945 (*Revolução dos covardes*, pp. 241-68).

18. Polícia Civil do Distrito Federal, *Polícia política preventiva (Serviço de Inquéritos Políticos e Sociais)* (Rio, 1939), pp. 9-10.

19. Walter Sharp, "Methods of Public Opinion Control in Present-Day Brazil," *Public Opinion Quarterly*, V, No. 1 (March, 1941), 6-7; Loewenstein, *Brazil under Vargas*, pp. 285-87.

20. Dispatch, Ritter to Berlin, March 30, 1938; see Francis D. McCann, Jr., "Brazil and the United States and the Coming of World War II, 1937-1942" (Ph.D. dissertation, Indiana University, 1967), p. 50; Simonson, "Nazi Infiltration," pp. 468-95.

21. Frye, *Nazi Germany and the American Hemisphere*, pp. 103-4. See also pp. 113, 116, 166, 173-74.

22. Hélio Jaguaribe, "The Dynamics of Brazilian Nationalism," in Claudio Veliz, ed., *Obstacles to Change in Latin America* (New York, 1965), p. 169. See also Luis Ratinoff, "The New Urban Groups: The Middle Classes," in Seymour Martin Lipset and Aldo Solari, eds., *Elites in Latin America* (New York, 1967), pp. 61-93. The federal government employed 131,628 persons in 1938, 145,991 in 1943, 217,135 in 1956, and 344,000 in 1960 (from Lawrence S. Graham, *Civil Service Reform in Brazil* [Austin, 1968], p. 132).

23. See Graham, *Civil Service Reform*, esp. p. 30; Bryce Wood, "The Federal Service," *Inter-American Quarterly*, II (1940), 46-47.

24. Nelson Werneck Sodré, *História da burguesia brasileira*, 2d ed. (Rio, 1967), p. 305; Paul Frischauer, *Presidente Vargas: Biografia* (São Paulo, 1943), p. 360;

Loewenstein, *Brazil under Vargas*, pp. 208-9, cited in Dulles, *Vargas of Brazil*, p. 177; John D. Wirth, "Brazilian Economic Nationalism" (Ph.D. dissertation, Stanford University, 1966), pp. 166-72 *passim*.

25. See John D. Wirth, *The Politics of Brazilian Development, 1930-1954* (Stanford, 1970).

26. Orlando de Carvalho, *Política do município (ensaio histórico)* (Rio, 1946), p. 165; Thomas E. Skidmore, *Politics in Brazil, 1930-1964* (New York, 1967), pp. 33-35.

27. Courtesy of Pedro Pinchas Geiger and Charles Wagley.

28. Orlando de Carvalho, *Política do município*, pp. 82-99; Graham, *Civil Service Reform*, pp. 22-37.

29. Kalman H. Silvert, *The Conflict Society: Reaction and Revolution in Latin America*, rev. ed. (New York, 1966), pp. 90-95, esp. pp. 91-92.

30. See, for example, dispatch, Ritter to German Foreign Ministry, Rio, Dec. 23, 1937, GV, referring to the visit to Berlin by João Daudt de Oliveira of the Commercial Association of Rio de Janeiro; J. S. Maciel Filho, "O homem providencial," special issue of *O Imparcial* (Rio), Jan. 1, 1938, esp. pp. 59-62.

31. The question of a possible new "legion" is discussed (and dismissed) in a letter from Luís Aranha (Lulú) to Ernani do Amaral Peixoto, Pôrto Alegre, June 3, 1938, GV.

32. Lawrence S. Graham and Walter Sharp use the term (*Civil Service Reform*, p. 27; "Methods of Opinion Control," pp. 14-16).

33. See George L. Mosse, "The Genesis of Fascism," in Walter Laqueur and George L. Mosse, eds., *International Fascism, 1920-1945* (New York, 1966), pp. 18-19; Harold Laswell, "The Psychology of Hitlerism," *Political Quarterly*, IV (July, 1933), 374; Herman Finer, *Mussolini's Italy* (London, 1935), pp. 365-73.

34. Finer, *Mussolini's Italy*, p. 373.

35. See Juan Linz's definition in his "An Authoritarian Regime: Spain," in E. Allardt and Y. Littunen, eds., *Cleavages, Ideologies, and Party Systems* (Helsinki, 1964), pp. 291-341. Ernst Nolte maintains that Italian fascism only adopted totalitarianism after 1925 (*Three Faces of Fascism* [New York, 1966], p. 217).

36. "Dictadura" means dictatorship; "blanda" means "soft"; "dura" means "hard." Gerhard Masur, *Nationalism in Latin America* (New York, 1966), p. 129. J. W. White of the New York *Times* refers to Vargas' blandness in a letter to Arthur Hays Sulzberger, Buenos Aires, Dec. 26, 1935, GV.

37. Skidmore, *Politics in Brazil*, p. 39.

38. Azevedo Amaral, *O estado autoritário e a realidade nacional* (Rio, 1938), p. 207, cited in Kenneth P. Erickson, "Labor in the Political Process in Brazil," MS, 1968, p. A-12. Cf. Eugen Weber, *Varieties of Fascism* (Princeton, 1964), p. 13. An excellent source for the political ideology of the Estado Nôvo is the DIP's monthly official journal, *Cultura Política*, 53 issues of which were published in Rio de Janeiro between March, 1941, and October, 1945. It is indexed in *Dados* (Rio), IV (1968), 221-46.

39. João Camilo de Oliveira Tôrres, *A democracia coroada* (Rio, n.d.), pp. 137-72; Amaral, *O estado autoritário,* p. 184, in Erickson, "Labor in the Political Process," MS, p. A-13; Francisco Campos, *O estado nacional: Sua estrutura, seu conteúdo ideológico,* 3d ed. (Rio, 1941), p. 23.

40. Campos, *O estado nacional,* p. 113. See also p. 42 *et passim.*

41. Oliveira Vianna, *Problemas de organização e problemas de direção* (Rio, 1952), p. 170, and his *O idealismo da constituição* (Rio, 1927), pp. xiv-xv, 213.

42. Weber, *Varieties of Fascism,* pp. 62-63; Silvert, *The Conflict Society,* p. 92.

43. Samuel P. Huntington, *Political Order in Changing Societies* (New Haven, 1968), pp. 196-208. Affonso Henriques, a bitter opponent of Vargas, offers as an example of pre-Estado Nôvo corruption the fact that 90 per cent of all Federal District governing expenses went for the salaries of officials, for the most part recipients of patronage (*Vargas, o maquiavélico* [São Paulo, 1961], p. 118). Cf. John J. Johnson, ed., *The Role of the Military in Underdeveloped Countries* (Princeton, 1962), and his *The Military and Society in Latin America* (Stanford, 1964); and Edwin Lieuwen, *Arms and Politics in Latin America* (New York, 1960), and his *Generals vs. Presidents: Neomilitarism in Latin America* (New York, 1964).

44. Wirth, "Brazilian Economic Nationalism," pp. 30-31; Skidmore, *Politics in Brazil,* p. 46.

45. Nolte, *Three Faces of Fascism,* p. 325. See also pp. 237-38, 261 (on Mussolini's Italy), 403-5, 407, and 413 (on Germany).

46. John Weiss, *The Fascist Tradition* (New York, 1967), p. 75.

47. Nolte, *Three Faces of Fascism,* pp. 11-15. For Portugal, see Oliveira Salazar, *Le Portugal et la crise européenne* (Paris, 1940), and A. Randall Elliott, "Portugal: Beleaguered Nation," *Foreign Policy Reports,* XVII, No. 19 (Dec. 15, 1941), 238-40. Analytical treatments of Salazar's long rule are sparse. Franco's Spain is discussed in Stanley G. Payne, *Falange: A History of Spanish Fascism* (Stanford, 1961), and Richard Pattee and Anton M. Rothbauer, *Spanien— Mythos und Wirklichkeit* (Graz, n.d.). Joaquín Arrarás, ed., *História de la cruzada española* (Madrid, 1940), 8 vols., offers an official version.

48. Getúlio Vargas, "Proclamação ao povo brasileiro," Nov. 10, 1937, reprinted in *A nova política do Brasil,* V, 32.

49. "Manifesto dos mineiros," Oct. 24, 1943, RP. See Dulles, *Vargas of Brazil,* pp. 251-54.

50. In April, 1939, Vargas had agreed to constitute a new body, the Political and Social Investigation Bureau (Serviço de Inquéritos Políticos Sociais, or SIPS), whose powers are indicated in Polícia do Distrito Federal, *Polícia política* (Rio, 1939).

51. Wirth, "Brazilian Economic Nationalism," p. 24; Skidmore, *Politics in Brazil,* p. 40.

Conclusion

1. Letter, Baptista Luzardo to Getúlio Vargas, Montevideo, Nov. 15, 1938, GV; memorandum, Sumner Welles to Franklin D. Roosevelt, Washington, Nov. 10, 1938, cited in Francis D. McCann, Jr., "Brazil and the United States and the Coming of World War II, 1937-42" (Ph.D. dissertation, Indiana University, 1967), p. 71. Müller, Campos, and Lourival Fontes were removed from their posts three weeks prior to Brazil's declaration of war against the Axis in August, 1942. Müller promptly joined the War Ministry. (*Ibid.*, pp. 191-92.) Müller and Campos exercised significant political influence after the 1964 *golpe*. Under President Garrastazu Medici in late 1969, Congressman Müller and ex-Integralist Raimundo Padilha were named to the highest posts in ARENA, the party identified with the government; Plínio Salgado and Miguel Reale also figured prominently in the post-Costa e Silva administration.
2. See Hélio Jaguaribe, "Political Strategies of National Development in Brazil," in Irving Louis Horowitz, Josué de Castro, and John Gerassi, eds., *Latin American Radicalism* (New York, 1969), p. 395.
3. McCann, "Brazil and the United States," pp. 63-65. See letter, Oswaldo Aranha to Sumner Welles, Rio, Nov. 8, 1938, OA.
4. Departamento Nacional do Café, *Atlas estatístico do Brasil* (Rio, 1941), p. 108.
5. Jaguaribe, "Political Strategies," pp. 394-95. See his "Política de clientela e política ideológica," *Digesto Econômico* (São Paulo, 1951). See also José Nun, "The Middle-Class Military Coup," in Claudio Veliz, ed., *The Politics of Conformity in Latin America* (New York, 1967), esp. pp. 83-91; and Raymundo Faoro, *Os donos do poder* (Pôrto Alegre, 1958).
6. See Azevedo Amaral, *Ensaios brasileiros* (Rio, 1930) and his subsequent *O estado autoritário e a realidade nacional* (Rio, 1938), and his laudatory *Getúlio Vargas: Estadista* (Rio, 1941); Francisco José de Oliveira Vianna, *O Idealismo da constituição* (Rio, 1927), as well as the significantly enlarged later edition (Rio, 1939); Paulo Prado, *Retrato do Brasil* (Rio, 1928); Francisco Campos, *O estado nacional: Sua estrutura, seu conteúdo ideológico,* 3d ed. (Rio, 1941).
7. Report, Felinto Müller to Getúlio Vargas, Nov. 26, 1938, GV.
8. T. Lynn Smith, *Brazil: Peoples and Institutions* (Baton Rouge, 1946), p. 688, cited in Emílio Willems, "Brazil," in Arnold M. Rose, ed., *The Institutions of Advanced Societies* (Minneapolis, 1958), p. 578. See also Thales de Azevedo, *Social Change in Brazil* (Gainesville, 1963), p. 24.
9. See Hélio Jaguaribe, *O nacionalismo na atualidade brasileira* (Rio, 1958), pp. 40-42, cited in David H. P. Maybury-Lewis, "Growth and Change in Brazil since 1930: An Anthropological View," in Raymond S. Sayers, ed., *Portugal and Brazil in Transition* (Minneapolis, 1968), p. 169.
10. Fernando Henrique Cardoso, "The Structure and Evolution of Industry in São Paulo: 1930-1960," *Studies in Comparative International Development,* I, No. 5 (St. Louis, 1965), 44.
11. Lourival Coutinho, *O General Góes depõe . . . ,* 3d ed. (Rio, 1956), p. 234.

12. Albert O. Hirschman, *Journeys Toward Progress: Studies of Economic Policy-Making in Latin America* (New York, 1963), p. 38. See his chapter, "Brazil's Northeast," pp. 11-91.

13. Gerhard Masur, *Nationalism in Latin America* (New York, 1966), pp. 131-32.

14. R. R. Palmer and Joel Colton, *A History of the Modern World*, 3d ed. (New York, 1965), p. 815.

Appendix A. Latin American Echoes

1. Eudocio Ravines, *The Yenan Way* (New York, 1951), pp. 164-66. The literature on communist and fascist movements in Latin America in the prewar period is extensive although lacking in depth. See Alton Frye, *Nazi Germany and the American Hemisphere, 1933-1941* (New Haven, 1967); Rodolfo Puiggrós, *Las izquierdas y el problema nacional* (Buenos Aires, 1967); Robert J. Alexander, *Communism in Latin America* (New Brunswick, 1957); Karl M. Schmitt, *Communism in Mexico: A Study in Political Frustration* (Austin, 1965); Rollie Poppino, *International Communism in Latin America: A History of the Movement, 1917-1963* (New York, 1964); John F. W. Dulles, *Yesterday in Mexico: A Chronicle of the Revolution, 1919-1936* (Austin, 1961); and "M.," "A Spate of Anti-Communist Provocations," *IPC*, March 7, 1936, pp. 324-25. For Chile, see Ernst Halperin, *Nationalism and Communism in Chile* (Cambridge, Mass., 1965), and John Reese Stevenson, *The Chilean Popular Front* (Philadelphia, 1942). See also Dorothy Dillon, *International Communism and Latin America* (Gainesville, 1962); Harry Kantor, *The Ideology and Program of the Peruvian Aprista Movement*, University of California Publications in Political Science, Vol. IV, No. 1 (Berkeley, 1953); Haya de la Torre, *A Dónde vá Indoamérica?* (Lima, 1936), and other works; and Ricardo V. Luna, "The Role of the Modern Peruvian Left," MS, Princeton University, 1962.

2. Stephen Naft, "Fascism and Communism in South America," *Foreign Policy Reports*, XIII, No. 19 (Dec. 15, 1937), 227.

3. See Poppino, *International Communism*, pp. 141-42. Thomas P. Anderson is currently engaged in a study of the 1932 El Salvador uprising.

4. Puiggrós, *Las izquierdas*, pp. 119-20.

5. New York *Times*, Aug. 18, 1935, p. 3; Aug. 7, 1936, p. 2.

6. *Ibid.*, Feb. 3, 1935, p. 27; Sept. 7, 1935, p. 6; "M.," "A Spate of Anti-Communist Provocations," pp. 324-25. See also Marysa Navarro Gerassi, "Argentine Nationalism of the Right," *Studies in Comparative Development,* Vol. I, No. 12 (St. Louis, 1965).

7. "M.," "A Spate of Anti-Communist Provocations," pp. 324-25; New York *Times*, Jan. 26, 1936, p. 27.

8. See Halperin, *Nationalism and Communism in Chile*, pp. 43-44; Ravines, *The Yenan Way*, pp. 164-66; Naft, "Fascism and Communism in South America," p. 233.

9. Halperin, *Nationalism and Communism in Chile*, pp. 45-53.

10. See Herbert S. Klein, "German Busch and the Era of 'Military Socialism' in Bolivia," *HAHR*, XLVII, No. 2 (May, 1967), 166-84.

11. New York *Times*, Jan. 6, 1935, Section IV, p. 8; Poppino, *International Communism*, p. 87.

12. Poppino, *International Communism*, pp. 80-81.

13. Schmitt, *Communism in Mexico*, pp. 16-19.

14. The Dorados and other Mexican fascist groups are treated in Albert L. Michaels, "Fascism and Sinarquismo: Popular Nationalisms Against the Mexican Revolution," *Journal of Church and State*, VIII (1966), 234-35.

15. *Ibid.*, pp. 238-50.

16. Dulles describes Garrido and his legions in *Yesterday in Mexico*, ch. 69. See also the New York *Times*, Jan. 6, 1935, Section IV, p. 8; June 2, 1935, p. 34; Feb. 11, 1936, p. 4; Feb. 19, 1936, p. 14.

GLOSSARY OF
BRAZILIAN PORTUGUESE TERMS

Anauê, Integralist salute, from the Tupí language.

Bacharel, holder of a baccalaureate degree. Plural: *bacharéis*.

Bancada, legislative delegation.

Bandeirante, pioneer of colonial Brazil, originator of armed expeditions into the interior to enslave Indians and seek gold.

Brasilidade, patriotic movement eulogizing Brazilian civilization.

Caboclo, Brazilian of mixed Indian and Caucasian parentage.

Cangaceiro, cowboy bandit of the northeast, especially during the 1890-1937 period.

Caudilho, local or regional chieftain; in Spanish, *caudillo*.

Cearense, native of the state of Ceará.

Charque, dried, jerked beef.

Chimangos, literally, "hawks." Members of nineteenth-century Rio Grande do Sul Republican Party; rivals of Federalists, or *maragatos*.

Colégio, secondary school.

Coronel, rural chieftain, often exercising political power. Title is usually honorific. Plural: *coronéis*.

Distritos, districts.

Estado Nôvo, literally, "New State"; the government proclaimed by Vargas on November 10, 1937.

Faculdade, university division corresponding to a school: e.g., Faculty of Law.

Farinha, flour, usually ground from the *mandioca* root.

Favela, hillside slum composed of wooden shacks, the most notorious of which are in Rio de Janeiro and São Paulo.

Fazenda, rural farm or plantation or ranch.

Fazendeiro, owner of a *fazenda*.

Fluminense, native of the state of Rio de Janeiro, not to be confused with *carioca*, a native of the city of Rio de Janeiro, formerly the Federal District, now the state of Guanabara.

Garôta, young girl.

Gaúcho, native of the state of Rio Grande do Sul.

Golpe, coup d'état.

Hora do Brasil, government-sponsored radio program of the 1930s to the present.

Indigenismo, movement exalting native themes.

Jagunço, rural ruffian.

Macumba, Brazilian voodoo-like cult which combines aspects of African folklore with primitive Catholicism.

Maloca, slum of Rio Grande do Sul. Cf. *favela.*

Maragatos, members of the Rio Grande do Sul Federalist Party, also known as *libertadores.*

Marujo, sailor, usually enlisted man.

Mineiro, native of the state of Minas Gerais.

Mocambo, rustic hovel, usually constructed on swampy land or at the waterside, particularly in the northeast.

Moradores, rural sharecroppers; contracted farm laborers.

Município, administrative division corresponding to a county.

Panelinha, informal group of persons mutually aiding each other's interests.

Patrão, boss.

Paulista, native of the state of São Paulo.

Pernambucano, native of the state of Pernambuco.

Potyguar, native of the state of Rio Grande do Norte.

Prefeito, mayor.

Provisórios, state militia troops.

Samba, rhythmic, improvised dance. *Escolas de samba* are clubs in *favela* areas which train during the entire year for competition during Carnival, prior to the advent of Lent.

Sertanejo, native of the *sertão.*

Sertão, arid rural backlands, found mostly in the northeast.

Sítio, rural property maintained as a retreat.

Tenente, literally, "lieutenant." Associated with *tenentismo,* a nationalistic and dissident movement among young military officers during the 1920s and early 1930s.

Tugurios, northeastern slang: rustic shacks.

Umbanda, folk cult of Bantu origin. Cf. *macumba.*

Usina, sugar refinery.

Viva, cry of adulation and allegiance.

BIBLIOGRAPHY

I. *Manuscript Sources*

A. ARCHIVES

1. Official (Brazilian government)

    Archivo Nacional, Rio de Janeiro, 1934-39

    Supremo Tribunal Federal dos Estados Unidos do Brasil, Rio de Janeiro, Palácio da Justiça, 1947-48

    Tribunal de Segurança Nacional (TSN), Supremo Tribunal Militar (STM), Rio de Janeiro, 1935-40

2. Police

    Delegacia de Ordem Social e Investigações, Natal, Rio Grande do Norte (RA), 1935-65

    Departamento Federal de Segurança Pública de Polícia Política e Social, Rio de Janeiro (RP), 1930-45

    Secretaria de Segurança Pública, Recife (RC), 1933-45

3. Other institutions

    Academia Brasileira de Letras, Rio de Janeiro, 1930-45

    Museu Histórico Nacional, Gustavo Barroso archive (GB), Rio de Janeiro, 1922-55

B. PRIVATE PAPERS

1. Rio de Janeiro

    Oswaldo Aranha archive (OA), 1930-40

    José Soares Maciel Filho archive, 1933-42

    Padre Ponciano dos Santos archive, 1934-37

    Roberto Sissón archive (RS), 1935-55

    Getúlio Vargas archive (GV), 1932-39

2. São Paulo

    Caio Prado, Jr. archive (CP), 1934-39

3. Natal

    Floriano Cavalcanti de Albuquerque archive, 1935-38

C. WRITTEN STATEMENTS TO AUTHOR

Agildo Barata, Rio de Janeiro

Guilherme Borghoff, Rio de Janeiro

João Café Filho, Rio de Janeiro

Hercolino Cascardo, Rio de Janeiro
Otto Guerra, Natal
Protásio de Mello, Natal
Roberto Sissón, Rio de Janeiro
Érico Veríssimo, Pôrto Alegre

D. UNPUBLISHED MANUSCRIPTS

Chacon, Vamireh. "Nacionalismo e anti-semitismo no Brasil." Recife, 1964.
Dean, Warren Kempton. "São Paulo's Industrial Elite, 1890-1960." Ph.D. dissertation, University of Florida, 1964.
Erickson, Kenneth P. "Labor in the Political Process in Brazil." New York, 1968.
Giffen, Donald W. "The Normal Years: Brazilian-American Relations, 1930-1939." Ph.D. dissertation, Vanderbilt University, 1962.
Lebovics, Herman. "European Fascism in the Interwar Years." Stony Brook, N. Y., 1967.
Linhares, Hermínio. "Levante Comunista em 1935." Rio de Janeiro, 1965.
Love, Joseph Leroy, Jr. "Rio Grande do Sul as a Source of Potential Instability in the Old Republic, 1909-1932." Ph.D. dissertation, Columbia University, 1967.
Luna, Ricardo V. "The Role of the Modern Peruvian Left." Senior Thesis, Princeton University, 1962.
McCann, Francis D., Jr. "Brazil and the United States and the Coming of World War II, 1937-1942." Ph.D. dissertation, Indiana University, 1967.
Silva, Hélio. "Rhapsódia verde em 5 atos." Rio de Janeiro, 1963.
Simonson, William Newton. "Nazi Infiltration in South America, 1933-1945." Ph.D. dissertation, Fletcher School of Law and Diplomacy, 1964.
Singer, Paulo. "Desenvolvimento econômico sob o prisma da evolução urbana." Ph.D. dissertation, Universidade de São Paulo, Faculdade de Filosofia, Ciências e Letras, 1966.
Wirth, John D. "Brazilian Economic Nationalism: Trade and Steel under Vargas." Ph.D. dissertation, Stanford University, 1966.

II. *Official and Semiofficial Publications*

A. BRAZIL

Bahia, Estado da. Directoria Geral de Estatística. *Anuário estatístico.* Salvador, 1937.
Brasil, Estados Unidos do. *Annais da Câmara dos Deputados.* Rio de Janeiro, 1934-38.
—— *Anuário estatístico do Brasil.* Rio de Janeiro, 1934-66.
—— Assembléia Constituinte. *Annais.* Vols. I-XXVI. Rio de Janeiro, 1934-36.
—— Departamento de Imprensa e Propaganda. *Brazil: A Political and Economic Study of the Country.* Rio de Janeiro, c. 1938.
—— Departamento Nacional do Café. *Atlas estatístico do Brasil.* Rio de Janeiro, 1941.
—— *Diario da Assembléia Nacional.* Rio de Janeiro, 1933-34.

—— *Da independência ao Estado Nôvo.* Rio de Janeiro, 1940.

—— Ministro da Fazenda. Directoria Estatística e Financeira do Thesouro Nacional. *Estatísticas econômicas, 1934-1944.* Rio de Janeiro, 1944.

—— *Brasil: 1935.* Rio de Janeiro, 1936.

—— Ministry of Foreign Affairs. Commercial Service. *Brazil: 1937.* Rio de Janeiro, 1938. [English edition.]

Diretoria de Estatística. Ministério da Educação e Saúde. *O ensino no Brasil (1932).* Rio de Janeiro, 1939.

Polícia Civil do Distrito Federal. *Arquivos da delegacia especial de segurança política e social.* Vol. III. Rio de Janeiro, 1938.

—— *Polícia política preventiva (Serviço de Inquéritos Políticos e Sociais).* Rio de Janeiro, 1939.

—— *Relação de comunistas fichados D.E.S.P.S.* Rio de Janeiro, May, 1940.

Rio Grande do Norte, Estado do. *Sinopse Estatística do Estado.* No. 1. Recife, 1936.

São Paulo. *A ação da bancada paulista por São Paulo unido na Assembléia Constituinte.* São Paulo, 1935.

B. UNITED STATES

Department of Commerce. "Trade Information Bulletin No. 767." Washington, 1931.

Department of State. *Papers Relating to the Foreign Relations of the United States.* Vol. V. "American Republics" Series. Washington, 1937.

War Department. *Survey of the Rio de Janeiro Region of Brazil.* Vol. I. Washington, Aug. 6, 1942.

III. *Major newspapers*

A. BRAZIL

Belo Horizonte	*Diario de Minas,* 1935-36
Fortaleza	*O Nordeste,* 1935-36
Natal	*A Ordem,* 1935-36
Pôrto Alegre	*Correio do Povo,* 1935-37
Recife	*Diario da Manhã,* 1935
	Diario de Pernambuco, 1935-36
	Diario da Tarde, 1935
	Fôlha do Povo, 1935
Rio de Janeiro	*O Imparcial,* 1934-38
	A Manhã, 1934-35
	O Observador Econômico e Financeiro, 1936-38
	A Offensiva, 1934-38
	A Ordem, 1934-36
	A Pátria, 1934-36
Salvador	*O Imparcial,* 1935-36
São Paulo	*Diario de São Paulo,* 1934-37
	A Platéia, 1935

B. FOREIGN

London   *International Press Correspondence*, 1935-38
    The Times, 1935-38
New York   *Communist International*, 1935-38
    New York *Times*, 1934-38

IV. *Other Works*

Abreu, Jaime, *et al. Anísio Teixeira: Pensamento e ação*. Rio de Janeiro, 1960.
Acção Integralista Brasileira. Secretaria Nacional de Propaganda. *Manifesto Programma com que a AIB comparecerá às eleições do Presidente da República*. Rio de Janeiro, 1937.
—— Secretaria Nacional de Propaganda. Cidade Integralista de Fortaleza. *O Integralismo em poucas palavras*. Fortaleza, 1936.
Alambert, Zuleika. *Estudantes fazem história*. Rio de Janeiro, c. 1963.
Alarcón, Euvaldo D. *E o sangue brasileiro correrá*. Pôrto Alegre, 1942.
Albuquerque, Epitácio Pessôa Cavalcanti de. *Getúlio Vargas: Esboço de biografia*. Rio de Janeiro, 1938.
Alexander, Robert J. "Brazil's Communist Party: A Case Study in Latin American Communism," *Problems of Communism*, IV, No. 5 (Sept.-Oct., 1955), 17-26.
—— *Communism in Latin America*. New Brunswick, 1957.
Almeida, José Américo de. *A palavra e o tempo (1937-1945-1950)*. Rio de Janeiro, 1965.
Almeida, Martins de. *Brasil errado*. Rio de Janeiro, 1932.
Alsberg, Henry G., ed. and tr. *Stefan and Frederike Zweig: Their Correspondence, 1912-1942*. New York, 1954.
Alves, Márcio Moreira. "1938: Golpe Integralista nasceu morto," *Correio da Manhã* (Rio de Janeiro), July 12, 1959, p. 18.
—— "Um govêrno comunista no Brasil," *Correio da Manhã* (Rio de Janeiro), July 11, 1959, p. 16.
Amado, Augusto. *A sucessão presidencial*. Rio de Janeiro, 1938.
Amado, Gilberto. *Depois da política*. Rio de Janeiro, 1960.
—— *Perfil do Presidente Getúlio Vargas*. Rio de Janeiro, 1936.
Amado, Jorge. *Seara vermelha*. 8th ed. Rio de Janeiro, 1961.
—— *A vida de Luís Carlos Prestes: O Cavalheiro da Esperança*. São Paulo, 1945.
Amaral, Azevedo. *A aventura política do Brasil*. Rio de Janeiro, 1935.
—— *Ensaios brasileiros*. Rio de Janeiro, 1930.
—— *O estado autoritário e a realidade nacional*. Rio de Janeiro, 1938.
—— *Getúlio Vargas: Estadista*. Rio de Janeiro, 1941.
Amaral, Rubens do. *A campanha liberal*. São Paulo, 1930.
Araujo, Oscar Egidio de. "Uma pesquisa de padrão de vida," *Revista do Arquivo Municipal*, Vol. LXXX, Supplement (1941).
Arrarás, Joaquín, ed. *História de la cruzada española*. 8 vols. Madrid, 1940.
Azevedo, Fernando de. *Brazilian Culture*. New York, 1950.
Azevedo, Thales de. *Social Change in Brazil*. Gainesville, 1963.

Baer, Werner. *Industrialization and Economic Development in Brazil.* Homewood, Ill. 1966.

Baptista, Pedro Ernesto. *Defesa prévia.* Rio de Janeiro, 1937.

Barata, Agildo. *Vida de um revolucionário (memórias).* Rio de Janeiro, 1957.

Barbosa, Edgar. *História de uma campanha.* Natal, 1936.

Barros, Adhemar de. *Discursos (1938-1939).* São Paulo, 1940.

Barros, João Alberto Lins de. *Memórias de um revolucionário.* 2d ed. Rio de Janeiro, 1954.

Barros, Souza. *Subdesenvolvimento, nordeste e nacionalismo.* São Paulo, 1964.

Barroso, Gustavo. *Brasil: Colonia de banqueiros: História dos emprestimos de 1824 a 1934.* Rio de Janeiro, 1935.

—— *O Integralismo de norte a sul.* Rio de Janeiro, 1934.

—— *O que o integralista deve saber.* 3d ed. Rio de Janeiro, 1935.

—— *Roosevelt es judio.* Buenos Aires, 1938.

—— *A sinagoga paulista.* 3d ed. Rio de Janeiro, 1937.

Basbaum, Leoncio. *História sincera da República.* Vol. III. São Paulo, 1962.

Bastos, Abguar. *Prestes e a revolução social.* Rio de Janeiro, 1946.

Bello, José Maria. *História da República.* 4th ed. São Paulo, 1959.

Bey, Essad. *A luta pelo petróleo.* São Paulo, 1935.

Bittencourt, Clemente Mariani. *O govêrno da Bahia e a defesa da República contra as agitações extremistas.* Rio de Janeiro, 1936.

Braga, Antônio Pereira. *Sentença . . . proferida no processo dos cabeças do movimento de onze de maio de 1938.* Rio de Janeiro, 1938.

B[randão], O[ctávio]. "The First Skirmishes in the Battle for Democracy," *International Press Correspondence,* XVII, No. 24 (June 5, 1937), 556-57.

—— "Important Events are Developing in Brazil," *International Press Correspondence,* XVII, No. 23 (May 29, 1937), 536-37.

—— "The Struggle for the Democratic Front," *International Press Correspondence,* XVII, No. 31 (July 24, 1937), 709-10.

Brandão, Octávio. "Government of Brazil Headed for Bankruptcy," *International Press Correspondence,* XVII, No. 1 (Jan. 2, 1937), 16-17.

—— "Luís Carlos Prestes, the Champion of National Liberation of the Brazilian People," *International Press Correspondence,* Vol. XVI, No. 15 (March 21, 1936).

Brandido, Octavio [*sic*]. "The Roman Octopus Stretches Its Tentacles to Brazil," *International Press Correspondence,* XVI, No. 16 (March 28, 1936), 434.

Brazilian Sailor, A. "Brazil—a Paradise!" *International Press Correspondence,* XVI, No. 15 (March 21, 1936), 406.

Bresser Pereira, L. C. *Desenvolvimento e crise no Brasil entre 1930 e 1967.* Rio de Janeiro, 1968.

Busey, William. "Brazil's Reputation for Political Stability," *Western Political Quarterly,* XVIII (Dec., 1965), 866-80.

Cabanas, João. *A coluna da morte.* Rio de Janeiro, n.d.

Café Filho, João. *Do sindicato ao Catete.* 2 vols. Rio de Janeiro, 1966.

Calmon, Pedro. *Curso de direito constitutional brasileiro.* Rio de Janeiro, 1937.

Câmara, Anfiloquio. *Cenários municipais (1941-1942).* Natal, 1943.

Câmara, Padre Helder. "Educação progressiva," *A Ordem* (Rio de Janeiro), X (April, 1933), 544-49.

Campos, Francisco. *10 de novembro*. Rio de Janeiro, 1938.

—— *Educação e cultura*. 2d ed. Rio de Janeiro, 1941.

—— *O estado nacional: Sua estrutura, seu conteúdo ideológico*. 3d ed. Rio de Janeiro, 1941.

Cardoso, Fernando H. "The Industrial Elite," in Seymour Martin Lipset and Aldo Solari, eds., *Elites in Latin America*, pp. 94-114. New York, 1967.

—— "The Structure and Evolution of Industry in São Paulo: 1930-1960," *Studies in Comparative International Development*, Vol. I, No. 5 (1965). St. Louis.

Carlos, Newton. "Tôda a verdade sôbre o plano Cohen," *Manchete* (Rio de Janeiro), Nov. 22, 1958, pp. 22-27.

Carneiro, Glauco. *História das revoluções brasileiras*. 2 vols. Rio de Janeiro, 1965.

Carone, Edgard. "Coleção Azul: Crítica pequeno-burguêsa à crise brasileira depois de 1930," *Revista Brasileira de Estudos Políticos*, XXV-XXVI (July, 1968–Jan., 1969), 249-95.

—— *Revoluções do Brasil contemporâneo, 1922-1938*. São Paulo, 1965.

Carrazoni, André. *Getúlio Vargas*. Rio de Janeiro, 1939.

Carter, Albert E. *The Battle of South America*. New York, 1941.

Carvalho, Affonso de. *O Brasil não é dos brasileiros*. São Paulo, 1937.

Carvalho, Apolônio de. *Os problemas da juventude brasileira*. Rio de Janeiro, 1947.

Carvalho, Hernani de. *Sociologia de vida rural brasileira*. Rio de Janeiro, 1951.

Carvalho, José Pessôa. "Tempos de Getúlio," *Jornal do Brasil* (Rio de Janeiro), Oct. 31–Nov. 5, 1965, various pages.

Carvalho, Orlando de. *Política do município (ensaio histórico)*. Rio de Janeiro, 1946.

Cascudo, Luís da Câmara. *História da cidade de Natal*. Natal, 1947.

—— *História do Rio Grande do Norte*. Rio de Janeiro, 1955.

Castro, Araujo. *A nova constituição brasileira*. São Paulo, 1936.

Castro, Josué de. *A alimentação brasileira à luz da geografia humana*. Pôrto Alegre, 1937.

—— *Death in the Northeast*. New York, 1966.

—— *Documentário do nordeste*. Rio de Janeiro, 1937.

—— *Geografia da fome*. 9th ed. São Paulo, 1965.

Cavalcanti, Carlos de Lima. *Manifesto ao povo pernambucano*. Recife, 1935.

[Ciano, Galeazzo]. *Ciano's Hidden Diary, 1937-1938*. Tr. Andreas Mayor. New York, 1953.

Cleven, N. Andrew. "Dictatorship in Brazil," *Events*, II, No. 12 (Dec., 1937), 468-71.

Correia de Andrade, Manoel. *A terra e o homem no nordeste*. 2d ed. São Paulo, 1964.

Coutinho, Lourival. *O General Góes depõe*. . . . 3d ed. Rio de Janeiro, 1956.

Couto, Miguel. *Para o futuro da pátria evitemos a niponização do Brasil*. Rio de Janeiro, 1946.

—— *Selecção social*. Rio de Janeiro, 1930.

Crawford, Henry P. "The New Brazilian Constitution," *Commerce Reports*, No. 48 (Nov. 27, 1937), pp. 939-46.

Cunha, Euclides da. *Os sertões*. 2d ed. Rio de Janeiro, 1903.

D'Albuquerque, A. Tenório. *Integralismo, nazismo, e facismo.* Rio de Janeiro, 1937.

Davis, Horace B. "Brazil's Political and Economic Problems," *Foreign Policy Reports,* XI, No. 1 (March 13, 1935), 2-12.

Davis, Horace B., and Marian Rubins Davis. "Scale of Living of the Working Class in São Paulo, Brazil," *Monthly Labor Review,* Jan., 1937, pp. 245-53.

Dean, Warren Kempton. "The Planter as Entrepreneur: The Case of São Paulo," *Hispanic American Historical Review,* XLVI, No. 2 (May, 1966), 138-52.

De la Torre, Haya. *A Dónde vá Indoamérica?* Lima, 1936.

Departamento de Pesquisa, *Jornal do Brasil* (Rio de Janeiro). "Comunismo de norte a sul," Nov. 7, 1967, Caderno B, pp. 2-4.

Departamento de Saúde Pública, Estado de Pernambuco. "Questionário sôbre o custo de vida," *Revista do Arquivo Municipal de São Paulo,* XVIII (Nov.-Dec., 1935), 171-74.

"Dependência do imperialismo: Dívidas do país, estados, e municípios." Rio de Janeiro, Aug. 20, 1935. Author unknown.

Dias, Everardo. *História das lutas sociais no Brasil.* São Paulo, 1962.

Dillon, Dorothy. *International Communism and Latin America.* Gainesville, 1962.

Duarte, Paulo. *Que é que há?* São Paulo, 1931.

Dulles, John W. F. *Vargas of Brazil: A Political Biography.* Austin, 1967.

—— *Yesterday in Mexico: A Chronicle of the Revolution, 1919-1936.* Austin, 1961.

Elliott, A. Randall. "Portugal: Beleaguered Nation," *Foreign Policy Reports,* XVII, No. 19 (Dec. 15, 1941), 238-40.

"Estado de Sítio," *Revista Brasileira de Estudos Políticos,* XVII (July, 1964), 199-210.

Eulau, Heinz H. F. "The Ideas Behind Brazilian Integralism," *Inter-American Quarterly,* III, No. 4 (Oct., 1941), 36-43.

Executive Committee of the Communist International. "May Day Appeal of the Communist International," *Communist International,* XII, No. 5 (May, 1936), 591-98.

Facó, Rui. *A classe operária: Vinte anos de luta.* Rio de Janeiro, 1946.

Faoro, Raymundo. *Os donos do poder.* Pôrto Alegre, 1958.

Fernandes, Florestan. *Educação e sociedade no Brasil.* São Paulo, 1966.

—— *Mudanças Sociais no Brasil.* São Paulo, 1960.

—— "Pattern and Rate of Development in Latin America," in Egbert de Vries and José M. Echevarría, eds., *Social Aspects of Economic Development in Latin America.* Vol. II. Paris, 1963.

—— Review of Jacques Lambert's *Le Brésil, Structure Sociale et Institutions Politiques* (Paris, 1953), in *Revista Brasileira de Estudos Políticos,* VII (Nov., 1959), 144-45.

Finer, Herman. *Mussolini's Italy.* London, 1935.

Fontes, Lourival, and Glauco Carneiro. *A face final de Vargas.* Rio de Janeiro, 1966.

Fontoura, João Neves da. *Acuso ! !* Rio de Janeiro, 1933.

—— *Memórias.* Vol. II. Pôrto Alegre, 1963.

—— *Razões finais da defesa do deputado federal Octávio da Silveira.* Rio de Janeiro, 1937.

—— *A voz das oposições brasileiras: Discurso em 1935 na Câmara dos Deputados.* São Paulo, 1935.

Franco, Affonso Arinos de Mello. *A alma do tempo (memórias).* Rio de Janeiro, 1961.

—— *Conceito de civilização brasileira.* São Paulo, 1936.

—— *Curso de direito constitucional brasileiro.* Vol. II. Rio de Janeiro, 1960.

—— *Um estadista da República.* Vol. III. Rio de Janeiro, 1955.

—— *Evolução da crise brasileira.* São Paulo, 1965.

—— *Introdução à realidade brasileira.* Rio de Janeiro, 1933.

—— *Preparação ao nacionalismo.* Rio de Janeiro, 1934.

—— "The Tide of Government: From Colony to Constitutional Democracy," *The Atlantic Monthly,* CXCVII, No. 2 (Feb., 1956), 152-56.

Franco, Virgílio de Mello. *Outubro, 1930.* 2d ed. Rio de Janeiro, 1931.

Freeman, Richard. "Arthur Ewert Is Being Tortured," *International Press Correspondence,* XVI, No. 20 (April 25, 1936), 556-57.

—— "A Peep into Vargas' Dungeons," *International Press Correspondence,* XVI, No. 23 (May 16, 1936), n.p.

Freire, Josué. *O exército em face das luctas políticas.* Natal, 1938.

Frischauer, Paul. *Presidente Vargas: Biografia.* São Paulo, 1943.

Frye, Alton. *Nazi Germany and the American Hemisphere, 1933-1941.* New Haven, 1967.

Fujii, Yukio, and T. Lynn Smith. *The Acculturation of the Japanese Immigrants in Brazil.* Gainesville, 1959.

Furtado, Celso. *The Economic Growth of Brazil.* Berkeley, 1963.

"G." "The National Revolutionary Uprisings in Brazil," *International Press Correspondence,* XV, No. 70 (Dec. 21, 1935), 1718-19.

Gabaglia, Laurita Pessôa Raja [Irmã Maria Regina do Santo Rosário]. *O Cardeal Leme.* Rio de Janeiro, 1962.

Gauld, Charles A. *The Last Titan: Percival Farquar, American Entrepreneur in Latin America.* Stanford, 1964.

Gerassi, Marysa Navarro. "Argentine Nationalism of the Right," *Studies in Comparative Development,* Vol. I, No. 12 (1965). St. Louis.

Graham, Lawrence S. *Civil Service Reform in Brazil: Principles versus Practice.* Austin, 1968.

Guilherme, Wanderley. *Introdução ao estudo das contradições sociais no Brasil.* Rio de Janeiro, 1963.

Halperin, Ernst. *Nationalism and Communism in Chile.* Cambridge, Mass., 1965.

Hambloch, Ernest. *His Majesty, the President of Brazil,* New York, 1936.

—— "The New Regime in Brazil," *Foreign Affairs,* XVI, No. 3 (April, 1938), 484-93.

Havighurst, Robert J., and J. Roberto Moreira. *Society and Education in Brazil.* Pittsburgh, 1965.

Heller, Frederico. "A carreira profissional de um pedreiro de subúrbio," *Sociologia,* IV, No. 2 (1942), 151-56.

Henriques, Affonso. *Vargas, o maquiavélico.* São Paulo, 1961.

Hervé, Egydio. *Democracia-liberal e socialismo entre os extremos: Integralismo e comunismo.* Pôrto Alegre, 1935.

Hirschman, Albert O. *Journeys Toward Progress: Studies of Economic Policy-making in Latin America.* New York, 1963.

Horowitz, Irving L. *Revolution in Brazil: Politics and Society in a Developing Nation.* New York, 1964.

Hunsche, Karl-Heinrich. *Der brasilianische Integralismus.* Stuttgart, 1938.

Huntington, Samuel P. *Political Order in Changing Societies.* New Haven, 1968.

Hutchinson, Bertram, ed. *Mobilidade e trabalho.* Rio de Janeiro, 1960.

Ianni, Octavio. *Estado e capitalismo: Estrutura social e industrialização no Brasil.* Rio de Janeiro, 1965.

—— *Industrialização e desenvolvimento social no Brasil.* Rio de Janeiro, 1963.

—— *Raças e classes sociais no Brasil.* Rio de Janeiro, 1966.

Ianni, Octavio, *et al. Política e revolução social no Brasil.* Rio de Janeiro, 1965.

"Integralismo reúne-se para tentar o retôrno," *Jornal do Brasil* (Rio de Janeiro), Jan. 15-16, 1967, pp. 1, 7.

"A intentona comunista de 1935," *Diário de Notícias* (Rio de Janeiro), Nov. 29, 1964, p. 4.

"A intentona comunista de 1935: Ordem do dia dos ministros militares," *Aviação e Astronáutica,* XXV, No. 316 (Dec., 1964), 2.

Ipanema, Marcello de. "Da liberdade à liberdade passando pela censura," *Jornal do Brasil* (Rio de Janeiro), Jan. 22, 1967, Caderno Especial, p. 4.

Jaguaribe, Hélio. "The Dynamics of Brazilian Nationalism," in Claudio Veliz, ed., *Obstacles to Change in Latin America,* pp. 162-87. New York, 1965.

—— "Political Strategies of National Development in Brazil," in Irving Louis Horowitz, Josué de Castro, and John Gerassi, eds., *Latin American Radicalism,* pp. 390-439. New York, 1969.

Johnson, John J. *The Military and Society in Latin America.* Stanford, 1964.

Johnson, John J., ed. *The Role of the Military in Underdeveloped Countries.* Princeton, 1962.

Kantor, Harry. *The Ideology and Program of the Peruvian Aprista Movement.* University of California Publications in Political Science, Vol. IV, No. 1. Berkeley, 1953.

Keiros [Queiroz]. "The Eve of Revolution in Brazil," *Communist International,* XII, No. 10 (May 20, 1935), 577-87.

—— "Struggles of the Communist Parties of South and Caribbean America: The Results of the Third Conference of the Communist Parties of South and Caribbean America," *Communist International,* XII, No. 10 (May 20, 1935), 564-76.

Klein, Herbert S. "German Busch and the Era of 'Military Socialism' in Bolivia," *Hispanic American Historical Review,* XLVII, No. 2 (May, 1967), 166-84.

Koestler, Arthur. *The Invisible Writing.* New York, 1954.

Lacerda, Carlos. "Rosas e pedras do meu caminho," *Manchete* (Rio de Janeiro), April-July, 1967, various pages.

Lacerda, F[ernando]. "The Fascist Coup d'État in Brazil," *Communist International,* XV, No. 1 (Jan., 1938), 41-47.

—— "The Recent Uprising in Brazil," *International Press Correspondence,* XVI, No. 9 (Feb. 15, 1936), 237-38.

—— "Regarding the Accusations Against Communists by the Reactionary Clique in

Brazil," *International Press Correspondence*, XVI, No. 10 (Feb. 22, 1936), 160-61.

—— "Revolt of the Political Prisoners in Rio de Janeiro," *International Press Correspondence*, XVI, No. 32 (Aug. 1, 1936), no page available.

Lacerda, Fernando, and Luís Carlos Prestes. *A luta contra o prestismo e a revolução agrária e anti-imperialista*. Rio de Janeiro, 1934.

Lafayette, Pedro. *Os crimes do partido comunista*. Rio de Janeiro, 1946.

Lamartine, Juvenal. *O meu govêrno*. Rio de Janeiro, 1933.

Lambert, Jacques. "Requirements for Rapid Economic and Social Development: The View of the Historian and Sociologist," in Egbert de Vries and José M. Echavarría, eds., *Social Aspects of Economic Development*. Vol. II. Paris, 1963.

Landucci, Ítalo. *Cenas e episódios da Coluna Prestes e da revolução de 1924*. São Paulo, 1952.

Laqueur, Walter, and George L. Mosse, eds. *International Fascism, 1920-1945*. New York, 1966.

Laswell, Harold. "The Psychology of Hitlerism," *Political Quarterly*, Vol. IV (July, 1933).

Leal, Hamilton. *História das instituições políticas do Brasil*. Rio de Janeiro, 1962.

Leeds, Anthony. "Brazilian Careers and Social Structure: An Evolutionary Model and Case History," *American Anthropologist*, LXVI, No. 6 (Dec., 1964), 1321-47.

Leff, Nathaniel H. *The Brazilian Capital Goods Industry, 1929-1964*. Cambridge, Mass., 1968.

Leite, Aureliano. "Causas e objetivos da Revolução de 1932," *Revista de História*, XXV, No. 51 (July-Sept., 1962), 139-66.

—— *Páginas de uma longa vida*. São Paulo, 1967 (?).

Leite, Eurico de Souza, and João Neves da Fontoura. *Defesa do Senador Abel Chermont*. Rio de Janeiro, 1937.

Levine, Robert M. "Brazil's Jews During the Vargas Era and After," *Luso-Brazilian Review*, V, No. 1 (Summer, 1968), 45-58.

Lieuwen, Edwin. *Arms and Politics in Latin America*. New York, 1960.

—— *Generals vs. Presidents: Neomilitarism in Latin America*. New York, 1964.

Lima, Alceu Amoroso [Tristão de Athayde]. *O Cardeal Leme: Um depoimento*. Rio de Janeiro, 1943.

—— "Catholicismo e Integralismo," *A Ordem* (Rio de Janeiro), XII (Jan., 1935), 405-13; XIII (Feb., 1935), 81-86.

—— *Da revolução a constituição*. Rio de Janeiro, 1936.

Lima, Areobaldo E. de Oliveira. *A imigração japonesa para o Estado da Parahyba do Norte*. São Paulo, 1936.

Lima, Cláudio de Araujo. *Mito e realidade de Vargas*. Rio de Janeiro, 1955.

Lima, Lourenço Moreira. *A coluna Prestes (marchas e combates)*. 2d ed. São Paulo, 1945.

Lima, Pedro Motta, and José Barbosa de Mello. *El nazismo en el Brasil: Proceso del estado corporativo*. Buenos Aires, 1938.

Lima Sobrinho, Alexandre Barbosa. *Interêsses e problemas do sertão pernambucano*. Rio de Janeiro, 1937.

—— *A verdade sôbre a revolução de Outubro*. São Paulo, 1933.

Linhares, Hermínio. "O comunismo no Brasil," *Revista Brasiliense*, XXV (Sept.-Oct., 1959), 146-66; XXVI (Nov.-Dec., 1959), 178-97; XXVIII (March-April, 1960), 122-42.

Linhares, Josephat. *O integralismo à luz do doutrina social catholica*. Rio de Janeiro, 1933.

Linz, Juan. "An Authoritarian Regime: Spain," in E. Allardt and Y. Littunen, eds., *Cleavages, Ideologies, and Party Systems*, pp. 291-341. Helsinki, 1964.

Lipiner, Elias. *A nova imigração judáica no Brasil*. Rio de Janeiro, 1962.

Lipset, Seymour Martin, and Aldo Solari, eds. *Elites in Latin America*. New York, 1967.

Lobo, Bruno. *De japonez a brasileiro*. Rio de Janiero, 1932.

Loewenstein, Karl. *Brazil under Vargas*. New York, 1942.

Luis, Pedro. *Militarismo e República (crítica e história)*. São Paulo, 1936.

"M." "A Spate of Anti-Communist Provocations," *International Press Correspondence*, March 7, 1936, pp. 324-25.

Maack, Reinhard. "The Germans of South Brazil: A German View," *Quarterly Journal of Inter-American Relations*, I, No. 3 (July, 1938), 5-23.

Machado, Augusto [Leoncio Basbaum]. *O caminho da revolução operária e camponeza*. Rio de Janeiro, 1934.

Machado, Luiz. "Revolution in Brazil," *International Press Correspondence*, XVI, No. 2 (Jan. 11, 1936), 31-2.

Machado, Raul. *Delitos contra a ordem política e social*. São Paulo, 1944.

—— *A incídia comunista nas letras e nas artes do Brasil*. Rio de Janeiro, 1941.

—— *Relatório e accordão do processo em que são accusados Luís Carlos Prestes, Harry Berger, Dr. Pedro Ernesto e outros*. Rio de Janeiro, 1937.

Maciel, Anor Butler. *Nacionalismo e o problema judáico no mundo e no Brasil e o nacional-socialismo*. Pôrto Alegre, 1937.

McKenzie, Kermit E. *Comintern and World Revolution, 1918-1943: The Shaping of Doctrine*. New York, 1964.

Magalhães, Juracy M. *Defendendo meu govérno (explicações à Bahia à propósito de um livro do Sr. J. J. Seabra)*. Salvador, 1934.

—— *Minha vida pública na Bahia*. Rio de Janeiro, 1957.

Mangabeira, Otávio. "A todos os brasileiros." Printed brochure. Recife, 1938.

Marighella, Carlos. "As idéias do movimento de 1935," *Novos Rumos* (Rio de Janeiro), Nov. 22-28, 1963.

Marini. "An Executioner of the Brazilian People: Felinto Müller, Head of the Special Police," *International Press Correspondence*, XVI, No. 27 (June 20, 1936), 726-27.

—— "Revolt of the Political Prisoners in Rio de Janeiro," *International Press Correspondence*, XVI, No. 32 (July 11, 1936), 860.

Masur, Gerhard. *Nationalism in Latin America*. New York, 1966.

Maybury-Lewis, David H. P. "Growth and Change in Brazil since 1930: An Anthropological View," in Raymond S. Sayers, ed. *Portugal and Brazil in Transition*, pp. 159-72. Minneapolis, 1968.

Medeiros, Estácio. "Padre Olímpio, 'o prefeito suburbano,' escreve as memórias," *Manchete* (Rio de Janeiro), Nov., 1966.

Medeiros, João. *Meu Depoimento.* Natal, 1937.

Medina, Carlos Alberto. *A favela e o demagogo.* Rio de Janeiro, 1964.

Mello, Manoel Rodrígues de. *Várzea do Assú.* São Paulo, 1940.

Mello, Olbiano de. *A marcha da revolução social no Brasil.* Rio de Janeiro, 1957.

—— *Razões do Integralismo.* Rio de Janeiro, 1935.

Menezes, José Rafael de. *José Américo: Um homem do bem comum.* Rio de Janeiro, 1967.

Mensário de Cultura Militar. *Guerra revolucionária.* Recife, 1962.

Michaels, Albert L. "Fascism and Sinarquismo: Popular Nationalism Against the Mexican Revolution," *Journal of Church and State,* VIII (1966), 235-50.

Moniz, Heitor. *Comunismo.* Rio de Janeiro, 1934.

Montalvo, Ricardo J. *Getúlio Vargas y la unidad brasileña.* Buenos Aires, 1939.

Monteiro, Pedro Aurélio Góes. *A revolução de 30 e a finalidade política do exército.* Rio de Janeiro, 1934.

Morais, Pessôa de. *Sociologia da revolução brasileira.* Rio de Janeiro, 1965.

Morel, Edmar. *A revolta da Chibata.* 2d ed. Rio de Janeiro, 1963.

Morse, Richard M. *From Community to Metropolis: A Biography of São Paulo, Brazil.* Gainesville, 1958.

Moura, Aloísio de Andrade. *Relatório das actividades comunistas no Rio Grande do Norte.* Natal, July 8, 1947.

Muricy, Antônio Carlos da Silva. *A guerra revolucionária no Brasil e o episódio de novembro de 1935.* Natal, 1966.

Myro, V. "The Struggle to Establish Inner Soviet Regions in the Semi-Colonial Countries," *Communist International,* XII, No. 4 (Feb. 20, 1935), 151-59.

Nabuco, Carolina. *A vida de Virgílio de Mello Franco.* Rio de Janeiro, 1962.

Naft, Stephen. "Fascism and Communism in South America," *Foreign Policy Reports,* XIII, No. 19 (Dec. 15, 1937), 226-36.

[Nasser, David]. Anonymous. *Eu fui guarda-costas de Getúlio.* Rio de Janeiro, 1949.

Nasser, David. *Falta alguém em Nuremberg: Torturas da polícia brasileira.* Rio de Janeiro, 1947.

—— *A revolução dos covardes.* 2d ed. Rio de Janeiro, 1947.

Niemeyer, Waldyr. *O japonez no Brasil.* 2d ed. Rio de Janeiro, 1932.

Nogueira Filho, Paulo. *Idéias e lutas de um burguês progressista: A guerra cívica, 1932.* 2 vols. Rio de Janeiro, 1965-66.

Nollau, Günther. *International Communism and World Revolution.* New York, 1961.

Nolte, Ernst. *Three Faces of Fascism: Action Française, Italian Fascism, National Socialism.* New York, 1966.

Nonato, Raimundo. *Bacharéis de Olinda e Recife (Norte-Riograndenses formados de 1832 a 1932).* Rio de Janeiro, 1960.

Normano, J. F. *Brazil: A Study of Economic Types.* Chapel Hill, 1935.

Nun, José. "The Middle Class Military Coup," in Claudio Veliz, ed., *The Politics of Conformity in Latin America,* pp. 66-118. New York, 1967.

Oliveira, Franklin de. *Que é a revolução brasileira?* Rio de Janeiro, 1963.

Oliveira, Xavier de. *O problema immigratório na Constituição brasileira.* Rio de Janeiro, 1937.

Oliveira Vianna, Francisco José. *O idealismo da constituição*. Rio de Janeiro, 1927. 3d ed. Rio de Janeiro, 1939.

—— *Pequenos estudos de psicologia social*. São Paulo, 1921.

—— *Populações meridionais do Brasil*. Vol. 1: *Populações do centro-sul*. São Paulo, 1920.

—— *Problemas de organização e problemas de direção*. Rio de Janeiro, 1952.

"Open Letter to Haya de la Torre," *International Press Correspondence*, XV, No. 22 (May 25, 1935), 593-94.

Pacheco e Silva, A. C. *Armando de Salles Oliveira*. São Paulo, 1966.

Palha, Américo. *Jornada sangrenta*. Rio de Janeiro, 1936.

Palmer, R. R., and Joel Colton. *A History of the Modern World*. 3d ed. New York, 1965.

Patric, Anthony. *Toward the Winning Goal*. Rio de Janeiro, 1940.

Pattee, Richard, and Anton M. Rothbauer. *Spanien—Mythos und Wirklichkeit*. Graz, n.d.

Payne, Stanley G. *Falange: A History of Spanish Fascism*. Stanford, 1961.

Pedreira, Fernando. *Março 31: Civis e militares no processo da crise brasileira*. Rio de Janeiro, 1964.

Peixoto, Alzira Vargas do Amaral. *Getúlio Vargas, meu pai*. Pôrto Alegre, 1960.

Peláez, Carlos Manoel. "A balança comercial, a grande depressão e a industrialização brasileira," *Revista Brasileira de Economia*, March, 1968, pp. 15-46.

Peralva, Oswaldo. "O Marxismo no Brasil," *Jornal do Brasil* (Rio de Janeiro), Nov. 5-6, 1967, Caderno Especial, p. 5.

—— *O Retrato*. Rio de Janeiro, 1962.

Pereira, Astrojildo. "Calúnia à moda nazista," *Novos Rumos*, Nov. 22-28, 1963, p. 4.

—— *A formação do PCB: 1922-1928*. Rio de Janeiro, 1962.

—— Series on the ANL, *Diretrizes* (Rio de Janeiro), June 5-July 24, 1945, eight parts.

Pierson, Donald. *Negroes in Brazil: A Study in Race Contact at Bahia*. Chicago, 1942.

Pinto, Heron P. *Nos subterrâneos do Estado Nôvo*. Rio de Janeiro, 1950.

Pires, Apollônio, and Manoel Machado Cavalcanti. *Indústrias de Pernambuco*. Recife, 1935.

Poppino, Rollie. *International Communism in Latin America: A History of the Movement, 1917-1963*. New York, 1964.

—— "O processo político no Brasil: 1929-1945," *Revista Brasileira de Estudos Políticos*, VI (June, 1964), 83-94.

Pôrto, Eurico Bellens. *A insurreição de 27 de novembro*. Rio de Janeiro, 1936.

Prado, Caio, Jr. *História Econômica do Brasil*. 9th ed. São Paulo, 1965.

Prado, Paulo. *Retrato do Brasil*. Rio de Janeiro, 1928.

Prestes, Luís Carlos. "A ANL e as lutas de novembro de 1935," *Novos Rumos*, Nov. 22-28, 1963, p. 5.

—— "Manifesto de 5 de julho," *A Manhã* (Rio de Janeiro), July 6, 1935, p. 1.

—— *Problemas atuais da democracia brasileira*. Rio de Janeiro, 1947.

—— *The Struggle for Liberation in Brazil*. New York, 1936.

Puiggrós, Rodolfo. *Las izquierdas y el problema nacional*. Buenos Aires, 1967.

Pujol, Victor. *Rumo ao sigma*. Rio de Janeiro, 1935.

Putnam, Samuel. "Fascist Penetration in Latin America," *Communist*, XVII, No. 5 (n.d.), 458-67.

—— "Vargas Dictatorship in Brazil," *Science and Society*, V, No. 2 (Spring, 1941), 97-116.

Ramos, Alberto Guerreiro. *Condições sociais do poder nacional*. Rio de Janeiro, 1957.

—— *A crise do poder no Brasil*. Rio de Janeiro, 1961.

Ramos, Graciliano. *Memórias do cárcere*. 4 vols. Rio de Janeiro, 1953.

Ratinoff, Luis. "The New Urban Groups: The Middle Classes," in Seymour Martin Lipset and Aldo Solari, eds., *Elites in Latin America*, pp. 61-93. New York, 1967.

Ravines, Eudócio. América Latina: Un continente en erupción. Buenos Aires (?), 1956.

—— *The Yenan Way*. New York, 1951.

Reale, Miguel. *ABC do Integralismo*. 2d ed. Rio de Janeiro, 1937.

—— *Perspectivas Integralistas*. 2d ed. Rio de Janeiro, 1936.

—— "Synthese da doutrina integralista," *Revista Brasiliense*, No. 8 (March, 1935), pp. 37-50.

Rios, José Arthur. "Italianos em São Paulo," in J. V. Freitas Marcondes and Osmar Pimentel, eds., *São Paulo,* pp. 75-91. São Paulo, 1968.

Robock, Stefan. *Brazil's Developing Northeast*. Washington, D. C., 1963.

Rodrigues, José Honório. *Conciliação e reforma no Brasil*. Rio de Janeiro, 1965.

—— *Teoria da História do Brasil*. Vol. II. 2d ed. São Paulo, 1957.

Rodrigues, Leoncio Martins. *Conflito industrial e sindicalismo no Brasil*. São Paulo, 1966.

Rosa, Virgínio Santa. *O sentido de tenentismo*. Rio, 1933.

Rose, Arnold M., ed. *The Institutions of Advanced Societies*. Minneapolis, 1958.

Rowe, James W. "The 'Revolution' and the 'System': Notes on Brazilian Politics," Part II, *American Universities Field Staff Reports*, Vol. XII, No. 4 (July, 1966), Brazil series.

Sá, Júlio. "Christianismo e Integralismo," *A Ordem* (Rio de Janeiro), Nov., 1935, pp. 420-22.

Saito, Hiroshi. *O japonês no Brasil*. São Paulo, 1961.

Salazar, Oliveira. *Le Portugal et la crise européenne*. Paris, 1940.

Salgado, Plínio. "Como eu vi a Itália," *Hierarchia* (Rio de Janeiro), March-April, 1932.

—— *Despertemos a nação!* Rio de Janeiro, 1935.

—— *O Integralismo na vida brasileira*. Rio de Janeiro, n.d.

—— *O Integralismo perante a nação*. 3d ed. Rio de Janeiro, 1955.

—— *Livro verde da minha campanha*. Rio de Janeiro, 1965.

—— *Páginas de combate*. Rio de Janeiro, 1937.

—— *Psicologia da revolução*. 4th ed. São Paulo, 1953.

—— *A quarta humanidade*. Rio de Janeiro, 1934.

—— *Was ist der Integralismus?* Blumenau, 1936.

Salles Oliveira, Armando de, and others. "Mensagem dos exilados brasileiros ao Presidente Roosevelt." Paris, Jan. 7, 1939.

Santos, Capt. Davino Francisco dos. *A marcha vermelha*. São Paulo, 1948.

Santos, Francisco Martins dos. *O fato moral e o fato social da década getuliana*. Rio de Janeiro, 1940.

Schmalhauser, Samuel D. *Recovery Through Revolution*. New York, 1935.

Schmitt, Karl M. *Communism in Mexico: A Study in Political Frustration*. Austin, 1965.

Sharp, Walter R. "Methods of Public Opinion Control in Present-Day Brazil," *Public Opinion Quarterly*, V, No. 1 (March, 1941), 3-16.

Sherwood, Frank P. *Institutionalizing the Grass Roots in Brazil: A Study in Comparative Local Government*. San Francisco, 1967.

Silva, Hélio. *1926: A grande marcha*. Rio de Janeiro, 1966.

—— *1930: A revolução traída*. Rio de Janeiro, 1966.

—— *1931: Os tenentes no poder*. Rio de Janeiro, 1966.

—— *1932: A guerra paulista*. Rio de Janeiro, 1967.

—— *1934: A constituinte*. Rio de Janeiro, 1969.

Silvert, Kalman H. *The Conflict Society: Reaction and Revolution in Latin America*. Rev. ed. New York, 1966.

Simão, Asiz. *Sindicato e estado*. Rio de Janeiro, n.d.

Simonsen, Roberto C. *Brazil's Industrial Evolution*. São Paulo, 1939.

Sissón, Roberto Henrique. *Carta aberta à marinha de guerra*. Rio de Janeiro, 1936.

Skidmore, Thomas E. "Brazil's Search for Identity in the Old Republic," in Raymond S. Sayers, ed., *Portugal and Brazil in Transition*, pp. 127-41. Minneapolis, 1968.

—— *Politics in Brazil, 1930-1964: An Experiment in Democracy*. New York, 1967.

Soares, Gláuco Ary Dillon. "The Political Sociology of Uneven Development in Brazil," in Irving Louis Horowitz, *Revolution in Brazil*, pp. 164-95. New York, 1964.

Sociedade Nacional de Agricultura. *Immigração: Inquérito promovido pela Sociedade Nacional de Agricultura*. Rio de Janeiro, 1926.

Sodré, Alcindo. *A gênese da desordem*. Rio de Janeiro, 1933.

Sodré, Nelson Werneck. *História da burguesia brasileira*. 2d ed. Rio de Janeiro, 1967.

—— *História militar do Brasil*. Rio de Janeiro, 1965.

—— *Introdução à revolução brasileira*. Rio de Janeiro, 1963.

—— *Memórias de um soldado*. Rio de Janeiro, 1967.

Sombra, S., *As duas linhas da nossa evolução política*. Rio de Janeiro, 1940.

Souza, O. de Carvalho de. *Komintern*. Rio de Janeiro, 1938.

Speigel, Henry William. *The Brazilian Economy: Chronic Inflation and Sporadic Industrialization*. Philadelphia, 1949.

Stein, Stanley J. *The Brazilian Cotton Manufacture: Textile Enterprise in an Underdeveloped Area, 1850-1950*. Cambridge, Mass., 1957.

Stevenson, John Reese. *The Chilean Popular Front*. Philadelphia, 1942.

Szulc, Tad. *Twilight of the Tyrants*. New York, 1959.

Tabajara de Oliveira, Nelson. *1924: A revolução de Isidoro*. São Paulo, 1956.

Tannenbaum, Edward R. "The Goals of Italian Fascism," *American Historical Review*, LXXIV, No. 4 (April, 1969), 1183-1204.

Teixeira, Anísio. "A universidade de ontem e de hoje," *Revista Brasileira de Estudos Pedagógicos*, XLII, No. 95 (July-Sept., 1964), 27-47.

"Tenente X." "Os acontecimentos no Recife," *Novos Rumos*, Nov. 22-28, 1963, p. 5.

Timbaúba [Epitácio da Silva Timbaúba]. "27 de novembro de 1935," *Diário Carioca* (Rio de Janeiro), Nov. 28–Dec. 1, 1963, pages unavailable.

—— "Também tivemos Gestapo," *Diário Carioca* (Rio de Janeiro), June 28, 1963.

Tôrres, João Camilo de Oliveira. *A democracia coroada*. Rio de Janeiro, n.d.

—— *Estratificação social no Brasil*. São Paulo, 1965.

Valladares, Benedito. *Tempos idos e vividos, memórias*. Rio de Janeiro, 1966.

Vargas, Getúlio. *Diretrizes da nova política do Brasil*. Rio de Janeiro, 1942.

—— *A nova política do Brasil*. Vols. I-IX. Rio de Janeiro, 1938-40.

Velloso, Cleto Seabra. "A alimentação do povo brasileiro," *Boletim do Ministério do Trabalho, Indústria e Commércio* (Rio de Janeiro), April, 1937, pp. 578-90.

Vergara, Luís. *Fui secretário de Getúlio Vargas: Memórias dos anos de 1926 a 1954*. Pôrto Alegre, 1960.

Vidal, Barros. *Um destino a serviço do Brasil*. Rio de Janeiro, 1945.

Vieira, Padre Arlindo, s.j. *A decadência do ensino no Brasil: Suas causas e remédios*. Rio de Janeiro, 1935.

Viveiros, Custódio de. *Camisas verdes*. Rio de Janeiro, 1935.

Waddell, Agnes S. "The Revolution in Brazil," *Foreign Policy Association Information Service,* VI, No. 26 (1931), 489-506.

Warren, Donald, Jr. "Portuguese Roots of Brazilian Spiritism," *Luso-Brazilian Review,* V, No. 2 (Winter, 1968), 3-33.

Weber, Eugen. *Varieties of Fascism*. Princeton, 1964.

Weffort, Francisco C. "Estado e massas no Brasil," *Revista Civilização Brasileira,* I, No. 7 (May, 1966), 137-58.

Weiss, John. *The Fascist Tradition*. New York, 1967.

Werebe, Maria José Garcia. *Grandezas e misérias do ensino no Brasil*. 3d ed. São Paulo, 1968.

Whitaker, Arthur P., and David C. Jordan. *Nationalism in Contemporary Latin America*. New York, 1966.

Willems, Emílio. "Assimilation of German Immigrants in Brazil," *Sociology and Social Research,* Vol. XXV, No. 2 (1940).

—— "Immigrants and Their Assimilation in Brazil," in T. Lynn Smith and Alexander Marchant, eds., *Brazil:Portrait of Half a Continent*. New York, 1951.

Wirth, John D. "A German View of Brazilian Trade and Development, 1935," *Hispanic American Historical Review,* XLVII, No. 2 (May, 1967), 225-35.

—— "*Tenentismo* in the Brazilian Revolution of 1930," *Hispanic American Historical Review,* XLIV, No. 2 (May, 1964), 161-79.

Wood, Bryce. "The Federal Service," *Inter-American Quarterly,* II (1940), 46-63.

Wythe, George, *et al. Brazil: An Expanding Economy*. New York, 1949.

—— *Industry in Latin America*. 2d ed. New York, 1949.

Young, Jordan M. *The Brazilian Revolution of 1930 and the Aftermath*. New Brunswick, 1967.

Zweig, Stefan. *Brazil: Land of the Future*. London, 1942.

INDEX